# STRATEGIC HUMAN
# RESOURCE TECHNOLOGIES

# STRATEGIC HUMAN RESOURCE TECHNOLOGIES

## Keys to Managing People

**ASHOK CHANDA**

**with**

**B. SIVARAMA KRISHNA and JIE SHEN**

Response
Business books from SAGE
Los Angeles ■ London ■ New Delhi ■ Singapore
www.sagepublications.com

*First published in 2007 by*

**Response Books**
Business books from SAGE
B1/I1, Mohan Cooperative Industrial Area
Mathura Road, New Delhi 110 044

**Sage Publications Inc**
2455 Teller Road
Thousand Oaks, California 91320

**Sage Publications Ltd**
1 Oliver's Yard, 55 City Road
London EC1Y 1SP

**Sage Publications Asia-Pacific Pte Ltd**
33 Pekin Street
# 02-01 Far East Square
Singapore 048763

*Second Printing 2008*

Published by Vivek Mehra for Response Book, phototypeset in 11/13 pt. Garth Graphic by Star Compugraphics Private Limited, Delhi, and printed at Chaman Enterprises, New Delhi.

**Library of Congress Cataloging-in-Publication Data**

Chanda, Ashok , 1965–
   Strategic human resource technologies : keys to managing people / Ashok Chanda with B. Sivarama Krishna and Jie Shen.
       p. cm.
   Includes bibliographical references and index.
1.   Personnel management —Technological innovations. 2. Management information systems. 3. Strategic planning —Data processing. I. Sivarama Krishna, B.  II. Shen, Jie, 1947– III. Title.

| HF5549.5.T33C53 | 658.3'01—dc22 | 2007 | 2007001024 |

**ISBN:**   978-0-7619-3558-2 (PB)        978-81-7829-717-0 (India-PB)

**The Sage Team:** Leela Kirloskar, Swati Sahi and Sanjeev Sharma

*This book is dedicated with love to my family, most desirably to Rupal who has been the balancing force in my work-life in true sense, Nupur whose innocent creativity has always inspired me, Aarnava whose naughty desire has been to play games on my computer and to my parents, 'Baba' and 'Maa', for gifting me this wonderful life.*

# Contents

## Part 3 Branding of HR Technologies

## Part 4 HR Word Power

# Foreword

In today's globally competitive and dynamic environment, companies need to be flexible, responsive and internationally-oriented. Traditional domestic markets and company structures are now giving way to global markets, and supply chains and virtual organisations are challenging the basic tenets of management practice. Employees, for their part, are now front-line workers who have greater interaction with customers. While technology is facilitating much of these developments, it is no longer the key factor in economic success. What is now important is people management and how it can create and sustain a competitive advantage for the company.

Although the human aspect of organisation has been studied since the ancient Greek civilisation it has not been seen as important as technologies and processes. Moreover, while many behavioural scientists have attempted to establish universal principles which can be applied across all cultures and countries, the results have been mixed. What has proven successful in one country has often been found to be counter-productive elsewhere. As a consequence, notions such as the best fit approach, which requires strategies to be responsive to the particular external and organisational environment, have come to the fore. This has led researchers and HR practitioners to search for new practices and to modify existing ones so as to accommodate the uniqueness of each organisation. These practices, however, all have similar aims: integrating HR strategies with the organisation's corporate strategies, building a high performance team culture, and attracting, retaining and nurturing the best talent.

Although these concepts are well established, and form the basis to many books on HRM, this book has a unique focus and structure. The book starts by applying the term 'technologies' to a variety of HR techniques. While such an approach is contestable, the book sheds new light on HR processes and provides an important guide to the practising HR professional. This is a welcome step and a useful addition to the libraries of those involved in research, people management, training and staff and management development. Two questions underpin the book. Is the discipline of HR moving towards a 'science' like many of the business areas, such as accounting, finance and production, are portrayed? Or does the human dimension make HR different and less susceptible to global principles?

These are some of the issues and questions that this book considers. The book, based on the author's research and industrial experience, presents 40 strategic 'HR technologies' and discusses their implementation. More important, each 'technology' is elaborated upon in terms of some of the recent management literature such as re-engineering, entrepreneurship and HR balance sheets. This differentiates this book from other HRM texts and provides HR professionals and managers more generally with a number of important HR issues to consider. In addition, the various levels of maturity of each of these practices are discussed and provides guidelines for the development of HR strategies for the different levels of an organisation.

The successful implementation of these 'strategic HR technologies', as elaborated in this book, would facilitate organisational growth and increase employee satisfaction and commitment. By doing so, HR becomes a strategic partner with the other functional areas of the organisation. The release of this book is both timely and refreshing and I would recommend it to all those interested in HR from a practical and academic perspective.

**John Benson**
Professor and Head
School of Management
University of South Australia
Adelaide, Australia

# Preface and Acknowledgements

This book is about an exciting and profound idea and is on a growing body of knowledge relating to that idea. The idea is this; it is possible to evolve Human Resource Management (HRM) practices as proven techniques which can be applicable across corporations for the purpose of attainment of goals and purposes of the organisations through HRM processes. I started on the path of this book in 2002, when I was heading HRM of a logistics organisation and just started to research for my proposed doctoral programme. After spending several months researching by both me and Shivarama, we decided to structure this book differently than the remaining literature. An idea stuck that the HRM proven processes are established technologies in the people management field and is to be presented in such a manner that it becomes easy for all levels of people involved in HRM to understand the concepts and practices prevailing in HRM. The involvement of Dr Shen came at the right time when I needed insights for the book from a researcher's point of view. We have researched a host of literatures and have also exchanged ideas with many corporates about the best HRM practices and found that most of the practices are being implemented keeping the core philosophy same but making changes in its implementation style. Thus, this book is the culmination of four years of research building a comprehensive book on human resource technologies that are universal and applicable across the organisations.

Human Resource Management is a growing discipline. With the culmination of innovative and refined approach to managing people, it is an extended behavioural science. We strongly felt that these HRM practices are in fact the 'technologies' which help in realising the potentials of people. Technology is described as the combination of all the knowledge, equipment, methods, etc. Human Resource practices help the organisation in increasing organisational productivity and in turn the profitability. Therefore, these practices are 'technologies' since these technologies enable releasing the potentials of people when implemented with the right kind of knowledge, methods, tools, etc. With the rising competitive environment, organisations would like to leverage their human resources as strategic advantage and hence every organisation would like to implement technologies which are strategic to the firm. This book helps understanding those HR technologies which are strategic with its usage, advantages, difficulties, instances where these are implemented. An attempt has been made to make this book more meaningful and result oriented. Examples of all those companies which have implemented these technologies are given to prove that these are beyond theories and are implemented in organisations successfully.

This book is more than just understanding the strategic HR technologies, but viewing these SHRTs as an integral part of the business. Our endeavour is to demystify the fact that the HR practices are meant for HR to survive rather than designed for the benefit of the organisation and driving productivity. We have avoided going into depth of each SHR technology, since lots of literature is available, if one thinks of implementing. If we would have made an attempt to do so, we might have ended up with a voluminous encyclopaedia or a series of books, which we are sure, would have been too taxing on the part of readers.

I would like to thank all those who have helped us directly or indirectly in getting the book published through sharing of ideas and experiences. My special thanks to Professor (Dr) Anil Saxena, National Police Academy, India for helping us in researching on a wide range of literature and Ms Leela Kirloskar, the editor of Sage Publications for constantly encouraging and supporting the fine tuning of this book.

**Ashok Chanda**

# Introduction

What do the terms 'strategy' and 'strategic thinking' mean to you? Think for a moment about a strategy for analysing learning needs and support in an organisation. What would be included in such a strategy? Is there a series of steps or phases to be worked through, either as a part of the continuous process at work or as a one-off identification exercise? What part does planning play in this strategy? What techniques could be included? An important aspect in using 'Strategy' is that it helps you to respond to the changing circumstances. Any effective and reliable strategy is the means to ask 'what if?' and 'what now?' questions. It helps to have a toolbox of techniques, i.e., systems and processes that can be called upon and that the choice of techniques is determined by particular circumstances. These techniques, systems or processes in HRM are the 'strategic technologies'. Thus, strategic HR technologies helps us anticipate events and plans for our needs; at other times they help us react quickly to events or when knowledge of needs become urgent. Human resource management is no less than a science. Tools and techniques used in managing people is no less than a technology normally spelled in science, computing and mechanics. Applied human resource management is bringing in all application of tools and techniques available in HRM. A plethora of research literature is available on the subject of HR and the need is to have concise and simple formulas for all relevant angles of managing human resources to have a better perspective and to appreciate the process.

The book is an attempt to provide all the relevant and important HR technologies proven in the industry under one umbrella. The technologies are so weaved that they are most important and are required quite often for application. As many as 40 such technologies have been compiled in this book. Each of these technologies have been elucidated in simple language and with a game analogy for better understanding and to give a holistic perspective. In HR, the games in training have great value, and many complex situations of management are addressed through simple simulated games and plays. On reading through each technology the reader would be in a position to know the concept and also comprehend:

- what the technology is all about and the purpose it solves?
- where it is useful? and
- how to implement the technology in an organisational setting?

Further, reading for better understanding and implementing is also suggested at the end. The books referred in further coaching would give further impetus to go into the depth and try to implement the same. However, there are certain technologies like the Psychometric Testing, where the help of the trained professional is a must. The authors would like to caution the readers that only after having complete knowledge about the same or in consultation with an expert these interventions can be planned. Similarly, for technologies like 360-degree feedback, Self Managed Teams, etc., the organisation needs to have maturity to absorb as well as the guidance of senior professionals who would be able to put the process in place at the right time. However, the technologies described, per se, will not give all the necessary inputs to implement. The book is not an user manual for one to start implementing the same in the organisation.

The authors have only made a sincere effort to provide a comprehensive view of all the technologies explained under various spectrums to enable the CEOs, HR professionals, line managers, students, etc., to have a bird's-eye view of the technologies and the purposes behind using these technologies. These HR technologies can be broadly divided into four spectrums:

Spectrum – I    HR Technologies for driving business
Spectrum – II    HR Technologies for building high performing individuals and team culture
Spectrum – III    HR Technologies for attracting and retaining talent
Spectrum – IV    HR Technologies for rethinking the future

- **HR Technologies for driving business.** These include technologies which primarily support the business processes. Though they are distinctive in nature than the normal HR practices, they have all that concerns the people processes. HR Balance Sheet, Business Process Outsourcing (BPO), etc., are integral with driving business with human resources.
- **HR Technologies for building high performing individuals and team culture.** The business scenarios are changing from individual driven processes to team driven. However, teams comprise individuals and have varied thinking. It is a challenging task to build a team and generate congruence and synergy so that the team operates with high spirit and productivity.
- **HR Technologies for attracting and retaining talent.** Attracting and retaining talent is the 'mantra' of HR, however, still one needs proper technologies to do so. Right from the employees' entry till exit, managing them in all spheres of the business cycle is important. The employees' recruitment, proper induction, training, compensation, appraisal, career advancement, etc., need a great attention while managing people on the job.

● **HR Technologies for rethinking the future.** Technological advancement has changed the scenario of the business. With the help of technology the distance barrier have literally vanished. Team members away from each other can operate easily with the help of technology as a virtual team. Massive database of the employees can be stored and retrieved at the finger tip of the decision maker and employees can themselves have access to the information of their own selves and others through employees' self-service approach.

# The Structure of HR Technology

The explanatory structure followed in this book has been detailed here.

## Intent

The various goals, which can be achieved by technology are being given to know why and how the technology would be useful in the organisation.

## Expression

Expression is a statement or presentation that indicates what a word or other expression refers to or otherwise means. The technology is being defined as what it means all about.

## Comprehension

Each technology is explained with a bird's-eye view of what the technology is all about. The comprehension would guide through the historical evolution, the importance of the technology in the organisational context, the process, and its uses and most important of all why the same is strategic.

## Experiential Application

### a) Prerequisite

The process is linkage of the theory with the application of technology. An understanding of the technology would always be the knowledge that would only be useful when the learning is transformed into application. The process shows the way of how technology can be translated into the organisational setting under this experiential application method.

## b) Process Steps

The process through which the technology can be implemented is given in a process flow chart method to provide a sequential approach. Whatever be the technology what is most important is the process through which it is implemented. Without a right process, the whole purpose of implementing the technology would go waste in terms of time and money, and may also be detrimental to the interests of the HR and the organisation. However no time stipulation is given for each step as the movement through each step depends upon the maturity of the organisation and the pace of implementation.

## Potential Gains and Areas of Concern

Each technology in an organisational context adds value by way of fulfilment of the objectives. Each technology if implemented would derive gains, but it needs to be implemented under conditions and various precautions need to be taken. The gains derived from the implementation of the technology are given. The potential gains are many, but only the important ones are given to illustrate how it will achieve the organisational goals and align with the business strategy.

The areas of concerns are important to take precautions so that the game will be won without any negative consequences. It is given so that sufficient measures can be taken to minimise the negative consequences and pave the way for potential gains, like the organisational culture, structure, strategy, skilled set of the people, etc.

## Measurability

## Try It Out

It comprises of five questions assessing the compatibility of the technology with the organisation under question. A five-point scale ranging from 1: not at all done, 2: moderately done, 3: to some extent done, 4: to a great extent done, and 5: excellently done, determines the extent to which the technology exists in the given organisation.

## Score Card

The score card is a measurement tool for the technology on various parameters. Here, an explanation of the elements of the HR Improvement Plan is being given.

- **Objective Elements.** They are organised into areas of performance called Indicators. These are the broader areas under which any HR normally functions. These areas can be increased or decreased depending upon the nature of function.
- **Unit.** It is the unit of measurement. The HR in pursuit of excellence tries to achieve each of these indicators. Many of the indicators are qualitative in nature and these need to be measured into an observable performance. The unit of performance can be a document, numbers, percentage of coverage, amount, etc.
- **Historical.** It is the performance in the past. Historically if the element is not practised, then it would be NIL, if not, the nature of achievement needs to be mentioned.
- **Last Year.** It is the performance done during the previous year. This is very useful and acts as a benchmark that needs to be surpassed. There are certain elements, which can be done only during certain periods like salary revision, performance appraisal, etc. If any innovation is being planned or a total change in the process, the parameters may also change.
- **Current Year.** It is the performance for the current year and the target date before which the element has to be completed. This is benchmarked against the performance in comparison to the last year.
- **Stretch Targets.** This is given to make the employees stretch to create newer benchmarks. The stretch targets ensure timely completion of the projects.
- **Status.** These are called the Stars. These stars are assigned against the status of performance by each element. At the start of the year no element will have a star and the endeavour of every employee in HR will be to attain 4 stars. Targets and stretch targets ensure timely completion creating 'next mark'. These stars are added in phases at the end of the completion of each stage in the technology. This can also be substituted in the form of Traffic Signals with Red, Amber, Orange and Green for better visibility.

(*: 25% achieved, **: 50% achieved, ***: 75% achieved, ****: 100% achieved)

| Technology | Objective Elements | Unit | Historical | Last Year | Current Year | Stretch Target | Status |
|---|---|---|---|---|---|---|---|
| No. | Element | Doc | Nil | No | Yes | NA | ** |

## Proven Track Record

The technologies mentioned in the book are not just theoretical or abstract, but which are being proven on application. Theoretically any concept will be good, but its worth will be proven only when it's being applied. Each technology is being dealt with examples of world-class companies, which have implemented the technology and have derived benefits. Some of the companies had made a turnaround by taking risk and implementing them. Various companies have used each technology, but to provide the examples, which have been laid down, two such examples are given to prove that the technology has delivered the objectives for which it is meant.

## Applied HR Case

The technology is being explained in a bird's-eye view by way of giving the concept and also learning through experiential approach. To enable the reader to know whether he has understood the technology, a case study is being given to enable him to read and answer the questions mentioned after the case study. A satisfactory answer to the technology application will fulfil the learning cycle.

## Supplementary Coaching

The technology mentioned earlier, per se, would not suffice to implement in the organisation, since the objective is to provide a bird's-eye view. Important books published and the Websites in each technology are given to enable the reader to further go through the technology thoroughly and make a platform for implementation.

## HR Branding

Brand is an integral part of consumerism. An organisation spends millions every year on brand promotion of products and services. This is primarily done to establish a recall on the mind of the consumer so that at the time of actual purchase, they recall the brand and make their purchase based on it. Internally within the organisation, the processes, which we put in, are also generally given a brand name. This is because the strategic processes through specific tools and techniques must travel to the lowest strata of the organisation. For making the technologies of HR more acceptable and bringing in recall in the mindset of employees, a suitable, easy-to-remember and relevant with the technology, brand names are given. Many organisations successfully run such internal brand, which becomes so popular that the initiative gets the synonyms and then the original name. Many examples are related to reward schemes in companies, which are branded so well that employees recognise it with the brand name attached to it. The focus of the book is to bring in some of those interesting brand names that are used in an organisation for popularising and disseminating the HR process deep within the organisation.

## HR Word Power

At the end, the book focuses on the meanings of various concepts of HR and those associated with HR. Since HR derives many of its theories, concepts, formula, etc., from other behavioural sciences, a comprehensive work should give the meanings of the concepts associated with HR to bring in clarity of thought.

# Conclusion

- Strategy for an organisation is the primary source of conceptualising developing and successfully growing business proposition.
- Strategy and Strategic thinking are linked and must be deep imbibed in the organisation culture of the company.
- As other business needs to define their long-term strategy, there is alarming awareness now to evolve strategic human resource processes in the organisation.

With advance research on various management tools and techniques, we all find numerous kinds of advancements, which keep coming quite often. It has become a trend and tendency for every manager to adopt such tools and techniques in all the fields of management and experimenting in their organisations. We also find that it does not work as easily as envisaged at the time of implanting. Every system, however good it may be, is successful only if the implementation is done properly. To do so it is essential that along with the system, the process of systems be clearly defined. By the process we imply the methodology or the means of conducting the whole system right from evolution to implementation.

# Part 1

## Strategic HR Technologies:
## A Framework

# 1 THINKING IN THE FUTURISTIC HRM

## Contents

## Learning Objectives

- Understanding the future scenario imperative in business environment.
- Dealing with change and business dynamics.
- Understanding strategic HR typology and applied HRM.
- Establishing relationship between science and HRM.
- Identifying the various stages of HR practices from contemporary approach to advanced practices.

# Future Scenarios

The past twenty years have seen dramatic changes in the types of work that people are called upon to do and the corresponding changes in the skills, knowledge and abilities required. An event that contributed most to these changes was the invention of the microprocessor in 1971. The innovation triggered other technological developments which resulted in many jobs becoming obsolete or adapting themselves to the changing demands. This effect has been felt everywhere including manufacturing, finance, services and areas of employment. In the nineteenth century most work was conveniently divided between 'doers' and 'thinkers'. On the doing side were mainly jobs based on motor skills such as that of the printer, turner, coppersmith, blacksmith, etc. Most of these jobs are obsolete or in serious decline today. On the thinking side were cognitive skill-based tasks such as those of a manager, foreman, clerk, lawyer and teacher. However, over the past twenty years there has been a steady growth in new jobs such as those of a system analyst, knowledge engineer, corporate manager, network engineer and consultants of various kinds.

Today, we all stand in a vortex of technological, economic, demographic and cultural change. Are we to deny it, resist it, or accept the fact that we too must change? Our brain must accept change and adapt to the changing environment. Our current assignment is evolutionary, nothing less than the remaking of man and woman into a more civilised form than our ancestors. We must do it, not within an extended family in a forest or on a vast savanna, but within what is becoming the human family in a global village. We cannot go backward; we cannot stand still. This is a personal journey and we must will the direction. There is no waiting for some evolutionary process of adaptation, because evolution as a biological process has no goal beyond reproduction and survival. We need to understand how the currents of technological change will affect our business and its place in the global market, how demographic and cultural changes will alter our self-perceptions, our perception of others and of human society as a whole. In short, we must know what the future would look like. Let's look at a few interesting scenarios.

## Scenario One: Personnel Information and Benefits Administration

Sitting down on her personal computer Jessey clicks on her HRIS icon, enters her password, and pulls up her own personal file. She edits her personal details by overwriting on the existing ones. She confirms that she wants her incentive payments directly deposited in the bank. Then she adds her newborn baby's name to her benefit package and designates the same as the beneficiary of her life insurance policy in case of any eventuality. She has to now confirm the changes with her password 'Signature'. When she types an incorrect number in her password, the system beeps and displays the error message, 'invalid password—please try again'. This is essential because error checking and exception control built into the system prevent Jessey from entering invalid data. The system is designed with sufficient control mechanism that prevents others to misuse the same. Jessey with the changes made in the HRIS is able to give the information to the HR department online without even contacting the HR department by ensuring her privacy and updating the data in the personal files.

## Scenario Two: Benefit Information Inquiries

Raman is in a hospital emergency room at 2:00 a.m., waiting for word about his 15-year-old son Prabhakar, who was found unconscious at a party that was raided by police. A preliminary diagnosis indicated that Prabhakar had consumed 'alcohol and some drugs'. Raman is fairly sure that his health care benefits cover dependents' emergency room treatment, but was not sure about the long-term care should so be needed. Also, what if he needed drug alcohol counselling? Raman remembers that his cellular computer phone PDA (personal digital assistance) is in his pocket. The PDA can connect to his firm's wide area network (WAN) from anywhere in the world. He dials with WAN's access number for Human Resource Services, logs on with his password, and listens to the interactive voice response menu, and goes on.

## Scenario Three: Employment

From the deck chair at the beach hotel in Tokyo, Kim is job-hunting via PDA and satellite to electronic job posting services. Kim, a freelance petroleum reservoir engineer, is taking two weeks off after six months of working for an oil company in Saudi Arabia. He is a professional contract employee, an increasingly common kind of worker. Before leaving Saudi, Kim signalled his availability by posting his resume, employment contracts, salary and benefit requirements and date of availability to an electronic bulletin board run by his professional manpower consultant. This bulletin board serves as a job posting system for both employers and employees worldwide. Accessing the bulletin board from his lounge chair on the beach, Kim finds that he has three indications of interest from prospective employers.

## Scenario Four: Team Placement

Rita, systems development manager for M/s Compulink Inc., a BPO in Bangalore, India, needs to assemble a multi-disciplinary team to integrate the information-processing department of two banks, one in Hong Kong and one in Los Angles. At her PC, Rita clicks on HRIS icon, followed by 'Team Builder' and then job/role requirements to specify competencies needed by team members: language skills, technical skills, industry knowledge and interpersonal competencies. After defining job/role requirements, she clicks on 'find team members' button. The computer immediately searches the personnel information records of the 3,000 regular and 2,200 contract employees available to the firm and identifies those system professionals who meet Rita's language, technical, business and personal competency requirements.

## Scenario Five: Online Coaching and Training

Michael, an MBA from a top business school with a reputation as a brilliant corporate self-analyst, is in his first line job: South Georgia Territory Sales Manager. Michael knows he was given this job to get line experience and to see if he has the right stuff to stay on the fast track to an executive position. This morning Michael faces a confrontation with one of his top salespeople, Joe. A customer has complained that Joe 'was drunk again when he called on us and embarrassed me in front of my boss. If you want to keep our account, you had better shape up Joe.' New to the territory and 20 years junior, Michael doesn't feel he knows how to handle a confrontation with Joe. He clicks IHRMIS icon on his PC, and then on management advisor for drug and alcohol abuse confronting an employee. When Joe was asked to sit on PC and he clicks 'yes' on HRM icon, he sees a ten-minute tape of an employee telling a boss about a decision to seek assistance for a personal problem, and how the employee can get help instead of getting fired.

## Scenario Six: Online Attendance and Pay Roll Management

Sofia, an expert in software security management is one of the few trained by SS Software Limited, which has a global clientele. In a month she travels to various countries. Her attendance is marked through the laptop she is carrying with her. Sofia gets updated through the e-mails received across the globe and has to look at the mails for every six hours. The moment she connects the system, the server at the Head Quarters catches the details and marks her attendance. Sofia can take leave by logging on to the intranet and submitting the leave form. The form reaches her boss and the leave letter pops up in her system for approval. Sofia gets details of her pay and the deposit details online the moment the banker confirms to the HR that the salary is being credited into the respective employee's account. Alternatively, she also gets an SMS from the HRIS which updates her about the attendance and the payment details.

### Scenario Seven: Human Resource Assets: Training Needs Assessment

When Ashley, CEO of Net Transport, boots his computer in the morning, his 'wallpaper' (opening screen) shows a message stating:

- Business Alert.
- Sales are down by 20.4 per cent in Eastern Europe.
- Problem causes: customer satisfaction down by 26.3 per cent.
- Human Resources Indicators.
- Front line employee's satisfaction: down by 0.9 per cent.
- Compensation: 4.3 per cent below market.
- Training Plan: 12 per cent completed.

During the night, various active agents, small expert systems software programmes triggered by a timer—call Net Transport's business and Human Resources Database around the world. These programme agents are part of an Executive Information System (EIS) that automatically uploads and analyses data, looks for patterns and problems that may explain business results and reports its finding to top management. The EIS provides him with up-to-the minute assessment of Net Transport's most valuable assets, its human resources.

# Change Makes All the Difference

The world does not stand still, and today, the pace of change is more rapid especially after the information revolution. The word 'change' has gained significance in business, economics, politics and society. One must be aware of the history of change in our world and be patient with transition. Change, per se, can be small and big, but it takes a long time to accommodate change, and the bigger the change, the longer it will take to adjust with it. Change is inevitable and one must not feel threatened by it. One need to see for the natural order of things and must have ability to separate positive change from negative ones. Resistance to change is like treading water and it wears you out if you stand against it.

Albert J. Dunlop, who has developed a reputation as a turnaround specialist, keeps an ornament on his desk of circling sharks. 'You must get rid of people who represent the old culture, or they will fight you,' he says. 'And you have to get rid of all old symbols.' If old symbols stay in place, too many people assume that nothing has changed and they need only wait out the new comers. When an organisation embarks on change, it must create new myths and symbols for its people. Some companies encourage change bringing in outsiders. Canon hires middle managers from outside the company. Honda does the same, and looks especially for those who it believes will bring in new ideas. Others like Pepsi rotate their people between field office, home office, marketing, distribution and product development to break up subcultures (Jennifer James, 1996: 29).

# New Business Reality

As we step in the new era of change, we see the emergence of borderless, interconnected global economy, fuelled by the spread of free market and democracy around the world. Since the Industrial Revolution, not only have we faced such forces in just two fundamental areas of world society, the electronic information revolution and global economic independence, but also in globalisation which is a new international system that is shaping domestic and international politics and changing the rules of the trade.

We lived in a well networked, interconnected world with computer devices embedded in telephones, cars, televisions and household appliances. The Internet and electronic commerce are dramatically changing our concepts on business. Our relationship with customers and suppliers has forever been altered and employees have access to information that they have never dreamt of a decade ago. Everyone is talking to everyone else in real time. The movement of people from office based to home-based work has already taken place in a number of organisations, and in some cases, the move has been towards almost total home working. If the trend continues we will have to review what is meant by the term 'organisation'. To help satisfy the technical logistics or the back-up needs of people who now work from home, there are 'tele-cottages' (small business centres), where information technology equipment is provided for the use of independent workers on a 'club' type arrangement.

In the twenty-first century, competition comes from all corners. Not only does the United States compete with Taiwan and Switzerland for jobs and customers, but businesses in Chicago must also compete locally with companies from Canada and Mexico. Furthermore, businesses in various countries are infiltrating one another's territories as never before. For example, European firms own large portions of the American publishing industry. Japan owns large portions of the world's automobile market and now entering the media, while Scandinavian companies provide a majority of the world's mobile telephones. India produces the world's tractors, France is the largest producer of glass, Chile is the leading supplier of copper and China produces many of the world's apples.

Global consumerism has skyrocketed, creating a proliferation of global brands while homogenising consumers' tastes. Global brands bring us together, linking people in Cape Town to unlikely partners in West Bank. People in the most remote regions of our world recognise the red Coke can, McDonald's golden arches and the silver medallion of Mercedes-Benz. International trade is burgeoning, as evidence by explosions of FDI (foreign direct investment); export expansion, and the growth of multinational corporations. Globally connected capital markets are producing open, transparent exchanges where investment flows seamlessly across the trading floor worldwide and the stock exchanges further enabling it.

Even within companies, cubicles and cabins are disappearing in favour of virtual teams. Companies seek suppliers, customers and employees globally for economies of scale rather than their own sons of soil or country of origin. Sharing techniques among industries and across national borders, they develop network organisations that are fast, flat and flexible knowledge companies. Their corporate cultures are characterised by less bureaucracy, more teamwork, better knowledge management and infectious entrepreneurship. In this competitive marketplace of winners and losers, there is a race of brainpower, creating whole new knowledge generating industries. The role of the government as a welfare state is also diminishing as the world moves from state controlled economies to market economies and the privatisation of business. Increasing pluralism and democracy accelerate the creation of one global community with common interest and concerns.

But not all is good news and global harmony. New threats proliferate like chemical and biological warfare, urban terrorism and digital espionage represent only a portion of our global minefield. Threats of nationalism and protectionism are lurking just under the surface. But still there is no turning back. This trend towards a fully integrated, borderless, global economy will continue and accelerate. To cope up with this growing pace of change and to bring in competitiveness in such a dynamic environment, there is a strong need for managing human resources.

# Science of HRM

The word 'technology' normally goes with science and technical subjects. The dictionary meaning of technology means a science of industrial and mechanical arts. Technology denotes proven methods or systems and the process for attaining output from a given input. Technology improves over a period of time by bringing in corrections in the process, with further research and by re-inventing the mechanics used in it. This is called technological advancement. For example, ever since the invention of the wheel, the usage of the wheel in various moving objects has dramatically undergone changes. Initially wheels were used in cart pulling, then subsequently in automobiles, then trains, and so on.

Human behaviour over a period of time has been captured through a definite science called behavioural science. This science from its inception till today advanced a lot with the changes in the business scenario. The people in the organisation need to cope up with technological advancement so that maximum output can be derived out of it. However, it is always a challenge for an organisation to match technological intervention with human skills. It has always been the endeavour of a behavioural scientist to find a success formula to harness human resources. The propounded theories of behavioural science, over a period of time, have challenged the changed environment and new avenues have been developed. The motivational theories, the interpersonal relationship orientation processes, the leadership theories, etc., have taken new shapes with changing time.

The science of HRM is one among the previous behavioural sciences and has brought in many new models, concepts, theories and processes which are being used successfully in the corporations for managing people. These tools and techniques are nothing but the technologies of HRM, similar to that of managing other natural resources. The tools are being designed in a scientific way using the logical methodology to predict human behaviour and the precision of such prediction has increased enormously with changing time. The technologies, which are available in the gamut of HR to manage the precarious and precious resources, are significant for any enterprise, and they always try to attain the equilibrium of human resources and other resources. Strategic HR technologies are the technologies used under the gamut of HR for effectively and efficiently managing HRM, which enable the organisation to optimise human resources and obtain a competitive advantage.

Definitions of technology vary widely among organisational writers. Technology is the term used to refer to the work performed by an organisation. More specifically, it refers to the knowledge, tools, machines, information, skills and materials used to complete tasks within an organisation as well as the nature of the outputs of the organisation. The definition implies that technology incorporates the idea of the way an organisation uses resources to produce products and services.

In other words, technology deals with the transformation processes, with the application of knowledge, skills and tools to problems or tasks. Technology deals with how people in an organisation carry out their tasks to produce the products and services of the organisation. Technology, however, applies to more than just those tasks directly involved with the transformation process. It also deals with how products and services are delivered and distributed, the supporting activities necessary to bring services and products to the market, and every other activity within an organisation. Some version of technology can be used to describe the nature of any task or job within an organisation.

Organisation Behaviour and Organisation Development have gifted many HR technologies to the corporate world. From the era of industrialisation till modern days of business processes, these technologies are put in practice in one form or the other. The travel of industrial relations to personnel management, and subsequently Human Resources Management has not significantly changed the concept but definitely brought in new processes that can suit the modern management philosophy. The new enterprise and the evolution of HRM have significantly influenced IR practices almost everywhere. Critics of HRM charge that its hidden aim is to wipe out pluralism at the workplace and establish the hegemony of the autocratic managerial authority. Developments in HRM literature have pointed out the possibility that IR issues are likely to be subsumed under HRM. Today's IR is being labelled as the 'New IR' or employees' relations. Corporate bargaining is another significant and noticeable trend in this new IR.

With the rising of the Web economy, HRM becomes more technology driven than ever before. This will also require an essential prerequisite development of human resource management skills and competencies in people working in various parts of the organisation. Human Resource managers will have to demonstrate greater technical competence, ability to use organisational development technologies and managing change. More than that they are expected to play the role of business partners and agents for change.

## Applied HRM

The science of human resource is not new. Management gurus, behavioural scientists, researchers and academicians have written ample literature on the management of human resource in different forms such as personnel management, industrial relations, industrial psychology, organisational behaviour, organisational development, social psychology, etc. Each of these disciplines has contributed in various forms of managing human resource in the life of corporations and individuals. The propounded theories are nothing but an applied research and a practical experience for a given subject. The management of human resource is not the outcome of the Industrial Revolution alone, but it has evolved since the days of the ancient civilisations, when managing human resources was always a challenge and many philosophers have attempted to map the patterns of behaviour and derive theories to manage them.

The concept of applied HRM can be related to applied mechanics of science and technologies. Applied HRM deals with the application side of HR. For example, applied physics means the application of theories of physics, emphasising the practical part of physics but not ignoring the theories. The 360-degree feedback and performance management are examples of applied HR concepts and have been a useful technique in managing human resources.

Human resource processes are an outcome of trial and error techniques, which is normally used in mechanics. As the organisation grows the complexity of managing people grows because of their increase in number, and the growing work pressure, which leads to personal as well as interpersonal problems among the employees. The corporations keep experimenting and introducing new ways and means to resolve such divergent views leading to interpersonal issues in the workplace. This gives birth to various new forms of applications because each situation varies with the previous one and more refined ways to deal with these situations evolve. Thus, over a period of time, though the status of human being in the company remains the same, the processes to manage the people in an organisation becomes more advanced.

If you look at theories and practices there is hardly a thin line between them. Theories evolve from practical experiences while practices are based on theoretical inputs. In all sense, theories are defined as something, which is propounded for universal application, are generally documented and moves around a model. Practices are real life case studies, experiential learning and have input and output in measurable terms. Applied HRM is a mix of human resource theories moulded in applications, which is easy to apply and implement in organisations.

## Strategic HRM

For remaining competitive and playing globally, the only factor that can make an organisation move is their people. All organisations have realised the strategic importance of human resources. Despite criticism, the usage of various HRM practices gives the management an edge over combating competition. This is done by systematically knitting them into well-articulated HRM processes. Strategic HRM refers to a central philosophy of people organisation and management and its translation into appropriate HRD tools and techniques.

As the dynamics of the human resource changes, the human resource functions become more strategic in nature. The companies that are enduringly successful will be those that begin as early as possible to define and embody in their activities a unique competitive position vis-à-vis human resource management. During periods of uncertainty in the development of an industry, its basic productivity frontier is being established or re-established. Strategic HR is a long-term direction of the HR function in an organisation. It describes the best options suitable to an organisation for managing its human resource in line with the available systems and processes, resources and the environment. Strategic HR includes: a case for change, the vision, the mission of the function, definitions of the customers to HR, the design criteria, relationships, the transition process and the implication for stakeholders. The customer definition and overall HR mission, while particularly troublesome to develop, ultimately would be helpful in building an integrated strategy.

## Strategy and Strategic Thinking

Strategy's original literary meaning is 'the art and science of directing military forces'. These days, the term 'strategy' is frequently used in the corporate world. It is used in describing the steps taken by an organisation in achieving its vision and mission. When the leader of a company or an organisation loses perspective, the results can be serious and long lasting. An obvious example is IBM, but there are many more from the auto makers of the 1960s and 1970s to the timber workers of the 1980s and the American Medical Association (AMA) of the 1990s. The IBM never saw the implications for the future posed by Microsoft DOS because the company operated in a self-sealing culture that deals with hardware, not software and shut out soft information (Lynch 1982: 29).

Jauch & Glueck (1988: 11) define strategy as '... a unified, comprehensive and integrated plan that relates the strategic advantages of the firm to the challenges of the environment. It is designed to ensure that the basic objective of the enterprise is achieved through proper execution by the organisation.' Basically any strategic process can be broken down into two phases—formulation and implementation. Strategy formulation is concerned with making decisions with regard to organisation's vision and mission, establishing long and short range objectives to achieve the organisation's vision, and selecting the best alternative to be used in achieving the organisation's objectives. While reviewing the strategic decisions in management, Johnson (1987: 4) suggests that they are likely to be concerned with some of the following:

- the long-term direction of the organisation;
- the scope of the organisation's activities;
- the matching of organisational activities to the environment and its resource capability;
- the major resource implications for an organisation;
- the higher degree of uncertainty involved in such decisions;
- the demand of an integrated approach in managing the organisation; and
- the change implied.

Strategy implementation is concerned with aligning the organisation structure, systems and processes with the chosen strategy. It involves making decisions with regard to matching strategy and organisational structure and providing organisational leadership pertinent to the strategy and monitoring the effectiveness of the strategy in achieving the organisation's objectives. Implementing change of strategic dimensions (i.e., decisions with long-term effects) is likely to involve the persuasion and readiness of people to change from what they are doing. Moreover, the expectation may be that they change towards something that is ill-defined, uncertain and unfamiliar. Not surprisingly the management of strategic change can be highly problematic (Johnson 1987: 6).

# Evolution of Strategic HR Technologies: Contemporary to Advance

Economic restructuring is noticeably practised in almost all the countries around the world. The concept of a welfare state has been diluted to make way for an alternative development paradigm. Most nations which resort to a new paradigm were forced to restructure their economies due to inflation, rising unemployment and fiscal deficits. These changes and challenges arising out of it could not be met without the adoption of alternative strategies, including policies involving greater resort to human resources management practices. American employers found the personnel policies in Japan quite attractive, and that attraction led to the popularisation of HRM. Later on, British and other European employers also started resorting to HR Strategies based on Japanese workplace practices. Such practices like 'JIT', '5s' are receiving greater attention from the Western world, especially from the USA and UK.

Traditional personnel management was obsessed with its power, whatever, it was, and did not shift its focus towards delivering any tangible achievement of organisational goals. It was accused of having a narrower functional outlook. The training of personnel managers did not enable them to speak the language warranted by business strategy, market competition and other internal customers in the organisation. Hence the need for travelling from contemporary to advanced practices was felt. The belief that the human resources were too important to be left to operational personnel managers grew and organisations realised the importance of having a HR Department rather than merely colouring the Personnel Department to a HR Department. The need for transferring HR related decisions to the top management was felt with managers eventually implementing decisions which were to percolate down. The prevailing opinion was that personnel managers were unable to fully utilise the inner potentials of the people. The comparison of contemporary with advance HRM can be seen in Table 1.1.

TABLE 1.1
**Comparison of Contemporary and Advance HRM**

| Dimensions | Contemporary | Advance |
|---|---|---|
| Ideology | Industrial relationship | Employee's relationship |
| Conflict perception | Unionised conflict | Individual conflict |
| Nature of contract | Compliance driven | Commitment driven |
| Systems and procedures | Rule dominated | Culture and value dominated |
| Planning perspective | Ad hoc, reactive | Integrated, proactive |
| Union acceptability | Acceptable | Not acceptable |
| Level of trust | Low | High |
| Key relationship | Employee–employer | Customer |
| Management role | Transactional | Transformational |
| Basis of job design | Division of labour | Team |
| Key role player | PM/IR specialist | Line and general managers |
| Skill acquisition | Training and development | Learning organisation |
| Reward management | Standardise job evaluation | Performance related |

# Stages of HR Practices and Its Related Approach

From the inception of an organisation to its attainment of maturity stage, an organisation undergoes phenomenal cultural change. To suit the organisation culture, the technologies used in HRM also undergo substantial changes over a period of time. The organisation passes through four stages of transformation, i.e., start-up, growth, maturity and decline. The HR technologies applied in each stage is different. The process of performance management and compensation in start-up phase is very different from the maturity stage. As the organisation passes through the volatility of different stages of growth, HR technologies also have four distinctive stages (see Table 1.2).

TABLE 1.2
**Stages of HR Technologies**

| Stage of HR Technologies | Approach to Managing People | Approach to HR Technologies |
|---|---|---|
| **Reactive** | Reacts only after the situation arise. | Very few formal systems. |
| **Compliance driven** | Implementing industry standards and complying with legislative requirements. | Complex formal systems. |
| **Risk management** | Identifies, assesses and reduces the risk inherent in the operations. | Performance through people aspects integrated into standard operation. |
| **Continuous improvement** | Actively seeks alternative approach to human processes to reduce the risk. | Most aspects integrated into standard operations. |

- When the organisation's HR system reacts with the issues, responds to the problem standing in the front and diagnose, such actions which are purely based on a situation in which HR is operating reactive in nature, in such a stage the organisation hardly ever emphasises on formal documented systems. The HR decisions are taken by an individual who is a decision-maker and the process is generally ad hoc. This pattern is seen more in small and medium organisations where the systems have not taken the roots and the decisions are made by the Manager. This stage is contemporary for HR technologies.
- There are certain norms prescribed by the government machineries or have been in practice along with the existence of the laws of the land, which organisations tend to follow meticulously. This is so purely to avoid legal consequences and to follow requisite formalities showing the abidance of the labour legislation. The HR practices are directed towards fulfilment of provisions stated for compliance under each law. They also follow the set standards of the industry and move on the same way as they did in the past. Approach to HR technologies is generally through complex formal systems. This stage too is contemporary for HR technologies.
- Risk management through mitigation plans in details is the priority for many corporations these days. The organisation having HR technologies, which identifies, assesses and reduces the risks inherent in the operations, is in the stage of risk management approach. The HR practices proactively plans and designs the systems to avoid the problems encountered in managing human resources in the organisation processes. This stage is being considered as the specialist approach to resolve organisational problems.
- The Japanese management believes that it is not possible for any corporation to reach perfection. Therefore, each organisation has to develop newer and newer ways and means through continuous improvement processes. Continuous improvement is the ultimate in business science. The organisation's HR technologies must choose such episodes to derive a lesson out of it. In such situations, most people integrate and align standard operations with that of continuous improvement.

# Conclusion

The world is experiencing dramatic changes in every sphere of life and the change is inevitable. Either one must change oneself along with the dynamics of change or the change would change the person.

- The future scenarios of personal information and benefit administration, employee self services, employment, team placement, on-line coaching and training has significantly changed the way in which HR is being perceived and viewed for future deliverables.

- The HR technologies can be defined from contemporary to advanced stages in which, it must travel from the reactive to compliance-driven technologies, risk management and continuous improvement stages, depending on the organisational maturity to accommodate such systems in the work environment.
- The HR technologies for different processes in the organisations should suitably be implemented such as for driving business, building high performing individuals and team culture, managing a large employee base and to keep pace with the technology revolution.

## References and Further Readings

Jauch, Lawrance R. and William F. Glueck. 1988. *Business Policy and Strategy Management*, Singapore: McGraw-Hill.

Lynch, James J. 1982. *Making Manpower More Effective: A Systematic Approach to Personal Planning*, London: Pan Books.

# Part 2

## Strategic HR Technologies

# Spectrum I
## HR Technologies for Driving Business

The management process such as planning and strategy development is the first to be touched by a customer value effort. Examining key business processes—those begin and end with the customers, and their sub-processes—billing, is also crucial. But there is another set of activities that must be aligned with strategy or process improvement or reengineering, those that support the employees and managers who must deliver customer value. Primary goal should be to raise employees' awareness of customers and promote an understanding of the customer needs. 'Training employees to interact with customers' and 'enabling frontline employees to exercise initiative in addressing customers needs' are the new goals in the progressive organisations.

The enchanted question of every HR practitioner is how to align its human resources and all the process of HR are integrated in such a way that they achieve the business plans of the organisation. The success of any organisation depends upon how the employees translate the resources with incremental approach towards providing the best products and the service. Only when the human resources are managed and developed to excel an organisation wherein all the employees would add value to the firm, which will lead to sustained competitive advantage over its competitors.

This requires that the organisation needs to apply those management techniques that fits the business plans and the rapidly changing environment. The relative strength of every organisation is only when the HR brings in the management techniques, which can interrelate various departments managing the business. The technology has so advanced that every department demands specialised competencies to manage and work in silos. Departments have their own goals and plans to achieve their key performance areas, but many times fail to appreciate the business plans as they are not in line with what the organisation wants. Organisations suffer due to excessive specialisation as they are not able to integrate with the business needs and everyone looks for vertical integration of the business process to achieve the desired goals. Human resource processes can no longer be a cost centre but has to definitely contribute in making profit for the organisations. This spectrum emphasises on how the HR technologies support enhancement of profit making, the main purpose of the organisational existence and building organisation culture to speed up the response time of organisation. Both these valuable requirements are imbibed by usage of the six technologies detailed in the entire spectrum.

# 2  PROFITING FROM HUMAN RESOURCES

## Contents

➟ Learning Objectives
➟ Human Capital as a Scarce Resource
➟ Driving Business Orientations

- HR Strategy Linking Business Strategy
- Productivity and Quality at Workplace
- Service Orientations and Innovativeness in Products and Services
- Enabling Structure Leading to Profiting

➟ Enable SHR Technology—Key to Success

SHR Technology-01  HR Strategy
SHR Technology-02  HR Performance Plan
SHR Technology-03  Organisation Structure
SHR Technology-04  Reengineering HRD
SHR Technology-05  Business Process Outsourcing
SHR Technology-06  HR Balance Sheet

➟ Conclusion

## Learning Objectives

- To understand the concept of HR strategy and its linkages with business strategy.
- To examine the evaluation techniques of HR systems through HR performance plan.

- To know the restructuring process and reengineering of human resource management function aligning with technology revolutions.
- To understand the BPO buzzword and outsourcing technology.
- To evolve the human resources balance sheet and ascertaining the worth of human capital.

# Human Capital as a Scarce Resource

According to Peter Drucker, 'The ultimate goal of the corporation is survival', and it remains as the ultimate legacy for every present and future organisations. Every organisation has to manage changes like increasing competitiveness, rapid technological changes, globalisation and information revolutions which have brought about uncertainty and instability. The key indicators of the success of an organisation are profitability, growth and precious manpower. The concept of 'economic man' has become obsolete. The only product that moved from the buyers market to the sellers market is manpower. The 'knowledge worker' has become the real capital. The skills and the cumulative experience of the employees are the most important asset in any organisation. Unlike other resources, human resources cannot be replicated and to attract and retain the right kind of people for the right job, is always a difficult proposition. It is every CEO's obsession to ensure that their human resources are satisfied and everyone contributes in achieving the goals of the organisation, i.e., winning in the marketplace.

Increasingly, the corporations are realising that managing human relations is the most important criteria and with rapid change in the advancement of technology has traversed the knowledge of managing human resources from 'Scientific Management theory' to 'Situational theory of Management'. In this globalised world various technologies have evolved with the sole intention to find out the way to channelise the energies so as to achieve a higher level of organisational performance and in turn the business goals.

Employees are now the key persons responsible for increasing the performance of the organisations thus giving a competitive edge to the organisation. This is only possible when new strategies are human centric rather than capital centric. Similarly, decentralisation and empowerment are required rather than centralisation. The organisations should move towards a cooperative and collaborative working relationship rather than a conflicting and confrontational relationship. Systems and practices need to be development oriented. The beliefs, values and guiding principles of the organisation altogether make the best place for everyone (i.e., employee) to work in, where they can enhance their competencies which leads to a better performance in the organisation. The organisation must invest in developing new skills among the employees so that they can be partners in the future and newer technologies.

# Driving Business Orientations

Increasing competition and technological changes have made organisations to respond very quickly to the changing needs and expectations of the customers. The effectiveness and efficiency of the organisation depends upon how fast it reaches the customer before the competitor. Organisations have to be highly innovative and creative to meet these challenges. The challenge of every HR practitioner is how to align its human resources, various processes of HR in relation with the business plans and meeting the customer requirements. The employees need to translate the resources with incremental approach towards providing the best products and services to the customer. It is necessary that organisations build in a culture of innovations and business orientation among its employees.

Every employee must be inducted appropriately with the business plan of the company. The orientation and attitude of each employee varies and may differ from time to time. The role of HR is to ensure the employees' development and their competencies in business orientation. Indeed, one of the most important concerns that organisations face is the improvement of productivity of every employee and in turn the organisational productivity.

Human resource is the only source where all the other resources are being converted into products and services. The products and services to be delivered at the customer end determines the level of increase in the bottom line that can happen. To do so, getting the right kind of resources is a must.

Hence, HR policies need to be impact oriented rather than activity oriented. The deliverables must add value to the business and practices rather than the activity being done only for the sake of doing it. For example, performance appraisal system is not an annual ritual for giving the increments to the employees but shall be used as a tool to anchor business plans along with individual plans, to clearly identify the Key Result Areas and evaluation against business plans.

## HR Strategy Linking Business Strategy

The strategy of HR is to design and integrate systems, processes and resources to suit the business strategy. It helps in ensuring the goals and accomplishing the objectives of an organisation. The HR strategy needs to enable the organisation to remain effective by building critical organisational capabilities to achieve the goals. The ability of the employees to provide high quality service and value to the customer depends upon the policies and practices that enable them to foster the bondage with the customers. The strategy needs to be looked up holistically aligning the systems, competencies and the culture with the business strategy. To work up for this strategy, people need to be competent and motivated to achieve the organisational goals. For example, the policies and systems must bring in the need for achievement among the employees so that they can drive the systems with the intrinsic rewards rather than external rewards.

The HR strategy for the organisation must comprise of what is being required and what would enable the company to derive the strategy to bring in the synergy between the systems, practices and activities in line with the business objectives. Organisations must realise that dynamic and creative workforce can only bring in sustained competitive advantage.

## Productivity and Quality at Workplace

The strategies of the corporations in managing human resources which require new kinds of capabilities to cope up with customers' requirements have been redefined from 'mass production' to 'quality production' because of the changing needs of the customers. Quality per se is not what the top management decides but it's a movement by the employees to bring in world-class standards in the products and services to meet the needs of the customers or even beyond their satisfaction. However, it does not mean to say that the top management role is not the sole factor for quality, but it is the determinant factor for quality.

Managing the diverse workforce that produces quality with productivity is important and it is possible only when the employees have the competencies to deliver excellence and superior performance. Competencies include knowledge, skill and attitude. While entering an employee has the knowledge and skill to an extent. But over the period of time, with training and development, an employee enhances his competencies to produce more with it or lesser energies thus raising the productivity. However, the key factor in driving the energies is the attitude. Time and again it has been found that if the majority of the employees have negative attitude, it reflects in the products and service that affect the bottom line of the organisation. Every organisation's dilemma is how to influence the attitude of the employees so that they work with utmost satisfaction, commitment and motivate others to achieve.

## Service Orientations and Innovativeness in Products and Services

The excellence in the organisation comes with how best they can serve the customer to the fullest satisfaction, which comes only when every employee in the organisation is focused on customer centric philosophy. It is not only that organisation must have customer centric philosophy but also must strive to be the best in the industry, which comes only when the products and services are served innovatively. This innovation need to be there continuously as the service rendered to the customer becomes obsolete and the customer looks for something more. The dynamics of the market forces will ensure only those who meet the expectations of the customers. Hence, only those organisations, which continually improvise products and services, can withstand the market pressure and still survive in the market against the competitors.

The future of industries depends upon the ability of the HR to innovate and bring in service orientation among all the employees from top to bottom. There have been many proven examples in the industry of how they have managed a turnaround being leaders. This requires a paradigm shift on the organisations to allow its resources to think beyond the boundaries and question the fundamentals of the organisations. The systems shall be designed in such a way that change is being accepted and allow employees to think beyond the laid down systems and procedures.

## Enabling Structure Leading to Profiting

A good business strategy is one, which yields results with the aid of a supporting structure. Even though it is said that a good structure cannot by itself produce good results, but a poor organisational structure definitely would hinder good performance. Hence, structure is not an end by itself, but it is a means for improving the performance of the organisation. Organisation structure must be flexible in various ways so as to respond to the present and future demands. It needs to adapt to the changing social environment and co-ordinate among all the functions/groups of the organisation.

The technology has become so advanced that every function/group demands specialised competencies to manage itself. The increasing specialisation has given the cutting edge to the organisation by providing the specialised skills required for effective management of resources but it has also led to each function working in silos. Function/group have their own goals and plans to achieve their key performance areas, but may at times fail to appreciate the business plans and the requirements of the organisation. Organisations suffer due to this excessive specialisation as they are not able to integrate with the business needs as every function/group looks for vertical integration of their process to achieve their goals rather than the goals of the organisation.

The organisation structure must integrate the horizontal integration of various functions/groups and also the people and the process. Hence, it has to be carefully designed to ensure business requirements and lead to high performance. A periodical review is needed to look into how the organisational structure is meeting the requirements. It has not only an impact on the organisational processes, but also the morale and job satisfaction of the employees. During the operationalisation, it is these employees who work within and give a shape to the framework, and if the organisation structure is not dynamic to suit the changing requirement whatever the best efforts put it, the customer does not get what he has expected to be delivered.

The relative strength of every organisation is only when HR brings in the management techniques, which can integrate various departments managing the business and bring in profit orientation. The most important goal of every business is how to increase the bottom line. The increase in the bottom line can only happen when each group/function works in tandem and harnesses the human resource by improving job skills, motivation, professional skills of managers, quality of work, etc., and ensuring that the product/service reaches the customer. The HR has to strategise those important aspects in the business plan, which can deliver business like process reengineering, job rotation, inducting fresh blood, etc. The innovative measure of driving Cross Functional Task Force which can drive both quality and quantity can be instrumental in increasing the productivity.

## Enable SHR Technology—Key to Success

The following technologies have been discussed in this chapter:

SHR Technology-01   HR Strategy—*Linking Business Strategy with HR Strategy.*
SHR Technology-02   HR Performance Plan—*Business Excellence through HR Performance Plan.*
SHR Technology-03   Organisation Structure—*Revamping Business through Restructuring Organisations.*
SHR Technology-04   Reengineering HRD—*Leaping Ahead of Others and Creating New Benchmarks/Next Mark through Re-engineering Human Resource Development.*
SHR Technology-05   BPO—*Focus on Core Processes and Outsource Peripherals through BPO.*
SHR Technology-06   HR Balance Sheet—*Evaluating the Value of Your Human Resource.*

These technologies primarily support the business processes. Though they are distinctive in nature than the normal HR practices, yet they have all that to do with people processes. Any business decisions has an impact on the HR and as HR has the knowledge of management of human resources, the participation with this knowledge would further add value and bring in sustained competitive advantage. Human Resources need to be strategic oriented, and a critical and value adding activity. The human resource strategy is a modern trend, which is imperative for any business to evolve to sustain long-term business plan. Time also has come to link the human resource strategy with business strategy, which is always a matter of debate among the HR professionals and the CEOs of the companies.

The human resource function is a management by itself and it has certain deliverables to achieve in the organisations. It is necessary that the HR is equally monitored for its performance and evaluated for non-performance as well. The HR performance plan is a right tool towards the performance monitoring and excellence towards human resource management. Every organisation's foundation lies with appropriate structure and design and what is most important is not to design the structure but to redesign the structure. The HR today plays an important role in the restructuring processes for bringing in the productivity, efficiency and effectiveness, cost reduction and becoming competitive in today's marketplace.

Most firms made changes in their organisational structure and processes as part of their enhancing customer orientation. Many firms recognise that their structure is primarily to enhance decision making and operates with fewer organisational layers. This required appropriate revamping business through restructuring organisation. To drive to deliver value, whether to shareholders or customers, has resulted in significant changes in the organisation design of corporations throughout the last decade. In general, the trend has been to flatten the organisation's hierarchical structure, remove layers of management, encourage cross-functional cooperation, and drive much of the day-to-day decision making down to those 'closest to the customers'. For example, Xerox is divided into worldwide business divisions organised by the market sector and further down the level as per the business requirements. For meeting the need of individual customers, there is no need to go through a hierarchy at the national level. The change in the structure or redesigning is made to enhance decision making, and the ability to operate with fewer layers and less hierarchy.

The traditional HR function has taken a new shape with the advent of technological revolution and opening up of the market economy. Outsourcing of human resource functions is the current trend that many companies are following and many more are in the process of making. The routine functions or non-value adding activities are looked upon for outsourcing and only developmental and qualitative aspects are more emphasised to be carried out within. There is a trend towards the re-engineering of human resource function in the corporate world. Self services and computerisation is taking the front seat in the management of human resource. Improving the cycle time and simplifying work processes in HR are also important goals which may entail both improving existing processes and a complete HRD reengineering.

Many organisations are asking questions about what is the ROI on every employee deployed in the organisations. The professionals are trying to evaluate the present value of human resource similar to that of calculating the present value of the future annuity in the financial term. Many progressive companies are attempting to evolve the balance sheet of human resource for leveraging the human assets within the company and the stakeholders to enhance the goodwill of the organisations.

# Conclusion

- Human resources as stated by each mission and vision statements of the companies as assets need to be realised in the real sense by the corporations.
- The HR functions must be viewed as a strategic function and aligned with business strategy of the company.
- Employees are to be treated as who drive the business objectives and therefore the people must be competent and aligned with the organisation's performance. Therefore, the HR role comes in to ensure that the employees develop the competencies of business orientation and be able to predict the future success of the organisation.
- The future of the industries depends upon the ability of the HR to innovate and bring in service orientation among the employees.
- The HR functions needs complete re-engineering and must focus its systems and processes towards employee orientation so as to bring economic value addition to the business.

# 'HR STRATEGY'
# LINKING BUSINESS STRATEGY
# WITH HR STRATEGY

*I am captivated more by the dreams of the future than by the history of past.*

—Thomas Jefferson

## Intent

- To link HR strategy with business strategy of the organisation.
- To build human capital for the present and future organisational needs.
- To make the organisation more competitive through HR strategy.
- To provide long-term direction to HR functions in the organisations.

## Expression

Human Resource strategy is a strategic look at HR functions in line with the business functions of the organisation. It is a sequential process of deriving alternative HR practices which are best suited to the business process to provide a competitive edge through expanding HR assets for the organisation.

## Comprehension

To build competitive advantage companies take proactive steps to define their business plans well in advance through proper strategic planning process. Through strategic planning process, the basic productivity frontier is rechristened for an organisation to bite the uncertainty. There can be growth in the business of a company due to innovation, but profits would shrink more and more since the industry witnesses imitation and cut-throat competition which ultimately affects the profitability. These damages can be repaired through strategic positioning of the HR.

The basic aim of HR strategy is to ensure that the structure, culture, quality and the competencies of employees contribute to achieve the organisational goals. Human Resource strategy provides a long-term direction to the HR function in an organisation to enable it to remain effective and efficient in managing the people in the dynamic business environment, by providing the best options suitable to align the human resource with the systems and procedures and resources.

Human Resource strategy is not reactive but proactive by way of achieving the business strategy through culture management, aligning the human resources and the processes. This paves the way in which the organisation can benefit through human resources by identifying the strengths and leveraging on them and at the same time overcoming the weakness through the development process. Human resources are viewed as strategic resources for obtaining the sustained competitive advantage. The evolution of HR strategy is based on the organisation's vision and mission and subsequently, the HR vision, its core competencies and current HR practices. Human Resource strategy defines a pathway for a short-term and long-term direction to the extent at which various HR systems and sub-systems are put into practices. It is evolved in line with the business processes since making of HR strategy takes consideration of business strategy as well.

Human Resource strategy covers vital issues such as change management, matching the resources, competency building, managing cultural change, etc. To achieve the business goals the implications of the HR processes need to be determined and how they enable to achieve the goals, which can include the skill-based recruitment, rewards and recognition, motivation, incentive scheme, etc.

Due to its inherent advantage many of the world-class organisations are realising and adapting a strategic focus on HR issues. Human Resource strategy plays an important role in helping an organisation to sustain in a dynamic environment and hence the strategy needs to be based on intuition and practical approach. The process of HR strategy cannot be done in silos by the HR, but requires commitment from the management, the efforts of the HR team, involvement of other functions and a council to continuously monitor whether the HR strategy is being aligned with the business process or needs some direction.

# Experiential Application

## A. Prerequisite

- The consent of the top management and support of business functions is a must for HR strategy evolution.

- Human Resource has to start thinking in line with the business requirement, appreciate the business, and has to plan all HR initiatives, considering the business requirement only. Effective implementation is everybody's prerogative, however, the HR has to play a lead facilitator's role.
- Besides building a long-term strategy, a yearly rolling plan revisit would enable necessary corrections and improvements in the HR strategy.
- A cross-functional task force if made for HR strategy evolution, then it would be more effective and close to reality.

## B. Process Steps

| Step | Process |
| --- | --- |
| Step – I | Formulation of Human Resource Vision. |
| Step – II | Scanning the environment on current HR trends in the relevant industry needs. |
| Step – III | Auditing of the organisational competencies. |
| Step – IV | Establish linkage of HR strategy with business strategy. |
| Step – V | Defining the long-term objectives of HR strategy. |
| Step – VI | Preparing an action plan to build Strategic Human Resource. |

# Potential Gains and Areas of Concern

- The HR strategy evolution process would give long-term direction to the HR function of the company.
- Human Resource strategy will not be an isolated approach but a fully integrated approach for linking business strategy with HR.
- It will help in building HR competencies in the company for the future and also would help in forecasting the future HR requirements based on the business needs.
- It is not enough to strategise if people do not know what your HR strategy is. It is not enough to know the strategy if you cannot implement. It is not enough to implement the strategy if you do not have the mechanism to review, to know where you went right or wrong.
- Human Resource strategy evolved without considering organisational need is a fancy and unnecessary burden on the employees as well as the organisation as a whole.
- In the absence of HR strategies, the human capital lying in the company is a liability rather than an asset.
- Faulty HR strategy can lead an organisation to explosive overheads without returns.

# Measurability

## Try It Out

(1: not at all done, 2: moderately done, 3: to some extent done, 4: to a great extent done, 5: excellently done)

- My organisation has willingness to invest in HR Strategy making process. ☐
- My organisation has documented long-term HR strategy. ☐
- It has a rolling plan which is revisited every year. ☐
- My HR function is taking lead role in HR strategy process. ☐
- Other business functions are participating in HR function deliverables. ☐
- There is an established link of business vis-à-vis HR strategy. ☐

Analysis: the average score would determine the extent at which HR strategy process exists in your organisation.

## Score Card

(*: 25% achieved, **: 50% achieved, ***: 75% achieved, ****: 100% achieved)

| Technology | Objective Elements | Unit | Historical | Last Year | Current Year | Stretch Target | Status |
|---|---|---|---|---|---|---|---|
| HR Strategy | Strategy Document | Doc | Nil | No | Yes | NA | ** |

# Proven Track Record

## Track One

### AT&T

AT&T has undergone significant restructuring and competitive repositioning in the face of challenges in the deregulated markets by integrating its strategic priorities with human resource priorities. AT&T's mission is to be the world leader in information movement and management; accomplishing the same by growing its core business, developing leadership in data networking services and increasing the global share.

The company considers its human resource as one of the competitive advantage. AT&T's human resource plans evolve around creating change—influencing the leadership and managerial changes required to succeed in the marketplace. These plans illustrate a top-down corporate-wide strategic thrust for managing human resources in order to enhance business competitiveness. The focus of AT&T was to accelerate leadership development, forging new partnership with unions to bring in quality improvements, to build diverse workforce to make employee diversity a competitive advantage and give human dimensions a quality. Company also made flexible compensation package and different benefits for a changing workforce and improves cost-effectiveness through reengineering.

(*Source*: Walker, 1992: 64–65.)

## Track Two

## Siemens Business Communications Systems Inc.

Siemens, a leader in providing the business solutions for private telecommunications systems, offers multinational companies a single point of contact for integrated sales and services in 120 countries across the world. The organisation strongly feels that strategy shapes the action.

According to Bonnie C. Hathcock, a senior executive at Siemens, strategy has two elements 'corporate strategy' and 'HR strategy'. Human Resource strategy is planned in line with the business strategy. The strategy of the company was to enhance the capabilities of enterprise by executing the business strategies; and HR strategy was to lead the people processes to maximise human assets for competitive advantage. To effectively deliver HR has been designed into service centres, strategy, design and consulting services. The HR service centres handle day-to-day repeatable transactions associated with normal functions of the HR. They are charged with operating, refining and linking the internal HR systems effectively. Strategy and design group is responsible for *'external translation'* of scanning the environment and then producing HR processes that create strategic impact for the organisation like organisational effectiveness, staffing, HR technology, communications, etc. Consulting services provide the business units consulting advice directed at implementation of business strategies. More focus is given to organisational learning, recruitment and change management.

This redesign and repositioning has helped the company deal with business trends and HR is taking the lead in providing HR services to drive organisational action.

(*Source*: Rothwell, Prescott and Taylor, 1999: 24–25.)

# Applied HR Case—'Sea Change'

## ABC Gas Company Limited

In the monsoon, mid-August of 2003, the CEO and top team was busy spending a large part of their time considering the reduction of non-gas cost and future growth of ABC Gas Company limited. In the nine years since its inception, ABCL has moved from its operations in one city to many cities and many joint ventures. Recently, it had been taken over by a multinational company trying to spread its presence in India. The new management is convinced that the international market and developing country particularly India were the key to ABCL's success but was wondering what the next step should be.

The company was formed in 1989, as a joint venture between State Government and a private sector corporate having its presence in textile, consultancy and financial services. The equity participation stood as 15 per cent and 47 per cent between State Government and the corporate while public holds the rest. It began its operation through piped distribution of natural gas. The distribution covered domestic, industrial and commercial sectors together. With this the company became the first of its kind in India in the distribution of natural gas to combined sectors.

It diversified in to the LPG parallel marketing business in 1985. It made a head start in this business by first, putting two bottling plants in two cities and second, launching through franchisees across the state. Importing LPG is crucial in this business and hence the company joined hands with petroleum major and put up an infrastructure project for port terminal.

The company has identified five distinctive stakeholders in its vision statement articulated through a shared process by its employees. The vision statement describes clearly the commitment the company expressed towards each of the stakeholders. The management has drawn a long-term business strategy for the company based on business environment and internal resources. With the long-term strategic planning process for the company as a whole, the business groups and the service groups are attempting their strategic business plans. The management has from the beginning emphasised on in-depth micro planning of individual businesses and thus developed a culture of planning till the individual level.

The management has adopted a participatory process of operations. Most of the decisions are initiated and taken in committees and task forces formed formally in the organisation. The hierarchical structure is flat in nature however currently having three different cadres comprising managerial, supervisory and staff in total of twelve different levels. The organisation has been structured as business divisions and central service groups.

Business units formulate their five-year strategic business plans in which they address sub-strategies like marketing, finance, operation, etc., in major ways. They also try to attempt basics on Human Resource angle in these strategies. The service group also attempts long-term plans but which is yet not formalised in the organisation. The consolidation of all these SBPs are made which then become the strategic plans for the company. The process of formulating this strategic business plan is highly participatory in nature because it is addressed through small teams formulated in each of the business and service groups.

The company has a decentralised form of managing HR functions. It has a central level corporate HR group with the business and service groups at the Corporate Office for maintenance of HR functions. The HR group comprises HR professionals and support staff. The Corporate HR Group is involved in HR systems and policies and chalk out plan of actions for implementations. The maintenance HR functions at the locational levels primarily deal with routine HR functions like timekeeping, salary and wage administration, facilitating implementation of HR policies, etc. The Corporate HR is instrumental in developing organisational level consensus on various HR issues. The employee relation, legal compliance, grievance handling, etc., is taken care by location HR groups.

The company since its inceptions has put emphasis on training and development for its employees. When the company started its operations in the distribution of natural gas, this technology was new to the industry. That technical staff required for such operations were not available from the marketplace. Supply of gas needs high level of safety and assurance of continuous supply. This commitment is possible only if the service staff and the technical employees are competent in managing technical and service related issues. The company identified this gap and established a training centre with requisite facilities at the hub of an industrial town where it had its major operation.

The company felt in the latter part of 1991 that training is just not enough but other HR interventions are required in the organisations. To initiate various HR systems in the company the corporate HR group was constituted for which a marketing head was chosen and assigned this task. Sufficient group members were recruited and based on the feedback of the employees various HR systems were evolved and implemented in the organisation. Some of the major systems, which are implemented in the organisation are Performance Management System emphasising open appraisal process, Training System, Internal Communication System, Reward and Recognition, Recruitment and Selection, Induction, etc. The employee issues are handled on a very proactive manner, the apex committee is essentially constituted of the HR committee to look after HR policy and its related issues. There is no union in the organisation and the location's HR department is expected to represent employees' issues to this apex committee for resolutions.

Till now the business of distribution of natural gas is monopolistic in nature. However, ABCL has always focussed on customer satisfaction. The available quantity of gas is not enough for expanding the business in more territories, which is essential for the organisation's growth. Over a period of time, the overhead expenses have increased due to various reasons. With the opening up of the market economy and entry of large multinational organisations, competition in this field is likely to crop up. Many organisations have opened shops in India and also Indian organisations to play a major role in natural gas distribution as well as LPG. This would certainly make ABCL's life tougher to live in comparison to other monopolistic situations. The margins on the amount of gas sold and services offered are reducing day by day due to competitions and alternative fuels. This would directly affect the bottom line of the organisation in the forthcoming years.

The new promoters of the company have vast experience of operating in natural gas but do not have business interest in other businesses other than natural gas and LPG. Can this approach of the new promoters become the decisive factors for future? The Promoter Company has higher standards in many areas such as employees' productivity, operations and maintenance, which at present are far below in the organisation. This may warrant a drastic new thinking and change process in the entire operations. Since the company has reached to a level of stabilisation after a period of nine years and many systems are time tested, it would look difficult at this juncture to substantially improve these standards.

## Questions

1. How do you conceptualise a long-term HR strategy for ABC Gas Company?
2. Do you think that the organisation has conducive environment for it and what would be your approach to the making of HR strategy for ABC Gas company?
3. If you were the head of HR, how you will strengthen the HR function in the competitive environment and align the business and your function?

## References and Further Readings

Bhatnagar Jyotsna and L. D'Souza. 2002. *Bridging the HR Strategy Gap with Assessment Centres, Indian Journal of Training & Development*, April–June.

Chanda, Ashok and Shilpa Kabra. 2000. *Human Resource Strategy—Architecture for Change*, New Delhi: Response Books.

Karen and Legge. 1995. *Human Resource Management: Rhetoric and Realities, Management Work and Organizations*, London: Macmillan Business.

Rothwell, William, J., Robert K. Prescott and Maria W. Taylor. 1999. *Strategic Human Resource Leader*, Mumbai: Jaico Publishing House.

Shaun, Tyson (ed.). 2001. *Strategic Perspectives in Human Resource Management*, Mumbai: Jaico Publishing House.

Stacey, D. Ralph. 1993. *Strategic Management and Organizational Dynamics*, London: Pitman Publishing.

Walker, W. James. 1992. *Human Resource Management*, New York: McGraw-Hill International Editions.

William, Anthony. 2002. *Human Rescue Management: A Strategic Approach*, Florida: Harcourt Inc.

# 'HR PERFORMANCE PLAN'
# BUSINESS EXCELLENCE THROUGH HR
# PERFORMANCE PLAN

*Where performance is measured, performance improves. Where performance is measured and reported, the rate of improvement accelerates.*

—Thomas S. Monson

## Intent

- To understand the HR performance plan concept.
- To examine the HR performance plan vis-à-vis deliverables of HR in business processes.
- How HR can add value.
- To examine the performance of the HR function in the organisation.

## Expression

HR performance plan is the plan of action with its measurement of deliverables. This includes the high performance work systems, external system alignment and efficiency of HR in an organisation.

## Comprehension

The HR's emerging strategic potential lies in its role in sustaining and developing intangible assets and intellectual capital for today and tomorrow's economy. In the competitive world, superior business performance requires a firm to continually embark upon its core competency and competitive advantage. The need of HR is to understand and implement the firm's strategy.

The HR system is the linchpin of HR's strategic influence. The HR strategy influences the rest of the foundation of high performing HR policies, processes and practices. However, given the conflicting demands that HR managers typically confront, the HR requires a set of measures, which keep the performance dimensions of those HR activities at the forefront of its attention. Such measures don't reflect what is as much as they remind managers of what should be. Therefore, they can be represented on the HR performance plan as simple toggles, indicating *'unsatisfactory'* or *'satisfactory'*. Or they can be included as metrics along a continuum.

Building a HR performance plan should not be considered a one time or even an annual ritual. To manage by measurement, human resource leaders must stay attuned to changes in the downstream performance drivers that the HR is supporting. If these drivers change or if the key HR deliverables that support them change, the performance plan must shift accordingly.

In building a HR performance plan for any organisation, a component to be included stating how the HR deliverables are, historical data and the timeframe to achieve. The same strategic perspective that guides the construction of the HR performance plan should also guide the management of HR. In particular, human resource professionals should keep line managers continually informed of the status of HR deliverables. The HR must feel free to invite line managers to identify potential deliverables on their own. This is all part of forging a powerful new partnership. The HR performance plan enables the HR to attain the sustained competitive advantage to build HR systems and practices, which are objective and measurable, in line with the business strategies

The HR performance plan is a road map for the actions that is being planned for performance. All the activities undertaken in HR have a definite and long-term impact on the people and business of the organisation. End of the day, it is necessary to measure and evaluate the essence of any programme being undertaken in the organisation. All HR initiatives and further planning is a must for effective HR functioning. Human Resource performance planning is a technology through which the performance of the Human Resource processes can be validated and hence it is strategic in nature.

# Experiential Application

## A. Prerequisite

- Human resource managers tend to focus more on HR performance drivers in attempting to demonstrate their strategic influence. But too often, they fail to recognise the aspects of employees' satisfaction as the most fundamental.

- The matrices they use and HR policies they institute between them is often not connected. Credibility of HR measures is particularly important when financial and non-financial performance measures are into conflict.
- The company has to identify the key HR performance drivers since they are unique for each firm. If an organisation identifies employees' productivity as a core performance driver then multi skilling might be an important enabler.
- The HR must focus on HR enablers so that HR performance drivers improve.
- The HR should evaluate the degree to which the organisation's entire HR systems support the business process of the company such as from selection to development and reward mechanism inside the company.
- For example, if R&D function identifies timeliness of marketable new products then innovation is the key performance driver. Thus the key HR enabler should be, generating a right kind of reward system that encourages marketable innovation and providing timely incentives to attract employees.
- Both the business and HR enablers shall comprehend each other.

## B. Process Steps

| Step | Process |
| --- | --- |
| Step – I | Define elaborate business strategy. |
| Step – II | Build a HR strategy for people being a strategic asset. |
| Step – III | Create a HR strategy map. |
| Step – IV | Identify HR deliverables within the HR strategy map. |
| Step – V | Identify HR deliverables and align it to HR architecture. |
| Step – VI | Design the strategic HR measurement system. |
| Step – VII | Implement measurement mechanism. |

# Potential Gains and Areas of Concern

- The HR performance plan reinforces the distinction between HR doable and HR deliverables.
- It helps control cost and create value.
- The plan measures leading indicators and it encourages flexibility and change.
- The HR performance plan brings in financial discipline in HR since it emphasises on Return on Investment (ROI), i.e., various measurement indicators for HR.

- It provides a means by which organisation's HR functions can collect rigorous, predictable and regular data that will help direct the organisation's attention to most important elements of the HR systems.
- The HR performance plan is not panacea. They will not cure the poorly run HR functions.
- The HR performance plan when built without proper support of HR systems is only a farce.

# Measurability

## Try It Out

(1: not at all done, 2: moderately done, 3: to some extent done, 4: to a great extent done, 5: excellently done)

- My organisation has pre-defined HR performance plan. ☐
- Our HR group operates based on the HR performance plan and performance is measured based on it. ☐
- Performance of HR team is based on the HR performance plan achievement. ☐
- The HR has all relevant data and benchmarking of each HR elements for measuring the HR performance plan. ☐
- Every year and periodically, the HR performance plans are re-visited and due consideration is made for improvement in targets. ☐

Analysis: the average score would determine the extent at which HR performance plan exists in your organisation.

## Score Card

(*: 25% achieved, **: 50% achieved, ***: 75% achieved, ****: 100% achieved)

| Technology | Objective Elements | Unit | Historical | Last Year | Current Year | Stretch Target | Status |
|---|---|---|---|---|---|---|---|
| HR Performance Plan | HR Performance Plan Document | Doc | Nil | No | Yes | NA | ** |

# Proven Track Record

## Track One

## Quantum Inc., USA

Quantum is one of the leading manufacturers of Hard Disk drives and computer peripherals in USA. At Quantum, executives emphasise something they call *'time-to-volume'*. In Quantum's view being first to market does not mean being first to announce or demonstrate a new product, rather it means that customers actually get the new products they want, when they want them, and in the quantities they require. Without the sacrifice of quality plus the ability to ramp up production *'time-to-volume'* enables rapid product development enough to meet the customers needs.

Quantum identifies a set of value behaviours, such as staying flexible and adaptable, taking initiatives for one's own development and resolving issues in an objective manner. Though there is nothing ad hoc or symbolic about the importance of these behaviours to the success of the company, but they are valued. Quantum integrates these value behaviours directly into performance criteria and gives them equal weight with more traditional performance measures. One half of the bonus and merit pay is based on financial results of the organisation and one half of bonus on employees' adherence to the value behaviour.

(*Source*: Becker, Huselid and Ulrich, 2001: 32.)

## Track Two

## GTE Inc., USA

A wide range of integrated tools has been developed by GTE to communicate its HR performance plans and to help managers make good decisions using the data. There were seventy-five different information systems in GTE, which have been now combined into a single system. This is further enabled through an intranet linked to a data warehouse. This system now places timely and relevant data on managers' desktops, which they can access using special software that enables them to set goals and track performances. The GTE has also developed an interactive CD-ROM simulation that shows managers how to use the system to improve their decision-making. Finally, GTE has prepared a wide range of reports and background material that an employee can access at any time.

In the GTE Balance Performance plan environment, there are different measures for major functions, such as staffing for each business units, which are accessible via intranet technology. This helps in building a virtual environment. In GTE the performance plan is also used as a teaching tool and as a key mechanism for helping to implement strategy. The HR performance plan is an evolving and highly valuable tool for both the HR management team as well as the business leaders.

(*Source*: Becker, Huselid and Ulrich, 2001: 32.)

# Applied HR Case—'Trend Setter'

## Premium Hydraulics Limited

Rosy is a Head of the HR of the hydraulics manufacturing company which supplies its machines across the world. The plant runs at its full capacity and has orders continuous throughout the year. Rosy was very happy with the nature of work she is doing and has planned various interventions to keep the morale of the employees, and she always does some activity or the other. However, since the unit was running with its capacity and attrition was less, there are no significant employee relations' issues. Rosy, after her assuming the office, has conducted the satisfaction survey and acted upon the issues, employee stock option plan, employee self service, etc., but the other Heads used to think that they directly contribute to the growth of the organisation where as the HR is not directly contributing to the growth, though they put in quality work. Rosy used to feel bad that even though she puts her maximum, she is not getting the right kind of treatment, which she should get.

On a weekend Rosy was looking at the HR journals and while reading she came across the HR Performance Plan, which she has learnt during the HR seminars. She recollected the process and structure on how to measure the performance of HR. She immediately sat on her computer and made a presentation and worksheet on the HR Improvement Plan comprising of what was in the recent past and what the HR is going to achieve in the current and next year. She decided that from the next monthly meeting onwards she would present the performance of HR only through the performance plan. Next Monday, she made a presentation to the HR team and they all felt excited about it. She also made a presentation to her Director who was also impressed by the details and the statistics and in fact, suggested that the same can be implemented by other functions. He also suggested that the same can be taken up in the next meeting.

## Questions

1. Do you think that HR plan would give a perspective to the function and impact on the future course of action? Why?

2. Do you subscribe to the MD that the same plan can be applied to other functions also?
3. Prepare a performance plan for HR with the existing data and suggest the action plan to reach the future? (Use the model given in this technology)

## References and Further Readings

Becker, Brian E., Mark A. Huselid and Dave Ulrich. 2001. *The HR Score Card—Linking People Strategy, and Performance*, Harvard Business School Press.
Dixon, Nancy, M. 1995. *Evaluation: A Tool for Improving HRD Quality*, New Delhi: S Chand & Company Ltd.
Fitz-Enz, Jac. 1995. *How to Measure Human Resource Management*, New York: McGraw-Hill.
Fitz-Enz, Jac and Jack J. Phillips. 1998. *A New Vision for Human Resources: Defining the Human Resources Function by Its Results*, CA: Crisp Publications.
Mager, Robert, F. and Peter Pipe. 1999. *Benchmarking for People Managers*, Mumbai: Jaico Publishing House.
Phillips, Jack J., Ron Stone and Patricia Phillips. 2001. *The Human Resources Scorecard*, MA: Butterworth-Heinemann.

**APPENDIX-2A**

## 'HR Performance Plan'

HR Performance Plan is basically a barometer to know where the HR is in the past, the present and the plan for the future. The HR function is divided into various areas and to enable the team to understand and bring in vision and achievements is difficult without proper focus. The HR Performance Plan tries to bring in the review mechanism and also the plan to build a progressive organisation. The following various areas could be identified.

- **Organisation Design:** To design and develop an organisation structure and its related processes which will enhance the business success. The area includes, Organogram, Role Directory, etc.
- **Human Resource Planning:** To ensure proper balance between work and personnel life. Planning the right kind of manpower in right place at right time is important for every organisation. The area includes the other process like Performance Management System, Productivity and Manpower Norms, etc.
- **Learning and Development:** It is a shared responsibility between the employee and the company. Company gives an opportunity to development through training and the employee has to encash the opportunity by learning.
- **Compensation, Rewards and Recognition:** Maximising the performance of the employee through the consistent provision of market and merit-based compensation structure and reward mechanism appropriate to the business needs.
- **Communication and Involvement:** It is necessary to promote a clear and consistent communication of business issue and encouragement for an open exchange of views among all the employees of the organisation.
- **Health, Safety, Environment and Welfare:** It is necessary that all the businesses of the company require to meet and maintain the set standard that have been established by the company under health, safety, environment and welfare policy.
- **Management Services:** Providing inputs in the areas of strategic management business improvement plans, TQM and ISO orientations as an internal consultant within an organisation.

- **Milestones:** These are the achievements, which are significant in nature and can bring in substantial improvement in organisational processes.

## Score Card

(*: 25% achieved, **: 50% achieved, ***: 75% achieved, ****: 100% achieved)

| Technology | Objective Elements | Unit | Historical | Last Year | Current Year | Stretch Target | Status |
|---|---|---|---|---|---|---|---|
| HR Performance Plan | HR Performance Plan Document | Doc | Nil | No | Yes | NA | ** |

# Beneficiaries of the HR Performance Improvement Plan

The HR Performance Improvement Plan is devised for the HR professionals as a measurable tool to know their performance. This can also be useful for:

- **The Director/Managing Director/CEO:** To know the performance and also during the performance reviews, he need not go through the total documents generated by HR.
- **Department Heads:** The sharing of information symbolises the transparency of the HR. This creates challenges before HR where they cannot afford to have no star or one star and to prove themselves, they need to achieve the stretch targets.
- **Head of HR:** The Head of HR uses it as a tool for improving the performance of the HR. The plan contains the important KRA (Key Result Areas) of all the employees of HR and a periodic review would enable him to judge the performance and take corrective and preventive actions.
- **Employees of HR:** This tool can be placed in the pin board before their table so that they are reminded of their key performance indicators. The KRA are derived into the plan and the status will remind them constantly the areas where they need to act upon and the stretch targets to be achieved to create next mark.

# Application of the Plan

Every function can have similar plans and can monitor their performance. Human Resources bring in change and value addition as they pioneer the learning organisations, knowledge management, change management, etc. Implementing this tool will compile the important KRA of the whole department and can be used during:

- performance appraisal;
- monthly meetings of the HR department;
- review with the Director/MD/CEO; and
- as a tool to make a transparent organisation.

## When?

The Plan can be used for a long-term HR Strategy that is ideally required for any organisation to leverage the human resources for the competitive advantage. The Plan is made annually and derives its key elements from the HR Strategy, which is made for a period of three to five years. From the Strategic Plan, the Rolling Plan/Performance Plan is being made which is for the present year.

## How?

HR Performance Plan is being made from the HR Strategy. The Plan is made at the beginning of the financial year. The Plan derives its strategy from the HR Strategy and the Business Strategy and hence, the Plan is dynamic in nature and is subject to change. The elements of HR are being analysed against the past record and performance and the same are being planned for the current year. The Plan also includes the KRA of the team members so that there is an integration of the KRA with the Plan. The targets and the stretch targets are being arrived at after discussion to encourage performance and achieve the goal before target time.

The HR Department uses the plan as a pivotal tool for the review and discussion goes as per the Plan. Each element is reviewed against the performance and the stars are changed depending upon the accomplishment. The tool is planned to be transparent and at the same time would give a perspective to the MD/CEO of the functioning of the HR in an easy manner. This tool is simple to understand and makes everyone on toes to turn one star into four stars and outperform.

# 'ORGANISATION STRUCTURE' REVAMPING BUSINESS THROUGH RESTRUCTURING ORGANISATIONS

*Society, community, family are all conserving institutions. They try to maintain stability, and to prevent, or at least to slow down, change. But the organization of the post-capitalist society of organizations is a destabilizer. Because its function is to put knowledge to work—on tools, processes, and products; on work; on knowledge itself—it must be organized for constant change.*

—Peter F. Drucker

## Intent

- To recognise the importance of alternative form of structure and the demand for flexibility through restructuring process.
- To bring an organisational competitiveness in the structural form which is more market and customer savvy with the changing demand of the marketplace.
- To improve on the organisational processes, better utilisation of resources and quick response to customers.
- To support the business strategy, attainment of business plan and fulfilment of employees' aspiration of growth through the structure that is mutually aligned.

## Expression

Organisation restructuring is a process of dismantling the current organisational structure and redesigning it for a better and suitable process for delivering the products/ services to the customer. All business processes are given a fresh look whether they are able to deliver the goals and the requirements of the customer in view of the competitive market scenario. It is not necessary to revamp the structure itself like wiping the slate and designing a new, but it is to look at the loopholes in the structure and strengthen it to enable the structure to deliver the strategy.

# Comprehension

The purpose of any organisation structure is division of labour, primarily among the three levels of the organisation. The managerial positions which are at the highest level of the management hierarchy is responsible for setting strategic goals, the middle and supervisory roles provide tactical support to the decisions while the lower categories such as workers/technicians/tradesmen etc., are for operation and implementation of decisions. Organisational structure is a framework enabling employees to divide responsibilities, reporting relationships, design of systems, ensure employee accountability and distribute decision-making authority.

Organisational structure helps the company to achieve its goal by providing a framework through which the responsibilities flow, make employee accountable for their work and effectively distribute the authority to make decisions. Similarly, organisation chart provides visual representation of how employees and tasks are grouped and how the lines of communication and authority flow.

Restructuring is examining the entire work process rather than just rearranging, changing the tasks and adjusting the boxes on the organisation chart. In this process, the organisation rethinks all the tasks, and those tasks that have become irrelevant are discarded. A new and more productive process is built that works better for the company and its customers. All those processes and procedures, which are a hindrance for the organisation serving their customers, are omitted and redesigned so as to enable customer satisfaction and in turn the survival of the organisation. The structure of a company is designed to respond to the changes, strong coordination across the functional areas, the strategy and the flexibility to meet the expectations of the customers and the changing market scenario. The benefit of such restructuring is achieving the speed, flexibility, innovation and quality objectives.

There is no scientific formula that gives an equation for a specific structure which can lead to success to a type of the organisation. The organisation structuring must always have contingency approach. The contingency approach takes the view that there is no best universal structure that exists to enable the success of the organisation. There are a large number of variables or situational factors, which influence organisational design and its performance. Therefore, organisation structure emphasises that there has to be flexibility and agility in the organisations to bring in change as and when required to survive and grow in the competitive market.

The study of organisation structure has gone beyond the organisation towards the conglomerate. It is a form of organisation, which adds an entirely unrelated business or product to its organisation design. For example, the Matsushita group has under its umbrella Asihi Bank, Panasonic, Nippon Life Insurance, etc. The benefit of these conglomerates is providing a network of organisations that are dependent on each other for products and services to create a competitive advantage.

No building can be constructed if the structure is not defined well before the construction. The effective management of corporation lies in appropriate structure through which the organisation processes and decision-making establishes. The structure is a foundation that helps organisation building on the common platform. Without structure no company can exist including the smallest of the corporations. For HR professionals, organisation design and to develop organisation structure is a strategic technology on which the entire organisation and its subsequent processes rest.

# Experiential Application

## A. Prerequisite

- The consent of the top management and support of business functions is a must.
- The organisational restructuring is a process, which may destabilise the organisation from top to bottom in one go and hence much thought must go, as to why the structure needs to be changed.
- Earlier approach to organisational management believed in one best form of structure and tended to concentrate on the limited aspects of organisations. They also tended to study the organisation in isolation from its environment. There are many variables which influence the most appropriate organisation structure and system of management, that is necessary to analyse the structure in terms of the relationships among its components.
- Attention needs to be given for greater flexibility of organisations and workforce, and the nature of the managers and subordinate relationship. The fit between the structure and systems of management will depend upon the situational variables for each variable organisation.

## B. Process Steps

| Step | Process |
| --- | --- |
| Step – I | Evaluation of organisation structure. |
| Step – II | Appraising the top management about the structural imbalances. |

*(Continued)*

*(Continued)*

| Step | Process |
|------|---------|
| Step – III | Creation of Cross Functional Task Force (CFTs) to evaluate the micro issue of imbalance and dwell on new structures. |
| Step – IV | Competent consultant's opinion and guidance can be taken to support the process. |
| Step – V | Findings of the CFTs to be deliberated, discussed and approved by top management. |
| Step – VI | Employees are explained the proposed changes and to incorporate any constructive suggestions. |
| Step – VII | Implementation of new structure with clear cut roles, responsibilities, reporting relationship and business partnering. |
| Step – VIII | Communication process initiated to inform the changes and mass awareness programme with promotion material across the organisation. |
| Step – IX | Role clarity workshops and the change management training across the organisation. |
| Step – X | Periodic Review of the changes and implementing any change in the structure, if necessary. |

# Potential Gains and Areas of Concern

- It helps organisation removal of non-value adding jobs, functions, hierarchies, etc., to rebuild afresh.
- It brings in dynamism in the organisations, which essentially overcomes on the conventional ways and means of dealing with the process with modern and advance outlook.
- Restructuring is a massive and complex process, which is a grassroot level change. It brings in new waves of change in the mindset of all the employees of the company, which ultimately helps bringing new vigour in product and services offering.
- Normally restructuring is aimed at improving the top and bottom lines of the company. It helps in reducing cost, improving productivity, faster decision-making, better utilisation of resources and quicker communication in the company.
- Restructuring is a movement of change within an organisation. All must participate whole-heartedly in this process of change.
- It is meant for improvement. It has to yield results and growth; else, the efforts made are futile.
- It is a large-scale change, if not thought over properly could aggravate the issue/problem that the company is facing instead of resolving it.
- Large-scale communication is a key to success for restructuring to establish route, miscommunication could lead to bigger failure.
- It demands the change of mindset of people and if the employees do not change their attitude towards new structure, there is a likely chance that it would delay stability in the company.

- Restructuring alone is not the answer to all the problems. It is one of the ways through which organisation complexities can be addressed.
- Restructuring is beyond drawing boxes and connecting lines. It is a process against which work is designed and performed.

# Measurability

## Try It Out

(1: not at all done, 2: moderately done, 3: to some extent done, 4: to a great extent done, 5: excellently done)

- The current organisation structure is proactive and supportive to the business growth of the company and is revisited quite often.  ☐
- The structure provided with complete role clarity and authority and responsibility for each employee within the company.  ☐
- Having identified structural bottleneck for the growth, management has rectified the issue by addressing it through new structure.  ☐
- Management recognises that the structure is beyond the line and box and is a route to business success.  ☐
- Communication is widely done for the existing as well as the timely proposed new structures.  ☐

Analysis: the average score would determine the extent at which organisation restructuring is done in your organisation.

## Score Card

(*: 25% achieved, **: 50% achieved, ***: 75% achieved, ****: 100% achieved)

| Technology | Objective Elements | Unit | Historical | Last Year | Current Year | Stretch Target | Status |
|---|---|---|---|---|---|---|---|
| Organisation Structure | Structural Correction | Doc | Nil | No | Yes | NA | ** |
| | Reporting Matrix | Doc | Nil | No | Yes | NA | * |
| | Role Clarity Workshop/Exercise | Doc | Nil | No | Yes | NA | * |
| | Span of Control | No. | 8 | 8 | 7 | 6 | * |

# Proven Track Record

## Track One

## Digital Equipment Corporation (DEC)

Digital Equipment Corporation has done restructuring in a very effective manner with the formation of cross functional and multicultural teams that encompass areas of marketing, manufacturing, design engineering, product development, customer support, sales and distribution. Most of the organisations are restructuring the work process rather than reengineering the boxes, changing the organisation chart or changing the individual's work.

In the process of re-engineering the organisation, DEC has to rethink on a group of tasks that has become irrelevant and created a new process, which is more productive, which adds value to the company and also brings in more customer focus. Since its implementation, the teams have reduced the time needed to develop new products from between one and three years to only six months.

(*Source*: Mescon, Bovee and Thill, 1995.)

## Track Two

## Four-Day Banking Holiday

An exceptional example of a leader providing insight into the importance of structure in an organisation was Franklin Roosevelt. During his radio announcement on 12 March 1933, he explained the 'four-day banking holiday' concept. In a time of panic, Roosevelt calmly explained how the banking system worked structurally.

> Let me state the simple fact that when you deposit money in bank, the bank does not put the money in to a safe deposit vault. It invests your money in many different forms of credit such as bonds, mortgages, etc. In other word, the bank puts your money to work to keep the wheels turning around.

He explains how banks were required to maintain reserves, how this reserves were inadequate if there were widespread withdrawals, and why closing the banks for four days was necessary to restore order.

(*Source*: Senge, 1999: 53.)

## Track Three

### General Motors

General Motors recognises the chronic managing issue within the company and has embarked on the most extensive organisational restructuring ever. Under the plan, GM would continue to market autos using the same five car divisions—Chevrolet, Pontiac, Oldsmobile, Buick and Cadillac. These three divisions have been consolidated in to two new divisions. Small cars would be engineered and built by the Chevrolet-Pontiac GM Canada group, while the Buick, Cadillac and Oldsmobile group would develop large cars. Each of these two groups would have its own group executive, who would report to the newly created position of Executive Vice President for North American Passenger Operations. Under the plan, GM's engineering thus have consolidated rather than spread throughout the corporation's various divisions, insofar as each of the two car groups would now have its own engineering group, created by consolidating the engineering staff from the existing car divisions. The five car divisions themselves would continue to exist, but primarily as marketing arms of the two car groups.

The top management of GM believes that the massive reorganisation would boost the company's organisational effectiveness. It would do this, for instance, by helping the company launch its new model on schedule, boosting quality control, providing more cost control and allowing the division to build more distinctive models instead of the current look-alike.

(*Source*: Dessler, 1985.)

## Track Four

### Asia Brown Boveri

Asia Brown Boveri is an 18 billion multinational company formed by the merger of Switzerland's Brown Boveri Company and Sweden's Asia. The strength of BBC is in basic research and that of Asia in applications-oriented research. The company's head-quarter is in Switzerland but 70 per cent of the employees are in other parts of Europe. In order to bring the research and development to the specific business units throughout Europe, several of the researchers were transferred with a hope in bringing the R&D closer to the marketing function. The objective is to push down responsibility, authority and accountability.

The company has moved restructuring, first, by quickly implementing the changes and second, by involving no outside consultants, instead, an internal taskforce of five top managers from each of the former group companies is created. With the advent of ABB, many new managerial positions became vacant and all the internal applicants were interviewed, and their emphasis was on the ability of the new managers to innovate, take risks and motivate others. The company looked at managers who are open and generous and capable of thinking in group terms. Due to its determination, ABB has become a company of the future.

(*Source*: Baird, Post and Mahon, 1990: 217.)

# Applied HR Case —'Designed to Redesign'

## Alva Engineers

Robert, an HR professional was recruited as HR Head with a hope that he will revive the organisation. Robert who did his masters degree from a premier institute had 20 years of experience in the field of HR. Alva Engineers is in the business of manufacturing engineering components and automobile parts to the major producers. It was doing very well, but the growth is not as per the expectations of the MD. The production was absorbed by the customers and the function of the marketing was to take care of the customers and the payments. Whenever the MD wanted to push the targets, there was resistance from the production and the marketing; hence, every year there was only an incremental increase of 5 to 10 per cent. But the MD had a vision and would like to take the company to greater heights and since there was resistance from all the quarters he did not take the risk of bringing any intervention.

Robert was recruited taking into consideration his vast experience and his reputation of bringing in a turnaround wherever he has worked. He went around the units and had detailed discussions with the heads of the departments. After careful study of all the facts, he found that each department was working in silos and since the existing customers were absorbing the production, there was not much work to be done. The production unit had 40 per cent of the manpower and the balance 60 per cent were in the field. Each unit had 10 to 15 employees to take care of service and marketing. However, the problem arose since they reported not to the geographical head, but the functional head at the corporate office, which was diluting the authority of the head of the unit. There was no interrelation between the departments as each one was working on their own KRA. There was no strategic planning and the only plan was the incremental plan of 5 to 10 per cent annual rise. The attrition rate was very less as the company existed since a long time and the people were comfortable with the structure and the pay. Robert was convinced that there was a need to restructure the organisation to bring in organisational renewal and to make the vision of the MD a reality. Robert discussed in detail his opinion with the MD and he was convinced about his observation. The MD asked him to make a presentation to the heads of the departments on the following Monday.

Robert made his presentation to the heads of the departments and his intention to restructure the organisation to bring in renewal. All the heads of the departments openly resisted the move since they believed that the organisation was doing well and any disturbance would hamper the process and that there was even a chance of losing the customers. They affirmed that the employees and the vendors were doing their best to give the results; they had also asked for massive recruitment of the people to increase the sales. The meeting ended with leaving the decision to the MD.

## Questions

1. What are the problems faced by Alva Engineers?
2. Do you think that Robert was correct in his judgement to opt for restructuring? If yes, then what structure you will propose?
3. If you were the MD of the company what will be your plans to restructure or to retain the structure? Why?

## References and Further Readings

Baird, Lloyd S., James E. Post and John F. Mahon. 1990. *Management—Functions & Responsibilities*, New York: Harper and Row Publishers Inc.

Daft, Richard L. 1997. *Management*, Florida: The Dryden Press.

De Meuse, Kenneth P. and Mitchell Lee Marks (eds). 2003. *Resizing the Organisation—Managing Lay offs, Divestitures & Closings*, CA: Jossey-Bass.

Dessler, Gary. 1985. *Management Fundamentals*, Virginia: Prentice-Hall.

Galbraith, Jay R. 1997. *Organisation Design*, USA: Addison-Wesley Publishing Company Inc.

Geroff, Edwin A. 1985. *Organisation Theory and Design—A Strategic Approach for Management*, New York: McGraw-Hill Book Company.

Huber, George P. and William H. Glick. 1993. *Organisational Change and Redesign: Ideas and Insights for Improving Performance*, New York: Oxford University Press Inc.

Khandwalla, Pradip N. 1992. *Innovative Corporate Turnarounds*, New Delhi: Sage Publications.

———. 1992. *Organisational Design for Excellence*, New Delhi: Tata McGraw-Hill Publishing Company Limited.

Mescon, Michael H., Courtland L. Bovee and John V. Thill. 1996. *Business Today*, New Jersey: Prentice Hall.

Sadler, Philip. 1992. *Designing Organisations*, New Delhi: Viva Books Pvt Ltd.

Senge, Peter. 1999. *The Fifth Discipline*, London: Random House.

# 'RE-ENGINEERING HRD'
# LEAPING AHEAD OF OTHERS AND
# CREATING NEW BENCHMARKS/NEXT
# MARK THROUGH RE-ENGINEERING HRD

*The future has waited for long enough; if we do not grasp it, other hands, grasping hard, will.*

—Adlai Stevenson

## Intent

- To step up the pace of technology and bringing in more agility in HR function through advancing in technological front.
- To build more on employee self-services concept and reducing the mundane and routine practices from the HR function.
- To provide value addition in HR rather than simple MIS and data generation.
- To make HR leaner and development oriented.

## Expression

Rethinking and redesigning of the human resource processes to improve the present and future performance, which are measurable in nature, and building human resource competencies for sustained competitive advantage is Re-engineering of HRD.

## Comprehension

The term 'Reengineering' is credited to Prof. Michael Hammer who defined it as *'Business Process Re-engineering'*. It means starting over from scratch. His approach has features of completely fresh start or blank sheet of paper approach. Another process is orientation approach to organisational analysis centred on a horizontal review of all activities involved in the process or set of activities in delivery of a product or services to the customers. Business Process Re-engineering (BPR) is a powerful tool and recommended only for those organisations, where there is stagnation and which really needs a change in the processes. If BPR has to be successful it has to be driven by a strategic plan and must have support from top management.

Re-engineering human resource is concerned with total restructuring of the HR process in the organisations in line with the business strategy. It starts from how one would like the HR processes to be to achieve the business strategy and the best practices in HR and work backward in an effort to achieve real gains in managing people. The routine and non-value addition tasks must be taken off from the HR and it must be oriented to build the 'human capital' to bring value to the organisation. The process involves redefining, re-aligning and reorienting the HR roles, systems and practices to suit the business goals.

The re-engineering of human resource would also lead to a radical change in the perception of HR bringing in the latest technology, which adds value and leadership to the organisation for the products and services it offers to the internal customers. Re-engineering human resource has major focuses in three phases. In Phase I, re-engineering cleans up administration, i.e., eliminating, outsourcing or automating all administrative paper work. Concepts like 'do it yourself' replaces 'paper work'. Phase II of re-engineering is development of virtual service delivery system, i.e., benefit advising and training replaces by HR kiosk and CD-ROM training. Phase III of re-engineering comprises of Executive Information System (EIS) for strategic planning. This is to do with recruiting, selecting, training, motivating and maintaining the performance of the people who can do the re-engineered job and provide competitive advantage.

'Human Resource Development' though a recently coined word has deep roots since the industrialisation process. It has undergone changes in the perspective as well as name from Industrial Relation to Knowledge Management dimensions. The HR needs to be rechristened often changing with line of business and the environmental change. As we always speak about re-engineering the business process, there needs a proper way to re-engineer the human resource function. Therefore, strategically, re-engineering the HRD time to time is a strategic technology.

# Experiential Application

## A. Prerequisite

- Re-engineering human resource function is similar to that of any other re-engineering efforts made in organisations. It is a fundamental rethinking of all HR processes and therefore requires commitment at the apex level of the organisation.

- The re-engineering of HR helps defining important and non-important activities that needs to be separated. Those non-value adding activities are wasteful and time consuming and therefore either to be eliminated or outsourced.
- Re-engineering would bring the latest HR technologies into practice and there would be quantum improvement in managing people. This requires high degree of innovativeness and creativity in conceptualising, strategising, implementing and reviewing.
- It is also necessary that not only the top management be committed to the re-engineering of HR processes but also the HR as well, as the line and other staff functions must own the desired changes.
- Success of any re-engineering effort including HR re-engineering depends on how well communication is established among the employees of the company.

## B. Process Steps

| Step | Process |
|------|---------|
| Step – I | Knowing the status of HR through HR Audit, ESS, Climate Study, etc. |
| Step – II | Scanning the environment on current HR practices of the most admired companies. |
| Step – III | Evaluating the systems and procedures and discarding those which does not add value. |
| Step – IV | Eliminating or outsourcing the non-value adding or routine activities. |
| Step – V | Redefining the present systems and introducing the best HR practices. |
| Step – VI | Reviewing the HR systems, procedures and practices for improvement. |

# Potential Gains and Areas of Concern

- Re-engineering HR is a step supporting business and bringing in dynamism in the HR processes.
- It helps organisation enhancing productivity and reducing unnecessary cost.
- With reengineering, non-value-adding processes in HR would either be eliminated or outsourced, hence would be cost effective.
- It will bring newness in the way the HR is being performed in the organisation.
- Re-engineering viewed as one additional fancy approach for the company could lead to failure.
- If the top management and rest of the employees do not whole-heartedly participate in the process, then the efforts would be fruitless.
- Re-engineering without creativity and innovation is no good. Exploiting technology is a must in the entire process. Without technology, it is off dated and may not attract participation.

# Measurability

## Try It Out

(1: not at all done, 2: moderately done, 3: to some extent done, 4: to a great extent done, 5: excellently done)

- My organisation has willingness to invest in HR Systems driven with ☐ technological advancement.
- As a proactive measure, some of the processes are eliminated and/or ☐ outsourced from HR in order to bring in efficiency.
- A complete re-look at HR processes and systems is done during the ☐ last two years to mitigate the HR challenges faced by the organisation.
- HR is facilitating the organisation re-engineering process depending ☐ on the business exigencies.
- Organisation has benefited from the re-engineering efforts of HR and there ☐ exists a mechanism measuring the benefits of the re-engineering efforts.

Analysis: The average score would determine the extent at which HR re-engineering process is been done in your organisation.

## Score Card

(*: 25% achieved, **: 50% achieved, ***: 75% achieved, ****: 100% achieved)

| Technology | Objective Elements | Unit | Historical | Last Year | Current Year | Stretch Target | Status |
|---|---|---|---|---|---|---|---|
| Re-engineering HRD | Non Value Adding Tasks Measured Benefits | Doc | Nil | No | Yes | NA | ** |
| | Re-engineering Efforts | Doc | Nil | No | Yes | NA | ** |

# Proven Track Record

## Track One

## Robert Bosch Limited

Robert Bosch Ltd., based at South Wales is part of the worldwide Bosch organisation with its headquarters at Stuttgart. Bosch has 170,000 employees working in 130 countries worldwide. Its belief in maintaining the highest standards of engineering design, product development and manufacturing systems is mirrored by its commitment to the people it employs and its customers. The HR is responsible for training and development, administration and secretarial, personnel and employment responsibilities. The demarcation of line and staff functions either formally or informally does not exist. As the industry is built new, the workforce needs to be recruited and trained before production begins. Better recruitment methods and training and development are given emphasis to create and maintain a highly qualified and motivated workforce.

Training and development starts at recruitment and selection. If proper workforces are recruited, it not only influences the quality of the workmen but also has the potential for further development. The main function of the HR is to identify those workforces, who are qualitative and are suited for future development. The functions of HR are seen holistically rather than with functional demarcation. Human Resources work together along with line managers to ensure that important decisions reflect complementary perspectives of employment and development in line with the business needs.

(*Source*: Megginson, Banfield and Joy-Matthews, 2001: 47.)

## Track Two

## Satyam Computers

Satyam Computers is the first software company to go public and achieve the CMM level 5 accreditation in India. CMM level 5 is a prestigious level in defining quality parameters for software companies worldwide. The HR plays a strategic support role wherein at all the locations HR representatives help the strategic business units in their functioning. All the employment processes are re-engineered using IT wherever practical, ensuring that the end result provides added customer value. It also re-engineered the role of HR away from the mundane works towards employment process design and audit. The recruitment process is done through E-mail. The paper-oriented glory is being replaced by direct access to information, i.e., pay slip, annual salary statement, tax computations, through mail. The HR was able to successfully integrate the Intranet to provide a seamless and intuitive medium for employees to interact with the organisation in general and the HR in particular.

Training is also imparted through Intranet in conjunction with the existing training process. The feedback on both effectiveness of training and surveys on employee satisfaction are obtained through Intranet to avoid geographical constraints and cover more employees. The performance appraisal is being done through HRIS (Human Resource Information System) and everything electronically transferred at the headquarters at Hyderabad. A knowledge database is created wherein employees can record their own experiences and viewpoints on an issue and react to others queries and comments.

The HR processes are re-engineered in such a way that the IT takes care of the mundane and routine matters and HR can take care of the developmental aspects.

(*Source*: Roshan and Ghosh, 2000: 15.)

# Applied HR Case—'Looking with a New Eye'

## Dove Power

Singh, head of HR has newly joined the Dove Power after a long period of working in an advanced software company. Singh was very enthusiastic about working in a power plant since he wanted to have a diversified exposure and opportunity to learn new things leaving behind the recruitment and attrition problems.

Dove Power was established two decades ago, but has considerably modernised its hardware and software recently. Singh wanted to start with understanding the whole business and how he can bring value to the HR. On the first day he had to encounter the problem of wrong calculation and printing of pay slips for which there was a large hue and cry. The department had two managers taking care of recruitment and compensation and eight other staff assisting these two managers. The software which was purchased from an outside vendor was never used to prepare the salaries, since there were certain bugs which neither the supplier nor the IT team was able to manage. He reviewed the whole function of HR and found that instead of having the advanced technology with them, they were still two decades back, using the same stationery and policies designed at that time. Singh was very disturbed and he immediately decided that the whole of routine HR needed to be automated to make the system self-sufficient and the HR must work for value addition by way of training and development. He made a plan to bring in IVR, Intranet and Employee Self Service software to assist the department to come out of the routines and work for the development of the self and the company.

## Questions

1. Do you think that Dove Power, which is having a two-decades-old culture and attitude, will be able to adapt to the new initiatives?
2. Would the people who are habituated to come to HR for solutions, use the new technology? How to sell the new concept to other departments?
3. If you were Singh, illustrate and brief how you will design the new systems and what are the facilities you are going to provide for the employees through the new technology?

# References and Further Readings

Gilley, Jerry W. and Ann Maycunich. 2000. *Organizational Learning, Performance, and Change: An Introduction to Strategic Human Resource Development*, New York: Perseus Publishing.

Megginson, David, Paul Banfield and Jennifer Joy-Matthews. 2001. *Human Resource Development*, New Delhi: Kogan Page.

Rao, T.V. 1999. 'Re-engineering HRD for Competitive Advantage—The HRD Scorecard Approach', in Udai Pareek and V. Sisodia (eds), *HRD in the New Millennium*, New Delhi: Tata McGraw-Hill Publishing Company Ltd.

Roshan, Joseph and Gautam Ghosh. 2000. 'The HR and IT Partnership at Satyam: Reaching Out to People', in Varkkey, Dutta and Rao, *Value Creation*, New Delhi: Tata McGraw-Hill Publishing Company Ltd.

Rothwell, William J., Robert K. Prescott and Maria W. Taylor. 1999. *Strategic Human Resource Leader*, Mumbai: Jaico Publishing House.

Spencer, Lyle M. 1995. *Reengineering Human Resources*, Canada: John Wiley and Sons.

Stolovitch, Harold D. and Erica J. Keeps (eds). 1999. *Handbook of Human Performance Technology: Improving Individual and Organizational Performance Worldwide*, San Francisco: Jossey-Bass/Pfeiffer Publishers.

# 'BPO'
# FOCUS ON CORE PROCESSES AND OUTSOURCE PERIPHERALS THROUGH BPO

*None of us knows what the next change is going to be, what unexpected opportunity is just around the corner, waiting a few months or a few years to change all the tenor of our lives.*

—Kathleen Norris in *Hands Full of Living* (1988).

## Intent

- To understand how an organisation concentrates on its core business processes and brings in change and value addition towards its products and services for better productivity and optimise the human capital.
- To understand the primary stimuli of Business Process Outsourcing (BPO) as sales and market share, development of new products, expansion into new markets and enhancing customer service and satisfaction.

## Expression

Business Process Outsourcing is a process of delegating back-end administrative and routine functions that are necessary to run a business but not a part of the core business, in order to concentrate on the core business and optimally achieve the desirable results.

## Comprehension

The knowledge led economy has created many challenges to HR in managing the human capital and concentrate on its core business process. Due to the immense competition and the globalisation of the economy, various products and services are available in the market, which are varied in nature adding value to the requirements of the customer. The organisations in order to survive and compete shall concentrate on its core business process and plan outsourcing the routine and administrative matters which does not add value to the main business process; while the organisation concentrates on its business and also takes the expertise and knowledge domain of other organisations which are specialised and provides the services at a lesser cost.

With the impact of technological revolution, the process has further enabled outsourcing as one of the key factors of determining the organisational agility and organising its business processes. The transnational organisations find it difficult to manage from their existing human resource to deploy huge operations and manpower and hence organisations re-engineer their developmental strategies and its execution to be adaptive and flexible to the 'speed, flexibility and economy'. Organisations find multi-location operations designed through economies of scale viable for product innovation, market penetration, after sales service and customer support. The organisations find it easy to outsource the process rather maintain the establishment and the manpower.

In this process, outsourcing has become the buzzword because of its inherent advantages of cost control and meeting the demands of the global economy. One way it can also be called as re-engineering the whole business process itself. Routine activities like customer service, data base and data processing, transcription and IT related services, are some of those areas which are being outsourced. Countries like India, Malaysia, China, etc., where there are abundant manpower and the cost of labour is cheap, many transnational organisations are outsourcing these activities, and in fact, some of the organisations in these countries have obtained expertise in these areas and have extended their services to many organisations worldwide.

At the same time, the BPO industries are becoming popular with their efficiency and cost-effectiveness and they are able to add value to the organisations. It has become one of the fastest growing multi-billion dollar industry generating growth and huge employment potential.

# Experiential Application

## A. Prerequisite

- The consent of the top management and support of business functions is mandatory.
- Organisations must plan for the activities that it wants to outsource very meticulously considering all pros and cons before taking decisions of outsourcing.
- The BPO for any processes that an organisation wants to take up must yield significant benefits back to the organisation in terms of revenue, customer satisfaction, cost effectiveness and bringing in ease for focused activities within the company.

- It should not be forgotten that the company undertaking outsource activity also have the prime objective to generate profit. Therefore, those activities that do not contribute to profit even after being outsourced would be rejected.
- It is not always necessary that processes which are non value adding processes are only outsourced. Sometimes in a business process even high value adding processes too can be outsourced if the core competency of the company does not support that activity to carry out internally.
- The following are the salient points that an organisation should consider while strategising the BPO activities:

  - Processes, which easily, can be outsourced and does not require direct involvement of the organisations, should be identified for the BPO.
  - A proper cost benefit analysis must be made in order to evaluate the outcome of process outsourcing.
  - A proper training is to be imparted to the BPO company so that outsourced processes are handled in equal or even in better manner for bringing in efficiency.
  - Organisations must educate the employees why processes are outsourced and its related impact within the company, so that employees are clear and no ambiguity exists.
  - Since outsourcing helps taking out many business processes to the third party, many experienced employees of the company would be excess and therefore, they need to be either redeployed in proper job or downsized in an utmost humane manner.

## B. Process Steps

| Step | Process |
|------|---------|
| Step – I | Mapping of all the Business Processes. |
| Step – II | Prioritising the processes which are most moderate and least important. |
| Step – III | Map the financial implications and the interdependencies of the process. |
| Step – IV | Cost benefit analysis of all the activities which are least important to business. |
| Step – V | Identification of a service provider with reference to quality and cost. |
| Step – VI | Periodically review the implementation of outsourced activity. |

# Potential Gains and Areas of Concern

- BPO helps the company to concentrate on the main business and add further value to the products/services.

- It also helps in obtaining the expertise available outside for guidance and skills but difficult to take as part of the organisation due to non-availability of manpower, scarcity of skills, economies of scale, etc.
- Business Process Outsourcing helps organisations in meeting the ever-changing requirements of the customers. Certain value addition services that are routine in nature can be outsourced. For example, post sales service is important but as various agencies are available to provide the services, a company can outsource the activity.
- It can facilitate revenue increase by way of increasing in the technology, application in new area, adapting to new technologies, etc.
- Only those jobs, which are routine and non-value addition in nature must be outsourced, if the key areas are planned, there is always a scope for the service provider to become a competitor.
- To enable economies of scale, the organisations in the short run can outsource but it has impact in the long run where it may lose focus on its core business.

# Measurability

## Try It Out

(1: not at all done, 2: moderately done, 3: to some extent done, 4: to a great extent done, 5: excellently done)

- There is a growing consensus in my organisation for increasing efficiency ☐ and reducing cost by various means.
- Through concrete efforts my organisation could reduce substantial cost ☐ and increase efficiency.
- There are more than one activities our organisation has outsourced and ☐ BPO has been a proven practice in our company.
- Business Process Outsourcing has generated an anxiety as well as resistance ☐ in the beginning which company managed through effective communication process.
- My organisation has made a strategic plan considering that the BPO trend ☐ in the long run will benefit the organisation substantially.

Analysis: the average score would determine the extent at which BPO process exists in your organisation.

## Score Card

(*: 25% achieved, **: 50% achieved, ***: 75% achieved, ****: 100% achieved)

| Technology | Objective Elements | Unit | Historical | Last Year | Current Year | Stretch Target | Status |
|---|---|---|---|---|---|---|---|
| Business | Reduction in Cost | Rs | Nil | No | Yes | NA | ** |
| Process | Improving | Rs | Nil | No | Yes | NA | ** |
| Outsourcing | Productivity Per Employees | | | | | | |

# Proven Track Record

## Track One

## JC Penney

In the late 1990s JC Penney decided to remove the burden of administering the benefit processes from their retail store managers so that they could focus on customer services. While examining, the company wanted a single source which can administer and benefit their workforce of 180,000 employees. To do such massive activity, it required a comprehensive software. However, JC Penney had old software, which was not able to take up such a massive job. Hence, it was decided to explore whether these processes can be outsourced or carried out internally. It was realised that outsourcing was the right approach since it was difficult for the company to keep pace with technology which becomes obsolete in no time, while, for a BPO company this forms a part of their core business and they can keep pace with the technological advancement. It was not advisable for JC Penney to incur huge investment for this technology. Besides, technology knowledge of specialising in benefit administration, was not the core competency of JC Penney.

The company selected Hewitt because they found some advantage of having one vendor deliver the various aspects of benefit management. By going live with a centralised system, JC Penney and Hewitt rolled out a Web based self-service application for areas of benefit administration enrolling almost 70 per cent of employees.

(*Source*: Hewitt Magazine.)

## Track Two

## Office Tiger

Mr Sigelman and Mr Randy Altschuler were concerned about the routine and mundane jobs affecting the organisation performance and looked at the possibility of doing business by offering to do the mundane office works through specialised service providers. They have found India as a better place, which has lot of potential for business with cheaper manpower by more than 50 per cent in comparison to the US and UK. Both have floated a BPO outfit—Office Tiger for office documentation work. Office Tiger became the fifth largest third party BPO in India with revenues over $25 million and employing more than 1,000 employees.

Besides office documentation work, it now caters to business research for the banking industry and analytics to 20 clients in the US and Europe. The projections for 2004 is promising and the revenues are expected to cross $50 million and to $150 millions in the next three years.

(*Source*: Singh, 2003: 30.)

## Track Three

## AFFINA

AFFINA is an Illinois-based customer interaction outsourcing company providing call centre solutions for government agency clients and Fortune 1,000 companies. Cutting labour costs to boost profits is a time-honoured tradition in the business world. When it comes to call centres which are typically labour-intensive, cutting staff can actually harm a company's bottom line, and this may not help because reduction of staff push the remaining employees to handle more calls in less time, which in turn would induce customer frustration. AFFINA handles almost 27 million customer interactions a year. To bring in more value to its customers, AFFINA has created a customer database to helps its clients increase their business.

AFFINA is using Oracle's E-Business Suite, which allows the company to track information on customer-by-customer basis and analyse the customer-buying pattern helping the clients in increasing their business. It has also helped AFFINA in the highly competitive call centre outsourcing marketplace. The company is also embarking upon to focus on revenue-generating offerings, rather than maintaining softwares and systems.

(*Source*: Shari, 2003: 59.)

# Applied HR Case—'Stepping in Stepping Out'

## Master Fertilisers and Chemicals Limited

Master Fertilisers and Chemicals Limited was established five years ago and since inception it was doing well. From the domestic market last year, they have gone for exports and the results were promising. There is a lot of scope for further development by way of either doubling the capacity or by setting up another unit in the other part of the country so that the cost of production gets reduced. When setting up of a plant at another location was mooted, which requires transferring of some of the key personnel, there was a lot of resistance from all the employees and the shareholders. Taking into consideration the economies of scale and the proximity to raw materials, the company embarked upon doubling the capacity.

Mani, Chief Operations Officer was of the opinion to give holiday for a month, dismantle the whole machinery and to install an automated machine, which had come new in the market that can work with 25 per cent of the manpower and double the capacity. The idea was well appreciated, but since the cost of the new machinery was too high, the plan was abandoned. It was decided to have a similar plant with a similar capacity and use the expertise internally. The plant was semi-automatic and requires considerable manpower.

Amit, a consultant was engaged to look into the overall requirement of the plant and personnel for the expansion. Amit had taken the total details of the plant, machinery and the production statistics. He was surprised to find that all the allied activities like the canteen, transportation, security, etc., were engaging company employees, which constituted 37 per cent of the manpower. Amit wanted to propose that the company needed to look at the production and concentrate on the core activity rather than other aspects, which could be given to outside contractors to handle.

Amit knew that there would be a lot of resistance. He wanted to ensure that the company concentrated on the core activity of production of fertilisers and chemicals rather than those activities that did not give much value addition. Amit had prepared his plan and submitted the same to the MD and the Heads of the Departments. There was a hue and cry among the members that it will be inhumane to downsize and they were in considerable number. Amit had proposed that since there was expansion, they could also be accommodated in the new plant. They needed to be sent for training in handling the machines and supervision, which would equip them to handle the new roles. By the time the new plant became functionable for commercial operations, the company would have a manpower to handle the new plant, and only the critical vacancies which were about 22 needed to be filled in. The MD had liked the idea of rationalisation and concentrating on core competency and outsourcing the allied activities. In the long run, outsourcing would be more economical and the company would grow by concentrating on expansion and diversification.

## Questions

1. Do you think Amit was right in suggesting the new structure?
2. If you were the Head of HR, what would be the activities which you would outsource and why?
3. If you were MD, do you intend to accept the proposal and go for implementation of the new plan in spite of the resistance? If yes, what would be your strategy to implement the new structure?

## References and Further Readings

Cooke, F.L., J. Shen and A. McBride. 2005. 'Outsourcing HR as a Competitive Strategy? A Literature Review and an Assessment of Implications', *Human Resource Management*, no. 4, Winter, pp. 413–32.

Caudron, Shari. 2003. 'From Call Center to Profit Center', Profit Oracle's e-business magazine, vol. 8, August.

Greaver, Maurice, F. 1999. *Strategic Outsourcing: A Structured Approach to Outsourcing Decisions and Initiatives*, New York: AMACOM/AMA.

Halvey, John K. and Barbara M. Melby. 2000. *Business Process Outsourcing: Process, Strategies, and Contracts*, New York: John Wiley & Sons.

Lawler, Edward E., David Ulrich, Jac Fitz-enz and James Madden. 2004. *Human Resources Business Process Outsourcing: Transforming How HR Gets Its Work Done*, US: Jossey-Bass.

Linder, Jane C. 2004. *Outsourcing for Radical Change: A Bold Approach to Enterprise Transformation*, New0 York: AMACOM/AMA.

Singh, Shelley. 2003. 'The BPO Status Report', *Business World*, New Delhi, 4 August.

# 'HR BALANCE SHEET'
# EVALUATING THE VALUE OF YOUR
# HUMAN RESOURCE

*If you don't measure it, people will know you're not serious about delivering it.*

—James Belasco, *Teaching the Elephant to Dance*

## Intent

- To assess the value of HR assets of the company.
- To quantify in financial terms, the worth of human resource in an organisation and how it adds value vis-à-vis the business results.
- To set the benchmark of value and return from the company's HR comparing its year-wise performance.

## Expression

Human Resource Accounting is a system of measuring the value of human assets of the organisation at a given point of time. The human resource accounting is tabulated as an asset and liability in the form of human resource balance sheet.

## Comprehension

Traditional accounting practice does not recognise human resource as an asset in the balance sheet of an organisation. Cost incurred for recruitment, training and development of HR are being charged with the wage and salary bills and accumulated along with general overhead charges. However, the definition of wealth as a source of income inevitably leads to the recognition of human resource as one of the several forms of wealth such as money, securities and physical capital. Compensation in any form must be considered a long-term investment, which yields returns far beyond the current physical year rather than short-term cost of doing business. For example, a company with a payroll of $60 million, from a cost of doing business perspective, a 5 per cent increase is viewed as a one-time $3 million expense. If viewed from an investment perspective, the increase would only add value when there is a growth of 5 per cent in the corresponding year.

Over a period of time, public and private sector corporations worldwide have started considering their human resource as an asset and are planning for improvement for their future usefulness. Most corporations, however, are making case-by-case advances beyond the traditional tasks of cutting personnel costs, organising pay schemes, reducing head count and carrying the basics of recruiting, retaining and developing talent. The objective of any organisation is to ensure maximum asset creation and one of them is their human resource. Brainpower is the most critical resource for any economy. The resource value of an employee arises from acquisition of knowledge and skill that has an economic value. Hence, during the last decade greater significance is assigned to effective utilisation of HR. Organisations incur continuous expenditure on HR so the economic benefits from these assets accrue to organisations on a continuous basis.

The human resource value shall be communicated to the shareholders, management and creditors. These in turn help these stake holders visualise the company's competencies and capabilities much better. The value of human asset in fact, depends upon by the services rendered by them. Human Resources not only adds value to the company but also enhance its ability to achieve vision continuously. The HR assets, in fact, focuses on the intangible aspects of the HR.

Asset value, replacement cost, present value of future earning, and value to the organisations have also been used to place value on the firms' human resource. However, a major limitation to all these approaches is focus on inputs and outputs. In other words, they do not relate a firm's investment in people with the output the people produce. Newer approaches attempt to put the money value on the behavioural outcomes produced by human resources in an organisation. Costs are determined for such behaviour as absenteeism, turnover, and poor job performance. This method measures the economic consequences of employee behaviour, but not the value of the individual. The HR balance sheet is one of the methods to assess the value of human capital.

Profit and loss management is the end result that every organisation looks at. A healthy balance sheet reflects the financial strength of the organisation. As the financial balance sheet covers mostly assets and the financial part of the business operation, the most important assets have been left out of the valuation of people assets. The human resource balance sheet is a technology through which people assets of the company get recognised and valuated to its actual value added level. Strategically, it is important that the valuation of the HR of the company does reflect the soundness of the internal health along with financial health.

# Experiential Application

## A. Prerequisite

- The organisation must have willingness to define the worth of human resources in absolute financial terms. These could lead to liability or assets depending on the value that they generate in the organisation.
- The HR balance sheet brings in financial ratios of human resources. The historical data are very important for establishing comparison year-wise.
- An appropriate financial tool is required to calculate the present value of future costs, derivatives, etc.
- The statistical HR data of the industry leader gives clarity of the assets and liability values of HR.

## B. Process Steps

| Step | Process |
|------|---------|
| Step – I | Assigning of data and targets to HR. |
| Step – II | Analysis of data with scientific tools. |
| Step – III | Interpretation of data with the financial terms. |
| Step – IV | Benchmarking the year-wise performance. |

# Potential Gains and Areas of Concern

- The HR balance sheet is a reflection of the human capital of the company similar to that of financial statement of the company.
- It gives an understanding of the worth of human resources in terms of assets and liability value.

- It is helpful in defining the output of HR in quantifiable terms, which is usually only qualitative in nature.
- The data used for the making of HR balance sheet must be authentic otherwise the value created could be misleading.
- Organisations must derive meaning out of the results of the HR balance sheet and develop appropriate HR strategy, else the entire exercise of making HR balance sheet will not have any purpose.

# Measurability

## Try It Out

(1: not at all done, 2: moderately done, 3: to some extent done, 4: to a great extent done, 5: excellently done)

- Human Resource has been treated as one of the most important asset in my organisation. ☐
- The company's vision, mission and strategy documents recognise people's assets explicitly. ☐
- The HR balance sheet making practices have been adopted in the organisation ☐ since long and it is part of the organisation's financial balance sheet.
- The HR balance sheet data are meticulously gathered and prepared and represents the health of the organisation's people. ☐
- The organisation chart out concrete plans to deal with the outcome of the HR balance sheet, annually. ☐

Analysis: the average score would determine the extent to which the HR Balance Sheet process exists in your organisation.

## Score Card

(*: 25% achieved, **: 50% achieved, ***: 75% achieved, ****: 100% achieved)

| Technology | Objective Elements | Unit | Historical | Last Year | Current Year | Stretch Target | Status |
|---|---|---|---|---|---|---|---|
| HR Balance Sheet | Strategy Document | Doc | Nil | No | Yes | NA | ** |

# Proven Track Record

## Track One

## ABB

ABB Sverige is Sweden's largest industrial company. It has 27,000 (approx.) employees and a turnover of 40 billion kroner (approx.). A major part of ABB's work with intellectual capital is a continuance of the T50 project initiated at the end of the 1980s. The purpose of this project is to reduce all times (especially various kinds of lead times) by 50 per cent. This has required considerable commitment from the employees. Part of the project was thus to mobilise employees, suppliers and customers in order to be able to locate and gain the 50 per cent. To support this strategy, which cannot be implemented overnight, intellectual capital accounts symbolising the companies' long-term commitment to a special competence developing strategy are necessary.

ABB is to be transformed into a state-of-the-art, *'flat'* company where the employees have a say in corporate decisions. ABB has become more productive with an increase in turnover per employee from approximately SEK 65,000 to approximately SEK 150,000. Add to this the important lead time reduction.

(*Source*: The Danish Trade and Industry Development Council, Memorandum on 'Intellectual Capital Accounts Reporting and Managing Intellectual Capital', 1997: 39.)

## Track Two

## Telia Communications

Telia communications is a Swedish telecommunication company. Time and again, it has been felt that investment in intangible goods is attaining importance, as these intangibles are increasingly important as determinants of enterprise growth, productivity gains, profitability and wealth creation. However, the importance of intangibles exceeds the current ability to recognise and measure them. One indication is the increasing gap between the market value and book value. The difference is wider in firms that are more dependent on human resources than in those that are not.

The Swedish Telecommunications Company for a number of years published an HR balance sheet as a supplement to the annual report using historical costs as valuation model. In the profit and loss account the recruitment and training capital are depreciated. Putting the people on balance sheet created a dominant image of HR organisation.

(*Source*: http://www.sveiby.com)

# Applied HR Case—'Is Training a Cost or an Investment'

## Irwin Software Solutions

Irwin Software Solutions (ISS) is a customised software solutions company with top IT companies as their clients. The company has been doing extremely well since its inception and has been able to continuously innovate and provide services as per the schedule.

ISS was able to perform well because it was controlling its costs through tough budgets, adhering to schedules and delivering results to all the stakeholders. Before the start of the financial year, the human resource department presented its budget as per the strategic plan of the organisation.

After working out internally, the finance department, before releasing the budgets, sent a copy to all the departments for their feedback. Tracy Johnson was the new intern who was given the assignment to go through the details and give the feedback before it was assessed by Mr Cyrus, who had been doing the budgeting for a long time. Looking at the various accounting heads under which all the outflow of money is projected disturbed Tracy. She pointed out to Cyrus that all outflow is being treated as 'costs', for instance, Recruiting Costs, Personnel Costs, Training Costs, Travelling Costs, etc.

Tracy was of the strong opinion that the unique proposition of ISS is its manpower and employees who drive the organisation. Hence any expenses made towards enhancing the competencies have to be regarded as an 'investment' rather than cost. Normal machinery is subject to depreciation, whereas the value of humans increases with longevity due to appreciation in their skill sets and knowledge. Any money that is spent on the employees to further enhance their competency would help the organisation to cope with the external and internal changes and lead the company towards success. Traditional accounting and costing procedures significantly influence habits in the organisation. The two main barriers encountered in ascertaining personnel cost as investment are (a) employees do not qualify as assets, and (b) the inability to establish a meaningful system of measurement. Human Resource Management deals with intangibles and measurement becomes difficult.

Tracy has worked on various statistics available with the department on employees like the number of engineers/graduates, their length of experience in the industry, number of employees specialised in specific disciplines, experiences in handling clients, etc. Initially the finance department resisted, but looking at the strategic advantages the company is creating, it started showing keen interest. Tracy is of the opinion that if these details are published in all communication to the stakeholders, like balance sheets of profit & loss, investment calculations, human assets, etc., the valuation of the company would be further enhanced and would leverage on the strength of human assets available within the company.

Appreciating Tracy for her efforts and looking at the function of HR in a new dimension, Johnson, Head of HR, has asked her to work on various methods to measure the intangibles and also to prepare details of its human assets for publication in the communication to stakeholders.

## Questions

1. Do you think Tracy was right in questioning the fundamentals of accounting practices?
2. What would the impact of publication of details of human assets in the communication to stakeholders be in terms of management accounting?
3. Do you think that the new dimension of looking at human resource accounting and valuation of the human assets would give a different outlook on the contribution of employees in an enterprise?

## References and Further Readings

Fitz-enz, Jac. 2000. *The ROI of Human Capital: Measuring the Economic Value of Employee Performance*, New York: AMACOM/AMA.

Flamholtz, Eric G. 2001. *Human Resource Accounting: Advances in Concepts, Methods and Applications*, MA: Kluwer Academic Publishers.

Kaplan, Robert S. and David P. Norton. 2004. *Strategy Maps: Converting Intangible Assets into Tangible Outcomes*, MA: Harvard Business School Publishing.

Malik, R.K. 1993. *Human Resource Accounting and Decision Making*, New Delhi: Anmol Publications.

Petitone, James S. 2000. *Human Performance Consulting: Transforming Human Potential into Productive Business Performance*, Texas: Gulf Publishing Company.

Raju, T., Ashok Kumar and Sangeetha Mohandas. 2004. 'Human Resource Accounting—An Accountant's Dilemma', *The Management Accountant*, March.

Sveiby, Karl E. 1997. *The New Organizational Wealth: Managing & Measuring Knowledge-Based Assets*, San Francisco: Berrett-Koehler Publications Inc.

# Spectrum II
## HR Technologies for Building High Performing Individuals and Team Culture

An organisation comprises man, machine and material. Product and services are delivered through applying these three resources in congruence and optimally utilising them. Most important among these three resources are the people resources which plays a vital role for their own inputs and output as well as bringing inputs and outputs from machines and material. If we examine the people resources of the company we find that an organisation has diverse people resources such as people with varied qualification, experience, learning ability, knowledge, cultural background and gender. Transforming their ability to perform their best with such varied nature is a challenging task for the corporations. Distinctively, people on the job behaves in two different forms: one, as an individual and second, as a part of a team. An organisation must recognise these two distinctive elements of human beings and accordingly draw all people processes focusing on the individual and the team. This spectrum deals with all HR technologies that essentially help in building high performance individuals and team culture.

In every organisation, the HR processes must recognise the current status of an organisation's people processes and build up systems which help understanding the present for the future. It is essential that each individual employee in the company values himself as well as is valued by others by leveraging sensitivity process and other organisational behaviour processes. In today's world, diversity is also an important factor. Focusing alone on an individual may not be enough when an organisation as a whole has to face a competitive marketplace. It is a team and other forms of group dynamics through which corporations can fight this fierce battle. Those days are over when we talk about division of labour and individualistic work processes. In today's modern world, group processes in the form of high performing teams is here to stay.

In this spectrum we have brought in 14 such strategic HR technologies which essentially focus on individual processes and group processes which would result in building high performing individuals and team culture.

# 3 DIAGNOSING THE HR SCENARIO

## Learning Objectives

- To diagnose the organisational current state of affairs in terms of employee satisfaction, i.e., the HRD climate through survey mechanism.
- To establish a two way communication process.
- To evaluate the HR system audit for all systems.

● To understand the process of Internal Customer Satisfaction Survey within each functions of the company.

## Satisfy Internally to Satisfy Externally

Motivated and satisfied employees are the greatest assets of the company because they can work hard and implement the policies and systems in its true spirit. Every organisation lays down policies and its effectiveness and efficiency would only be seen when they are implemented, e.g., an organisation may have a charter for ensuring the customer service which may have been hung on every table, wall, or used as screen savers. However, unless and until the concept goes into the rational thinking process of effective customer service, every employee will not go out of the way to accommodate customers with courtesy and good cheer.

Creativity and innovation are encouraged for improving effectiveness. Employees should have concern, respect and a caring attitude within the organisation, i.e., the internal customers, so that they are expected to share externally with the customers. The customer service must come from their heart, which genuinely have love for the customers and value their contributions, however small it may be. Customer satisfaction must be the philosophy driving the top management and they need to ensure that every customer is given the best treatment for the first time, and every time. The management must consist of true leaders and do the acts, which the employees would learn by watching, and in turn, will imitate the same to bring in customer satisfaction.

True commitment to the value can be brought if the employee is being trained in all the areas of the core business process of the organisation and appreciate the business that they are doing. The organisation must bring in the highest standards by providing a suitable work atmosphere having the opportunities for learning and for personal growth. The organisation should make the policies, systems, procedures and practices that are employee friendly to build trust and commitment. Rules and regulations are meant to provide the guidelines, but they must not be the ends. An employee needs to be empowered to be flexible and drive that extra mile to try accommodating the requirements. This is because he needs to provide the best customer service, and the present rules and regulations framed does not give enough room for such an individualised service.

This requires adequate skills among the employees who are especially in the front end. All the employees need to be given on the job training and thus learn by observation and examples for better services. The employees need to work in other functions so that they can understand the business and will be able to deliver the best to the customer.

This helps ordinary people to do extraordinary things. The sense of achievement motivation would have an impact on the self and the individuals, intra and inter-departmental cooperation, to ensure customer satisfaction.

# Review of Organisational Human Resource Systems

Human Resources take care of recruitment, training, development, etc., in accordance with the objectives of the organisation. The HRD system helps to build the competencies and commitment of the individuals, groups, teams and the organisation as a whole through various technologies like induction, training, performance planning, etc. In other words, while the HR makes its own objectives, components, processes and values in line with the company's objectives, in order to achieve these objectives, the organisation builds its own HR system. If one of the objectives is training and development to enhance the competencies, the appropriate system would be a training policy which defines the goals, deliverables, nature and number of programmes, the feedback mechanism and MIS (Management Information System).

The HR systems need to be reviewed with the changing environment and hence, bringing in the changes in the system to make it more dynamic. However, the environment needs to be scanned to check whether the prerequisites to enable the changes to happen does exist, if not, the HR manager must bring in interventions to bring in the environment to effect the changes. For example, if the industry is moving towards a 360 degree feedback, unless the level of employee maturity reaches a stage where they are capable of reviewing their performance and indicating their flaws along with the corrective action to be taken at their end, the implementation of the system would be a failure.

Periodical assessments of the HR systems at regular intervals are needed to indicate the maximum achievable levels along with any changes and innovations. If no assessment is made, then the systems may not be in tune with the requirements of the business and HR cannot play the role of a strategic partner, but may become a hindrance for the achievement of the business objectives. For example, if the organisation's culture is open and transparent with increasing business targets, the appropriate system would be an open appraisal system and if the HR system is struck at closed appraisal system, it would become a hindrance to achieve the business objectives because the HR systems does not support the business strategy. The HRD audit thus helps to assess the orientation, processes and mechanisms, degree of participation, cost-effectiveness and efficiency of the overall HR system and helps to identify areas of improvement for meeting the organisational needs and building the sustained competitive advantage.

# Surveys in Contemporary Organisational Life

Survey is a method of obtaining information about attitudes, beliefs, opinions, behaviours, etc., of the employees. Organisational surveys are very prominent due to current management emphasis on employee involvement, customer satisfaction, quality, service excellence, etc. The three basic purposes of organisational surveys are first, to gather information on a wide range of issues like employee attitude towards policies. For example, Exit Interviews gives the feedback of the reasons why an employee is resigning and what sort of actions can be initiated by the management to overcome any deficiencies. Second, it helps to improve communication by way of establishing a link between the lower level employees and the management. The employees may not like to give the opinion directly during the meetings, suggestion schemes, etc. The survey method ensures that the employees are free to give their negative or positive feedback, which will be useful to the management to take corrective actions. It also gives the employees a feeling that their input is important to the organisation. Third, periodical surveys enable an organisation to detect the changes in the employee attitude and can plan to minimise their discontentment. The organisation can also have the feedback of how the employees perceive the changes in the processes initiated in the organisation, which can help in fine-tuning to achieve the optimum results.

The organisational surveys bring in a sense of empowerment, which enhances motivation, productivity and brings in a transparent organisational climate. Organisational surveys are used extensively to gather data but they are not the answers to a problem. It is a process to identify the potential sources of problems and act as a catalyst for organisational changes.

# How Effectively are Organisational Surveys Done?

Organisational surveys enable us to know the opinions, insights and facts about the current situation regarding various aspects like organisational climate, training and development, customer satisfaction, employee satisfaction, etc. The outcome of the survey enables the management to gauge the present situation and to plan for interventions to change the desired situation, in case of any deficiencies. The management has to give the objectives of the survey to be conducted and if the information is available, it means that there is no necessity to conduct a survey. But in case the survey is a must, it is necessary to determine the type of survey to be conducted, the size of the study, i.e., all the employees or only part, the nature of the group, sensitivity of the questions, the amount of time and money available, the types of questions to be asked and the means of tabulating the data and analysing the answers. Surveys vary greatly in amount of time and money required and in complexity. The method of survey needs to be chosen based on the data required and in case the information is scattered or critical, one or more methods of survey techniques are needed.

Before conducting a survey especially when the sample size is huge, it is desired to have a pilot testing, i.e., test the method for a few and derive the data required and analyse. If the method gives the requisite data then the survey method can be conducted on the total sample chosen, if not, necessary changes are to be made in the method or a different method is to be used to get the information. It is better to make the method foolproof so that it would not be needed to go back to the employee again to give his opinion and at the same time, the employee may not feel discomfort and may not participate in the same way he had done for the first time.

There are various methods of surveys like face-to-face interview, telephone interview, written questionnaire, etc. Face to face interview method is used when exploring complex questions that require explanatory answers like the effectiveness of training, what changes are required in the current training policy, the focus of training, etc. Telephone interview is used to get non-sensitive data of what the employee like/dislike, yes or no, etc., which is basically close ended. The questionnaire method is used to collect quantifiable non-sensitive data, for example, to know the opinion of the employees about the policies and practices. This method is also used for getting the sensitive data when the group size is large. The sample chosen for conducting the survey is very important, as it would determine whether the chosen one would give the information about the whole organisation. It also depends upon the size, the time available to conduct the survey and the money involved. The sample needs to be a cross section of the employees and large enough to give the opinion as a whole.

The data collected need to be tabulated and analysed using a proper statistical tool. If proper tool is not chosen, the data generated will give a different opinion. The report to be submitted has to have the same meaning of what the survey has revealed and that is the ethics of the survey. Whether the feedback is good or bad must be given to the management and it is for the management to decide about the action plan. The nature of data generated has to be with utmost confidence and if the respondents are committed to give the feedback, then the necessary feedback is needed to be given to them.

Surveys are the most prominent form of getting the feedback of the employees about the various aspects among the organisations. The quality of survey depends upon the method used and the analysis and presentation of the feedback. Surveys would enable the organisation to take action on the areas deficiencies, if any.

# Enable SHR Technology—Key to Success

This chapter brings in the following Strategic HR Technologies:

SHR Technology-07    Internal Communication—*Communicate, Communicate and Keep Communicating.*

SHR Technology-08    ESS—*Measuring Satisfaction Levels through Employee Satisfaction Survey.*

SHR Technology-09    HRD Climate Study—*Evaluating Prevalent Environment of Employee Friendliness and Organisational Culture through HRD Climate Survey.*

SHR Technology-10    HRD Audit—*Analysing the Effectiveness of HR Systems through HRD Audit.*

SHR Technology-11    ICSS—*Building Customer Centric Organisation through Internal Customer Satisfaction Survey.*

Universally making and breaking lies with effective and non-effective communication. Organisations must strengthen their communication process so that the communication channel travels from top to bottom and from bottom to top. Communication may involve multiple channels from print and video to electronic mail, teleconferencing, and large and small group meetings among management and employees. Philips Electronics devotes a section of its 'Philips Quality' guide to suggest to its managers an alternate approach to communication. Those choosing to deploy a company's wide initiative needs to be prepared to make a major effort.

As an organisation's health is reflected through the balance sheet of a company and the employees' satisfaction is measured through the ESS, the employee satisfaction survey is a reflection of what employees expect the organisation to provide to attain their satisfaction level. The employees start feeling dissatisfied the moment they realise that there are no such offers made by the organisation.Conducive working environment, enabling culture, respect for individual dignity and a learning culture is what every employee expects from the organisation. The custodian for providing all such intrinsic needs lies with the HR. It is obvious that this kind of a climate needs to be provided. The survey is a reflection of the existing HR oriented climate in the organisation and the desired level, so as to create an environment where the expectations of employees are met.

It is essential to evaluate the task, structure, systems and technology used in the organisation process, whether these processes are timely and appropriate, through a diagnosis process. The outdated processes need to be replaced with advance processes. The HR function, its deliverables and the processes also need to be evaluated through systematic processes. The HRD audit is a tool, which helps auditing the inherent strengths and weaknesses of HR functions so that more improvements are made. All employees are the internal customers to HR. Internal customer satisfaction survey is a technique through which HR functions can evaluate their customer orientation in the company.

# Conclusion

- Customer satisfaction comes when the internal employees of the company are satisfied within the systems of the organisation. Needless to say, that if employees are not tuned and motivated, the level of customer satisfaction that they bring in will have detrimental effect.
- Every organisation must strengthen the process of communication both ways, i.e., from above to below and vice versa. Communication is a key for organisational success.
- The HR systems implemented in the company require a periodic review and that can be done through the employee satisfaction survey, HRD climate survey and HRD Audit.
- The feedback mechanism provides the current status and situation at which the organisational HR processes are existing and it helps defining an action plan for improvement.

# 'INTERNAL COMMUNICATION' COMMUNICATE, COMMUNICATE AND KEEP COMMUNICATING

*If you are an enthusiast, it communicates. And nothing communicates so much as the lack of it.*

—Rowland Whitehead, *Country Life* (1996)

## Intent

- To understand the barriers to interpersonal communication.
- Discuss and formulate systems and procedures for effective and improved communication.
- How an individual can be an effective communicator.

## Expression

Communication is the evoking of a shared or common meaning in another person. Interpersonal communication is the communication between two or more people in an organisation.

## Comprehension

The most important leadership role in an organisation is to communicate and to ensure that proper communication is going on throughout the organisations. For building effective relationships with the employees this is needed. However, many of our current organisational moves are attributed to its absence. Also, a great deal of management time is spent on it. Nothing is wrong in any of that. The problem is that most of the time what we actually do is just inform, not communicate.

Inform means to tell off, while communicate means to impart and share with. Reading, listening, managing and interpreting information, and serving clients are few such interpersonal communication skills. The communicator is the person originating the message; the receiver is the person receiving the message. The receiver must receive the message and understand it. The message, the language and the data are the means of communication. In an organisational set-up one-way communication from top to bottom or bottom to top alone does not work. There is a possibility that some sort of communication distortion would take place which would generate more confusion rather than clarity. Therefore, a two-way communication in the organisation is very important. Two-way communication is an interactive form of communication in which there is an exchange of thoughts feelings or both or through which shared meaning offer occurs. A good communicator is also a good listener, and a good listener would always get more than what he wants and get better with others. Problem solving and decision-making are often examples of communication.

Communication can be defensive or non-defensive. Defensive communication in an organisation brings in aggressiveness, attacking and angry or passive and withdrawing, while non-defensive communication is assertive, direct and powerful. Defensive communication in an organisation can create barriers in people whereas non-defensive communication helps in opening up relations. Language is a central element in communication. It may be a barrier if its use obscures meaning and distorts intent. Although English is the language of aviation, it is not the language of business. Where the native language of employees and managers differs, the risk of barriers to communication exist. These days there are increasing businessmen and women who are bilingual or multilingual. There are various non-verbal elements of communication, such as the study of facial and eye behaviour, sign language, etc.

Computer mediated communication was once used only to be technical specialists but now this influences virtually all managerial behaviours in the work environment. Informational database is becoming more commonplace. Electronic mail, video conferencing, voicemail, chatting, etc., has become the order of the day. This has improved the communication substantially in the business.

Every problem has one reason, *'miscommunication'*. This communication is something so deep an issue that ultimately all things are attributed to it only. How is it possible to strengthen communication processes within the company? It is an issue of process or people. The reason could be anything but one thing is clear the better the communication within the company, higher is the productivity and better is the clarity amongst all employees. Communication flow and its distortion is common phenomenon. There are various means through which communication strengthening needs to be done so that the upward and downward flow is maintained. Communicate, communicate and keep communicating is the *'mantra'* in modern business environment and effective process associated with communication is a strategic move in organisational business effectiveness.

# Experiential Application

## A. Prerequisite

- To deal with the communication barrier, the following strategies have been listed here. Seek to clarify your ideas before communicating:
  - be sure your actions support your instructions;
  - consider the total physical and human situation whenever one gives instruction;
  - follow up on communication—get feedback.
- Formal channels of the communications are the officials' paths by which official messages travel. Informal channels stem from the unofficial, social relationships existing between individuals who work together and serve to transmit unofficial messages.
- In the informal channel, the major modes of communication are friendship cliques. They are important because such cliques generate and sustain loyalty to the larger organisation and because they are groups in which natural leaders develop their talent for leadership.

## B. Process Steps

| Step | Process |
|------|---------|
| Step – I | Projection of manpower is made basing on the factors like plant expansion, contraction, attrition, etc. |
| Step – II | The HR department to review its management skill inventory to identify the management talent now employed. |
| Step – III | Using multiple review method, an inventory of permutable employee to be found out. |
| Step – IV | Define and determine high potential employees with their availability. |
| Step – V | Management replacement charts drawn to fill the management and individual development needs. |
| Step – VI | Each higher level management reviews the recommendations and makes revisions. |
| Step – VII | Assess candidates against competencies and criteria. |

# Potential Gains and Areas of Concern

- Good and effective communication plays a significant role in determining the overall success of any organisation.

- If effective cooperative behaviour is to exist in an organisation, communication must be understood, believed, accepted and acted upon.
- When the communication process between the staff and line is poor and less than effective, problem can develop.
- Many a time it is felt that top management is frequently out of touch with its workers' thoughts and feelings about work related matters since there exists a communication gap.

# Measurability

## Try It Out

(1: not at all done, 2: moderately done, 3: to some extent done, 4: to a great extent done, 5: excellently done)

- My organisation has defined communication strategy and all are aware of it. □
- Employees are able to express freely about their issues within the organisation and they are addressed diligently. □
- We have frequent meeting only with an agenda to communicate certain organisation policies and decisions and they are deliberated widely. □
- A periodic assessment of the effectiveness of communication is done through structured survey administered to all. □
- Post feedback actions are taken to improve the communication within the organisation. □
- Many effective mediums are effectively used in the organisation. □

Analysis: the average score would determine the extent to which communication exists in your organisation.

## Score Card

(*: 25% achieved, **: 50% achieved, ***: 75% achieved, ****: 100% achieved)

| Technology | Objective Elements | Unit | Historical | Last Year | Current Year | Stretch Target | Status |
|---|---|---|---|---|---|---|---|
| Communication | Communication Effectiveness | Scale | Nil | 3.5/5 | 4/5 | 4.24/5 | ** |

# Proven Track Record

## Track One

### Wal-Mart, USA

Sam Walton, founder of Wal-Mart store, Inc., opened his first Wal-Mart store in 1962. Focusing on the sale of discounted name, he begun to set up more and more stores in Sun Belt. He, at the same time introduced effective marketing and inventory control systems. Today, it is not only the largest retailer but is one of the biggest firms in the world. Although Sam died several years ago, his legacy and cultural value remains. Walton himself used to stress, and the current management staff continue to emphasise the importance of encouraging associates to develop new ideas. If the policy does not seem to be working, the company quickly changes it. Executives continually encourage associates to challenge the current system and look for ways to improve it.

To make sure that the culture values get out to all associates, the company has a communication network worthy of the Pentagon. It includes everything from six-channel satellite to a private airforce of numerous planes. Every one is taught this culture and is expected to operate according to the core cultural values of hard work, efficiency and customer services.

(*Source*: Luthans, 2002: 128.)

## Track Two

### Xerox, USA

Xerox is a global corporation of 85,000 employees, a Wall Street favourite basically a document company. Keeping people well informed about the direction the organisation was heading, in addition to giving them detailed information about current and future changes is very essential. This helps management to remain as a part of solution rather than part of the problem. In Xerox this is highly emphasised. Xerox believed in clear communication and frequent updates, which enabled people to be excited rather than, frightened by the prospect of a major organisational change.

Managers and executives would be required through the use of frequent meetings, e-mail updates, and printed reports to keep all members informed of any information on the progress of the changed programme. In Xerox, they were required to create a feeling of ownership among all employees of the company. Xerox has learnt that open communication is the natural prerequisite to team building.

(*Source*: Carter, Giber and Goldsmith, 2001.)

# Applied HR Case—'Wireless'

## Wizard Technologies

Raman was a young and energetic chartered accountant who had gained immense experience in the area of budget preparation, control and analysis. He had good command over the subject and used to offer solutions to other departments on anything related to accounts and finance. He used to invite people into his room and used to discuss the matters. Though he had good knowledge, he was considered as being '*attached to books*' or an '*expert advisor*'.

Looking at his experience and expertise, Raman was made head of finance and accounts, which was hitherto run by two heads. Raman immediately accepted the challenge and was quite enthusiastic about his new role.

The purview of Raman had increased enormously and he was getting less time to concentrate on the activities and hence, he had taken special permission to recruit fresh CAs as trainees. He would train them and subsequently they would occupy important roles in the company as the organisation grew. Raman used to think that out of all the activities he was handling, the most trivial one was budgeting since he had good exposure and could easily find any mistakes. The trainees were very eager to work with him since he was considered to be an authority on the budget. Initially when they used to get the reports to Raman, he used to see and give advice so that they could be sent across to respective departments. Raman became more and more busy and he asked the trainees to handover the papers to the secretary and he would take them home, read and give them the feedback. Since Raman did not have the time to go through, he used to just give the papers back. The trainees were confused whether they were correct in making the budget.

Slowly they got good hold of the subject and started sending the reports directly to the head of the departments sometimes without the knowledge of Raman since they knew that he did not have time looking at the budget. The HODs started interacting with the trainees directly and sometimes they used to take undue advantage and make the plans to their benefit at the cost of others. Soon the budget section, which was considered as sacrosanct, was now considered as no-man land and everybody started dictating their own terms and conditions.

With the starting of the budget year, Raman had to submit the new budget to the HODs and since he had less time to go through he just took the papers before the meeting and copied the presentation to be presented. Raman had presented the budget with a deficit which need to be fulfilled with the borrowings and he was upset by the way budget was being prepared. All the HODs had complained his inability to handle the budget. The Managing Director was very upset with the performance of Raman and he left the meeting in middle. Raman was taken aback and he did not have any answer to the questions raised. The next day Raman was summoned to the Director's office to give his explanation.

## Questions

1. Do you think the management was correct in giving both accounts and finance to Raman? If yes, please explain why?
2. Do you think trainees have behaved highhandedly and overtook Raman in making the budget? If yes, why?
3. Do you assume that there was utter lack of communication between Raman, the trainees and HODs?
4. Prepare an action plan for Raman to improvise the state of affairs.

## **References and Further Readings**

Carter, Louis, David Giber and Marshall Goldsmith (eds). 2001. *Best Practices in Organization Development and Change*, LA: Jossey-Bass.

Dobson, Ann. 2002. *How to Communicate at Work*, Mumbai: Jaico Publishing House.

Francis, Dave. 1989. *Unblocking Organisational Communication*, England: Gower Publishing Company Limited.

Griffin, Ricky W. 2000. *Fundamentals of Management*, Chennai: All India Publishers and Distributors.

Hannagan, Tim. 1995. *Management—Concepts and Practices*, Delhi: MacMillan India Ltd.

Hersey, Paul, Kenneth H. Blanchard and Dewey E. Johnson. 2002. *Management of Organisation Behavior—Leading Human Resources*, New Delhi: Prentice Hall of India Private Limited.

Luthans, Fred. 2002. *Organisation Behavior*, New York: McGraw-Hill.

Mohan, Krishna and Meera Banerji. 2001. *Developing Communication Skills*, Delhi: MacMillan India Ltd

Rao Chalapati. 1999. *Communication and Leadership-Skills and Strategies*, Hyderabad: Booklinks Corporation

Weihrich, Heinz and Harold Koontz. 1994. *Management—A Global Perspective*, New York: McGraw-Hill Inc

# 'ESS'

*Winning Companies.... Realize they are only as strong as the intelligence,*
*judgement and character of their employees.*

—George Bush, Washington DC (1990)

## Intent

- To analyse the existing level of employee satisfaction among the employees of the company through scientific survey technique.
- To identify the areas requiring improvement and areas maintained efficiently from the survey.
- To set a benchmark on the level of satisfaction persisting among the employees and set the next mark for strategic improvement.
- To give a feel of employees being heard and have a voice to communicate the level of satisfaction through survey technique; and for the management to have a data to work on improvement plans.

## Expression

Employee Satisfaction Survey (ESS) means use of questionnaire survey to help determine the satisfaction level of members of the organisation. The ESS provides the feedback to the top management and to work groups for interpretation and analysis. Group members participate in discussion on the implication of the information, the diagnosis of problems and the development of action to overcome the problems identified.

# Comprehension

A satisfied employee would be an asset to the organisation since it helps the organisation to have a longer life cycle, increased motivation, better performance and commitment towards the goals. Motivating employees to perform at their highest potential is one of the many challenges managers face on a daily basis. However, it is often difficult to judge just how satisfied and motivated employees are at work, especially for managers who oversee a large number of employees. Therefore, many managers find out about their employees' true feelings through surveys. Employees are asked how they feel about their responsibilities, work objectives, management support, communication with co-workers, level of control over their work and other pertinent questions. Responses are scored and analysed to provide managers with an overall view of employee satisfaction and morale.

Employee Satisfaction Survey can be considered as a powerful tool of diagnosis, evaluation and measurement and a foundation upon which strategic thinking and plan of action can be established. It depicts and reflects the perception of the organisation's realities as experienced and understood by the employees. The ESS are normally conducted across different divisions, locations and levels of the employees.

The ESS results provide the information on the present health of the company, the style of management in the organisation and the areas where the organisation is strong in and the areas where it needs to improve, to evolve new improved methods/systems of working in order to enhance organisational effectiveness and efficiency of operations as well as taking systematic steps towards enhancement of organisational employee satisfaction and happiness.

The information derived is normally discussed in various forums, meetings, Intranet, notice boards, etc., so that every employee knows how their organisation is taking care of them. If the comparative figures of the past and the present are shown, it will have better impact. The results need to be shared with the employees so that they feel that the organisation is transparent. Confidentiality can be maintained, if the feedback tends to give a different picture, which may act detrimental to the organisation. The measure will have greater impact if the head of the organisation shows concern, being part of the process and driving the areas, which needs improvement. Without having done periodic ESS, the direction on which HR processes are moving would be questionable and hence, having ESS is strategic technology in HR management.

# Experiential Application

## A. Prerequisite

- The ESS must adopt a comprehensive multi method approach with a robust design that ensures a high degree of validity and reliability of survey findings.
- These multi pronged approach encompasses a questionnaire made up of three distinct sections:
  - a questionnaire section made up of close-ended questions in a five-point scale;
  - quantitative opinion analysis section made up of open-ended questions that elicit opinion/ideas/perceptions of the candidates; and
  - the background information that schedule the categorisation and sorting of data.
- The comprehensive questionnaire must be administered to all the employees of the company across all sections and levels.

## B. Process Steps

| Step | Process |
| --- | --- |
| Step – I | Discussion with the top management to identify the objectives and the scope for the survey to be done. |
| Step – II | Understanding the systems, policies, practices and the culture of the HR through manuals, reports, discussion and observation. |
| Step – III | Preparing the ESS questionnaire. |
| Step – IV | Pilot study and validation of the questionnaire. |
| Step – V | Administering the questionnaire across the organisation or the sample size as determined in the objectives. |
| Step – VI | Compilation and analysis of the gathered data. |
| Step – VII | Presenting the facts to the top management and the HR about the satisfaction levels. |
| Step – VIII | Human Resources to make an action plan on gaps and with the approval of top management make a strategy to implement. |

# Potential Gains and Areas of Concern

- It helps in understanding the level of satisfaction amongst the employees.
- It sets a target for the organisation to decide on what are the measures to be taken to increase the level of satisfaction.
- The ESS done periodically gives a clarity of the effectiveness of the various HR initiatives in the organisation.

- The ESS some times give skewed results if the questionnaire is not designed properly or administered properly.
- Employee sometimes gives feedback very casually or without active interest hence data can be misnomer.
- Credibility of the administration of questionnaire and its analysis may be questionable due to methods used and its acceptance in the organisation.
- Management may not take appropriate corrective measures on the results hence, interest on the feedback get lost.

# Measurability

## Try It Out

(1: not at all done, 2: moderately done, 3: to some extent done, 4: to a great extent done, 5: excellently done)

- There exists management consent to evaluate periodically the level of employees' satisfaction in my organisation. ☐
- Organisation makes sincere efforts to know the level of employees' satisfaction periodically through structured surveys. ☐
- A periodical employees' satisfaction is determined and an action is made to mitigate the low employees' satisfaction level areas. ☐
- A year-wise comparison on employees' satisfaction is drawn and a positive trend of growth is maintained in the organisation. ☐
- The ESS level is discussed among all the important business meetings across all levels in the organisation. ☐

Analysis: the average score would determine the extent at which Employees' Satisfaction level exist in your organisation.

## Score Card

(*: 25% achieved, **: 50% achieved, ***: 75% achieved, ****: 100% achieved)

| Technology | Objective Elements | Unit | Historical | Last Year | Current Year | Stretch Target | Status |
|---|---|---|---|---|---|---|---|
| ESS | Employees' Satisfaction areas | Scale | Nil | 2.5 | 3.0 | 3.25 | ** |

# Proven Track Record

## Track One

### Monsanto

Many companies are beginning to pay a lot more attention to non-financial factors that contribute to profits. Employee satisfaction, customer satisfaction and financial results seem to be linked when employee commitment and customer loyalty are important. Monsanto has conducted a survey of customer and employee's satisfaction. They have found out that employee satisfaction was one of the strongest predictors of customer satisfaction.

Dick Clark leader of financial services unit says, 'It's common sense, when people feel great about the place where they work, they provide better customer service.' The survey was useful in gauging the satisfaction level of the employees and how it could enhance the external customer satisfaction.

(*Source*: Hellriegel and Woodman, 2001: 53.)

## Track Two

### Cellular One

Cellular One is the leading wireless communication company in San Francisco, with its main aim being enhancing customer solutions by being 'dedicated to providing the best total solution to meet a customer's unique needs.' One of its long-term strategy was retention of employees and management development. The company's urge to know the satisfaction of the employees has embarked upon the annual ESS, since satisfied employee means longer employee life cycles, increased motivation, stronger commitment to the organisation and better business performance. Every year, two weeks are dedicated and the survey is conducted for all the employees and the participation is always more than '94 per cent'. The information regarding the survey is being made through voice mails, internal marketing, posters at the conference rooms, rest rooms, break rooms, etc. The posters also exhibit what actions they have implemented based on the feedback of the previous survey.

The HR personnel go to each nook and corner to administer the questionnaire. The company went electronic to have quick access and timely results of the survey. Some of the areas where top management worked towards increased satisfaction levels are Career Development, Company Communication, Development of Management Skills and Perceived Fairness of Organisational Policies and Procedures.

# Applied HR Case—'Turning to the Trend'

## Samson Projects

Samson Projects is into Business Process Outsourcing (BPO) and takes up the projects on turnkey basis or on a long-term venture. The short-term projects can be telemarketing for events, products, etc., and at the same time taking up the sale of Credit Cards, Loans, etc. The competition in the sector is very high in spite of the periodic rise in the salaries. Francis, the HR head is worried since much of the time is being spent on recruitment and retention and he has little time to spend on the development of the competencies.

Francis used to always think that if the satisfaction of the employees is high then there is a scope for employees to have a longer life cycle, motivation and commitment to perform well. He has been struggling to keep these three elements high and was finding it difficult to hold on to the people and hence, not able to make any strategic plans except to periodically rise the salaries.

Francis was bothered by two factors: employee satisfaction and retention and he had hired a consultant to work on the same since it is objective and employees would be open to speak to an outsider. ABC Surveys, which is predominantly in doing surveys, has suggested two types of surveys to get a better picture—one is the ESS and the other is surveying the effectiveness of the retention practices. The results of both will be displayed on prominent places so that employees will come to know how the satisfaction level has moved and the mere information may give them an idea how the company is taking care of them.

## Questions

1. Do you think that Francis is right in engaging the external consultant for the project?
2. Do you think that in spite of knowing what is going wrong; still he needs the help of a consultant.
3. If you were the consultant, design the questionnaires on ESS and retention management practices to be administered across the company.

## References and Selected Readings

Church and Waclawski. 1998. *Designing and Using Organizational Surveys*, England: Jossey-Bass.

Dwivedi, R.S. 2001. *Research Methods in Behavioral Sciences*, Delhi: MacMillan India Ltd.

Hellriegel, D., J. Slocum and R. Woodman. 2001. *Organisational Behavior*, US: South Western College Publishing.

## APPENDIX-8A

## 'Employee Satisfaction Survey (ESS)'

## FAQs

- **What is ESS?**
  Employee Satisfaction Survey is a tool to measure the opinions and feelings of the employees about their job and the organisation. This survey gives a chance to give confidential feedback to the organisation and also a window to let know how you feel about working in the company.
- **Will my feedback have an impact?**
  The result will help the organisation to know what it is doing with its own employees, compare with the best standards in the industry and take measures to improve upon the present conditions.
- **How confidential is my information?**
  Information given by you will be maintained with utmost confidentiality, and in fact, the questionnaire is designed in such a way that you need not mention your name.
- **Are there any right or wrong answers?**
  There are no right and wrong answers; you need to just give your opinions and perceptions. Your answers should reflect your honest opinions and perceptions only.
- **How shall I answer the questionnaire?**
  The questions are designed in such a way that answers are to be marked on a 5 point rating scale. All you need to do is just to tick mark against each question.

## Employee Information: (Please encircle)

1. What is your current location
   (A) CO    (B) Zone    (C) Branch    (D) Franchisee    (E) .............. (Pl. specify)

2. How long you have been working in this company?
 (A) Less than 1 year
 (B) 2 years
 (C) 5 years
 (D) 10 years
3. Working in the present level since
 (A) Less than 1 year
 (B) 2 years
 (C) 4 years
 (D) More than 4 years
4. Current Level:
 (A) Managerial    (B) Non-Managerial    (C) Trainees
5. Gender
 (A) Male    (B) Female

## Tick mark the answer

| | Item | Strongly Agree | Agree | Agree to Some Extent | Dis-agree | Strongly Disagree |
|---|---|---|---|---|---|---|
| 1. | I really feel like 'part of XYZ Family'. | | | | | |
| 2. | I feel an act of encouragement to stay with this company. | | | | | |
| 3. | I am proud to work for this organisation. | | | | | |
| 4. | At work, I often do things that are 'above and beyond' my duty and my superiors support me. | | | | | |
| 5. | I feel highly motivated to do my work. | | | | | |
| 6. | I am treated with dignity by my superiors. | | | | | |
| 7. | The organisation trusts me and gives me freedom to do my job. | | | | | |
| 8. | The organisation shows genuine care and concern for me. | | | | | |
| 9. | I have a good understanding of what I am supposed to do at work. | | | | | |
| 10. | Ideas and suggestions are appreciated by the organisation. | | | | | |
| 11. | I get a real sense of achievement working for this organisation. | | | | | |
| 12. | I believe that the pay I get for my work is good. | | | | | |
| 13. | The policies are framed and carried out are fair and just. | | | | | |
| 14. | Periodical Review of my KPA is being done in right perspective. | | | | | |

(Continued)

*(Continued)*

| | Item | Strongly Agree | Agree | Agree to Some Extent | Dis-agree | Strongly Disagree |
|---|---|---|---|---|---|---|
| 15. | I manage my work within the shift timings. | | | | | |
| 16. | I have control over the resources I use to do my work. | | | | | |
| 17. | Employees are encouraged to innovate and implement ideas. | | | | | |
| 18. | Employees are provided training to help do work effectively. | | | | | |
| 19. | Organisation provides help whenever I am in emergency. | | | | | |
| 20. | Organisation provides family–friendly benefits to employees. | | | | | |
| 21. | My Manager shares my concerns and views. | | | | | |
| 22. | I get fullest support from my Team members during my work. | | | | | |
| 23. | Management makes clear what they expect of me at work. | | | | | |
| 24. | Organisation has a process of getting feedback and ideas. | | | | | |
| 25. | Information is communicated in time and in a correct way. | | | | | |
| 26. | I am satisfied with my work. | | | | | |
| 27. | My job provides me chances to grow and develop. | | | | | |
| 28. | I have a well-defined job. | | | | | |
| 29. | Organisation provides the right man on the right job. | | | | | |
| 30. | People who contribute are being rewarded. | | | | | |
| 31. | My office has the right kind of work environment. | | | | | |
| 32. | I get enough time to spend with my family. | | | | | |
| 33. | My company adheres to the quality standards. | | | | | |
| 34. | My superior supports me as leader, trainer and coach. | | | | | |
| 35. | All the employees work towards customer satisfaction. | | | | | |
| 36. | My company has a concern for my safety. | | | | | |
| 37. | My grievances are being attended immediately. | | | | | |
| 38. | My outstanding contribution is recognised and rewarded. | | | | | |
| 39. | I am given sufficient authority to carry out my job. | | | | | |
| 40. | Company has a good strategic planning to bring in fresh ideas. | | | | | |

*(Continued)*

(Continued)

| | Item | Strongly Agree | Agree | Agree to Some Extent | Dis-agree | Strongly Disagree |
|---|---|---|---|---|---|---|
| 41. | I get timely and constructive feedback about my performance. | | | | | |
| 42. | My Manager encourages sycophancy. | | | | | |
| 43. | I prefer to go to the HIGHER BOSS than the immediate superior to redress my grievances. | | | | | |
| 44. | My Manager asks me for my input to help make decisions. | | | | | |
| 45. | There is a high sense of belongingness in the company. | | | | | |
| 46. | My Managers and peers help me out when I am held up in my work. | | | | | |
| 47. | My job is challenging and I love it. | | | | | |
| 48. | The company has a good career development plan. | | | | | |

# 'HRD CLIMATE STUDY' EVALUATING PREVALENT ENVIRONMENT OF EMPLOYEE FRIENDLINESS AND ORGANISATIONAL CULTURE THROUGH HRD CLIMATE SURVEY

*The achievement of excellence can only occur if the organization promotes a culture of creative dissatisfaction.*

—Lawrence Miller

## Intent

- To define the Organisation Culture and understand the Organisational Culture and performance.
- To define the Organisation Culture as OCTAPACE values.
- To evaluate the level of Organisation Culture through climate survey approach and action plan for improvement.
- To bring in the desired level of Organisational Change through structured intervention process.

## Expression

Organisation Culture is a two-level construct that includes both observable and unobservable characteristics of the organisation. At the observable level, culture includes many aspects of the organisation such as architecture, dress, behaviour pattern, rules, stories, myths, languages and ceremonies. The unobservable culture is composed of shared values, norms, beliefs and assumption of organisational members. Culture is the pattern or configuration of these two levels of characteristics that orient or directs organisational members to manage problems and their surroundings. A pattern of basic assumption that is considered valid and that is taught to new members is the way to perceive, think and feel in the organisations.

# Comprehension

The concept of culture in organisations was alluded as early as Hawthorne studies, which describe work group culture. Many definitions of organisation culture have been proposed. Most of them agree that that there are several levels of culture. And these levels differ in terms of their visibility and their ability to be changed. Culture attains significance since it is the key component in the achievement of the organisation's mission and strategies, the improvement of organisational effectiveness and the management of change.

Every formal organisation of prescribed jobs and structural relationships includes an informal organisation characterised by unofficial rules and interconnections. These informal organisations arise, as employees make spontaneous, unauthorised changes in the way things are done. As stated culture is a pattern of basic assumptions—invented, discovered or developed to poke with problems of external adaptation and internal integration—that has worked well enough to be considered valid and therefore to be taught to new members as the correct way to perceive, think and feel in relation to those problems. Culture is a cumulative crystallised and shared lifestyle of people as reflected in the preference of some state of life over others (values), in the predisposed response towards several significant issues and phenomena (attitudes), in the organised filling time in relation to certain affairs (rituals) and in the ways of promoting desire, and preventing undesirable behaviour (sanction). It can help an organisation by way of creating an environment, which is conducive to performance orientation and adapting to the change.

The most important aspect of Organisation Culture are the value (OCTAPACE) it perceives; these are *openness*—the degree of transparencies in the organisations on important factors determining the business processes; *confrontation*—related to putting the problem in the front rather than back and working with others to find its solutions; *trust*—level of mutual understanding without seeing with suspicion; *authencity*—the willingness of a person to acknowledge the feeling he has and accept himself as well as others who relate to him as person; *proactive*—anticipating issues and acting to take advantage of this understanding or responding to the need of the future; *autonomy*—willingness to use power without fear and helping others to do the same; *collaboration*—working together and using one another's strength for a common cause; and *experimenting*—emphasising the importance given to the innovations and trying out new ways of dealing with the problems in the organisation.

Congenial and cordial environment within the organisational set-up always attracts new talents as well as a motivation for the existing talents for retention; an environment where creativity is fostered, openness is cherished and forthrightness in dealing brings a positive state of organisation climate. No matter what the size and the volume of business is, positive work culture and environment is something all employees always look for. If an organisation lacks these basic climates, the efforts should be on to strengthen those positive climates which can allow employees to perform in ease. Climate survey is a technology through which organisation climate can be examined and corrective measures can be initiated to bridge the gap between positive and non-conducive environment. This is the technology through which this is possible and therefore, it is strategic in nature.

# Experiential Application

## A. Prerequisite

- Many organisational scientists argue for assessing organisational culture with quantitative methods, others say that organisational culture must be assessed with qualitative methods.
- Quantitative methods such as questionnaire are valuable because of their precision, comparability and objectivity.
- Qualitative methods such as interview and observations are valuable because of the detail descriptiveness and uniqueness.
- Many quantitative assessment instruments are used, some of them are Organisational Culture Inventory (OCI), Hillmann–Saxton culture—gap survey and most proven HRD Climate Survey.

## B. Process Steps

| Step | Process |
|------|---------|
| Step – I | Create a simple and clear mission statement. A shared mission can unite individual from diverse cultural background. |
| Step – II | Create a system that ensures an effective flow of information. |
| Step – III | Create a matrix mind among the managers, i.e., broaden the managers mind to allow them to think globally. |

*(Continued)*

(*Continued*)

| Step | Process |
|------|---------|
| Step – IV | Develop career paths, ensuring not only employees get new avenues of working but also have job rotations. |
| Step – V | Use cultural differences as a major asset, i.e., using various cultural diversity organisational activity. |
| Step – VI | Implement management education and team development programme which establish a shared identity. |
| Step – VII | Unified training efforts that emphasise corporate values. |

# Potential Gains and Areas of Concern

- Organisation Culture is a pattern of basic assumption that are considered valid and that are taught to new members as the way to perceive, think and feel in the organisation.
- The most visible and accessible level of culture is an artifact, which includes personal enactment, ceremonies and rites, stories, rituals and symbols.
- Organisational Culture has four functions: giving members a sense of identity and increasing their commitment, serving as a conscience for members, reinforcing organisational values and serving as a control mechanism for shaping behaviour.
- Leaders shape and reinforce culture by what they pay attention to and how they react to crisis, how they behave, how they allocate rewards, how they hire and fire individuals.
- Organisation culture is a deep-rooted phenomenon for any organisation. Simple efforts to bring change in the culture is not possible to attain.

# Measurability

## Try It Out

(1: not at all done, 2: moderately done, 3: to some extent done, 4: to a great extent done, 5: excellently done)

- The organisation culture is a prime important area for the management in my organisation.  ☐
- The company frequently makes attempt to gauge the prevailing cultural climate that exists and the concern areas requiring improvement.  ☐
- There is consensus among the senior management team on commonly shared culture building efforts and all contribute equally in the process.  ☐

- The organisation has shown exemplary punitive action when some
  employee found acting beyond the boundaries of cultural barriers.  ☐
- The company has framed certain explicate policies which bind the
  employees within the boundaries of good conduct on cultural ground.  ☐

Analysis: the average score would determine the extent to which positive organisation climate exists in your organisation.

## Score Card

(*: 25% achieved, **: 50% achieved, ***: 75% achieved, ****: 100% achieved)

| Technology | Objective Elements | Unit | Historical | Last Year | Current Year | Stretch Target | Status |
|---|---|---|---|---|---|---|---|
| Climate Survey | Climate Survey Outcome | Survey | Nil | No | Yes | NA | ** |

# Proven Track Record

## Track One

## SouthWest Airlines

An important reason for the commitment of SouthWest employees is the culture that strives inside the company created by their CEO. The CEO sends cards to employees on their birthdays and anniversaries to thank them for the job well done. Furthermore, letters from customers are often delivered to employees with a note from CEO saying *'keep up the good job'*. SouthWest is also sensitive to the personal and family life of the employees. For example, people can swap jobs and shifts if they need time off for any reason and management makes a point of providing employees with access to the information they need to do their job most effectively. Management believes that when employees have the critical information they need, they solve the problems quicker.

SouthWest seems to be doing all the right things to motivate the employees and keep the morale high. It may be hard to believe that such a company exists in the world today, but perhaps the philosophy of Kellener, CEO of SouthWest Airlines, on company–employee relations explains it all, 'I feel that you have to be with your employees through all their difficulties, that you have to be interested in them personally. They may be disappointed in their country. Even their family might not be working out the way they wish they could. But I want them to know that South West will always be there with them.'

(Source: Mescon, Bovee and Thill, 1996.)

## Track Two

## Amway

Amway is a network marketing organisation that earns 7 billions in sales per year through its 3 million Amway distributors around the world. It is a multilevel marketing organisation in which distributors sell products face to face, without a central business location. An in-depth study of Amway was conducted using observation, interviews and archival data to know how Amway fosters strong culture. The research question was how does Amway manage numbers, i.e., its organisational identification. The results of the study show that two basic processes are used at Amway to manage worker identification: sense breaking and sense giving. Sense breaking practices include helping distributors, and set personal and sales goals. This induces in the distributor when the current and ideal selves are compared. Distributors are encouraged to link their ideal selves to possessions, and that they have a long way to go to achieve the dream life style of their dreams. Sense giving practices involve helping distributors surround themselves with uplifting and supportive Amway people who encourage them to achieve their dream. When both types of practices are successful, members positively identify with Amway. When either sense breaking or sense giving practices fail, members misidentify the organisation. This study of Amway may be important in understanding how other organ-isations cause members to identify with them.

(Source: Debra and Quick, 2003.)

# Applied HR Case—'Weather Forecast'

## Susan Futuristic Company Limited

De'costa has high regard for his mother and he remembers his mother's saying that '*if you want to aim high think what your customer wants in the next ten years*'. De'costa has named the company in memory of his mother and is into the business of dealing with hardware and software technologies. The company is recognised for its innovativeness and creativity. Within a span of three years the company has grown tremendously, but he was never satisfied with the performance.

One day while on his journey to meet his client De'costa met his old friend James and he shared his success story with him. James along with his friend Vijay are running an HR consultancy firm and are doing good business having six to seven clients. De'costa shared his thought to make the company one of the 500 future companies of the world and one of the world's best employers.

James shared his thoughts on the performance organisation and briefed him of how an organisational culture affects the performance. If the climate is positive, people are motivated, have the freedom to do their job and excited about what they are doing; hence, the performance of the organisation will definitely go up. De'Costa was excited about the concept of organisational culture and he asked James to take up the project and give him a report and action plan of how to fulfil his dreams.

## Questions

1. Do you agree with James that organisational culture has a bearing on the performance? If yes, how?
2. Was De'costa right in choosing James as the consultant for the project? Why?
3. If you were James prepare the action plan and questionnaire of how you are going to implement the Culture Survey.

## References and Further Readings

Ashkanasy, Neal M., Celeste P.M. Wilderom, Mark F. Peterson. 2000. *Organisational Culture and Climate*, Thousand Oaks, Sage Publications Inc.

Debra, Nelson L. and James Campbell Quick. 2003. *Organisational Behavior: Foundations, Realities & Challenges*, USA: Thomson Learning.

Fischer, James R. (Jr). 1998. *Six Silent Killers: Managements Greatest Challenge*, Florida: St Lucie Press.

Hodge, B.J., William P. Anthony and Lawrence M. Gales. 1996. *Organisational Theory: A Strategic Approach*, New Jersey: Prentice Hall International.

Mescon, Bovee and Thill. 1996. *Business Today*, New Jersey: Prentice Hall.

Pattanayak, Biswajeet, Vipin Gupta and Phalgu Niranjana (eds). 2002. *Creating Performance Organisations*, New Delhi: Response Books.

Rao T.V. 1992. *HRD Missionary*, New Delhi: Oxford & IBH Publishing Co.

Sachdeva and Arora. 1988. 'Improving Employee Relations Climate—HRD Shows the Way The Eicher Experience', Rao, Verma, Khandelwal and Abraham (eds), *Alternative Approaches and Strategies of HRD*, Jaipur: Rawat Publications.

Sarupria, D.S., T.V. Rao and P. Sethumadhavan (eds). 1996. *Measuring Organisational Climate*, Academy of HRD, India.

Schein, E.H. 1992. *Organisational Culture and Leadership*, San Francisco, CA: Jossey-Bass.

# 'HRD Climate Study'

## HRD Climate Survey

### Instructions

A number of statements are given below describing the HRD climate of an organisation. Please give your assessment of the HRD climate in your organisation by rating your organisation on each statement using the following five-point scale:

4 = Almost always true; 3 = Mostly true; 2 = Sometimes true; 1 = Rarely true; 0 = Not at all true.

### Questionnaire

1. The top management of this organisation goes out of its way to make sure that employees enjoy their work.
2. The top management believes that Human Resources are an extremely important resource and that they have to be treated more humanely.
3. Development of the subordinates is seen as an important part of their job by the managers/officers here.
4. The personnel policies in this organisation facilitate employee development.
5. The top management is willing to invest a considerable part of their time and other resources to ensure the development of employees.
6. Senior officers/executives in this organisation take active interest in their juniors and help them learn their job.
7. People lacking competence in doing their job are helped to acquire competence rather than being left unattended.
8. Managers in this organisation believe that employee behaviour can be changed and people can be developed at any stage of their life.

9. People in this organisation are helpful to each other.
10. Employees in this organisation are very informal and do not hesitate to discuss their personal problems with their supervisors.
11. The psychological climate in this organisation is very conducive to any employee interested in developing himself by acquiring new knowledge and skills.
12. Seniors guide their juniors and prepare them for future responsibilities/roles they are likely to take up.
13. The top management of this organisation makes efforts to identify and utilise the potential of the employees.
14. Promotion decisions are based on the suitability of the promote rather than on favouritism.
15. There are mechanisms in this organisation to reward any good work done or any contribution made by employees.
16. When an employee does good work his supervising officers take special care to appreciate it.
17. Performance appraisal reports in our organisation are based on objective assessment and adequate information and not on favouritism.
18. People in this organisation do not have any fixed mental impressions about each other.
19. Employees are encouraged to experiment with new methods and try out creative ideas.
20. When any employee makes a mistake his supervisors treat it with understanding and help him to learn from such mistakes rather than punishing him or discouraging him.
21. Weaknesses of employees are communicated to them in a non-threatening way.
22. When behaviour feedback is given to employees they take it seriously and use it for development.
23. Employees in this organisation take pains to find out their strengths and weaknesses from their supervising officers or colleagues.
24. When employees are sponsored for training, they take it seriously and try to learn from the programmes they attend.
25. Employees returning from training programmes are given opportunities to try out what they have learnt.
26. Employees returning from training programmes on the basis of genuine training needs.
27. People trust each other in this organisation.
28. Employees are not afraid to express or discuss their feelings with their superiors.
29. Employees are not afraid to express or discuss their feelings with their subordinates.
30. Employees are encouraged to take initiative and do things on their own without having to wait for instructions from supervisors.

31. Delegation of authority to encourage juniors to develop handling higher responsibilities is quite common in this organisation.
32. When seniors delegate authority to juniors, the juniors use it as an opportunity for development.
33. Team spirit is of high order in this organisation.
34. When problems arise people discuss these problems openly and try to solve them rather than keep accusing each other behind the back.
35. Career opportunities are pointed out to juniors by senior officers in the organisation.
36.' The organisation's future plans are made known to the managerial staff to help them develop their juniors and prepare them for future.
37. This organisation ensures employee welfare to such an extent that the employees can save a lot of their mental energy for work purposes.
38. Job-rotation in this organisation facilitates employee development.

## Administration

The questionnaire uses a five-point scale. It could be administered to all employees (specially supervisory and managerial staff) and an HRD climate profile can be drawn up. The scores may range from 0 to 156 when the scores on all the 38 items are added to get a composite score. Scores **above 114** indicate a good HRD climate.

Scores **closer to 150** indicate an excellent climate (which is rare).

Scores **below 76** indicate that there is considerable scope for improvement.

The scores of all the respondents may be analysed item-wise and areas needing improvement should be identified and discussed in small groups. Annual surveys of HRD climate could be conducted and profiles maintained.

(*Source*: Rao T.V., 1992, *HRD Missionary*, New Delhi: Oxford and IBH Publishing Co.)

# 'HRD AUDIT'
# ANALYSING THE EFFECTIVENESS OF HR SYSTEMS THROUGH HRD AUDIT

*We are entering a new phase which is more counterintuitive because now globalness is assumed.*

—Anonymous

## Intent

- To audit the current HR practices of the company to establish alignment with the business processes.
- To analyse the competency of HR professionals and effectiveness of HR systems in the organisation.
- To identify the area requiring improvements in the HR sub-systems.
- To analyse the level at which HR practices are currently being used and bringing in the advanced HR practices for continual improvement.

## Expression

HRD Audit is a comprehensive evaluation of the current HRD strategies, structure, systems, style and skills in the context of the short and long-term business plans of the company.

## Comprehension

The HRD Audit is generally attempted to find out the future HRD needs of the company, after assessing the current HRD activities and inputs. In today's competitive world in order to get the best out of people, HR functions introduce different HR initiatives in the company. These initiatives should be aligned with the business goals and strategy. Besides these alignments, the skill and the style of the HR staff, line managers and top management should be in line with the HR goal and strategy. The HRD audit is an attempt to identify the extent of this alignment existing among them.

Human Resource Development audit focuses on competency, commitment and culture building from the practices that the HR is implementing in the organisations. These three are needed to make an organisation function well. They need to be identified and implemented cost effectively, reviewing and revising them from time to time to enhance their effectiveness and appropriateness.

The HR department is the most crucial department to play a role in HRD Audit. The HRD Audit is likely to point out the weak areas of the HRD functions. Since the responsibility for the weak areas lies in the HR Department, there needs a good deal of maturity on the part of the HR Manager and the top management about the concern raised and working out the action plan to mitigate. On the other side, HR department must use HRD Audit as a step to build the desired awareness among the managers.

The HRD Audit helps HR in many ways. It makes the HR function business driven, for expanding diversifying and entering into fast growth phase and it helps promoting professionalism among HR employees.

Auditing is a conventional approach in pure Finance and Account terms. Audit is checking and finding faults in order to get the correct procedure. Unlike the traditional audit, HRD Audit is a recent phenomenon. The audit here means taking a holistic view of evaluating the current state of HRD affairs in the organisation. It generally focuses on the existence of developmental and learning culture as well as HR sub-systems prevailing in the organisation in a proactive manner. It helps analysing an organisation where it stands in terms of its effectiveness of its HRD practices and brings out the areas requiring focus and improvements. Without being taken this holistic approach, it is difficult to take corrective and improvement steps in the HR processes. The strategic point of view of the HRD Audit is one of the most important technologies in the HR gamut.

# Experiential Application

## A. Prerequisite

- The HRD Audit initiated in the organisation should have the confidence and courage to accept the weaknesses in the organisation and plan for its improvement. The HR Department should play a very proactive role in releasing the facts of audit and come out with a constructive action plan to mitigate the areas requiring improvement.

- As the findings of the HRD Audit have consequences on HR, the sample taken for the audit should be universal in nature consisting of employees of different levels and functions/groups which have to be identified by the external consultants rather than the internal HR department personnel.
- The tool used for the HRD Audit should be simple in nature and the questions should be designed in a close ended manner. It should also generate an atmosphere of openness among the employees to respond to the questionnaires whole-heartedly.
- The respondent should not be insisted upon for identification, since some of the respondents might not like to reveal their identity for such questionnaires.
- The analysis should be done scientifically and with utmost confidentiality and the facts of the report with all truth to be kept open to the management and subsequently all other employees of the company.
- From the credibility point of view, it is desirable that the HRD Audit is normally being conducted by an external consultant rather than the internal HR department. The frequency should not be too short or too long.
- The actions taken at the end of the HRD Audit gives credibility for the next HRD Audit, otherwise the exercise will be futile, if employees don't see any change happening in HR practices and systems based on the previous HRD Audit carried out. This is not applicable if the HRD Audit is being conducted for the first time.

## B. Process Steps

| Step | Process |
|------|---------|
| Step – I | Senior Management and stakeholders to be interviewed to know their future plan and HR related issues. |
| Step – II | Interviews to be conducted for groups in 4–8 to know the group dynamics. |
| Step – III | Conducting workshop for a large-scale interaction to analyse the performance of the HR Systems. |
| Step – IV | To observe by visiting the departments, workplace, canteen, etc., which gives a view of the system of HR. |

# Potential Gains and Areas of Concern

- HRD Audit is a comprehensive evaluation of the current HR strategies, structures, systems, style and skills in the context of the short and long-term business plans of the company.
- HRD Audit brings out the HRD score on various dimensions of HR that exist in the organisation, which in turn provides the inputs required for HR to improve its deliverables.

- The HRD Audit's main objective is to align the HR functions—structure, systems and processes, with business goals or create a business driven HR function.
- The company's goals for HRD Audit are: growth and diversification, promoting professionalism, improving HRD strategies and enhancing the direct contribution of HRD to business.
- The HRD Audit is fruitless if the credibility of the survey is at question.
- It is not one more fancy of the HR initiative but to be taken as a sole searching process for the HR function as well as for the organisation's HR angle.

# Measurability

## Try It Out

(1: not at all done, 2: moderately done, 3: to some extent done, 4: to a great extent done, 5: excellently done)

- My organisation has willingness to invest in periodical HR Audit process.  ☐
- HR Audit and the subsequent improvement plans are meticulously  ☐
  followed-up and are implemented in the organisation.
- There is a considerable amount of improvement is visible subsequent to  ☐
  the last few HRD Audit in my organisation.
- The HR department's graph of internal customer orientation is improving  ☐
  in my organisation.
- The last HR Audit has opened up many areas for improvement of the  ☐
  HR team of which otherwise they were ignorant.

Analysis: the average score would determine the extent to which HR strategy process exists in your organisation.

## Score Card

(*: 25% achieved, **: 50% achieved, ***: 75% achieved, ****: 100% achieved)

| Technology | Objective Elements | Unit | Historical | Last Year | Current Year | Stretch Target | Status |
|------------|--------------------|------|-----------|-----------|--------------|----------------|--------|
| HRD Audit | Overall areas requiring improvement | Scale | 2.5 | 2.75 | 3.5 | 3.75 | ** |

# Proven Track Record

## Track One

### Roy Rogers Restaurants

Roy Rogers Restaurants, a major division of Marriott Corporation, operates 657 restaurants, primarily in the northeastern part of the US. Entry-level managers are drawn largely from workers between age 20 and 24. Company audit reveal an annualised turnover of 80 to 90 per cent, the costs of which are conservatively estimated at $3 million a year. It has been found out from the audit that 31 per cent of the reasons for turnover lie with the HR department. Armed with this knowledge, the department was able to address the managers' perception and began addressing the turnover problem.

(*Source*: Werther, Davis and Werther Jr., 1996: 566.)

## Track Two

### Gati Limited

An HRD Audit for Gati Limited, a leader in the Express Cargo Industry was conducted by a leading HR consulting firm of India. Gati's operations were controlled from 10 regions and in order to improve the HR processes, T.V. Rao of TVRLS was assigned the task to conduct the HRD Audit.

A total of four places of Gati were covered under the intervention, which consists of three regions and corporate office. The audit has opened up areas where the HR was doing well and where they were lacking. Basing on the audit report some of the policies are amended and some of the policies are reinforced to bring in efficiency and effectiveness in the HR.

(Author's self experience.)

# Applied HR Case—'HR Check-Up'

## J&G Projects Limited

Tom was heading the HR Department of the J&G Projects, which is into the construction of large projects around the world, and they are considered to be the best executing companies in hydroelectricity. Founded by two progressive engineers Jim and Gillespie, the company has gained its reputation over a period of 25 years. Being a management graduate, Tom was impressed by the plans of Jim and Gillespie. When Tom joined the organisation 25 years back, it was a small firm and he used to take care of HR and Accounts. Hence he is considered to be the seniormost in the company and most knowledgeable.

Being the Head of HR, he was confident that he knew the business and that the systems designed for HR were suitable to the diverse employees. Tom had a team of 22 employees in the department to handle the HR processes in the company with one HR representative at the project. The HR processes are highly centralised.

Tom used to feel that the HR for this particular business needs a centralised structure and it has been working since 25 years and the same was expected to work in future also. Jim was getting worried since many young and bright engineers were leaving because of the unfriendly HR policies.

Jim called and told Tom that he needs to look into the policies since they are becoming one of the causes for attrition among the bright young engineers. They are staying for the training period and are leaving once they have learnt the trades of the business. When Jim spoke to them why they are leaving, many trainees complained that it was because of the HR policies. Tom defended his policies stating that since the industry is diversified an uniform policy will enable the uniform application of the policy. Jim told Tom to take the advice of Johnson and conduct the HRD Audit to have a third opinion and plan his HR programmes depending upon the feedback. Jim left the option to Tom to decide the future course of action.

## Questions

1. Do you think that Tom should accept Jim's offer to conduct the HRD Audit?
2. If you were Tom, would you like to do the audit internally or through a consultant? If yes, why?
3. If you were Johnson, design a questionnaire to elicit the opinion of the employees on the HR policies.

## References and Further Readings

Mathewman, Tim. 1992. *HR Effectiveness*, London: Institute of Personnel and Development.

Rao, T.V. 1999. *HRD Audit*, New Delhi: Response Book.

Werther, William B., Keith Davis and William Werther Jr. 1996. *Human Resources and Personnel Management*, US: Irwin McGraw-Hill.

# 'ICSS'
# BUILDING CUSTOMER CENTRIC ORGANISATION THROUGH INTERNAL CUSTOMER SATISFACTION SURVEY

*Customers have come to expect that we do things their way,*
*rather than they do things our way.*

—Anonymous

## Intent

- To analyse the mutual working cohesiveness among the departments.
- To gauge the level of satisfaction that is being generated by the function on other functions.
- To arrive at areas requiring improvement to enhance internal customer satisfaction level.
- To build an organisation culture where constructive criticism and appreciation are freely shared and taken with a whole-hearted spirit and freedom.

## Expression

ICSS is a means to evaluate the level of satisfaction generated by a function to other internal function for which they operate. Attitude towards internal customer determine how inclined a function is in satisfying the needs of others.

# Comprehension

Organisation in a system with interrelated and interdependent functions and the efficiency and effectiveness depends upon how well the functions are aligned among themselves to achieve the organisation goals. With the growing functional specialisation each function works in silos thereby creating an ivory tower, which is detrimental to the interests of the organisation. Whatever may be the capability and competency of the function if the same is not being appreciated and add value to the process, it may not serve the purpose of existence. Hence every function needs to know how its 'customers', i.e., other functions are viewing their functions and whether they are able to serve to their best to achieve the organisation goals.

Internal customer satisfaction survey generally focuses on the satisfaction level that a function generates on other functions beside the capabilities and effectiveness of the function independently. The recipient department employees are free to comment on the level of their satisfaction in various areas in terms of timeliness, quality of services, the behaviour of the functional employees, etc., through a structured, close and open-ended questionnaire being administered periodically. Sometimes a third department normally Management Services Group or TQM group is entrusted with the survey task to arrive at the satisfaction level of one department to another. The important thing here is after having known the level of satisfaction that one is generating on the other a concrete action plan is required to work on the implementation of the satisfaction level. This helps in generating mutual cohesiveness, open and transparent environment of giving and taking positive and negative feedbacks and constructive suggestions of what improvement other functions have to do to satisfy other related needs and priorities. The ICSS is a relatively modern tool and requires maturity among the functions on which the survey is being administered as well as responses received.

The HR function is a shared service and it exists to serve employees within the organisation. The well-being of employees and the fulfilment of their needs so that they perform at the highest productivity level is the main objective of its existence. Since employees in an organisation are spread across all of its functions, complying their requirements is a challenging task indeed. The employee of each function, therefore, becomes a direct customer of HR. The employees are essentially internal customers. Satisfaction level of the internal customer thus becomes an area worth examining time to time which reflects the effectiveness and efficiency of HR function vis-à-vis other functions. Internal Customer satisfaction survey is a strategic technology through which this level of satisfaction existing within other functions can be judged and right and corrective measures can be initiated to bridge the gap if any.

# Experiential Application

## A. Prerequisite

- Each function beside their core competency and specialisation must be aware of the needs of other functions that they are going to fulfil and satisfy. Unawareness of what is being expected from them is the root of cause and concerns generated in the other function.
- It is generally not spelled out what is being expected by the function from others. The other functional employees may not explicitly express the needs and support they want from the given function, but through this structured ICSS process, it could be revealed.
- While administering the survey, third party involvement is desirable since it helps developing credibility and also keeps the respondent's anonymity.
- The questions of the survey should be so designed that it gives the clear meaning of what is being expected and the level of satisfaction that is being generated before.
- It is not necessary to take 100 per cent sample but simple stratified sampling technique for deciding the respondents is enough to generate authenticity in survey techniques.
- Before the survey, the personal belief or values about the necessity of certain surveys should not overpower the survey mechanism. Although, the outcome may not have been the intention of the members of the survey team when advocating their issue, it can easily be the end result.
- Use enough items to measure what you need on a given topic but not too many. These days time is a precious commodity for people in organisations and they do not look favourably on people who waste their time. Hence, surveys should not be too lengthy and time-consuming.
- One of the common mistakes in item construction is attempting to measure more than one item at a time. These items need to be avoided. The item such as *'to what extent you are satisfied with your salary and benefit?'* should not be used.
- It is better to be clear and concise with the survey item. Consider carefully and understand the respondent group or audience that will ultimately be surveyed when developing survey items. Survey items should provide an appropriate range of options, and the wording of the item itself made to be as free of value judgement as possible.
- Regardless of the format or content of all the items, the survey should be internally consistent.

## B. Process Steps

| Step | Process |
| --- | --- |
| Step – I | Pooling the resources with the right people, appropriate supports and resources. |
| Step – II | Designing and developing survey questions, content, response, options and the scale, the layout or presentation. |
| Step – III | Communicate the purpose, objective and content of the survey initiative clearly and effectively with those involved in survey. |
| Step – IV | Establishing a clear comprehensive and reasonable project plan with appropriate milestones and checkpoints. |
| Step – V | Collecting the data as per the questionnaire made. |
| Step – VI | Once the data are collected they are to be analysed for result. |
| Step – VII | Delivery of survey results to organisational members both in various forms and throughout different levels. |
| Step – VIII | The analysis and the results are put in practice for the organisational development. |

# Potential Gains and Areas of Concern

- Surveys can be particularly useful when the resultants are linked to other measures of performances.
- Linking survey results to these hard measures enable organisations to identify relationship between various aspects of organisational functioning and desired performance of outcome.
- The ICSS can be used to target areas of change, which will enhance organisational effectiveness as well as demonstrate improvements in the way one function works for others.
- The authenticity if missed, the results could be skewed.
- The function undertaking the ICSS, if does not take the result in the right spirit, the future performance can be jeopardised.

# Measurability

## Try It Out

(1: not at all done, 2: moderately done, 3: to some extent done, 4: to a great extent done, 5: excellently done)

- My organisation is equally concerned for both external as well as internal ☐ customers' satisfaction.

- Internal customer satisfaction is a well accepted process amongst all the ☐ employees of the company.
- There is a defined policy for periodical measurement of internal customer ☐ satisfaction level amongst all the departments.
- The level of internal customer satisfaction determines one of the ☐ performance parameter for annual performance review of the employees.
- There is an open culture to accept and give feedback on the internal ☐ customer satisfaction and employees are encouraged to take positive steps.

Analysis: the average score would determine the extent at which internal customer satisfaction exist in your organisation.

## Score Card

(*: 25% achieved, **: 50% achieved, ***: 75% achieved, ****: 100% achieved)

| Technology | Objective Elements | Unit | Historical | Last Year | Current Year | Stretch Target | Status |
|---|---|---|---|---|---|---|---|
| ICSS | Overall ICSS level | Scale | 3.0 | 2.75 | 3.25 | 3.5 | ** |
| | Finance Department | Scale | 2.75 | 2.75 | 3.25 | 3.5 | ** |
| | HR Department | Scale | 2.5 | 2.75 | 3.25 | 3.5 | ** |
| | Administration Function | Scale | 2.25 | 2.75 | 3.25 | 3.5 | ** |
| | IT Department | Scale | 3.0 | 3.0 | 3.25 | 3.5 | ** |

# Proven Track Record

## Track One

## RINL

Rashtriya Ispath Nigam Limited, a conglomerate of steel industries having a plant in Visakhapatnam, India, has embarked upon Internal Customer Satisfaction. This is a very new concept for the public and private sector and it is very easy to identify the outside buyer who purchases goods and services. However, there is a large chain of customer–supplier relationship, which needs to be addressed. The need of the external customer cannot be fully satisfied without satisfying the internal customer. A workshop has been conducted by the HRD Department to inculcate the culture and after the workshop a survey was conducted, which has brought to the limelight the significance of the internal customer satisfaction.

The biggest benefit of the workshop has been the awareness that all the employees are customers within the company. There has been a significant improvement in the approach of one department with the other department, thus smoothening the business process.

(*Source*: Chandrasekhar, 1994: 85.)

## Track Two

## Austin Community College

The Austin Community College in Texas has a group of colleges at various campuses and in order to enhance its ability to meet the needs of its employees, an ICSS is conducted during spring and accordingly the survey was conducted since 1996 and is continued till date. The ACC employees are surveyed each spring regarding their satisfaction with services in the previous fall. The forms are changed every year to suit the requirements and are being approved by the Executive Vice President. The form contains the details of all the 90 offices organised by the administrative area. The employees are asked to give their opinion about the services provided by the various functions like Compensation Services, Purchasing, Bookstore, Admission and Records, Duplication Services, etc.

The results of the survey are being communicated to the employees and also put on the Internet to make it more transparent and its commitment to improve the services. This brings every department to work at its best to increase the satisfaction level of the services it gives to the employees. The Internal Customer Satisfaction will help in serving the external customers, i.e., the students who attend the college.

(*Source*: http://www.austincc.edu/oiepub/pubs/ics/index.html)

# Applied HR Case—'Make Their Day'

## First Telecom Limited

Katherine was made the Chief Operating Officer of the First Telecom Limited, which is into the business of providing basic and cellular services in the city. The unit was started by two entrepreneurs who dreamt of a telecom company for the city to cater to the local needs exclusively so that they can be given personalised service. Initially the company did not make many inroads into the business, but looking at the value added service and the facilities which it was providing, the First Telecom Limited has 72 per cent of the basic and mobile services in the city.

But, since last two years, the business has stagnated and it has remained at 72 per cent only despite the fact that the number of connections increased. Katherine was working as the customer service manager and since the COO had resigned she was given the responsibility since she knew many of the valuable customers. Katherine was more concerned about her function and had taken keen interest in resolving the problems of the customers, sometimes even going out of the way. This attitude had given her the advantage of becoming the COO.

Katherine had good experience in the customer service and she knew that the problem was lack of coordination among the departments. Each department used to feel that their function was the most important one and they were the revenue earners. Since the First Telecom is the largest service provider, the employees have taken the business for granted. Katherine found the scope to increase the business from 72 per cent to 82 per cent over a period of six months. The key to success lies with the departments coordinating with each other. Katherine was worried of how to bring in internal customer service among all the departments.

Katherine contacted Sandy who is a consultant of how to bring in internal customer service among the departments and she had suggested going for an ICSS to be done every fortnight and the department which gets the highest percentage will be given monetary reward. Katherine asked Sandy to prepare the survey and administer for two months and then handover the same to the HR department.

## Questions

1. Do you agree with Sandy that the company requires a periodical internal customer satisfaction survey to bring in better coordination among departments? If so, justify your argument.
2. Do you feel that Katherine is justified in giving the task to Sandy rather than her colleagues at the company?
3. If you were Sandy, prepare a survey questionnaire and action plan to implement the scheme across the company.

## References and Further Readings

Ashkanasy, Neal M., Celeste P.M. Wilderom, Mark F. Peterson. 2000. *Organisational Culture and Climate*, Thousand Oaks, Sage Publications Inc.
Church and Waclawski. 1998. *Designing and Using Organizational Surveys*, San Francisco: Jossey-Bass.
Sripada, Chandrasekhar. 1994. 'Imbibing Internal Customer Orientation, The RINL Experience in Training for Corporate Turnaround', in Uddesh Kohli and Dharni P. Sinha (eds), *HRD Global Changes & Strategies in 2000 AD*, New Delhi: Allied Publishers Ltd.

## 'ICSS'

## Expectations from Other Departments

**Team No:**
**Representing Department:**
**Expectations from:**

Please mark everything in a 10 point rating scale:

  2: No response.
  4: Response but no further action.
  6: Delayed Action. Able to get the work done. Needs follow up.
  8: On time action. Needs follow up.
10: Get things on time without any reminder.

| Sl. No. | Expectations | Unit of Measurement | Expected | Existing |
|---------|--------------|---------------------|----------|----------|
| 1. | | | | |
| 2. | | | | |
| 3. | | | | |
| 4. | | | | |
| 5. | | | | |
| 6. | | | | |
| 7. | | | | |
| 8. | | | | |
| 9. | | | | |
| 10. | | | | |
| 11. | | | | |
| 12. | | | | |

# 4 UNDERSTANDING THE PRESENT FOR THE FUTURE

## Contents

## Learning Objectives

- To define the role of an individual in the organisation set-up.
- To recognise the elements of diversity in the context of present day's corporate culture.
- To appreciate individual dignity for oneself and others and becoming sensitive to one another in the organisational set-up.
- To examine 'walk the talk', philosophy in real sense perceived and practised in the organisation.

# Importance of the Individual in an Organisational Concept

The large manufacturing plants of the companies are 'societies' by itself. It comprises machine, material, manpower and of course, money. The organisation is true representative of the culture, creed and values that we practise in the society. No organisation can remain aloof of the social norms. What we believe as perfect and acceptable in society is preached and practised in organisations too. How does this happen? The answer lies in the simple phenomenon, which takes place in an organisation, that is, recruitment of individuals. Each individual who starts his career with the company brings with him a discrete behaviour based on the culture he/she learned and belongs to since his/her childhood. Organisations are built around these individuals. Organisation culture, hence, is nothing but the imbibed culture of the promoter and his followers. Each individual adds to the existing culture and remains with it. Over a period of time organisation culture becomes so powerful that any newcomer has to adjust to the culture of the organisation else, he will not be able to survive. In the US, software companies developed its unique culture; employees coming from different parts of the world have made such a culture. Any average US citizen though being in the country had to adjust to such diverse culture that cherish within such software organisations. Similarly, the Korean and Japanese companies have their distinctive culture.

An organisation can not be described without the individuals within it. The organisation is existing because there is product or services it delivers to the customers. These products and services are manufactured or delivered by the employees. The workforce, the supervisors, the managers—all work towards setting common goals for the company. Each individual plays direct or indirect role in the fulfilment of the promises of the company to its customers. The individual has different levels of tasks to perform and thus generates a division of labour, hierarchical structure, reporting relationship, span of control and productivity norms. Small or large, national or multinational, manufacturing or service, consumer goods to pharmaceuticals, no company can exist without the individual employee in it. No technology can replace the people power; the individual is a must and would remain forever.

# Managing Diversity

Ever since trade and business came in existence with mankind, each clan travelled beyond their boundaries and established early trading processes. In pursuit of economic independence and well-being people travelled far flung and established themselves in a new country. Even within one country people travelled from villages to towns and from towns to cities, and thus gave birth to metropolitan cities. Companies grew within the country and beyond with the same fashion. From being local and regional players, companies moved beyond the boundaries of the countries and set shops around the world. Today's multinationals are so big that they run in almost 50 or more countries with a size equal to any economy of a country in terms of revenue and the manpower employed.

Global companies such as GE, Microsoft, Mobil Oil, Toyota motors are all operating worldwide. They are virtually small globes within the company. Such companies have people from all around the world with different social, religious and cultural background. The cultural diversity is so immensely varied that it is a complex and challenging task to weave all such people under common thinking processes and common shared goals. Managing such magnitude of task required set systems and processes explicitly spelled out for the company. Diversity has many elements. It is beyond culture and creed. It has dimensions of providing equal employment opportunity, trying to ensure gender balance, equal opportunities for the minority, physically and mentally challenged, and having no prejudice to age and colour of skin.

Beside the laws enacted in many countries on diversity management such as laws pertaining to equal employment opportunity in the US, the issue lies in the hands of the organisation. The HR plays a vital role in manifesting the diversity management of the company. The recruitment policy, opportunity to the ladies, jobs for physically and mentally challenged, pay policy for them, promotion and career opportunity, etc., reflect the organisation's commitments towards diversity management.

## Dealing with Self and Being Sensitive to Others

An organisation is a sum total of individuals. The self, dyad, group, team, department, Strategic Business Units, etc., are the different forms in which an individual operates. It is not possible that an individual remains aloof in the organisation. For all-purposes, one has to deal with other individuals. The goods and services produced and offered are collective efforts of all members of the organisation either directly or indirectly. Since an organisation has to remain competitive, there lies a performance pressure on each functionary. This demands giving and taking situations within each individuals members, each departments, teams, etc. In such a situation it is likely that the dynamics of interpersonal behaviour will play a critical role.

Each individual has to recognise that their isolation and independent thinking alone cannot work in the organisation. Each person has its distinctive views and ideology. The clash of ideology could result in to conflict and distrust among other players. It is necessary that one must introspect within and become sensitive to others. Listening to what is said is easy, but listening to what is not said is the capability that each one of us has to develop to become sensitive to others. One must learn to decode the unstated and reflected behaviours of the individuals around us.

## Bringing Organisational Discipline

In order to build future from the present, setting footsteps of 'Walk the Talk' is absolutely necessary. What is said and what is done cannot be different. If an organisation value states that 'bribery is in no case acceptable but for practical purposes the organisation permits or encourages such dealings, then the organsation completely violates the commitment stated in the value statement'.

An organisation externally as well as internally must follow the set practices, explicitly stated for the company in its fullest capacity. It is possible for an organisation to stand on one principle, only through a defined business ethics policy. All the dealings of the company must be transparent and should be made open to pass through any evaluation for public scrutiny. Each employee must follow the ethical principles of the company. Any deviation must be viewed seriously and should warrant penal action.

To bring uniformity in their behaviour and making them disciplined, it is necessary for all employees internally, to implement a code of conduct. With code of conduct implemented in its right spirit and value, one can develop a strong disciplined workforce and obviously the output and the productivity standards achieved could be very high.

## Enable SHR Technology—Key to Success

The following are the technologies being discussed in this chapter:

SHR Technology-12    360-Degree Feedback—*Turnaround in PMS through '360-Degree Feedback'.*

SHR Technology-13    Managing Diversity—*Making the Organisation a place for all through Managing Diversity.*

SHR Technology-14    Emotional Intelligence—*Harnessing the Mind and Heart through Emotional Intelligence.*

SHR Technology-15    Business Ethics—*Directing Behaviour through Code of Conduct and Business Ethics.*

With globalisation and expansion of transnational organisations every company has virtually become a global tiny village. The organisations though try to build their own culture, the place at which they are present have a variety of diverse culture such as language, customs, creed, religion, etc., which pose to be a greater challenge to the HR in their efforts to build an intact organisation culture. The success of an organisation depends on how best they are culturally bonded since organisations are the reflection of society and society has a diverse culture.

Though an organisation is divided vertically and horizontally with specific functions of specialisation and hierarchies among the employees specifically for division of labour and distribution of skill set, there is a need that a cohesion exists in all these functions and hierarchies similar to that of all limbs and parts of the human body towards the common goal of keeping the life moving.

Sensitivity process is a process which in a behavioural science emphasise on reflecting on individual sensitivity towards others. Intelligent quotient has moved towards emotional intelligence now. Intelligence is not only an arithmetical and mathematical ability of the mind but it has a close linkage with the heart as well. The behaviour of an individual with different emotions reflects different performance orientations which in turn reflects the level of intelligence.

Since businesses are crossing the boundaries of countries, it has become a necessity that the business community operates according to international standards rather than a local standard of the country. As we practice within the company 'walk the talk' through code of conduct, organisations have to set standards of ethical practices that warrants the highest degree of ethical standards in their dealings with society, other organisations, government and people at large.

# Conclusion

- In an organisational set-up individuals are the key to a business. A true organisational culture is a sum total of all the individual that it represents.
- Since the organisations are enlarging the operations beyond the boundaries of their respective countries, building a uniform work culture through ethical principles as guiding factor for business operation is imperative.
- The global corporations are engaging employees from different culture, ethnic group, varied religion and gender. With changing awareness of equal employment opportunity, diversity issues are becoming an important element to deal with every organisation.
- An organisation has to build external goodwill, at the same time building an internal code of conduct. Each employee is governed by an organisational explicit code of conduct of the company.

# '360-DEGREE FEEDBACK'
# TURNAROUND IN PMS THROUGH
# '360-DEGREE FEEDBACK'

*Before jumping headfirst into 360-degree appraisals, consider what you want the system to accomplish and design process that support those outcomes.*

—Rao (2000)

## Intent

- To identify strengths and areas requiring improvements in terms of leadership role, style and personal qualities in the employee.
- To understand his/her impact on others in the organisation due to the style of his/her functioning.
- To know his/her all the good actions and behaviours which are valued by colleagues and subordinates.

## Expression

360-degree feedback is a multi-rater evaluation/appraisal and feedback technique wherein individuals evaluate themselves and receive appraisal in the form of feedback from other employees and organisational members.

## Comprehension

The 360-degree feedback is being used to serve multiple objectives to bring changes in the management tool for leadership development to a mechanism for assessing the potential of the employees. It is used as a tool for getting the performance feedback data of an individual or group derived from stakeholders and senior managers. The annual appraisal had traditionally been done by the manager and had resulted in a pay hike or a promotion, a practice which hitherto had not helped him in developing the qualities. To remove the lacunae in the appraisal process the US consultancy firm McBer first pioneered the approach of 360-degree feedback, a shift from the solo appraisal by the boss to multiple appraisals.

Performance feedback, generally from the appraiser, plays a major role towards employee's development, while the 360-degree feedback mechanism is to increase the manager's awareness on his or her performance to make it more effective. It is a self-appraisal vis-à-vis feedback from others, i.e., superiors, managers, customers, stakeholders, peers and subordinates. These set of people are called 'significant others'. The process gathers the information on the participants' current performance on each competence from the self and from the 'significant others' against the standards expected at their level in the organisational context. The candidates need to be educated of how the process can help them in developing themselves in the continuous learning culture.

Though there is scope for the subjectivity creeping in, but the system helps in providing a detailed and a comprehensive picture of the current performance of the participant and he is expected to take the feedback in a positive manner and leverage on the strengths and work on the improvements.

In this process of 360-degree feedback, the participants are asked to make a detailed action plan to enable them to develop their qualities further. They are also advised to have a 'mentor' who would facilitate him to further work on his qualities, which is optional but never a mandatory.

We need to recognise that 360-degree feedback can be a fad if used only as a tool and a one-time event. If one integrates it into the performance strategy of an individual, then it will support the HR process like appraisal, succession planning and leadership development.

Some organisations may implement 360-degree feedback without clearly defining its mission and scope. Many new systems appear to focus on the improvement of employee's work pattern and the increase of their performance level as the primary outcome. But, if the process is not designed to make improvements, then those expectations will not be fulfilled. Hence, it will generate disappointment and the disillusion, and ultimately 360-degree feedback will prove to be ineffective. The individual and organisations must continually work on the improvements since the 360-degree feedback is not a one time event, but a continuous process and need to be seen from a holistic perspective.

# Experiential Application

## A. Prerequisite

- While designing 360-degree feedback process, the management of the organisation must be clear with the objectives.
- The process must be thoroughly discussed among the peer teams, to develop a list of behaviours and accountabilities needed from each other in order to achieve success.
- A shared understanding of the process must be arrived at. The issues such as *'who would be the owner of the feedback'* and *'whether it would be linked to the performance evaluation and reward mechanism'* must be discussed.
- First, consider the range of possible outcome. These could be strengths and weaknesses, improvement in employees work behaviours to increase their performance level, which in turn may lead to leadership development.
- Over a period of time, the technology might increase in getting the feedback from employees and increase self-awareness with relevance to competencies needed to meet the excellence in performing a job. By this individuals get a broader perspective of how others perceive them.

## B. Process Steps

| Step | Process |
| --- | --- |
| Step – I | Defining the objectives for introduction of 360-degree feedback. |
| Step – II | Identifying the levels of employees for whom the tool is aimed. |
| Step – III | Defining variables to incorporate in tool. |
| Step – IV | Identification of dimensions of variables. |
| Step – V | Creating the rating scale, instructions and format of tool. |
| Step – VI | Pilot testing, report generation and validation of the tool and making changes wherever required. |
| Step – VII | Final questionnaire and its administration to all concerned and report generation. |
| Step – VIII | Results communication and individual counselling sessions. |
| Step – IX | Action plan for the improvements based on the feedback. |
| Step – X | Periodic review. |

# Potential Gains and Areas of Concern

- The 360-degree feedback provides more acceptable feedback, as it is a multi-rater assessment process.
- It can also serve all conventional purposes of appraisal such as developmental needs, rewards management, performance development, etc.
- It helps to focus on internal customer satisfaction and can enhance customer services and quality of inputs and services to internal customers.
- It participates and enhances the quality of HR decisions.
- It improves organisational culture and employee moral, which is being promoted by most world class organisations.
- Empowering, delegating and providing feedback to subordinate should be much more in practice.
- Transparency in sharing information down the line has to be developed.
- Preconceived notion should not be a hindrance and an element of trust and bonding has to be cultivated.
- The 360-degree feedback requires a great deal of maturity of the participants, in absence of that it is an effort without yielding desire results.
- It provides subordinates and other appraisers an opportunity to criticise and provide negative feedback if bias and prejudice persist.
- After receiving feedback if an individual does not work on the areas requiring improvement then the purpose of 360-degree will be fruitless.
- The 360-degree feedback gives many surprises, as the results provided are straight feedbacks, which are usually not expected. The participants must cultivate the habit of seeking feedback from all sources at regular intervals of time.

# Measurability

## Try It Out

(1: not at all done, 2: moderately done, 3: to some extent done, 4: to a great extent done, 5: excellently done)

- The 360-degree feedback process is an acceptable process among all the ☐ managerial employees of my organisation.

- Taking and giving candid feedback on performance, conduct, as well as on behavioural areas for any employee is taken in a positive way and is always appreciated by all managerial employees. ☐
- My organisation have made systematic attempt time to time for implementing 360-degree feedback mechanism and it has taken time to stabilise in the organisation. ☐
- All managerial employees work on the areas requiring improvement based on the feedback received by the 360-degree process. ☐
- The company uses 360-degree feedback for the developmental purpose rather than using it as a performance evaluation technique. ☐

Analysis: the average score would determine the extent to which 360-degree feedback process exists and is implemented in your organisation.

## Score Card

(*: 25% achieved, **: 50% achieved, ***: 75% achieved, ****: 100% achieved)

| Technology | Objective Elements | Unit | Historical | Last Year | Current Year | Stretch Target | Status |
|---|---|---|---|---|---|---|---|
| 360-degree feedback | System document | Doc | Nil | No | Yes | NA | ** |

# Proven Track Record

## Track One

## Wipro

Wipro, which started as a small factory manufacturing vegetable oil has grown and diversified into engineering, software, health care, etc. The organisation has the performance management system in process since one and a half decades. The organisation has also the culture to express their views. With the steady influx of fresh blood from the campuses, the managers started accepting new ideas. The organisational commitment towards openness, expressing the views openly and managing the mistakes with focus to learn has given the preparedness for the people to receive feedback. The tool, which started with application on the top management soon percolated down to senior and middle management. The feedback was used as a tool to develop the leaders. The 360-degree tool is called as 'Wipro Leaders' Qualities Survey' (WLQS), where the top management and the consultants arrived at imbibing vision, aggressive commitment, high energy, commitment to excellence, self-confidence, building star performers/teams, etc.

The tool has been changed to depending on the feedback received and strengthening the tool further. The process has been outsourced to bring in objectivity. To develop the employee the development part of the feedback is given to the superior and the evaluation part is kept confidential. Initially, there was a lot of resistance even before starting the process, but the cultural changes brought in the system made the managers accept the feedback and act upon it.

(*Source*: Acharya, 2000.)

## Track Two

## Motorola

Motorola is a leading name in wireless communications, semi-conductor technology and advanced electronic equipments, and it employs more than 140,000 people in 87 countries with an annual turnover of US $ 30. To succeed in the ever changing market, Motorola has identified and defined 15 competencies which are essential as part of Totality of Motorola Leadership (TOML). 360-degree feedback is being used to solicit feedback from varied quarters to assist in accelerating the growth of leaders. Since the instrument has strong emphasis on leadership behaviour, its relevance was focused on leadership positions. Motorola university has tied up with Selection Testing, Assessment and Research (STAR) organisations to assist the implementation across the levels identified. Reports are being sent to the participants directly. An in-built analysis identified the top 25 percentile leadership dimensions allowing departmental plans to focus on traits falling outside the range. To enable the participants to cope with the developmental needs, qualified, professional coaches were engaged.

The 360-degree feedback process gave Motorola two distinct, competitive advantage: first, it was able to establish a shared understanding of what it collectively stood for, through the definitions of TOML competencies. In the words of its CEO Chris Galvin: 'Imagine the power of 140,000 Motorolans marching in one direction with one motto—linking people's dreams with technology's promise.' Second, the company was able to translate the feedback obtained from multiple sources to formulate and implement individual development plans.

(*Source*: Busrai, 2002: 28–35.)

# Applied HR Case—'Gauging All Around'

## Stone Publishers

Keshav is the Chief Executive Officer of the publications and he is the person who has changed the destiny of the company from the publishers, which are dealing with school-books to that of publisher of world-class academic books where every big writer would like to publish his book. Keshav has learnt the traits of business through his experience in the business and his sheer acumen. He is always of the opinion that leaders can be groomed with the requisite inputs. Keshav has put in lot of efforts to enable the company to reach to this extent and he does not want the company to go back to the place of origin. He very well knows that his only son cannot handle as efficiently as he can and he thought of building strong systems so that the systems will drive the business.

To create an atmosphere of performance culture and right kind of leadership to drive the organisation, Keshav was trying for a method through which he can build the leaders who would have freedom, but within the limits and drive the business process. Keshav wanted to build a healthy organisation in which the culture and performance orientation are very important. Keshav has a friend Tarun who is into HR consultancy business. Keshav explained to Tarun the whole history of how he has transformed the whole company and would like to sustain the movement with strong systems and dynamic leadership. Tarun has suggested implementing the 360-degree feedback appraisal system which will guide in building right kind of leaders. Keshav was impressed by the process and immediately gave the consent to implement the same. Tarun was quite surprised at his enthusiasm and initiative to drive the process.

## Questions

1. Do you think that 360-degree feedback process will drive the managers towards proper leadership and stabilisation of the systems? Explain.
2. Do you suggest that the 360-degree feedback process be linked to the annual appraisal system? Elucidate.
3. If you were Tarun, give an action plan for implementing the feedback and the qualities that you look at assessing and implementing.

## References and Further Readings

Acharya, Ranjan. 2000. '360 Degree Feedback Experience in Wipro', in T.V. Rao, M. Vijayalakshmi and Raju Rao (eds), *360 Degree Feedback and Performance Management System*, New Delhi: TVRLS/Excel Books.

Antonioni, D. 1996. 'Designing an Effective 360-Degree Appraisal Feedback Process', *Organizational Dynamics*, Autumn.

Busrai, Aquil. 2002. 360 Degree Feedback Experience: 'The Imperatives and the Impetus' in Radha R. Sharma (ed.), *360 Degree Feedback, Competency Mapping and Assessment Centre—For Personal and Business Development*, New Delhi: Tata McGraw-Hill Publishing Company.

Nowack, Kenneth M., Jeanne Hartley and William Bradley. 1999. 'How to Evaluate Your 360 Feedback Efforts', *Training & Development*, April.

Rao T.V., M. Vijayalakshmi and Raju Rao (eds). 2000. *360 Degree Feedback and Performance Management System*, New Delhi: TVRLS/Excel Books.

Rao, T.V. 2002. *360 Degree Feedback and Performance Management System*, New Delhi: Excel Books.

Rao, T.V., Gopal Mahapatra, Raju Rao and Nandini Chawla. 2003. *360 Degree Feedback and Performance Management System*, New Delhi: TVRLS/Excel Books.

Walter, Tornow W. and Manuel London. 1998. *Maximizing the Value of 360-Degree Feedback*, San Francisco: Jossey-Bass Publishers.

Ward, Peter. 1999. *360 Degree Feedback: A Management Tool*, New Delhi: Jaico Publishing House.

# '360-Degree Feedback'

## Case on 360-Degree Feedback

As a part of bank's new commitment to customer services, Jessica was charged with the responsibilities of improving the branch's level of customer services. Her boss told her that the number of accounts closing would be his way of measuring Jessica's success in this area. She was not completely happy with that measure, as many things beyond her control affected account closing. But that was her boss' measure so she was stuck with it. She also knew that the number of accounts closing meant little to the bank tellers, so she could not use the measure with her people.

For several weeks she puzzled over how to measure improvements in customer service by her tellers. Then she hit upon the idea of asking her teller for their ideas. They flooded her with many ideas, with measures like: smile, use the customer's name, maintain a neat, business-like appearance, make at least one non-business comment and say 'hello' in the beginning and 'thank you' at the end.

Employees agreed to evaluate their fellow workers daily using those measures. Jessica took all those who scored 'good' for a special lunch. Within weeks she found a distinctly friendlier and warmer atmosphere in the bank. Her boss commented on the friendly feelings as well.

Jessica knew that her bank was not rare competitive, so she felt that a lot of the impact of the improvement in her teller's customer service was washed away. The number of accounts closing fell somewhat, though not as much as either Jessica or her Manager expected. But her branch was the only one in the 37 outlets to show a decrease in closing during this period.

# 'MANAGING DIVERSITY'
# MAKING THE ORGANISATION A PLACE FOR ALL THROUGH MANAGING DIVERSITY

*With strength of a character, nothing is impossible, when your heart expands,
to embrace the impossible, you are able to lead the path.*

—Tao

## Intent

- To understand the diversity in the context of present day's business.
- To determine the extent to which the diversity principles are applicable in the organisation.
- To analyse the present Equal Employment Opportunity laws and its implications in the work environment.

## Expression

Diversity means recognising all form of individual differences, including culture, gender, age, ability, religion, personality, social status and sexual orientation. Cultural diversity raises the issues of fair treatment for workers who are not in a position of authority. Equal Employment Opportunity (EEO) is the provision of equal opportunity to secure and earn rewards regardless of conditions unrelated to job performance.

## Comprehension

With the advent of globalisation and an increasing demand of skilled persons, employess come with diverse culture. The industrialisation and modernisation has enabled organisations to employ people irrespective of culture and gender. Hence, every organisation's attention is to manage the diversity. In gender diversity, the feminisation of the workforce has increased substantially. Thus, diversity can be related to age, ethnicity, gender, race, region, sex, etc.

Managing diversity means taking steps to optimise the potentials available in the diverse workforce while minimising the barriers, which undermine such potentialities. Managing diversity is paramount especially due to the manager's responsibility to motivate the workforce and effective communication strategy to bind the employees who are from diverse culture and languages.

Due to the demographic changes the workforce in the next decade will be more diverse culturally, employing more female and the older than ever. The graying of the world's industrial workforce is another source of diversity in an organisation. The manager faces challenges of integrating the diverse workforce into a cohesive group, which has differences in attitudes and values due to generation gap. The current workforce is full of individuals with different abilities presenting another form of diversity. This is being supported by legislation and newer technologies. Individuals who are physically and mentally challenged are under utilised human resources. An estimated 54 millon individuals with disability live in the US and their unemployment rate is to exceed 50 per cent.

Organisations derive advantage due to diversity by way of attracting the best talent available and improve on their human capital and in turn gain the sustained competitive advantage. Diversity can promote innovation and creativity. It also gives results in better problem solving and enhances organisational agility and flexibility.

Diversity is not a forceful need of organisation but it is a representation of our society at the work place. The global village and crossing the boundaries of the nations have given emergence of transnational organisations and are the order of the twenty-first century. Today's society does not differentiate religion, creed, culture, language, gender, and other physical and mental disabilities while rights and dignity of human being are issues of concern. The workplace and the organisation are the reflection of this diversity. A large number of organisations are imbibing diversity related approach in all their work processes specifically no difference is observed in gender while recruitment, promotion, compensation and work allocation. Diversity has taken place in regulation and laws in many countries.

Equal Employment Opportunity (EEO) is a widely used term in today's organisations. Keeping pace with this trend, the diversity management is a strategic technology and organisation ought to manage it very diligently in order to keep the organisation's goodwill intact. The equal employment opportunity is a battle against racism and prejudice and managing the diversity is a battle to value the difference among the individuals and bring in increased productivity and improved organisational health.

# Experiential Application

## A. Prerequisite

- Every organisation, which honours the human potential, aims at valuing the diversity to optimise the potential. The main basis of diversity is an attempt to change the underlying attitudes of discrimination, which was encompassed by unfounded assumptions.
- In the organisational set-up, difference needs to be recognised, acknowledged, appreciated and used to collective advantage.
- All employees of the company need to explore their cultural differences, learn from others around them and use that information to build a stronger organisation.
- All levels of management including top management should be committed to the entire programme. If employees perceive a lack of commitment from management, then the programme might fail.
- Every employee should understand fully the organisational policy on diversity. Managers and employees need to be aware of both their obligations and their rights.
- The top management should ensure that the organisation does not discriminate against any qualified job applicant of employees because of him being mentally and physically challenged or disabled.
- The manager should consider establishing result-oriented goals and time tables to eliminate the under-utilisation of minorities and females throughout the organisation.
- The manager should be careful not to limit, segregate or classify employees in any way that would tend to deprive them of employment opportunities or adversely affect any employee's status because of sex, race, colour, religion, age, national origin, etc.

## B. Process Steps

| Step | Process |
|------|---------|
| Step – I | Written Equal Employment policy and a statement indicating commitment to diversity. |
| Step – II | Appointment of top officials to head and implement the programme. |
| Step – III | Survey to be conducted to get the data on the various aspects of diversity. |
| Step – IV | Preparation of action plans and time tables to utilise the potentials of minorities, females, etc. |
| Step – V | Reviewing the personnel management systems in line with the EEO. |
| Step – VI | Establish an internal committee to audit and review the implementation of EEO and diversity. |

# Potential Gains and Areas of Concern

- Recognising the diversity elements provides a powerful cultural force to which employees must adapt in the organisation.
- Diversity principle in the company taboo against discussing differences among people, and creates a process to overcome that restriction.
- Diversity raises the issue of fair treatment for workers who are not in a position of authority.
- Changing one's own or another employee's attitude is seldom easy, yet there are constant political, social, economical and technical pressures on people and organisations to change.
- Due to diversity laws, although some progresses have been made, it has often been slow, and the problem still remains.
- Discrimination is an action and prejudice is an attitude, therefore, the problem still remains because of this key difference between discrimination and prejudice.

# Measurability

## Try It Out

(1: not at all done, 2: moderately done, 3: to some extent done, 4: to a great extent done, 5: excellently done)

- Diversity is the subject very close to the values and conduct in my organisation. ☐
- Diversity is practised and preached while recruiting new employees. ☐
- There is a diversity policy and all the provisions of EEO Act is complied and voluntarily exceeded. ☐
- Gender balance in the company three years before was much skewed which is corrected with modest attempt to balance gender in my organisation. ☐
- Many jobs are ear-marked for physically challenged people in my organisation in order to give diversity boost. ☐

Analysis: the average score would determine the extent to which the diversity process exists in your organisation.

## Score Card

(*: 25% achieved, **: 50% achieved, ***: 75% achieved, ****: 100% achieved)

| Technology | Objective Elements | Unit | Historical | Last Year | Current Year | Stretch Target | Status |
|---|---|---|---|---|---|---|---|
| Diversity | Diversity Document | Doc | Nil | No | Yes | NA | ** |
| | EEO Document | Doc | Nil | No | Yes | NA | ** |

# Proven Track Record

## Track One

## Microsoft

Microsoft is one company that is progressive when it comes to promoting diversity in its corporate culture. In fact one of the reason of Microsoft achieving success is promoting the diverse work environment. To meet this objective the company sponsors scholarships, promote diversity activities within the company, maintain ties with organisations committed to diversity and equality, and sends managers to conferences throughout the US to find new and diverse candidates for Microsoft work pool. In addition, Microsoft supports many diverse groups within the company through Microsoft diversity advisory council.

Such groups include blocks at Microsoft; gay, lesbian and bisexual employees at Microsoft; Microsoft women group and Native American at Microsoft. These and other groups provide support and advocacy for their members, and they promote understanding among all Microsoft employees and managers.

(*Source*: Mescon, Bovee and Thill, 1996.)

## Track Two

## Pepsico Foods and Beverages International

Pepsico is an international organisation with about 81,000 employees worldwide having global imperatives like global mindset/synergies, great products/quality, customer focus/service, sales/operating excellence, exciting product new/quality, innovation/ideas, aligned/skilled/empowered people and organisations. The company has a management team of 300 executives from 45 countries out of which two-thirds are non-Americans.

Four of six senior field presidents are from India, Peru, Mexico and Canada who oversee the manufacturing and distribution of products in 180 plus countries. The corporation constantly strives to be result-oriented, customer-focused and value driven. The organisation believes that the goals of the organisation can be achieved through managing the diversity.

The company (a) celebrate diversity, (b) make it an ongoing, everyday part of the organisation's fabric, (c) use diversity in it's broadest sense, (d) accept the differences, (e) be ruthless about the sharing of best practices, and (f) have a childlike wonder about what is new.

(*Source*: Odenwald, 1996: 91.)

## Applied HR Case—'Chocolate Treat'

### Nation Engineers Limited

Dilbert was a nationalist to the core and because of his engineering background and entrepreneurial skills, he named the company as '*Nation*'. To foster the oneness of nationality he used to celebrate all the national festivals in the office and distribute gifts and sweets. Every year he used to organise '*Family day*' so that he can foster the oneness among all the employees and their families together. His recruitment process also followed the same wherein he would invite applications from all over the country and select them basing on the merit and also the cultural diversity. The organisation looks like a true cosmopolitan structure and people used to cherish the moments, but the interpersonal relations among the employees haunted Dilbert. He used to get disturbed especially whenever such issues cropped up and used to think that if a small organisation will have such problems, then the country would also be facing similar problems. When it comes to work and work related problems they used to unite and ensure that the process gets smoothened and never was there any disruption in the production and the output was as per the targets.

Dilbert wanted to bring in cohesiveness among all the members and has taken the help of '*easy survey*', the firm that was famous for conducting the surveys only to find out the interpersonal issues. The firm conducted the survey and found the following:

- since there are cultural differences and each one is not being fully aware of other's culture there arose always a scope for misunderstanding;
- no measure is being taken to train them to handle the cross-cultural, communication, gestures and their significance;
- flexibility and adaptability needs to be filled in by various OD (organisational development) exercises.

Dilbert was first perplexed about the findings and later on reconciled that this is the reality that he cannot run away. He immediately asked the HR head to start training for all the employees across the organisation on the importance of diversity, habits and cultural factors of various prominent cultures.

## Questions

1. Do you feel that very small and trivial issues can create performance hurdles? Explain.
2. Does diversity enable the organisation to attract the best of talent? Elucidate.
3. If you were the HR head, how will you plan to conduct the training across the organisation and how will you ensure the return on investment.

## References and Further Readings

Daft, Richard L. 1997. *Management*, Florida: The Dryden Press.

Gardenswartz, Lee and Anita Rowe. 1998. *Managing Diversity: A Complete Desk Reference and Planning Guide*, New York: McGraw-Hill.

Harris, Phillip R. and Robert T. Moran, 2000. *Managing Cultural Differences: Leadership Strategies for a New World of Business*, Houston: Gulf Professional Publishing.

Lebo, Fern. 1996. *Mastering the Diversity Challenge*, Florida: St Lucie Press.

Mescon, Michael H., Courtland L. Bovee and John Thill. 1996. *Business Today*, New Jersey: Prentice Hall.

Odenwald, Sylvia B. 1996. *Global Solutions for Teams*, Chicago: Irwin Professional Publishing.

Sonnenschein, William. 1999. *The Diversity Toolkit*, Illinois: Contemporary Books.

Thomas, Roosevelt R. (Jr.). 1991. *Beyond Race and Gender: Unleashing the Power of Your Total Work Force by Managing Diversity*, New York: AMACOM.

Thomas, Roosevelt R. (Jr.), et al. 2001. *Harvard Business Review on Managing Diversity*, USA: Harvard Business School Publishing Corporation.

# 'EMOTIONAL INTELLIGENCE' HARNESSING THE MIND AND HEART THROUGH EMOTIONAL INTELLIGENCE

*The test of a first-rate intelligence is the ability to hold two opposed ideas in the mind at the same time, and still retain the ability to function.*

—F. Scott Fitzgerald, *American Novelist, The Crack-Up* (1945)

## Intent

- To understand the specific roles that emotions and intelligence play in Emotional Intelligence (EI).
- To identify those factors which enable the EI in an organisational success and promote the knowledge sharing.

## Expression

Emotional Intelligence is defined as the capacity for recognising our own feelings and those of others, for motivating ourselves, and for managing emotions well in us and in our relationships.

## Comprehension

In Indian mythology, the synergy of emotions and intelligence is very well described in the Bhagavad Gita when Lord Krishna preached Arjuna to work with balance of intelligence and emotions. The phrase Emotional Intelligence could sound new to all of us, but the essence has been existing ever since mankind started learning.

Emotion and intelligence together bring a unique congruence in life. After considerable research, Danial Goleman (1998) coined the concept of EI. He explained that success and effectiveness depends more upon the EI rather than the traditional intelligent quotient (IQ), technical expertise and experience itself. The EI is not the same as IQ, but not necessarily opposite from one another. While the IQ is mostly associated with the neocortex region, the thinking brain, located near the top of the brain, the EI is associated with the inner subcortex, one related to the emotional impulses.

Emotional Intelligence is really to do with the notion that intelligence always needs to be accompanied by emotional competence if we are to be truly effective. Indeed, many claim that EI is twice as important as IQ or technical expertise. Large companies are getting so excited by the idea that questionnaires that measure EI are now routinely being used to identify and develop leaders and to create better teams.

Emotional Intelligence typically measures:

- *self-awareness*—how you experience your feelings and your ability to control them;
- *resilience*—how you perform under pressure and your ability to change your behaviour;
- *drive*—the amount of energy you need to achieve your goals;
- *sensitivity*—how aware you are of other people's needs and the degree to which you take such needs into account;
- *influence*—your ability to bring other people around to your point of view;
- *decisiveness*—your ability to make clear and unambiguous decisions, even when you may not have all the information you would like; and
- *integrity*—your ability to stick to a course of action and to do what is right.

Emotional Intelligence is the buzzword in today's corporate. Organisations have all kinds of people and each one of them could be differentiated on the basis of intellectual ability. Along with competencies and intelligence, the most important aspects to recognise are people's emotions. Emotional Intelligence is beyond just competencies. It is Intelligence with Emotions. All activities performed in the organisation have sentiments and emotions attached such as right from the CEO's decision-making process to an assistant's type writing job. The importance of EI is enormous and hence is a strategic technology for Human Resources Management.

# Experiential Application

## A. Prerequisite

- There are basically two ways to increase EI in an organization.One, hire people who are emotionally intelligent, or two, develop EI in current members.

- Hiring is one of the quickest ways to increase EI. But unless the organisation hires a critical mass of emotionally intelligent personnel, it may not see an impact.
- In addition, if the organisation's climate does not support or reward emotionally intelligent behaviour, it is likely that the people it is trying to keep will leave. Therefore, it is necessary to develop the EI in their present employees' pool.
- Strategy for enhancing EI through HR is as follows:

  - selecting right people with high EI;
  - understanding competency cluster vis-à-vis EI;
  - selecting for different types of jobs;
  - create an encouraging environment and proper training and development opportunities;
  - provide performance feedback; and
  - communicate effectively.

## B. Process Steps

| Step | Process |
| --- | --- |
| Step – I | Create an encouraging environment in the organisation. |
| Step – II | Help learners to set clear, meaningful and manageable goals to gain EI. |
| Step – III | Encourage practice of new skills and provide feedback on performance. |
| Step – IV | Inoculate learners against setbacks. |
| Step – V | Build in follow-up support. |

# Potential Gains and Areas of Concern

- The EI plays a role in helping organisational leaders make good decision about new products, market and strategic alliance.
- It affects the development of talents—how relationship helps improving the effectiveness at workplace.
- The EI of mentor, boss or peer will influence the potential of a relationship with that person for helping organisational members develop and use talents that is crucial for organisational effectiveness.
- Though from a decade the research in EI is on, there still is much that is unclear about the nature of EI.
- It is difficult to quantify and measure the nature of EI, the ways of measurement and its actual impacts on individual performance and the organisation's effectiveness.
- Individual and group EI is a matter of dilemma. Having few people with high individual EI is not enough to generate the conditions necessary for teamwork and group effectiveness.

# Measurability

## Try It Out

(1: not at all done, 2: moderately done, 3: to some extent done, 4: to a great extent done, 5: excellently done)

- My organisation has recognised the importance of EI at the workplace. ☐
- Concerted efforts are made in order to improve the EI amongst the employees. ☐
- The recruitment practice of my organisation is well equipped with identifying the EI quotient of any incumbent. ☐
- Company has recognised certain decisions taken by managers based on EI and then the same have been prescribed in management practices. ☐
- Emphasis is given on training to improve EI knowledge amongst the employees of the organisation. ☐

Analysis: the average score would determine the extent to which EI process exists in your organisation.

## Score Card

(*: 25% achieved, **: 50% achieved, ***: 75% achieved, ****: 100% achieved)

| Technology | Objective Elements | Unit | Historical | Last Year | Current Year | Stretch Target | Status |
|---|---|---|---|---|---|---|---|
| Emotional Intelligence | Document | Doc | Nil | No | Yes | NA | ** |

# Proven Track Record

## Track One

## American Express Financial Advisor

American Express uses intensive and recurring training to create support to its employees to know and use emotional competencies through training programmes. An initial programme was offered to the financial advisors, designed to help them sell life insurance products by improving their ability to cope up with the emotional strains associated with the selling process. After the first programme proved successful, the programme staff developed a second version for the advisor's regional managers, designed in part to make them emotional coaches.

The programme was conducted further encouraging the regional management teams to go through the training together. Eventually, several versions of the training on EI were given to the new advisors, new managers and the corporate office management groups to understand the concept of EI and implement it in their roles.

(*Source*: Cherniss and Goleman, 2001: 221.)

## Track Two

## IBM

The key for the success of 'System 360' is due to *'Creative tension'* the tension between vision and reality. The most effective people are those who can *'hold their vision while remaining committed to seeing current reality a reality'*. Fortune wrote, 'IBM staked its treasure, its reputation and its position of leadership in the computer field.... radical new concept, series of compatible machines serving the broadest possible range of applications, from the most sophisticated scientific applications to the relatively small business needs'. IBM CEO Tom Watson Jr. introduced *'Stretch'* a high-end machine. The machine project was killed at an early stage only after a few were sold as it was found uneconomical and the machine did not satisfy the customer requirements.

Watson spoke, *'our greatest mistake in Stretch is that it walked up to the plate and pointed at the centre field stands. When we swung, it was not a homer but a hard line drive to the outfield. We're going to be a good deal more careful about what we promise in the future'.* The learning from *Stretch* led to the introduction of 'System 360' 3 years later, which proved to be the platform for its extraordinary growth over the next 10 years.

(*Source*: Senge, 1990: 226.)

## Track Three

## Xerox Palo Alto Research Centre (PARC)

The gap between the vision and reality can create hopelessness but it is a source of energy. This gap is called as creative energy or creative tension. The possibility is to resolve either to reality or vision and the success depends upon how one holds steady to the vision. Mr Alan Kay who directed the research at Xerox Palo Alto Research Centre, which led to many features of the personal computer, actually had a vision for a different machine, which he called the *'Dynabook'*. The computer is meant to make it interactive with the child to test his understanding, play games and creatively rearrange the static presentation of ideas.

But the *'Dynabook'* never became a reality, however, the prototype machines developed at PARC achieved the functionality of windows, pull-down menus, mouse control, iconic displays that was introduced in the computer machines later. The present day computers owes to Alan Kay for his vision.

(*Source*: Senge, 1990: 150.)

# Applied HR Case—'Do as Heart Say'

## Futuristic Business Systems

Naidu was working as the Chief Operating Officer of the Futuristic Business Systems, which is dealing with the office automation products selling under the brand name *'Easy'*. As the brand name suggests the products are made simple to operate and designed to give a better ambiance in the office with various colours. The company was doing well and was able to reach the targets, but they were not able to encash upon their USP (Unique Selling Proposition). The marketing executives would always negotiate on the prices rather than the USP, which worried Naidu. The products had advance features and also pleasing look. Naidu observed that the executives and managers in order to achieve the target would like to negotiate on the prices and the customer understood well the tense situation of the executive and wanted to cut down the prices further.

Naidu was worried that if the trend went on, he may not be able to lead the company further with the expected growth rate. Mary, the HR head had been in the company since two years and understood the concern of Naidu and his urge to market the USP. Gary, the marketing head was celebrating his 10th marriage anniversary and had called all his colleagues for a lunch. Mary had given her car for maintenance and Gary had promised her that he would take her to the hotel and get her back to the workplace. After completing lunch and while they were returning back, Gary received a call from one of his executives that he needed his help in finalising a deal which could take care of two months of production. Gary was happy and since he did not want to miss the opportunity, he requested Mary if she would accompany him for the negotiation for which she agreed reluctantly since she had already fixed up a meeting with one of the consultants.

Mary observed the whole negotiation discussion and found to her surprise that Gary and his executive were under immense pressure while the customer was putting undue pressure to reduce the cost. By looking at the face one could easily find out that the customer was ready to take but was also keen in reducing the cost.

Mary was sleepless during the whole night remembering the whole negotiations and the next day she discussed with Naidu that all the managers needed to undergo training on *'Emotional Intelligence'*, which would bring in creativity and innovation under tension. Naidu liked the idea and he shared the thoughts with other heads. Everybody made a mockery of EI and remarked that the market goes by negotiation and relationship rather than intelligence. However Mary was committed to do the programme and took up the challenge to prove her point.

## Questions

1. Do you think that Mary will be successful in her endeavour to bring value addition to the organisation? Why?
2. Do you subscribe to the concept of EI?
3. If you were Mary, how you would plan selling the concept and conducting the training programme for all the marketing personnel.

## References and Further Readings

Cherniss, C. and D. Goleman. 2001. *The Emotionally Intelligent Workplace*, CA: Jossey-Bass.
Cooper, K. Robert and Azman Sawaf. 1997. *Executive EQ/EI in Business*, London: Orion Business Books.
*Executive EQ*, New York: Grosset/Putnam.
Goleman Danial. 1998. *Working with Emotional Intelligence*, New York: Bantam Books.
——. 1996. *Emotional Intelligence*, London: Bloomsbury.
Segal, Jeanne. 2000. *Raising Your Emotional Intelligence*, Mumbai: Magna Publishing Company Limited.
Senge, Peter M. 1990. *The Fifth Discipline*, UK: Random House.
Singh, Dalip. 2001. *Emotional Intelligence at Work*, New Delhi: Response Books.

# Appendix-14 A

## 'Emotional Intelligence'

### Additional Case Study—I

Taylor is working as a technician in the assembly line of the Automobile giant and he is considered as a good worker. Since he has been doing the job since four years in the same assembly line he set his own standards, which are above the standards set by the organisation. He was being awarded the best performer award consecutively for two years.

The organisation has decided to change one of the machines in the assembly line to increase the productivity. Taylor along with another technician was taken as the trend-setters where the organisation can set the speed of the assembly rolling. Taylor was happy with the proposal and was jubilant.

When the machinery was installed and the engineers were explaining about how to increase the production by 30 per cent, Taylor was worried initially about the functioning of the new machinery and its impact on others. Martin, HR Head who was observing Taylor realised that he was emotionally disturbed and need to be taken care. After the lecture he called Taylor in his room and discussed with him about the installation of the new machinery in the assembly line. Taylor replied that apparently it is good but there are concerns, which need to be addressed. Taylor asked him to give him one day time to him to talk to him at length.

Next day, Taylor came and discussed with Martin of how the production can be even doubled changing the assembly line and also installing new machinery. He explained in detail how it can be done, but the team needed to be empowered in lines of SMT. Martin was very happy to listen to his suggestion and he immediately rushed to meet the Director to explain him the new proposal.

### Questions

1. Was Taylor right in proposing a new method of production activity?
2. What prompted him to think 'out of box' and redesign the whole production activity?
3. How did emotional intelligence help him to propose the new method?

## Additional Case Study—II

Mr Richard joins as Sales Manager in an upcoming Insurance company. His previous experience had been of a sales coordinator with little exposure to direct marketing. As the previous company closes its doors due to downsizing, Mr Richard has no other option but to immediately grab the opportunity of becoming a Sales Manager with a better pay packet. By all standards Mr Richard is an average profile and with utmost difficulty he has been passing on examinations and has also cleared his license for a certified insurance advisor.

Mr Robert, who is the Head of Sales and Marketing, is worried about his performance, as his performance is crucial for achieving the targets. During every meeting, Mr Robert argues with Mr Richard about the performance.

Mr Richard is worried about his job in the new role. Though he is trying his level best but is not able to deliver as per the expectations of the organisation. Meanwhile, Richard's wife, who used to work as a teacher and support the house, has a fracture to her neck bone and he has to incur expenditure for her treatment besides losing the additional income for maintenance. His daughter is admitted in a good school and the fee is very high. Mr Richard is in a fix.

Due to sudden change and the unforeseen happenings Mr Richard starts blaming himself and his fate for his performance and the personal life. This further affects his performance and the sales figures starts having a downward trend.

Mr Robert knows that Mr Richard can perform well and has the potential to grow in the company. He wants to help him so that he can come out of the problems and can become one of the best sales managers of the company.

### Questions

1. If you were Mr Richard, how you would overcome the performance and personal problems?
2. If you are Mr Robert how would you help him out in becoming the best sales managers of the company?

## Additional Case Study—III

Mr Kiran is the CEO of Anurag Software Corporation and he is doing well in the business. Having started as an enterprise, which basically works for the data entry job, gradually with the help of his contacts and the friends, he started foray into the software industry. With his knowledge, timely decisions and risk-taking ability, he has been able to get good overseas projects.

Having started with only five employees, he has now about 1,100 employees. Anurag Software has both the data entry division and the software division. He is being recognised as the person having enchanted for taking the right kind of decisions under any circumstances. When all the companies were reeling under the downtrend in software, he never bothered and firmly believed that the technology is going to stay. Anurag Software has consistently performed during such tough periods as well.

Kiran has recently attended an international seminar on IT and he came across a similar entrepreneur, Robinson from US, who has come here to explore the possibility of a tie-up. Robinson is a software engineer by profession and he has recently set up his own firm in Los Angles, presently employing about 52 employees. He has both data entry and as well as software projects.

The preliminary discussions has been completed and both of them understand each other. Robinson has agreed to give him good returns. However, as his firm is a a new one, he needs to clear some of his loans and has asked Kiran to settle for small returns for three years after which he will double the returns.

Kiran is confident about the order, but since the return of investment is very negligible he is in a dilemma. Robinson has invited him to come to US for a final discussion so that the matter gets settled.

Kiran is in a dilemma, whether to accept the offer given by Robinson, which enables him to enter the overseas market or to confine himself to the local business. Kiran needs to take a decision within a week to go to US.

## Questions

1. Do you think that Kiran can take the risk of accepting the overseas business?
2. How do you think with so minimal a return and without much guarantee such a huge project can be accepted?
3. If you are Kiran, how will you take a decision with your EI and gut feeling?

# 'CODE OF CONDUCT AND BUSINESS ETHICS' DIRECTING THE BEHAVIOUR THROUGH CODE OF CONDUCT AND BUSINESS ETHICS

*An individual without information cannot take responsibility; an individual who is given information cannot help but take responsibility.*

—Jan Carlzon, Swedish Business Leader, Cambridge (1987)

## Intent

- To define the code of conduct and business ethics for the organisation and communicate effectively to all employees of the company.
- To provide a sense of morale and psychological support to the employee in his work.
- To provide an understanding in the helping and guiding of day-to-day decisions through defined code of business ethics policy of the company.
- To drive the organisation towards value driven and transparency.

## Expression

Code of conduct and ethics are the written statements setting forth the principles that should guide an organisation's decisions. It is a systematic study of morale (ethical) matters pertaining to business industry or related activities, institutions or practices and belief.

# Comprehension

Ethics sets the standards as to what is good and what is bad in conduct and decision making in the organisational context. Ethics deals with the internal values and culture of the organisation and shapes the decisions of the employees in pursuance of the conduct of business concerning the social responsibility. The decisions taken by the employee on behalf of the organisation may also have an impact on the stakeholders including the society and any unethical decisions may harm the society and the company itself.

Many of the present organisations are concerned about the way business is being done and are enforcing business ethics to bring in transparency in the deals and corporate governance. Large number of companies have developed a written code of ethics governing the business, defining the values and principles that should be used to guide decisions. A code of ethics cannot accomplish much by itself. The code of ethics only gives the expected behaviour from the employees whether they can be tolerated. The principles must be upheld by the top management not in the form of declarations and policies but being transparent in its actions and business strategies. The top management must also set tone along with the senior managers throughout the company. The organisation must also disseminate information, training and a system through which an employee can get help in difficult situations. Organisations at the same time take the liberty to demand fair and ethical employee behaviour just as it attempts to initiate the same through its policies, procedures and practices.

The rise of business ethics is due to the changing nature of employment. Employees are now from various cultures as a result of the rapid spread of new technology. At work, the employees may experience ethical dilemma and/or even disagree with others, because of doubt about of how to proceed, or because of clash of values or cultural differences. The question arises of how one is to choose between various ethical standpoints. The ethics programme provides a guide for self-introspection before taking any business decisions. One way is by giving a handout on the principles guiding the business decisions, through usage of Intranet, Graffiti in Cafeteria, etc.

Ethical structures provide the system through which a company can establish the code of ethics like the 'Ethical Committee' which looks into the implementation of ethics and the 'ethics ombudsman' an official appointed by the company to look into all the complaints and points out the ethical failures to the management. Some organisations have gone ahead in laying down the 'corporate aspirations' in terms of ethical standards stating that the rise given to the employees would depend upon his contribution towards upholding these standards.

Values, code of conduct, organisation principles, credos, etc., are the different forms under which the values of the organisation have been reflected. The presentations of values are in different forms but after all it speaks the same language that the organisation wants to adhere. Ethics are based on the values that the organisation wants to cultivate. Ethics teaches the organisation and its employees the principle under which the organisation wants to operate. Any deviation and challenge to ethics are firmly tackled with. The start of the company's good practices depends on how ethical the organisation is, which generates ultimate goodwill for the organisation. Ethics are the strategic needs since it is the foundation on which the organisational process rest.

# Experiential Application

## A. Prerequisite

- The policy of business ethics is a statement of ethical principles of the company and therefore, shall be evolved collaboratively and must be shared by all the employees. It cannot be imposed, but are the principles, which are practised and valued by the organisation since long.
- The business ethics and code of conduct are not merely for documentation but it has to be imbibed and internalised in every action that is being carried out by an individual employee in their day-to-day working process.
- Right from the top management to the bottom of the pyramid of the organisation, all the employees must be involved and committed to adhere to the code of business ethics of the company.
- 'Walk the talk' should be the mantra for all. A strict implementation of norms must be followed including disciplinary actions for those who violate the code of business ethics.

## B. Process Steps

| Step | Process |
| --- | --- |
| Step – I | Management to identify business principles and values. |
| Step – II | Announcing business ethics and code of conduct. |
| Step – III | Communication through oath taking, training, posters, booklets, Intranet, etc. |
| Step – IV | Strict disciplinary action in case of violation. |
| Step – V | All the business related processes must be run with the business ethics and code of conduct. |

# Potential Gains and Areas of Concern

- Business ethics gives a guideline for the company stating the dos and don'ts for all activities that it undertake keeping all the stakeholders in mind.
- Ethical principles are a mirror of the company. It shows the society, a true picture of the company.
- It is a common platform, clarifying all the ambiguous situations which otherwise could not stand at public scrutiny.
- It is a tool through which organisational discipline and a bonding can be initiated among business processes as well as employees of the company.
- Business ethics is a fine and rigid line of guidelines crossing which could be unethical. Hence, at times, it is difficult to manage the situation within the guidelines of the ethical principles.
- Though explicitly written and well communicated, the violation of principles and code of conduct is bound to be there due to the human factor. Punishment could be possible only for those who are caught red-handed.

# Measurability

## Try It Out

(1: not at all done, 2: moderately done, 3: to some extent done, 4: to a great extent done, 5: excellently done)

- My organisation has a defined code of conduct and business ethics policies in place.                                               ☐
- Management takes all efforts to communicate these policies to all the employees of the company especially as a part of induction for the new entrants.                                                              ☐
- There are examples through which the management has shown their commitment to the code of conduct and business ethics and follow the 'walk the talk' policy within the company.                          ☐
- Management has taken senior actions on the employees not adhering to the code of conduct and business ethics in recent past.        ☐
- Code of conduct and business ethics are the number one agenda in all the business meetings of the company.                           ☐

Analysis: the average score would determine the extent to which business ethics process exists in your organisation.

## Score Card

(*: 25% achieved, **: 50% achieved, ***: 75% achieved, ****: 100% achieved)

| Technology | Objective Elements | Unit | Historical | Last Year | Current Year | Stretch Target | Status |
|---|---|---|---|---|---|---|---|
| Business Ethics | Strategy Document | Doc | Nil | No | Yes | NA | ** |

# Proven Track Record

## Track One

## McDonnell Douglas

At McDonnell Douglas, a short version of the ethics code and an ethical decision-making checklist are printed on cards so that the employees may carry them in a pocket or purse. The company expects the employees to display ethical behaviour that are required by law. The contents of the card have been explained here.

Integrity and ethics exist in the individual or they do not exist at all. They must be upheld by individuals or they are not upheld at all. In order for integrity and ethics to be characteristics of McDonnell Douglas, we who make up the corporation must strive to be:

- honest and trustworthy in all our relationships;
- reliable in carrying out assignments and responsibilities;
- truthful and accurate in what we say and write;
- cooperate and constructive in all work undertaken;
- fair and considerate in our treatment of fellow employees, customers and other persons;
- law abiding in all activities; and
- dedicated in service to our company and to improve the quality of life in the world in which we live.

(*Source*: Daft, 1997: 160.)

## Track Two

## Texas Instruments

Texas Instruments has successfully implemented the ethics programme with an innovative method of communication of what is being expected from the employee. A formal training is imparted to every employee who joins the organisation and a 14-page booklet to communicate its expectations for ethical behaviour. The booklet also provides for a tear-out wallet size card that includes the tips for help during the ethical implications of situations. The card contains the following:

- Is the action legal?
- Does it comply with our values?
- If you do it, will you feel bad?
- How will it look in the newspaper?
- If you know it's wrong, don't do it!
- If you are not sure, ask.
- Keep asking until you get an answer.

Ethics is not only for the business of the organisation but for the employee also who has to follow the corporate values and ethics in business transactions.

(*Source*: Bernardin, 2003: 258.)

## Track Three

## Sundstrand

Sundstrand is large defense contractor that was prosecuted for unethical behaviour by Pentagon officials and in order to embark on a programme to emphasise ethical behaviour, including encouragement of internal whistle blowing by its employees so that illegal and unethical practices could be detected and corrected. As a result, the employees guilty of such behaviour suffer harsh consequences such as suspension, dismissal, unappealing work assignments and social ostracism by fellow workers.

To create an ethical climate, Sundstrand took several actions like created the position of a Corporate Director—Business and Ethics, who reports to the President directly. All the employees need to undergo orientation session during which each are given a book in which everyone need to sign indicating that they have read the book, understood and realised their obligations to follow the ethical guidelines presented in it. The director and his staff wrote a manual detailing the kinds of ethical dilemmas that occurred most frequently in the defense industry. Covered were legal interpretations for contract pricing, receipt and payment of gratuities and conflicts of interests, a hot line was also included. To evaluate the success of the programme, the director's office monitored the (a) total number of calls received; (b) total number of self-conduct checks by employees wondering about the ethics of behaviour; (c) the number of hot line callers; and (d) the number of reports of ethical violations that the team has investigated.

The whistle blowing programme has been instrumental in shaping the ethical behaviour at Sundstrand.

(Source: Hellriegel, Slocum Jr. and Woodman, 2001: 173.)

## Applied HR Case—'*Dealing Dilemma*'

### Susan Life Corporation

Susan Life Corporation is an upcoming industry in the manufacture of detergent soaps. Mr Daniel, the founder Managing Director of the company has got 15 years of experience in the industry and has set up his own company, since his wish was to become the MD. Starting with the initial investment of 50,000 US$ in a small way with 1 employee Mr Roger, he expanded the business to 5 million US$ with 40 employees. The main strength of the organisation is the quality of the product and the '*goodwill*' it has created in the market that they never sell any product which is substandard. The eldest son of MD, Mr Simon who did his Masters Degree in Management took over the business from his father, but Mr Daniel continued to be in the board. Since the detergent business is going at a good pace, Simon wanted to diversify to sell fruit juice in cans of exotic fruits available in other countries. Mr Daniel found the idea very good since the product can be moved through the retail outlets, which are already selling the detergents. He was able to get the bank loan easily, since it's an established organisation and the production stared within 1 year. Initially there was problem of sale since they are exotic fruits and the cost is high, but the quality is good since the product is made to stand the quality standards and goodwill gained by the detergent soaps.

Mr Simon has reviewed the sales for the first six months, but the product has not moved as per the expectations and through the survey done by the external consultants found that the price of the product is high in comparison with others. Mr Simon in order to push the product by selling at reduced prices got liquid concentrates and mixed them with the natural juices. After reducing the prices and the packaging costs, the product has picked up well and has been able to sell in the market. The company has achieved highest profit of 45 per cent, which is a all time high in the history of Susan Corporation.

Mr Roger, when he casually visited the plant, which is beside the detergent plant, observed that the product is being adulterated and was worried that if the food authorities detect the same, the company will be prosecuted and at the same time the company will lose its reputation. He immediately brought it to the notice of Mr Simon, who struck down stating that these are very common practices in the business, that regulatory authorities can be managed and asked him not to enter the premises again as it is not his job. Since the company has stood for its quality and standards, Mr Roger immediately went and spoke to Mr Daniel and told him about the incident.

## Questions

1. What are the ethical issues in the case study?
2. If you were Mr Daniel, will you justify the action of Mr Simon?
3. If you were Roger what course of action you would take? If Mr Daniel asks you to leave the organisation, how will you react and what will you do?

## References and Further Readings

Bernardin, H. John. 2003. *Human Resource Management: An Experiential Approach*, New Delhi: Tata McGraw-Hill Publishing Co. Limited.

Daft, Richard L. 1997. *Management*, Florida: The Dryden Press.

Hall, William. 1993. *Making the Right Decision—Ethics for Managers*, New York: John Wiley and Sons Inc.

Hellriegel, Don, John W. Slocum Jr. and Richard W. Woodman. 2001. *Organizational Behavior*, US: South Western College Publishing.

MacKinnon, Barbara. 2001. *Ethics—Theory and Contemporary Issues*, 3rd edn., Australia: Wordsworth Thomson Learning.

Mike Woodcock and Dave Francis. 1989. *Clarifying Organizational Values*, England: Gower Publishing Company Limited.

Newell, Susan. 1995. *The Healthy Organization*, London: Routledge.

Parker, Martin. 1998. *Ethics in Organization*, London: Sage Publications.

Petrick, Joseph A. and John F. Quinn. 1997. *Management Ethics Integrity at Work*, New Delhi: Response Books.

Sadri Sorab, Dhun S. Dastoor and S. Jayashree. 1999. *The Theory and Practice of Managerial Ethics*, Mumbai: Jaico Publishing House.

# 'Code of Conduct and Business Ethics'

## Additional Case Study—I

Mr Tom Andrews who was recruited into the company as Manager Facilities was extremely doing well in his new job. He had developed a good rapport even with government authorities.

The telephone line of the Director Operations Mr Daniel was not working since two days causing much inconvenience to Mr Daniel. He was on an important project which was going to be finalised and he had given his phone number to those concerned with the project. The telephone was connected to the Fax and the Internet. This meant that further progress in the finalisation process was impossible till the line was been restored. When Mr Daniel called upon Mr Chhabra, an executive in concerned with the restoration, he stated that since there was a fault of the cable in the main line, it would take another week to restore the line. Mr Daniel called Mr Tom to take up the job immediately and restore the same on war footing.

Mr Tom went to the local exchange and met Mr Dighe, who was in charge of the local telephone exchange. He agreed to restore the line only if he was paid an amount of Rs 2,000 towards the purchase of the cable through private parties for which he could not provide any bills as this was being done at the request of the party.

However, Mr Tom's organisation had a code of conduct for the employees which that laid down the norms of employee's behaviour while on duty and the business ethics to be maintained in dealings.

Mr Tom went back to the office and discussed the same with Mr Daniel. Mr Daniel was of the opinion that as their behaviour was guided by corporate ethics the amount could not be paid. However, the telephone line needed to be restored very urgently as an important and valued project was at stake.

## Questions

1. If you are in the position of Mr Tom what will you do to get the telephone line restored?

2. Is it justifiable to pay Mr Dighe the requisite amount to restore the telephone line?
3. If the amount is paid and telephone line is being restored will the act be against the business ethics and corporate values?

## Additional Case Study—II

Mr Anthony was an upcoming marketing manager. He had done his Bachelor of Engineering from one of the premier institutes in the country and had an MBA degree with a specialisation on Marketing. He was rated the best student and had been a topper in the college. An Express Cargo Industry took him as a management trainee. He was in the period of training for one year, after completion of which he was put on to the direct job of Branch Manager in an industrial area.

Mr Anthony who had taken the stock of the functioning of the unit, was surprised to see that the claims for damages had been lying for some time, from one of the largest customers Excel Auto Spares, which manufacture Engine Spare Parts for many automobile manufacturers. The contract was on a verge of being lost and it was one of the main sources of the revenue for the branch. Mr Anthony had taken up the challenge to revive and ensure that the branch retained the customer and also added value to the customer.

Mr Anthony observed the nature of damages and after coming to a conclusion of the nature of the problem, approached the Managing Director, Mr Srinivas Nayar. Before meeting him, he had taken the permission to go around the plant to look at the process.

During the discussion with the Managing Director, Mr Anthony explained that the cause of damage was due to faulty packaging rather than transportation. The packaging used to be done in corrugated boxes. He suggested that as the material was in bulk, instead of using thermocole sheets for protection, wooden boxes could be used to hold the material in good condition. The products could have a corrugated box but circumvented into a wooden box to enable it to reach safely.

The Managing Director was surprised that no one in the industry had looked into the matter earlier, and within a span of two months, the claims had turned to be zero. Mr Nayar was very happy as the products reached the dealer in good condition, which also helped them in selling the product in the market.

Mr Nayar offered Mr Anthony a gift worth Rs 30,000 to appreciate the business acumen of Mr Mathew. Mr Anthony was in a fix whether to take the gift or decline. The organisational ethics says that no employee must take undue advantage of the position and accept any gift from its customers in what so little form it may be. Mr Anthony feels that if he refuses to take, besides his personal interest, Mr Nayar may get offended and may decline to give the business further.

## Question

1. If you were Mr Anthony what would you have done? Would you accept or decline the gift?

## Additional Case Study—III

Mr John is one of the senior employees in the company and is known for his integrity and good disposition to his other employees. He is always seen as a person to help any one in the industry and to understand and alleviate the problems of his colleagues and his subordinates. Mr Unnikrishnan, who is one of the senior subordinates is often facing severe health problems, for the cause of which he is not in a position to come to the company regularly.

Mr Shravan, who has come from the service industry has joined as Head, HR. He is very strict in the matter of discipline and never compromises on values and principles. Mr Shravan has analysed the attendance of all the employees and has found that Mr Unnikrishnan has too many pay losses and hence asks Mr John to take action against Mr Unnikrishnan. Mr Shravan is of the opinion that absenteeism is not only hampering the production process but also the general discipline in the organisation. He feels that it is also affecting the work schedules and hence Mr Unnikrishnan should either be given early retirement with some benefits or be subjected to certain disciplinary proceedings. The top management is in agreement with Mr Shravan as they also believe that for proper maintenance of production schedules discipline is very essential.

## Question

1. If you are in the position of Mr John how will you resolve the problem? Will you take disciplinary action or support Mr Unnikrishnan?

# 5 BUILDING ONE GREAT LEGENDARY FAMILY

## Contents

## Learning Objectives

- To understand the essence of team building for bringing in achievement orientation among the employees.
- To recognise the strength of operating in Cross-functional Task Force for creativity and innovativeness in the workplace.

- To learn HR technologies on 360-degree feedback, understanding mentoring and coaching process and draw lessons of leadership from transformational leadership style.
- To build self-managed team by providing sense of entrepreneurship and empowerment.

# Transforming the Workplace

In order to comprehend the changes in the external environment and to survive in the competitive market, the organisation has to constantly adjust itself to the changes. Modern organisations are transforming their workplace. One of the methods of workplace transformation is reorganisation on the basis of team. Two or more people working collaboratively to achieve a common set of goals form a 'team'. The necessity of the team arises when the task is difficult to be completed by one individual and hence there is a requirement of a group of people to accomplish the task. Thus, when the team starts functioning, it becomes the fundamental units of the organisation and helps in improving the functioning of the organisation.

The traditional hierarchy in an organisation has changed and in the modern organisation consists of a team member, team leader, etc. The emphasis is on the importance and recognition of each team member's contribution to the achievement of goals. Due to the change in the nature of workplace, a manager is expected to understand when to make a 'team' and how to get the work done from the 'team members'. The knowledgeable team member is expected to take initiative and play a positive role on various tasks rather than sticking to one particular job. A team works together and creates a climate in which the energies of all the team members are channelised to achieve the goals of the organisation.

The nature of work has become so dynamic that people do not have a single job but multiple jobs to perform, being participant in various teams, as well as being leaders of individual teams as well thus leading to the formation of a matrix structure. Managers face the problem of achieving the goals by grouping and regrouping and changing the strategy to suit to the needs of the future. The situation has become so complex that it has become imminent that a Manager cannot by himself take a decision, but by discussing and brainstorming can arrive at a decision in a team.

The advantage of the formation of teams is that they boost up the morale of the employee in the organisation and enable them to accomplish greater tasks. Teamwork is one of the most essential features of modern organisations and many HR interventions are based on team approach. The greatest advantage of team based functioning is that they can be formed quickly; and once the task is finished the teams may be disbanded or restructured to meet the next goal.

## Generalist to Specialist Trend and the Role of the Team to Break the Silos

The changes in technology have created employees who have expertise in a specific function and thereby creating functional or vertical structures of specialisation. Each one looks inward to their department and upward to their bosses, but seldom looks at the customers who are serviced. This leads to process fragmentation and specialisation leading to the scuttle of innovation and creativity in the organisation. When problems arise, in such organisations, each one tries to blame the other rather than taking the mantle to settle the issue. Teams can percolate down the hierarchy and groups to accomplish the task and ensure customer satisfaction. The teams must have cohesion and must cooperate to perform. This is possible especially when a cross-functional task force is being created to overcome a problem by way of open discussion and honesty, which is the cause of concern for the performance of the organisation.

The teams built across the functions can improve the quality of the products/services rendered to the customer. The Japanese style of management has proved that the quality initiatives like six sigma, kaizen, etc., when implanted in the group, can bring in changes in the product, which adds value to the customer by way of bringing in better quality. It also brings in innovation in the products, as each team member would contribute his ideas and thoughts, which can improvise the production process and bring in changes that are far more superior to an individual working in silos. The members in the group can be motivated with fewer efforts when the group is cohesive and organised as the group regulates human behaviour.

## Dynamics of the Team—Cross-functional Task Forces

An individual who is determined can bring in improvement in the process and can make a big difference in the organisation. But due to constraints of human capacity and time sometimes individuals are not in a position to perform. This is also not possible when a group of employees form a team from a particular section because every activity in an organisation involves various functions. A team requires employees from various functions to solve a critical problem is called the Cross-functional Task Force (CFT). The significance of the CFT is that each department has a stake in the team and everyone would try to achieve the objectives for which the CFT is being built.

# The Essence of Leadership

A team requires leaders who can lead. The leaders need to take the risk, motivate the teammates and utilise the resources to the optimum extent to accomplish a goal. Leadership is not directing and forcing the team members to perform, but plays the role of a facilitator and coordinator channelising the energies. Leadership is not what you perceive in view of the position but it is the acceptance of the team members and other teams.

The leader needs to set up the goals so that the team members can know the purpose of the team formation. The goals must be realistic, challenging and positive. Reiteration of the goals during meetings and discussions would reinforce thereby strengthening the process. It is not going to solve the purpose when the team is formed and asked to perform without proper authority. Empowerment would facilitate the team members to perform the given responsibility and solve the problem. The leader needs to seek the ideas, opinions and reactions of the team members. Empowerment can also happen when the member comes with a problem and when his opinion is asked and valued; he personally takes the responsibility of getting it done as he feels that it is his decision and has to ensure its implementation. Leaders need to act swiftly when tough tasks are accomplished which will motivate team members to own the goals. Thus the role of a leader will be that of a coach, mentor, resource provider, etc.

It is always better to attain the consensus for taking certain critical decisions. This is possible only when a leader acts along with other members. It is done by the process of eliciting the opinions, ideas and conflict on surface and helps the members to find out the best possible solution. The leaders need to ensure that the team is cohesive, cultured and promotes mutual cooperation. Periodical review of the process is vital. The lines of communication between the team and the organisation need to be open and the leader needs to remove the blocks in the team's success when it faces the problem. However, the effectiveness of the team depends upon how the group accepts or rejects the goals of the organisation and the standards that the group maintains either to increase or decrease the output.

# Enable SHR Technology—Key to Success

This chapter brings in the following Strategic HR technologies:

SHR Technology–16    Teams—*Making of High Performance Teams.*
SHR Technology–17    Cross-functional Task Force—*Breaking Hard Nuts through Cross-functional Task Force Approach.*
SHR Technology–18    Mentoring and Coaching—*Prepping the Next Generation through Mentoring.*
SHR Technology–19    Transformational Leadership—*Building leadership through Transformational Leadership.*
SHR Technology–20    Self-Managed Team—*Imparting the Sense of Entrepreneurship through a Self-Managed Team.*

Individuals in the organisations cannot produce the desired result because the product and services which the company offers, require multiple supports. Unlike a stand-alone researcher, today's organisation processes are based on team approach and are not individual driven. Even though organisations operate in functional processes, they are striving to build teams among the functions so that the desired efficiency and performance can be achieved. Most of the business processes either in the shop floor or at the marketplace are now redesigned in many companies through a team approach, the cross-functional task forces approach being the most popular one. This technique owes to the Japanese industry to a great extent and is being used worldwide for improvement projects and for bringing in business efficiency.

In order to prove the customer as the focal point, Rank Xerox aligned all the business processes from design to delivery as per customer expectations. The company has organised its teams around six key processes: customer relationship management, customer service management, demand management, manufacturing flow management, procurement and fulfilment.

The company encourages its managers to adopt 'the process ways'—stretching themselves to think and cooperate cross-functionally to transform input from suppliers into output for customers in a way that focuses on the creation of customer benefits, looking at the total value added chain before any one element, reducing the total cycle time, and increasing the 'throughput' of the total system rather then reducing resources.

A close appraisal process has travelled substantially towards open appraisal and now appraisal has further progressed in the form of 360-degree feedback. Under 360-degree feedbacks, the appraisee is appraised from subordinates, superiors and peers as well as sometimes by customers too. This is a very successful and popular handy tool for developing leader-ship among the managerial employees of the company.

Besides the formal hierarchies in which boss–subordinate relationship exists, there has always been a need felt for an individual to overcome certain personal and professional issues in the workplace. These issues if unresolved could result into frustration, anger and non-performance. Mentoring is a process through which an identified mentor of a superior calibre could provide a sense of belongingness in the workplace and appropriate guidelines for improving competencies and emotional bondages.

Organisation processes are multi-layered and decision-making rests with different levels. However, it is observed many a times that instead of taking decisions of that respective level, employees tend to indulge into the decision-making process of a lower level and entangle into lower level activities. This makes the subordinates and juniors suffocated since they are not allowed to take decisions on many areas in which they would otherwise have been operating. Empowerment is no more a science but recognising the need for achievement orientations of the subordinates and allowing them to take their own decisions with an assumption that they are competent and they would do better without close monitoring and supervision.

Unlike empowerment processes leadership has to do with providing directions and guidelines rather than entering into lower level decision-making process. It is proved that leadership style of an individual has to be situational oriented which warrants total flexibility as and when the situation arises. For subordinates who are immature and for the subordinates who are mature, the leadership style varies with situations. Today's work demands that the team engaged in delivery services and products is responsible for everything that they can offer to the customer. To bring in a sense of involvement, self-directed teams or self-managed teams are the latest scientific methods through which a team can manage all its businesses and be responsible for the delivery of goods and services.

# Conclusion

- The traditional organisational hierarchical approach of operating in individual status has changed to team building approach in present day organisations.
- The team should have in-depth performance orientations to achieve the set and desired goals of the organisation.
- The formation of teams in a company has many approaches. Cross-functional Task Forces, self-directed work teams, self-managed teams, etc., are the different forms of organising teams in the workplace.

- Leadership development of an individual depends on the kind of mentoring pro-vided, empowerment given and adjusting of oneself to a variety of situations.
- Organisations must look at each individual as an entrepreneur rather than merely as a job seeker or a salary earner. The processes such as self-managed team could be the right way to build entrepreneurship development among the employees of the company.

# 'TEAMS'
# MAKING OF HIGH PERFORMANCE TEAMS

*We have to recognize a new paradigm; not great leaders alone, but great leaders who exist in a fertile relationship with a Great Group.... The leader and the team are able to achieve something together that neither could achieve alone.... The leader finds greatness in the group.*

—Bennis and Biederman, *Organizing Genius: The Secrets of Creative Collaboration*

## Intent

- To understand the formation and functioning of high performing teams.
- To build high performance teams.
- To understand the issues concerning teamwork and overcoming them.

## Expression

Team means two or more people collaboratively work to make something happen. Whenever someone teams up with someone else to agree on an action, they are for those moments a team. High performance team is collaborative approach of working together in organisational functioning to produce desired results for which they hold mutually accountable.

## Comprehension

Modern organisations are changing the way the whole business process is being organised from a hierarchy based division of labour to that of building teams (cellular working) with shared responsibility among all the members. Organisations are encouraging high performance workforce and teamwork across all levels. The business process that was once considered carried out by the bastions of top and middle management, is now being carried out by team leaders and workers. What drives the organisation is the achievement of goals in the competitive environment with contribution from every employee. High performance teams are vital to foster the process as they can be formed quickly for a specific task or projects and then disbanded or restructured to meet the next need.

The tendency of the organisations is to become flatter as the layers of hierarchy is being stripped to create the aura of teamwork. This brings in change in the style of the manager who needs to delegate the responsibilities to the team and have a larger span of control. The rapid changes in the information technology has only speeded up the process of team building since many of the manufacturing and the service organisations have changed their functioning with the change in technology.

Due to the intense competition and the opening up of the economy and free movement of labour, there is a high turnover in the industry and companies are looking for the scope to improve the morale, employee motivation and retention. The only solution to achieve the goals is to form high performance teams. Research shows that teams are a valuable resource that can improve work methods, increase attraction and retention of the workforce and improve concern for quality and output. If the organisation wants to guarantee the desired results and put organisations on the right track, building high performance teams is a must.

Tuckman, has identified four stages of team development, *forming*—when there is anxiety, dependence on the leader and testing what sort of behaviour is acceptable; *storming*—where there is conflict, emotional resistance to demands of the task and even rebellion against the leader; *norming*—when group cohesion is developed, norms emerge, views are exchanged openly and mutual support and cooperation increases giving the group an identity; and finally *performing*—when the team functions fully without any problems and there are constructive attempts to complete the tasks.

Teams are structured while teamwork is a process. Teams form the way to organise, while teamwork is the product of a person's thoughts and actions. Teamwork is more than skill. It is more than a structure and it is more than force group cooperation. Teamwork, at its best, is a spirit, the spirit of cooperation fuelled with a desire to excel. Teamwork is both an individual process and an organisational process. For it to really work, it must be infused into the daily operations of an organisation.

Some of the organisations have gone further by creating the SDWT (Self-Directed Work Teams) also called SMT (Self-Managed Teams), which are empowered to carry out the task and conduct their jobs. The team members' involvement is at its peak since the team is responsible for all the tasks assigned to them and they are free to plan, spend, monitor the results and plan for the future without much of management interference. However, they are accountable to the top management.

An organisation is a pool of people having common objectives related to Vision and Mission fulfilment. Hierarchies and division of work is the method through which a variety of tasks are performed in order to provide goods and services to the consumers. Individuals alone cannot perform unless a group of people together work on common goals. Teamwork and team spirit are the means through which difficult tasks are accomplished. Teams for processes, special tasks, etc., are the order of modern management practices. Formation of proper team, task distribution process, team member's evaluation and rewards, etc., demands systematic and strategic approach. Team building technology cannot be ignored in any organisation if the organisation wants to fight the competitive forces.

# Experiential Application

## A. Prerequisite

- For a high performance team to stay alive and function well, a definite strategy needs to be formulated. Members of the team need a reason for being and working together. The goals of the team rationalise its existence.
- Without clear goals, people become apathetic or use the group to achieve their own personal goals.
- Whether the group has a formal leader or the leadership is shared, the group needs people who are willing to take the risk of leadership. Leaders help coordinate the work of the team, have good communication skills and know how to involve everyone.
- To achieve synergy and group spirit, all team members must contribute actively. Therefore involvement is must.
- The team should have ample time to communicate, share information, discuss issues and use informal channel of communication to pass on information, make suggestions and bring up new ideas.
- The work of the team should centre on the things it has the power to influence. For people to function well together as a group, attention must be paid to the process used to do the work and to the content of the work. Trust depends on how the leader and members treat one another.
- Members and the team members may need to discuss how their behaviour and attitude effects trust. Team members must feel they can disagree and differ from one another without being punished.

## B. Process Steps

| Step | Process |
| --- | --- |
| Step – I | Organisation to define the formation and goals of team. |
| Step – II | All resource to support the formation of the team. |
| Step – III | Bringing in consensus among the group to achieve similar goals. |
| Step – IV | Establishment of clear goals, rules and tasks to each member to bring in collective work processes. |
| Step – V | Operational freedom and support to the team, its leader and the team members to accomplish the task. |

# Potential Gains and Areas of Concern

- The team brings in commonality of purpose, a shared vision and understanding of how to compliment one another's efforts.
- The team's accomplishments can set the tone of success and become a sense of honour for all the members as well as for the organisation.
- Teams need to be compensated well for their efforts since it reinforces the team efforts. Further, more plans can be made to reward teams based on the company's performance enabling the team to align with company's goals and profits.
- The fundamental characteristic of relatively unaligned team is wasted energy. Individuals may work extraordinarily hard, but their efforts do not efficiently translate to team efforts.
- Individuals do not sacrifice their personal interest to the larger team vision; rather the shared vision becomes an extension of their personal visions.
- Eliciting the top management support is vital, if not, the team collapses over a period of time.
- The characteristics of the team need to be built in the team and any laxity would lead to the team working against the objectives.
- Patience is required to get the results out of the team. Making a team is not the panacea of all the problems. Developing effective teams is difficult, and the path to success is time consuming full of obstacles.

# Measurability

## Try It Out

(1: not at all done, 2: moderately done, 3: to some extent done, 4: to a great extent done, 5: excellently done)

- The organisation structure of my company gives scope for team operation □ rather then functional silos.
- There are many teams operating today than they used to a few years □ back.
- Employees are encouraged and given the opportunity to work in a team in □ different positions from time to time.
- Teams currently existing in the company are evaluated for their □ performance and recognised with rewards.
- The management and the employees believe that team and teamwork can □ only bring a competitive advantage over others.

Analysis: the average score would determine the extent at which Team process exist in your organisation.

## Score Card

(*: 25% achieved, **: 50% achieved, ***: 75% achieved, ****: 100% achieved)

| Technology | Objective Elements | Unit | Historical | Last Year | Current Year | Stretch Target | Status |
|---|---|---|---|---|---|---|---|
| Teams | Strategy Document | Doc | Nil | No | Yes | NA | ** |

# Proven Track Record

## Track One

## Toyota Motor Manufacturing, USA

In Toyota, team building begins with the firm's commitment to the teamwork principles. Toyota's *'Team Member Handbook'* states their commitment. All factory work is organised around work teams. There are teams of about five to ten people in charge of door installation, assembly team, power train conveyance, stamping tool and die and body weld. There are no individuals on the plant floor. Every employee belongs to the work team. Toyota uses several practices to ensure the smooth functioning of work teams. There is a team member handbook and a team member activity association.

Rigorous teamwork training is repeatedly provided. Letting work teams recruit and select their own new member enhances closeness. The feeling that they are all there to share the groups' work comes across when speaking with team members themselves.

(*Source*: Dessler, 1997.)

## Track Two

# Nokia

The Finland based telecommunications company with top market share in the cell phone industry, stretches the concept of teamwork far beyond technical definitions, while rivals pay lip service to motivational tool, Nokia puts teams at the core of the innovative management system allowing employees directly involved in projects to make decisions regardless of their positions on the corporate hierarchies. The CEO of the company believes that empowering teams to take the lead in directing growth allows for greater creativity, remarkable flexibility and unique ability to stay competitive. Every aspect of Nokia's operation from design and engineering to manufacturing and sales is assigned to the team. With a workforce of more than 60,000 spread around the globe is not an easy feat.

People from different cultures, disciplines and background work together, harnessing diverse capabilities for better informed, more effective decision making. Teams are given the responsibility to figure out how they get things done, and each member has the opportunity to develop beyond the conventional business roles. As experts envision a world in which handset technology usurps the personal computers as the communication tool for the future, Nokia's teams are set to meet even greater challenges.

(*Source*: Wagner III and Hollenbeck, 2002: 251.)

## Track Three

# Infosys Technologies

Software house Infosys Technologies depends on teamwork throughout its organisation. The organisation resembles Californian rivals more than India's traditional hierarchical behemoths. Teams enable synergy among the members, and capitalise this energy. Team members are selected basing on their functions, previous performance on projects, task forces, product teams and they fit well in a particular team.

Depending upon the job, teams form, do the work and then disband. The work processes are designed on the basis of teams forming and after completion disbanding and forming another team for a different job, which made Infosys truly a global corporation.

(*Source*: Odenwald, 1996: 109.)

# Applied HR Case—'Giving a Punch'

## Colts Agri-Products Limited

Sam was very happy to assume the office of the Head of HR in the prestigious company, which everyone would like to work and it is ranked as one of the top *Best Employers to Work'*. He was dreaming to join a company, which can give leverage to his career and grow professionally. The departmental structure of HR is as follows:

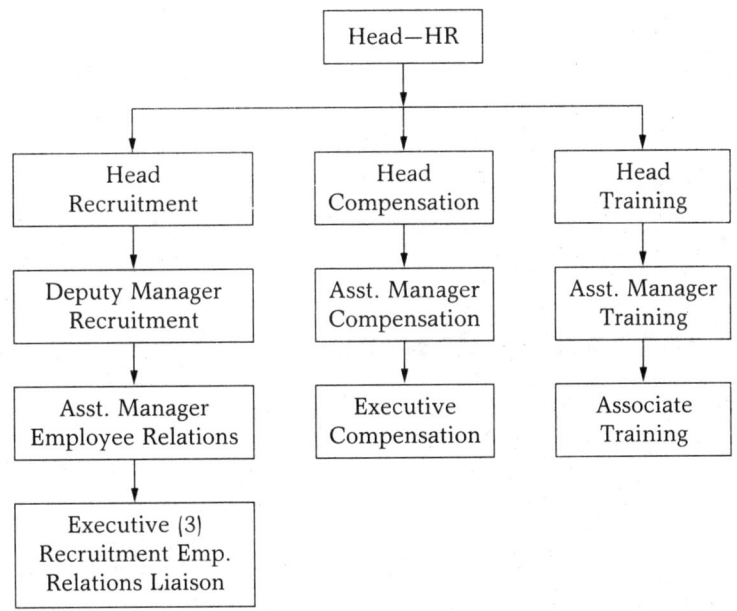

Alex, Joe and Mathew were the heads as given in the above organisation chart and Alex was the senior most of all. Sam met the MD before assuming the role and while discussing casually he has mentioned about Alex and told him that he may face some trouble from him, but he will be with Sam for all the decisions taken.

Sam has called for the departmental meeting and everybody came on time, but Alex has not come to the meeting. Sam wanted to take the consensus of all to start the meeting and everybody told that Alex has asked all not to start the meeting until he joins as he needs to take the interview for the Office Assistant for the Infrastructure Department. While they were discussing Alex arrived and asked Sam to start the meeting. While Sam was introducing himself and what is his vision about the company and how to improve upon, Alex started speaking loudly to advocate. Everyone got irritated and Alex exactly wanted to create this sort of an atmosphere. When he was asked to switch off the mobile during the meeting, he sarcastically replied that it was a matter of dismissal of an employee and since the MD has asked him to look after it personally, he cannot avoid. In spite of his seniority he neither took interest in what Sam was discussing nor was he giving any constructive criticism and his standard reply was that he tried to implement many things, but it will not work in this company.

The meeting concluded without any result. Sam has reviewed the whole situation and worried how he will go about in building a strong team. He felt his paradise was shattered.

## Questions

1. Do you think that the MD should have spoken to Sam about the whole process of recruitment before giving him the formal offer?
2. Was Sam right in his approach to meet all the HR personnel without discussing with Alex?
3. What techniques of team building Sam needs to make so that he can drive the department to achieve what he had visualised?

## References and Further Readings

Katzenbach, R.J. and Douglas K. Smith. 1993. *The Wisdom of Teams: Creating the High-Performance Organization*, New York: Harper Collins.

Biech, Elaine (ed). 2001. *Successful Team-Building Tools*, San Francisco: Jossey-Bass/Pfeiffer.

Blake, Robert R., Jane S. Mouton and Robert L. Allen. 1987. *Spectacular Teamwork*, Mumbai: Sachindra Publications.

Dessler, Gary. 1997. *Human Resource Management*, New Jersey: Prentice Hall.

Fisher K., S. Rayner and W. Belgard. 1995. *Tips for Teams*, New York: McGraw-Hill.

LaFasto, Frank M.J. and Carl Larson. 2002. *When Teams Work Best*, New Delhi: Response Books.

Montebello, Anthony R. 2001. *Work Teams that Work*, Mumbai: Jaico Publishing House.

Odenwald, Sylvia B. 1996. *Global Solutions for Teams*, Chicago: Irwin Professional Publishing.

Rees. Fran. 2001. *How to Lead Work Teams*, San Francisco: Jossey-Bass/Pfeiffer.

Skopec, Eric and Dayle M. Smith. 1997. *How to Use Team Building to Further Innovation throughout Your Organization*, USA: Contemporary Books.

Tuckman, Bruce. 1965. 'Developmental Sequence in Small Groups', *Psychological Bulletin*, 63: 384–99.

Wagner J.A. III and J.R. Hollenbeck. 2002. *Organizational Behavior*, 4th edn. FortWorth, TX: Harcourt Inc

Woods, John A. 1997. *10 Minute Guide to Teams and Teamwork*, New York: Alpha Books.

# Appendix-16A

## 'Teams'

### Hi-tech Team Development Worksheet

**Instruction:**

Write at least four items under each of the heading as given under. Devise a punch line that depicts your group.

- **Strengths that you bring to the team:**


- **Abilities you bring to the team:**


- **Your most important values:**


Punch line description:

# 'CROSS-FUNCTIONAL TASK FORCE' (CFT) BREAKING HARD NUTS THROUGH CROSS-FUNCTIONAL TASK FORCE APPROACH

*The essence of strategy is cross-functional, cross-activity integration.*
—Anonymous

## Intent

- To streamline or reengineer the current tasks or process to bring in effectiveness and efficiency.
- To develop a cross-functional perspective among functional silos of the company.
- To resolve conflict that frequently takes place due to people with different perspectives, skills and values and bringing in harmony for a heterogeneous group.
- To develop competencies among individuals to be a breakthrough team player to apply their knowledge.

## Expression

Cross-functional teams are ongoing teams that are formed to address problems that cut across the organisational boundaries. Task team members are appointed from one or more departments to work on specific high priority assigned problem. When the problem is solved the task team is disbanded.

## Comprehension

Most of the activities of a business firm are performed through formal organisational structure and hierarchy. When a large number of people cooperate in performing a task, individual roles and responsibilities are decided by sub-dividing the work into a number of different elements and structuring those elements. An organisation tailored to the task is then set up and the work is performed by it. When the work is structured skillfully and the organisation structure matches it well, the organisation is considered to be good. In practice, it is not easy to create a good organisation due to various reasons. No matter however the organisation's activities are performed, there would be many processes which would be either performed well or poor as a company as a whole. Whenever, an attempt for improvements are made, sectionalism in each function and division cause greater hurdles since they have their own interests and the sectoral improvement activities are not effective for the entire organisation. Because of this, it is necessary to manage such a kind of overarching activities from a standpoint that transcend organisations through cross-functional task forces.

The cross-functional task forces are one of the important elements in the quality improvement programmes. Generally, quality improvement programme contains three elements—one, policy deployment; second, cross-functional task forces for quality improvement teams; and finally quality in daily work life. Most problems addressed by cross-functional task forces are either those caused by an upstream part of the work flow but are not tackled because they affect downstream in a different part of the organisation, or workflow congestion problems because of poor coordination among different functions. In cross-functional task force, a problem is given as a project to the entire team to work on its resolution. The seniormost member of the organisation is given the responsibility to lead the task force and to bring in the desired result with a good cohesive team approach.

The cross-functional task force team members undergo extensive training and this is one area in which the HR systems have a major impact. The team members are trained on special tools and techniques of problem solving such as statistical quality control, group decision making techniques such as brain storming, work book, case studies, video presentations, etc.

There is an increase complexity in the organisation due to dynamic changes in the marketplace and with the changing customers' expectations. Maintaining speed and innovation are the keys through which organisation can remain competitive in this complex scenario. In the organisation context addressing such complex scenario arising frequently cannot be resolved by few and from a given function, but there need a composite and collective wisdom and thinking. Going to the grassroot level of the problem can only bring solutions to the complexity. A very powerful technology that can make such scenario easy is solving problems through a cross-functional team or a task force. No organisation can claim that they are free of any issues or problems. They are bound to exist. The approach through cross-functional task force can bring the problem closer to diagnosis and a resolution can be arrived at meaningfully. Thus, technology of cross-functional task force is the right means in today's business world.

# Experiential Application

## A. Prerequisite

- In cross-functional task force, it is better to gather people from different functional areas to coordinate their efforts from the beginning, and then turn them loose.
- The facilitator or the leader must trust the group. The leader must act mostly to reconcile the conflicting opinion.
- The cross-functional task force team member must look at the problem from the broad, multidisciplinary perspective. The team player must have effective cross-functional skills to understand the perspective of various disciplines.
- The team member must keep in mind the vulnerable analogy of wearing different hats.
- To bring in a breakthrough success the team player must apply their knowledge about conflict resolutions.
- The ideal approach to resolving the conflict is to confront the real issue and solve the problem; identifying facts, logic or emotions that account for the differences with another person of the team.
- Confrontation can proceed gently in a way that preserves a good working relationship.

## B. Process Steps

| Step | Process |
| --- | --- |
| Step – I | Identifying the issues which are chronic in nature. |
| Step – II | Team is selected across the functions and levels. |
| Step – III | Identification of a Team Leader. |
| Step – IV | Necessary training in cross-functional task force and quality tools is imparted. |
| Step – V | Allocation of responsibility depending on capability. |
| Step – VI | Necessary data being collected by the team members on the issues confronting the organisation. |
| Step – VII | Various problem solving techniques and tools are used to go into the root cause of the problem. |
| Step – VIII | Team brainstorms on the problem and gives an action plan to overcome. |
| Step – IX | Implementation of action plan as suggested by cross-functional task force. |

# Potential Gains and Areas of Concern

- Cross-functional task force helps bringing cross-functional approach to problem solving.
- It brings in thinking line *out of the box* due to involvement of cross-functional members and fosters innovation and creativity.
- Many chronic issues of the organisation can be resolved though cross-functional task force which otherwise difficult to addresses with the regular functional approach.
- Members would refrain contributing their best in cross-functional task force since it is out of their performance parameters.
- In the absence of proper encouragement, the desired result may not be arrived at.
- Working in cross-functional task force could lead to additional burden on the members since they have to work and contribute additionally over and above their current assignments.

# Measurability

## Try It Out

(1: not at all done, 2: moderately done, 3: to some extent done, 4: to a great extent done, 5: excellently done)

- My organisation is concerned with many overriding issues which are chronic in nature and shows interest in resolving them.  ☐
- Gravity of these issues are well understood and a mechanism of cross-functional task force is well placed to address such issues within the organisation.  ☐
- Currently we have many cross-functional task forces in existence and they are functioning well within the organisational norms.  ☐
- Due to cross-functional task forces' recommendations, in the past few years our organisation could address some of the chronic issues and it has resulted in significant financial gains.  ☐
- Employees are encouraged to participate in CFT and they are well rewarded and recognised by the management time to time.  ☐

Analysis: the average score would determine the extent to which cross-functional task force exists in your organisation.

## Score Card

(*: 25% achieved, **: 50% achieved, ***: 75% achieved, ****: 100% achieved)

| Technology | Objective Elements | Unit | Historical | Last Year | Current Year | Stretch Target | Status |
|---|---|---|---|---|---|---|---|
| Cross-functional Task Force | Strategy Document | Doc | Nil | No | Yes | NA | ** |

# Proven Track Record

## Track One

### Komatsu

At Komatsu cross-functional task forces are used for profit management, quality assurance and quantity management. These committees are intended to improve the systems of the company and upgraded to the level for better results. Since each CFT deals with the improvement of the systems, it tries to identify any malfunctioning in the system and make the recommendation for improvements. For instance, the committee may find that the malfunctions arise from inappropriate rules; in that case, the committee makes recommendation to the departments concerned on reviewing and revising the rules.

When the cross-functional task forces working on profit management finds that the profit targets have not been achieved, it studies why the initial target was not achieved, and identifies the areas for improvement. Although it is the job of each line department to achieve the target, cross-functional task force reinforces the efforts of line departments by providing direction for the systems improvement. At Komatsu the planning and co-ordination group at each plant takes care of various cross-functional task forces. Regular meetings are organised to review the progress in each of the task forces operating for various purposes.

(*Source*: Imai, 1991.)

## Track Two

### AT&T

In 1988 when AT&T started developing its first ever cordless phone, the company hoped to reduce the product development time by 50 per cent. For doing this there was a requirement of making major changes. The main obstacle that the company was facing was a tightly formed hierarchical structure. In the past AT&T approached product development through a process resembling a relay system in which the product development group would handover a design to the manufacturing group, and subsequently, the manufacturing would hand over the product to the marketing to be sold to the consumers. In the entire chain there was no complete connection. It was then decided that there is a dare need to revamp the process by forming teams whose membership will include engineers, manufacturers and marketers. Team members were granted the authority to decide about how much the product would cost, how it would work, and its appearance as well. Rigid speed requirements were established before design requirements were fixed. The decision of cross-functional team was overwhelmingly successful.

The team achieved tight deadlines since they were highly empowered and did not have to send decisions of the hierarchies for approval. As a result of the shift to approach of cross-functional task force, AT&T cut development time from two years down to one year. Equally significant, the cost of manufacturing was substantially lower and the product quality became more customer-oriented.

(*Source*: DuBrin, 1995.)

## Applied HR Case—'Be a Businessman'

### Advanced Computer Systems

Lawrence, MD of the company has the dream to set up one of the biggest computer hardware manufacturing companies in the world and he continually strives for achieving the same. He, along with his classmates Jane and Prasad, established the company and with their technical support, Lawrence was able to sell his computer under the name 'genie'. 'Genie' is a small and cute model, which has all the features of other brand computers and is faster. The model was a moderate success and it was not able to penetrate the market as planned. While analysing some of the features and problems faced in the operation in the review meeting, the team felt that these might have been handled if there is sufficient information. Lawrence was of the strong opinion that each department has worked on his own which has led to the launching of a system and which is not complete in all aspects.

This has created further challenge to Lawrence that he needs to build a system, which is different from all the existing models and would surpass all in the technologically advanced features. He asked Prasad to do a market survey of the present and future requirements of the valued and highly critical customers so that they can come out with a model that can give answers to all the questions.

Lawrence was still not satisfied with the progress and wanted that the gaps that existed during the production of 'genie' does not repeat again. Hence he decided to have a team called 'Critical Brains' consisting of the cream of all the departments to brainstorm and build a model that can challenge the future.

## Questions

1. Was Lawrence right in designing a team 'Critical Brains' and do you feel that it's going to work?
2. Do you think that the efforts of Lawrence would be fruitful in developing a model for the future? Why?
3. What are the advantages of having 'Critical Brains' in advanced computer systems?

## References and Further Readings

Donnellon, Anne. 1996. *Team Talk*, MA: Harvard Business School Press.
DuBrin, Andrew J. 1995. *The Breakthrough Team Player*, New York: American Management Association.
Imai, Masaaki. 1991. *Kaizen*, New York: McGraw-Hill Inc.
Kartzenbach, R.J. 1998. *Teams at the Top*, MA: Harvard Business School Press.
Nash, Susan. 2001. *Turning Team Performance Inside Out*, Jaico Publishing House.
Odenwald, Sylvia B. 1996. *Global Solutions for Teams*, Chicago: Irwin Professional Publishing.
Singh, Kuldeep, T.V. Rao and Baburaj V. Nair (eds). 1996. *Selected Readings in HRD*, New Delhi: Tata McGraw-Hill Publishing Company Limited.

# 'MENTORING AND COACHING' PREPPING THE NEXT GENERATION THROUGH MENTORING

*Mentoring is a brain to pick, an ear to listen, and a push in the right direction.*
—John Crosby

## Intent

- To provide psychological support to the subordinate and new entrants of the organisation to get accustomed and work in a new organisational environment.
- To provide a work relationship that encourages development and career enhancement for people moving through the career cycle.
- To support the junior management and middle management to build competency for moving laterally in the organisations for career development.

## Expression

A mentor is an individual who provides guidance coaching, counselling and friendship to a protégé. Mentoring is defined as a relationship of a mentor (organisation member) who can share, guide and provide feedback to the mentee. Coaching is defined as bringing out the best in a person and improving personal skills.

## Comprehension

The word 'mentor' appeared in Homer's Greek classic, the *Odyssey*, while Odyssey is away at the Trojan War, Mentor serves as a tutor and guide to his son. The dictionary meaning of mentor is *'a close, trusted and experienced counsellor or guide'*. The current method of management development, which is being advocated throughout the world, include skills of mentoring and coaching. Mentoring in the organisational context involves deliberate pairing of the experienced and skilled staff with the less experienced. Mentor is a person who enters into an informal contact with the learner and gives independent advice affecting the learner. The meetings go on for a long time and the details of the meeting are kept very confidential.

Mentoring provides for proper induction of the new incumbent into the organisation and enables him to adjust with the organisation culture. Since the mentor is revered for the qualities and skills he possesses, the new incumbent is likely to imbibe which will create performance orientation. The mentor will have satisfaction that he is being recognised as a learned man, gains confidence by helping others to grow and in the process develop his own knowledge and skills by updating what is new.

Organisational mentoring may be formal or informal. Informally, of course, middle and senior level managers often voluntarily take up and coach employees coming under their wings not only to train them but also to give career advice and to steer them through political pitfalls. Many employers also establish a formal mentoring programme. Here employers actively encourage mentoring relationship to take place and may, in fact, pair protégés with potential matters. Role modelling occurs when the mentor displays a behaviour pattern for the protégé to emulate. This facilitates social learning.

Mentoring has had a strong impact in shaping the identities of many firms. Many companies are moving towards formal mentoring programmes. It requires a set of skills that include the role of a coach, i.e., counsellor, networker or facilitator. Benefits to be gained from mentoring are obvious and include managerial effectiveness, communication improvement and promotion of equal opportunities and self-learning.

Coaching and mentoring are the aspects which everyone needs from time to time. No matter where and in what position one is, each one of us needs a support from a person whom you can rely and relate with. Mentoring is such a process that gives us a direction from the dilemma that we face in day-to-day organisation and personal life. Mentoring is a voluntary process but these days it has increasing acceptability in the corporations. There are special sessions organised by the HR to generate awareness about mentoring. Mentoring helps reducing individuals' issues, which are bothering them and it also helps seeing the situation with practical approach. Mentoring is a technology; it requires maturity and understanding of managing individuals' problems and competencies to relate with the employee seeking mentoring, hence it is strategic in nature. Good mentoring practices in many large corporations has helped reducing employees' turnover, brought teamwork and an increase in organisational commitment.

# Experiential Application

## A. Prerequisite

- A good mentor is able to perform any one of the many supportive roles. The major mentoring functions include that of the trainer, sounding board, coach, counsellor, and political advisor.
- The mentor should not be an immediate supervisor or in a direct reporting line with the mentee.
- Mentoring must be purely voluntary; it cannot be implemented forcefully on anyone. Similarly to accept the mentor or to be a mentee should also be a voluntary decision.
- It is not necessary that the mentor is responsible for the success or failure of the mentee. The mentee must set the pace of the process of making mentoring effective.
- If the mentee does not approach the mentor at all, the mentor cannot play any role to help the mentee.
- The most important point in the success of mentoring is that the mentor should become obsolete as soon as possible. This indicates that the mentee can now live on his own and does not require any mentoring support.

## B. Process Steps

| Step | Process |
| --- | --- |
| Step – I | Organisation identifies the employees/new incumbents requiring support in the mentoring process. |
| Step – II | Organisation identifies the competent mentor. |
| Step – III | Proper training is imparted to both mentor and mentee explaining the role, relationship and goal congruence. |
| Step – IV | Each mentor is assigned with one mentee and they are left for working out their own process. |
| Step – V | Taking the feedback from the mentor and mentee to evaluate the process. |

# Potential Gains and Areas of Concern

- Mentoring enhances self-esteem for the mentor. It is a respect from the organisation.

- Mentoring brings in new perspective to the job for the mentor. Mentor leaves his/her mark on the organisation.
- Mentee can plan his/her professional development activities with the mentor rather then doing it alone.
- Mentee can take correct decision and spend less time since with the help of the mentor, who knows the organisation well would arrive at right decision faster.
- Mentoring is an art in which each mentor passes on his/her insights and skills in the way that is unique to that mentor.
- Mentor has to spend a lot of time, which hinders pursuing his/her own objectives.
- Mentor can sometimes so strongly identify with the mentee that mentee's decision becomes normally the mentor's decisions and for the mentee, it becomes difficult to be in a favoured position.
- Mentee would be in a difficult situation if the mentor does not keep to the commitment and put up unreal expectations.
- There are many different opinions regarding what mentoring is, such as, who should conduct it, and what are its values and functions.

# Measurability

## Try It Out

(1: not at all done, 2: moderately done, 3: to some extent done, 4: to a great extent done, 5: excellently done)

- Periodic analysis of employees' satisfaction is done in my organisation          ☐
  through planned surveys.
- Requirement of support and guidance is understood by management and          ☐
  hence the mentoring programme is placed in the company.
- Mentors are chosen based on their competencies and also given additional          ☐
  input for effective managing process.
- Mentees are given fair opportunity to interact with mentors and their          ☐
  majority of the issues are being managed through the mentoring process.
- A definite improvement in the employees satisfaction level is observed          ☐
  after the mentoring programme is put in practice by the company.

Analysis: the average score would determine the extent to which mentoring and coaching process exist in your organisation.

## Score Card

(**\***: 25% achieved, **\*\***: 50% achieved, **\*\*\***: 75% achieved, **\*\*\*\***: 100% achieved)

| Technology | Objective Elements | Unit | Historical | Last Year | Current Year | Stretch Target | Status |
|---|---|---|---|---|---|---|---|
| Mentoring and Coaching | Mentoring System | Doc | Nil | No | Yes | NA | ** |

# Proven Track Record

## Track One

### Brinker International

Mentoring is a key element of Brinker's ability to establish a fast growing restaurant like 'Chillies'. Part of the management's philosophy is to face bright, energetic young people in positions of higher authority and then coach them through a mentor/student relationship. The influence of Norman Brinker's mentoring can be seen all over top restaurant chains and many of his protégés are referred to as the Brinker Boys. Brinker uses casual dining method which tries to help everyone who wants to learn. Mentoring is one way Norman Brinker was able to sustain a high level of performance through out his career.

(*Source*: Nelson and Quick, 2003: 569.)

## Track Two

### Eli Lilly

At Eli Lilly, an executive mentoring process has been put in place to encourage senior decision makers to actively support the learning and development of potential junior managers. A primary objective of this initiative is to actively develop high potential women and minorities for executive positions. Recognising that in all likelihood senior executives needed help in learning how to build relationships across gender and racial boundaries and how to facilitate others' learning of personal and social competencies, the executive development staff has continuously offered training and follow-up meeting that provides this critical support. In this way the human resource components of the organisation is contributing to the potential of development relationships to enhance emotional competencies.

(*Source*: Cherniss and Goleman, 2001: 221.)

# Applied HR Case—'Qualify for Mentoring'

## Softech Solutions

Softech Solutions is a software company with 1,200 employees working round the clock to meet the software requirements of the clients who include the fortune 500 companies. Established about eight years ago, the company has grown to be one of the best software companies. The recent employee satisfaction survey conducted to know the feedback of the people is the cause of concern for the top management. Compensation, training, welfare measures, etc., were given good rating but when it comes to career opportunities it is as low as 26 per cent, which shook every one from HR to the top management. They found that the present career opportunities is not meeting the expectations of the employees which may be one of the causes for the attrition in the organisation, since the compensation, training and welfare are being taken care. The feedback is clear that there will be performance implications since they are not satisfied with the jobs and career opportunities in the organisation. Softech also recognises that in order to make the organisation competitive they need to develop certain competencies, which are vital to have a sustained competitive advantage. The market is also not responding to the requirement of the organisations since the people with the skill set are not available.

To bring in a sense of ownership and growth in the organisation Softech approached HR Consultants who also did the ESS for them. After careful study, they have suggested to have mentoring process where many high performing employees will have a mentor to take care of their career prospects and learning. The seniors will have mentors from the external sources, where as the internal employees will be mentored by select seniors. Besides the mentoring, Softech has also carried career prospects workshops throughout the organisation explaining the growth that the organisation gives provided the skill set is being developed.

## Questions

1. Do you think that career opportunities are the concern of Softech?
2. If you were the HR Head of Softech, can you think of alternatives to Mentoring?
3. If you are asked to handle the mentoring process for the whole organisation, please give a method; time frame and action plan to implement the process.

# References and Further Readings

Caldwell, B. and E. Carter (eds). 1993. *The Return of Mentor: Strategies for Workplace Learning*, London: The Falmer Press.

Cherniss, C. and Daniel Goleman. 2001. *The Emotionally Intelligent Workplace: How to Select for, Measure, and Improve Emotional Intelligence in Individuals, Groups, and Organizations*, CA: Jossey-Bass.

Choen, Norman. 2002. *Effective Mentoring*, Mumbai: Jaico Publishing House.

Clutterbuck, D. 1991. *Everyone Needs a Mentor*, 2nd edn, London: IPM.

Hamilton, Reg. 1993. *Mentoring: A Practical Guide to the Skills of Mentoring*, New Delhi: Sterling Publications.

MacLennan, Nigel. 1997. *Handbook of Coaching and Mentoring*, Mumbai: Jaico Publishing House.

Megginson, D. and D. Clutterbuck. 1995. *Mentoring in Action: A Practical Guide for Managers*, London: Kogan Page.

Nelson, D.L. and J.C. Quick. 2003. *Organizational Behavior: Foundations, Realities, and Challenges*, Ohio: Thomson Learning.

Parsloe, E. 1995. *Coaching, Mentoring and Assessing—A Practical Guide to Developing Competence*, London: Kogan Page.

Whittaker, Mike and Ann Cartwright. 2000. *The Mentoring Manual*, London: Gower Publishing Limited.

# Appendix-18A

## 'Mentoring and Coaching'

### Mentoring Aptitude Survey Tool

**Instructions:** Statements given below pertain to effective mentoring. Please read each item carefully and circle the number on the scale that corresponds with how much you agree with the statement. As this is an important questionnaire please fill in the responses without any prejudice as there are no right or wrong answers, but this is merely a tool to identify your attitude to become a mentor.

**Scale:** Strongly Disagree-1; Disagree-2; Neutral-3; Agree-4; Strongly Agree-5

1. I am both people oriented and task oriented.
2. I am a good listener.
3. During my weekdays I spend my time with my friends and help them out in their problems.
4. I always learn new things and help others to learn.
5. I extend all possible support to enable my subordinates to make decisions.
6. I know my areas of strengths and weaknesses and how I can help others.
7. I sympathise with others' problems but try to help others in finding a solution rather than only being a sympathiser.
8. I feel that it is my duty to help others to develop professionally.
9. I am always recognised as a professional.
10. I understand the organisational structure and am comfortable with peers, superiors and subordinates.
11. I feel happy in doing my job and also assist others in doing theirs.
12. I can recognise when people need guidance and when they can become independent.
13. I am good at working out alternatives and making decisions.
14. I am patient when working with the others' problems and concerns.
15. I have actively sought mentors myself.

*Interpretation Sheet*:

There is no predetermined score for qualifying to become a mentor, but the survey gives you a feel for how ready you are to become a mentor.

If your score is between **75 and 61**: You clearly have the awareness and confidence to become a mentor. You understand the need for a mentor in an organisation who has the ability to coach and guide the new incumbents.

If your score is between **60 and 46**: You have the necessary skills and perspectives to provide mentoring but still need some experience. You need to build confidence in certain areas by looking at your strengths and working on them.

If your score is between **45 and 30**: You have the ambition and talent to be a mentor, but require a lot of improvement. You can talk to your mentor of how to become an effective mentor.

If your score is between **29 and 0**: Your ambition to become a mentor is good but you need to do lot of pre-work before taking up the responsibilities of a mentor. If you do not have a mentor yourself, actively seek one out who can show you the secrets of mentoring. You can also undergo a formal mentoring training process.

# 'TRANSFORMATIONAL LEADERSHIP' BUILDING LEADERSHIP THROUGH TRANSFORMATIONAL LEADERSHIP

*The prince is like the wind and the people like the grass; it is the nature of grass to bend with the wind.*

—Confucius, *Analects* (6th century BC)

## Intent

- To understand transformational leadership and its model.
- To examine how leadership style can revitalise the organisation.
- To analyse the usage of transformational leadership in different situations within the organisation.

## Expression

Transformational leadership means a leader having charismatic qualities uses them to transform and revitalise the organisations. These leaders have the ability to innovate and change by challenging the people with exceptionally high levels of morality, motivation and performance.

## Comprehension

James McGregor Burns in 1978 in his famous book *Leadership* drew distinction between transactional leadership and transformational leadership. A transactional leader operates within the existing system or culture, has a preference for risk avoidance, and generally prefers process over substance as a means of maintaining control. Such type of leadership is suitable in a stable and predictable environment where the strategy is to maintain the status quo. Transformational leaders, on the other hand, are those who use charisma to motivate the followers highly and seek new ways of working so as to achieve more for both themselves and from the followers. In this process both the leader and followers raise one another to higher levels of motivation. It results in increasing the morality of the collective group to transcend the individual and result in the achievement of significant changes in the effectiveness of the work unit.

The transformational leader always seek new ways of working, seek opportunities by facing the risk and always want change rather than maintaining status quo. The leaders try to induce and raise our level of awareness, consciousness about the significance and value of designated outcomes of the followers; raising individual needs and inducing them to transcend self-interest for the sake of the organisation. Due to rising expectations and needs, the followers of the transformational leaders tend to perform better and report greater satisfaction than those of transactional leaders. The followers possessing certain freedom and needs tend to develop autonomy within the leader's vision and demonstrate free choice in behaviour and empowerment. By giving them the authority, the leader motivates them to think 'out of box' to challenge their values and beliefs and think in new ways.

The qualities possessed by the transformational leader are: creating a *vision*, *inspiring* about the vision and encouraging thinking of ideas or problems by *stimulating* and *coaching* people to take greater responsibility for developing and improving the performance. Bass developed an instrument to measure both transactional and transformational leader's behaviour to investigate the nature of relationship between these two relationships in terms of styles, work unit effectiveness and satisfaction. He named the questionnaire as Multifactor Leadership Questionnaire (MLQ) which was able to differentiate between the two kinds of leaders. The tool is validated through study in various research, organisations and military institutions and stood the test of time. The transformational leadership affects organisational effectiveness in diverse cultures and organisations.

Leadership as taught in the classroom having examples of the world's political, business and spiritual leadership has a limitation in practical life. Leadership as portraits of certain qualities cannot be practised in a given situation. Business, today, demands leadership which can bring about change and transformation. The solution lies only with the transformation leadership process. It evaluates the scenario and situation to determine the kind of leadership quality required. Transformation leadership is totally situation based and is quite flexible in nature since in the organisation's context leadership depends on the situation. Variation in leadership style with changing scenario and change in management is essential and this technology evaluates the same in detail.

# Experiential Application

## A. Prerequisite

- Transformational leadership is an answer to the rapid changes in economy, effecting the functioning of organisations; hence an organisation must be receptive to a vibrant leadership style and be prepared to change.
- The old bonds of loyalty and relations are broken and the organisation must encourage the employees towards greater performance and commitment.
- The new economy demands 'out of box' thinking to do things in newer ways and methods to improvise the process which is possible only through a leader who can inspire, raise the expectations and motivate the employees towards achievement.
- Development of such transformational leaders is a must. The organisation would be at its best if the organisation is lead by such a leader, if not, the organisation must look at developing such leaders.

## B. Process Steps

| Step | Process |
| --- | --- |
| Step – I | The management identifies the transformational leaders within the organisation having requisite qualities. |
| Step – II | A learning workshop on Transformational Leadership to be organised for the selected one and transformation leadership traits and its effectiveness to be taught. |
| Step – III | Management to analyse periodically the qualities of transformational leaders. |
| Step – IV | Leaders to apply the techniques of transformational leadership in their functioning. |

# Potential Gains and Areas of Concern

- Transformational leadership process helps in bringing turnaround and creating a new culture in the organisation.
- Transformational leadership provides an atmosphere of empowerment, freedom and taking challenges to achieve higher form of goals and thereby achieving the stretch targets.
- Transformational leaders when exist at the middle and/or lower level may cause the problem of hierarchy and may lead to disobeying or intimidating.
- Transformational leadership processes cannot be successful where the culture is status quo oriented.

# Measurability

## Try It Out

(1: not at all done, 2: moderately done, 3: to some extent done, 4: to a great extent done, 5: excellently done)

- If we have to choose a few transformational leaders from within my organisation, I am able to identify a handful of leaders.  ☐
- Our organisation believes in developing leadership from within which reflects on the upgradation of the internal leadership.  ☐
- A great deal of emphasis is given on training and development of leadership style development for many of us to take up future leadership positions.  ☐
- My organisation has experienced that leadership is the key in making difference and can sustain a company to grow in the competitive environment.  ☐
- My organisation avoids, to the extent possible, lateral entry of leadership and encourages growth of leadership within.  ☐

Analysis: the average score would determine the extent to which Transformational Leadership process exists in your organisation.

## Score Card

(*: 25% achieved, **: 50% achieved, ***: 75% achieved, ****: 100% achieved)

| Technology | Objective Elements | Unit | Historical | Last Year | Current Year | Stretch Target | Status |
|---|---|---|---|---|---|---|---|
| Transformational Leadership | Number of Leaders Identified | No | Nil | 10 | 15 | 18 | ** |

# Proven Track Record

## Track One

## Este'e Lauder Cosmetics

Este'e Lauder has transformed the cosmetic business and she accounts for 45 per cent of the cosmetic business of cosmetics markets in US Departmental Stores over a period of more than 50 years, three times as much as the company's closest competitor. When founding her mesmerising ways were influential in getting counter space in some of the most exclusive departmental stores. It is through her charisma that she was able to make the organisation one of the leading cosmetics manufacturers.

(*Source*: Greenberg and Baron, 2004: 489.)

## Track Two

## St Charles Medical Systems

Jim Lussier, Chief Executive Officer of St Charles Medical Systems (SCMS), Oregon has captivated the people all over the world because of his vision and breakthrough results causing many to question existing paradigms. The breakthrough results of lower costs, reduced length of stay, higher patient satisfaction, award-winning service and a waiting list of nursed desiring employment, all demonstrate the skills of leading trans-formation and building an organisation of meaning. SCMS was able to breathe new life into the possibility that authentic caring can return to a medical system, which for many patients and their families is currently sterile and heartless. And for many doctors, nurses, and other categories, the medical systems in which they exercise their vocations are frequently places where the spirit is thwarted. St Charles Medical Systems under Jim's leadership has created something quite different from the norm in health care ser-vices. Jim employed 250 task forces to look at how existing care processes and hospital procedures must change to serve patients better.

Through this five-year effort, Jim and his staff redefined healthcare delivery by rec-ognising that the spirit of love and compassion must be partnered with technology and intellect in healing the body. Every process and hospital procedure was re-engineered and the staff was trained in patient-relationship-centred approach to care. Innovation and experimentation was encouraged among the staff and creativity continues to flourish.

(*Source*: Hacker and Roberts, 2003: 13.)

## Track Three

## Mary Kay Limited

Mary Kay a single mother established the company in her name, which is into direct selling. Her success is being attributed to her charismatic leadership of being an orator, reputation for hard work, struggling with adversity and giving meaning to the lives of the distributors by appealing to higher ideals of women's independence. She also made innovative reward schemes of target achievement, rewarding with things which they value and is making *'female friendly'*. The organisation has enabled women to compete with men on equal footing and in fact the company has women earning more than 50,000$ than any other US company. The outstanding employees are given pink Cadillacs, holidays, jewellery and expensive clothes in carefully staged *'Pageant Nights'*.

(*Source*: Shackleton, 1995: 116.)

## Track Four

## Chrysler Corporation

One of the most dramatic examples of transformational leadership and organisational revitalisation is the leadership of Lee Iacocca, the Chairman of Chrysler Corporation. He provided the leadership to transform a company from the brink of bankruptcy to profitability. He created a vision of success and mobilised large factions of key employees toward enacting that vision. To bail out the company, Lee has taken guaranteed loan and he has decided to change the organisational culture from a loser to a winner. Lee extensively used internal communication as a vehicle to signal change but also his personal appearance in Chrysler advertisements to reinforce the changes. The internal culture changed to that of a lean and hungry team looking for victory. As a result of his leadership the company had made a turnaround and made profits, attained high levels of employee morale and helped employees generate a sense of meaning in their work.

(*Source*: Tichy and Ulrich, 2001.)

# Applied HR Case—'Leap First Ask Later'

## Catharine Corporation

Catharine was born and bought up in a middle class family. Her father was a teacher in the school and mother used to work in a departmental store. Her father was a true nationalist and used to tell stories of the leaders who fought for justice and independence. He used to always say that one has to take the name of the country high whether it can be in the field of politics, business, literature, etc. Being brought up in such an atmosphere, Catharine obtained her masters degree in Business Management from the premier schools. Since her childhood because of upbringing, she had a vision to make big and raise the name of the country in that field. Her vision is being appreciated at school and college levels and teachers used to encourage her.

Catharine had taken up a job in a financial firm as a business analyst, but she was not satisfied by the job since she wanted to pursue her dream. Instead of cursing herself for working in a financial company, she started strengthening her dream by coming in touch with various venture capitalists and bankers. Soon the clients started identifying her name rather than the company and she became the most wanted by the employees and customers of the company.

Catharine was getting a good name but she was not satisfied with the job since she had a vision to make it big and one day in an informal meeting she had shared her vision to two of her colleagues Kim and Nelson. Both of them started getting interested in her plans and they also started crystallising her thoughts to start a firm which no one had ventured, an area which was critical and had a lot of scope to develop. Catharine decided to venture into Artificial Intelligence and Robotics where there was a lot of scope for development and could create a niche for her. Her vision was to take the technology to every house where her product would be made available. To ensure that there is continuous flow of money she wanted to make dolls of various types so that the children may enjoy, get a name for herself and the company and finally the cash flow.

Catharine shared her vision with one of the professors of Artificial Intelligence and he assured that he will be part of the team in giving technical advice and also enable her to set up the industry. Catharine, owing to her contacts, was able to get sufficient funds from bankers and venture capitalists and thus was successful in creating Catharine Corporation. She started with 20 employees and while recruiting she would look whether the incumbent had a vision, because she always felt that a person with vision could work with zeal and commitment.

Her initial products of dolls were an instant success since they were cute and affordable. Soon she spread her products to various departmental stores across the country and she was in the news. Catharine alternatively worked on robots where they could be applied in automobile manufacturing, packaging, etc. Initially she had a problem in convincing about the product and the value addition it will bring in, but soon the industrial robots were also a hit. Not satisfied with the achieved success she expanded her network to other countries and soon she was in 54 countries selling her products. In spite of her busy schedule she always used to attend the induction of the new recruits and interacted with each one to know whether they had any vision and she used to tell her story of how vision can help in making big in the life. She used to motivate the new recruits to expand their purview and look towards higher goals for mutual benefit. Her efforts and vision has made Catharine truly a global company.

## Questions

1. What are the qualities that Catharine possess to become successful in her life?
2. Do you think that Catharine has transformational leadership qualities? Why?

# References and Further Readings

Bhargava, Shivganesh. 2003. *Transformational Leadership Value Based Management for Indian Organizations*, New Delhi: Response Books.

Bushe, Gervase R. 2002. *Clear Leadership*, Mumbai: Jaico Publishing House.

Greenberg, Jerald and Robert Baron. 2004. *A Behavior in Organizations*, Delhi: Pearson Education (Singapore) Pvt. Ltd.

Hacker, Stephen and Tammy Roberts. 2003. *Transformational Leadership—Creating Organizations of Meaning*, Wisconsin: ASQ Quality Press.

Hersey, Paul H., Kenneth H. Blanchard and Dewey E. Johnson. 2002. *Management of Organization Behavior—Leading Human Resources*, New Delhi: Prentice Hall of India Private Limited.

Hersey, Paul. 1996. *Situational Leader*, Malaysia: Synergy Books International.

Lynton, Rolf P. and Udai Pareek. 2000. *Training for Organizational Transformation*, New Delhi: Sage Publications.

Pearman, Roger R. 1999. *Hard Wired Leadership*, Mumbai: Jaico Publishing House.

Shackleton, Viv. 1995. *Business Leadership*, London: Routledge.

Tichy, Noel M. and David O. Ulrich. 2001. 'The Leadership Challenge—A Call for the Transformational Leader', Craig M. Watson (ed.), *Dynamics of Leadership*, Mumbai: Jaico Publishing House.

Watson, Craig M. (ed.). 2001. *Dynamics of Leadership*, Mumbai: Jaico Publishing House.

# 'SELF-MANAGED TEAM'
# IMPARTING THE SENSE OF
# ENTREPRENEURSHIP THROUGH A
# SELF-MANAGED TEAM

*When spider webs unite, they can tie up a lion.*

—Ethiopian proverb

## Intent

- To promote business culture that can adapt quickly and react wisely to a competitive market.
- To bring in decentralisation over achievements of goals and decision making responsibilities through a team approach.
- Having team of employees solving problem without the intervention of the management to save company time and fill its employees with a sense of trust and empowerment.

## Expression

Self-managed teams (SMT) are highly trained workgroup that use consensus decision-making and broad authority to self direct their activities. The group assumes greater autonomy and responsibility for effective performance of the group.

## Comprehension

With increasing waves of decentralisation from centralisation culture, the organisational decision-making is now vested horizontally and vertically through the lowest strata in the organisational hierarchies. If an organisation wants to succeed in a competitive environment, managing business should be left to individuals and teams who are straight in the marketplace, but not to those sitting in the corporate offices.

Since, the organisation has multifunctional roles at each location and unit where they operate, it becomes necessary that each representative of the functions collaborates together and operates on a common goal. Normally, each individual operates on isolation with different key result areas or key performance indicators to achieve. The self-managed team is the solution to such flaw, which is by design or default built in the organisation structure of any company. Organisations that are highly technology oriented finds easy to get the work done through small but close-knit group whose goals are high and are linked to the unit's performance. These groups are formal, permanent organisational units. Members of SMT handle their own job responsibilities and specialised tasks to carry out interdependently. The teams decide their own leader, solve job-related problems, design jobs, plan work, control material and inventory, maintain equipment, improve quality and work methods and take break as decided among them.

Self-managed teams are empowered to manage themselves and their daily work. Empowering the team and enriching their jobs enable them to commit to the goals. Empowerment gives them the skills, authority and discretion to perform their tasks. Job enrichment allows them to change their job content, building challenges and achievement orientation to look into their own schedules. Empowerment without skills is a sham and the team is provided with sufficient decision-making skills and training to enable them to perform a new role. Job enrichment by way of changing their job content, building challenges and achievement orientation into the team would enable them to inspect what they have produced, make their own balance sheets and deliver the results. Proper documentation, flow charts and the total details of the tasks that need to be accomplished are given to plan their assignments. Training is the tool that makes them a better team and it is continuous to enable them to discharge the responsibility and authority.

Management however must clearly define their boundaries of authority. It is important that the top management provides an appropriate team structure and facilitate the move towards the decision making to the lowest level. The managers must allow the team to use their authority to do their jobs and not to interfere in their activities. The management must provide continuous training to the team members to adapt to the new roles, otherwise the chances of failing is very high. The management must allow free and fair communication with the SMT to gain their commitment to the goals as these groups work with sufficient autonomy linked to the organisational goals. The team must be aware of the organisational priorities and plans. Management should have absolute trust and must take all steps to disseminate the information and authority. To make the SMT to be effective, an incentive plan needs to be placed on achievement of certain goals, creating newer benchmarks and improvement in the processes. The SMT must decide the sharing of the incentive itself.

Organisation structures are undergoing changes and more refinement based on the context and complexities are done. Unbundling of business, decentralised decision making, formation of special task forces, independent profit centres, etc., are the latest phenomenon in the business processes. Empowering a group of people in the frame of a team and allowing them to operate independently to take all decisions regarding business is the underline principle behind the SMT concept. An organisation which has a long-term vision and have belief in team, the SMT is the right solution for adaptation.

# Experiential Application

## A. Prerequisite

- An organisation that wants to have SMT needs to transit slowly and carefully. It is a process that must be supported by training initiative.
- The management must develop a clear vision of where they want to lead their organisation to and a plan to accomplish their goal.
- The SMT has its own income and expenditure and therefore would generate fund and spend money and thus bring profitability or loss.
- The decision of performance lies with the leader and the team member. Since the income and expenditure is controlled by SMT itself, the team must strategise its functional efficiency and effectiveness, which could bring them a healthy bottom-line and thus organisational productivity.
- Initially people might tend to resist the SMT idea because they perceive it as a threat. Knowing and understanding these fears or failure will help SMT to mitigate them. A strategy should be drawn to provide the members of SMT with a clear sense of the future direction. This will help them understand where they stand.
- Emphasise any small success. A series of small success will make people more receptive to change.

  - Experiment with new approaches and welcome positive change.
  - Use outside resources and benchmark other organisations.
  - Encourage breakthrough thinking and overcome self-limiting paradigms.
  - Encourage risk taking and learning from honest mistakes, do not punish people for making errors.
  - Seek creative and novel solutions.

■ De-emphasise status symbols, e.g., reserved executive parking space, dining areas, rest rooms, etc.

## B. Process Steps

| Step | Process |
|------|---------|
| Step – I | Identification of the need and the requirement of SMT and the determination of top management for implementation. |
| Step – II | Mapping of the process to identify and formalise the team structure and its authority and responsibility. |
| Step – III | Define roles, responsibilities, norms, standards and expectations from the SMT. |
| Step – IV | Training to be provided to SMT on team, technical, management and other backward areas in a systematic manner. |
| Step – V | Periodically reviewing and revisiting the process and providing proper inputs to streamline the process. |
| Step – VI | To build in control process, monetary awards, process flow and continuous monitoring untill the stage of maturity. |
| Step – VII | Delegate responsibility and full-fledged SMT only when the team is ready to accept the responsibility. |

# Potential Gains and Areas of Concern

- The SMT denotes independence and empowered approach. Each one of the SMT manages themselves and the entire team.
- It brings in a change in the process of managing the business which is decentralised and acts like a strategic business unit (SBU).
- The SMT is not a replacement of functions, but it's a collaboration of functions.
- As the process from formation to action to results is time-consuming, it requires a lot of patience, but once it starts, it surges ahead leaving behind all the erstwhile benchmarks.
- The SMT needs to be operationalised very cautiously by way of scanning the environment, studying organisational culture, market scenario and business process itself.
- It is a major cultural change away from traditional hierarchies and bringing in dimensions of openness and sharing. The SMT are not panaceas of the problems, as it has its own weaknesses, which need to be addressed to ensure its success.

# Measurability

## Try It Out

(1: not at all done, 2: moderately done, 3: to some extent done, 4: to a great extent done, 5: excellently done)

- Many of our business decisions are taken through team approach. ☐
- Our organisation has formal mechanism for formation of team and its evaluation process. ☐
- Our organisation has many teams in place and the SMT is one of such an innovative process. ☐
- All the members of the teams and their leaders are trained thoroughly on the functioning of the SMT and they are evaluated as well. ☐
- Management takes all the interest of effective functioning of the SMT and invests sufficient time to review its process. ☐

Analysis: the average score would determine the extent to which the SMT process exists in your organisation.

## Score Card

(*: 25% achieved, **: 50% achieved, ***: 75% achieved, ****: 100% achieved)

| Technology | Objective Elements | Unit | Historical | Last Year | Current Year | Stretch Target | Status |
|---|---|---|---|---|---|---|---|
| SMT | Team Document | Doc | Nil | No | Yes | NA | ** |
| | Number of SMTs | No | Nil | 2 | 3 | 3 | ** |

# Proven Track Record

## Track One

### Harley–Davidson

Harley–Davidson was facing competitive pressure like never before and the motor cycle manufacturer had to make radical changes in the way it conducted the business when it opened its Kansas City plant. These required unique partnerships with the union, the establishment of self-managed teams and a revamping of the organisation culture. The true taste could only be measured in terms of results. The manufacturing productivity increased by 88 per cent, production cost decline between 35–45 per cent, and the dealer preparation work was cut in half. Most significantly, customer satisfaction with Harley–Davidson sportster went up by 200 per cent. The 16–24 months' waiting period that customers have had earlier had declined to less than two weeks.

Inside the organisation, the progress was made in moving from a traditional and command and control culture towards shared decision making, team oriented environment. Employee satisfaction is at its highest levels, the employees feel more empowered than ever. The changes at Harley–Davidson did not happen quickly or easily. They required extensive planning, shared leadership, and many organisation development efforts. They also required partnership with the unions and commitment to changing the culture. Harley–Davidson has faith that the culture of self-managed team would allow it to continue to manage the challenge of global competition.

(*Source*: Nelson and Quick, 2003.)

## Track Two

## Hewlett-Packard

Hewlett-Packard is a good example of teamwork. Although the firm has long been admired as one of the best companies in America, its distribution organisation was second rate. On an average, it took 26 days for an HP product to reach the customer. The employee had to shuttle information through a tangle of 70 computer systems. This is when the company decided to recognise the distribution system and reduce delivery time. A team of 35 employees was drawn together and they began examining the workflow. They examined the current process and began noting the ways of eliminating work steps and shortening the process.

The team completed the two-week training and orientation programme to familiarise team member with the current process. Then the team redesigned the entire work process and finally, they implemented the process and made changes to correct errors remaining in the system. In the process, they were allowed to empower the workforce and managed to get delivery time down to eight days. This enabled the firm to cut its inventories by nearly 20 per cent while increasing the service levels to customers.

(*Source*: Luthans, 2002: 478.)

# Applied HR Case —'Sea Change'

## Ken Food

Ken Food is into the processing and canning of fruits and selling worldwide. The company has attained laurels because of the quality and the packing. The quality is uniform in all the batches and all the varieties are being made with utmost care. Kim was working in Japan in an electronic manufacturing company and was keen to come back to his native country and was looking for an opportunity. Through an advertisement in the Internet he appeared for the interview and got selected as Production Manager of one of the units. Kim was very happy to go back and was looking for a glorious career since Ken food is well known all over the major cities.

Kim completed one month of service and when he was analysing the productivity of the plant he was handling, he was surprised to find that the costs were very high and the profit margin on each product was very low. He observed that there was too much of manpower and various other processes which were not necessary and could be cut down. He found that the people were enterprising and could understand the issues faced by the company.

Kim made a plan to organise the production not on the lines of the production line but on the team concept. He discussed with the MD about the new process, which if implemented would increase the profitability by 35 per cent while reducing the manpower and the processes. The MD was quiet impressed by the new method of production planning and asked Kim to prepare an action plan to implement the same in his unit, and if it was successful the same process would be implemented across all the units.

## Questions

1. Do you agree with Kim that a change in the production process would enhance the profitability and reduce the cost and the manpower?
2. If you were Kim, prepare an action plan addressing the cultural and behavioural issues during the implementation.

## References and Further Readings

Bone, Diane and Robert F. Hicks. 1990. *Self-Managing Teams*, California: Crisp Publishing Inc.

Luthans, Fred. 2002. *Organizational Behavior*, New York: McGraw-Hill.

Nelson, D.L. and J.C. Quick. 2003. *Organizational Behavior: Foundations, Realities and Challenges*, Ohio: Thompson Learning.

Osburn, Jack, Linda Moran, Ed Musselwhite and John H. Zenger. 1990. 'Self Directed Work Teams', *Business One*, Illinois: Irwin.

Wilson, Patricia. 1996. *Empowering the Self Directed Team*, England: Gower Publishing Limited.

# Spectrum III
## HR Technologies for Attracting and Retaining Talent

Companies are investing today in efforts to heighten the employees' sensitivity to customers, and to develop their skills in listening and interpreting the customer input. They are training them to align customer needs with the process required to deliver products and services that the customer will value. In future, the new recruits will be expected to exhibit these capabilities or have the capacity to develop them in a short time. For example, in addition to training current employees on communication skills, the senior management group at Searle's American Division is reformulating its recruitment criteria. New hires will need to have the skills to carry out specific functions, but the management will also be looking for people who have grounding in business finance and economics, as well as the basics of the pharmaceutical industry. They want people who are team players, have listening skills, can deal with ambiguity, can make concrete decisions in a fluid environment, and can be creative and innovative within an overarching set of business and boundaries.

The people resources are scarce resources and it is always difficult to build the right kind of cadre in the company, despite all efforts being made by the company. The reason is simple that people resources are free to choose their own destiny by way of employment in one organisation to another. No law could forbid any employee to choose a company and to leave a company. Therefore, in such circumstances, attracting and retaining talent becomes a task equivalent to conquering Everest.

Attracting people from the vast ocean of labour force and labour market is something like choosing a star from a galaxy. You never know the life expectancy of a star and whether you are hitting the right spot in the bull's eye. Until you interview and make a person's placement on the job, the HR people keep their fingers cross whether the selected candidate would prove to be good or not, no matter whatever selection process and techniques are put into application. Similar analogy applies while retaining the people on the job. Having attracted and placed on the job, the difficult task starts of moulding them into the organisation culture. Keeping them motivated and vibrant is even more a challenging task. Organisational HR processes has to keep being innovative in the various ways and means through which the right kind of people are attracted and retained on the job.

This spectrum deals with how HR planning could consider to produce more with less, how the concept of pay for performance could be implemented, how competencies could be built and how could employee first rather than the customer in the organisational context be established. The complete spectrum comprising of 16 technologies divided into three broad chapters essentially deals with attracting and retaining talent.

# 6 DOING MORE WITH LESS

## Content

→ Learning Objectives
→ Effective Span of Control and Optimum Size
→ Bringing in the Right Attitude Rather than Skill
→ Selecting the Future CEO
→ Where Are We?
→ Enable SHR Technology—Key to Success

→ Conclusion

## Learning Objectives

- To understand the building of organisations around optimum size and productivity of employees through job design and Human Resource planning process.
- To make use of scientific selection techniques for the recruitment process.
- To draw a career and succession plan for the perspective growth of the employees.

- To develop clarity of role through role clarity and understanding advance performance management systems.
- To evaluate the implications of undertaking downsizing activity in the company.

# Effective Span of Control and Optimum Size

Theory of organisation and management can be dated back to the centuries, but has taken its concrete shape especially after the Industrial Revolution. The Industrial Revolution has created organisation structures, which are far complex than the previous ones. The standardised organisation hierarchy of most of the organisations was suitable for managing the employees when the growth rate of the product cycle was high. When the organisation grew, the method of enhancing production was by way of increasing more number of hands for production and also more people to manage them. Fredrick W. Taylor, father and guru of Scientific Management, has propounded various practices of producing more with less number of people by giving better incentives, organising work methods, etc.

With the growth in the demand for the products of mass production, the organisations just added the people at the bottom of the pyramid and increased the middle management accordingly. However, the middle management was bulky as their sole contribution was to manage the people below and give periodical reports to superiors. The management of such an organisation was simpler and easier because the tasks were divided and distributed among the employees and the management found it justifiable and easy to monitor smooth production. Since the tasks were simple and routine in nature the training of the employee had been reduced to a smaller extent.

As the number of tasks grew, however, the overall processes of producing a product or delivering a service inevitably became increasingly complicated and managing such a process became difficult. The mass production of goods in the line assembly has changed to customised products. The new technology is demanding employees who are more competent and have the requisite competencies. The middle level managers are normally involved in managing people working under them and sending reports upwards. They are fragmenting the structure between the top and bottom and are highly priced. Another cost is the increasing distance of senior management and the end users of the product or services. Due to the number of layers involved in reaching the complaint/request of the customers, their response to the company's strategy becomes a set of faceless numbers that bubbles up through layers.

Modern organisations are leaner and effective teams. Jobs need to be designed as per the requirement of the organisation. Job design has a tremendous impact on the effectiveness of the organisation and the quality of work life of the employees. Job design is the blueprint of the tasks required to accomplish the job successfully. This can be done with job analysis. It means obtaining all the necessary information about the job, the tasks to be done on the job and the personal characteristics like education, training, etc. If a clear clarification and demarcation is made with the interrelations, specifying the responsibilities, it would help in promoting efficiency and minimising overlap and duplication. Job design needs to be built with the overall strategy of the organisation. With frequent changes especially in a larger organisation and with a multitude of jobs to be performed, it is difficult to design an appropriate job. Also when any change takes place in technology, it reduces the quantitative job and increases the qualitative job.

## Bringing in the Right Attitude Rather than Skill

Recruitment and placement of right kind of manpower is always a challenge for any manager, as they have to keep the right people in the right job. The supply of competent manpower is always scarce and to select the right kind of candidate among the pool is an onerous job. Manpower planning is the process of acquiring and utilising Human Resources. It is the sum total of all the activities planned by recruitment, compensation, training, promotion and work rules. This manpower is being utilised for achieving the short-term and long-term goals of the organisation. Organisations can plan for manpower either proactively or react to the situation. Manpower planning can be done in advance by looking at the total manpower available for productive use and their skill sets. Taking into consideration the strategic business plans of the company, growth, market share, launch of new products, retrenchment and attrition, an organisation can plan for recruitment of manpower. The organisations start hiring for the manpower one or two years before, so that they can be groomed in the organisation culture for future projects.

Organisations have to take certain strategic decisions while initiating the recruitment process such as whether to bring people with right attitude and less skilled or pay more and get the skilled manpower. People with the right kind of skills and who have been already trained to do certain jobs would demand more compensation. The strategic advantage would be to give such an employee induction training and put them on to the job immediately. The new incumbent would immediately start giving the results. However, the dilemma is that whether one can fit into the culture of the organisation, go along with the teams and motivate the employees working with him.

The other way is to recruit less skilled employees or freshers and train them thoroughly to ensure standardisation. This would help in moulding the attitude of the new incumbent to the organisational culture and hence we may not get immediate replacement for any vacancy. Putting people with the right kind of attitude ensures proper teamwork. Organisations who does proper manpower planning, always keep a certain percentage of workforce as apprentice/trainees, who would be trained in all the areas of the organisation and as and when vacancy arises they could be put on to the job. Such a system incurs the cost of hiring certain percentage of employees as trainees and training them.

Mergers and acquisitions provide a challenge for the HR department, as the whole strategy has to change to suit the changed environment. There are conflicting corporate cultures which need to be assimilated—reconstitution of the employees, reassignment of jobs, transfers and retrenchment/lay offs.

Business Process Re-engineering has paved the way to look at the various processes involved in business and the necessity of various roles for a particular task. It is evaluating whether systems built in the organisation are delivering the value to the customers or not. This has given newer challenges to the HR. As explained above, re-engineering helps in looking at all the processes and tries to shred off all those roles, which does not add value. Automation has brought in the better ways of making things that needs less manpower and produce more, both qualitatively and quantitatively. These are the heart of the manpower planning. The task is much more complex when the organisation is very big and is divided into various divisions or Strategic Business Units. These units must also have their own HR planning in line with the corporate plan.

# Selecting the Future CEO

The task of selecting the candidates is an art, because, over a short span of time a manager is expected to select the right kind of candidate. As there is variability among the individual's abilities, aptitudes, interests and personality traits, we can only expect that similar candidates would perform comparably. Normally, the goal of any selection process is to identify applicants, who scores high on measures like assessing knowledge, skills, abilities or other characteristics that are important to job performance. However, in an organisation, there is assessment only once when an employee is being taken in and during the assessment centre for placement and promotion.

While selecting the candidate, the subjectivity would always be there, as managers are influenced by the culture, religion, origin, etc., which is detrimental to the interests of the organisation. One of the methods of objective evaluation is a psychological testing and questionnaires to test the intelligence. These tests are administered to assess the qualities of the candidate. Various aptitude tests are designed to the specific job to measure skills and abilities of the candidate. However, there has been a criticism that the verbal and mathematical knowledge needed to excel in these tests does not match with the skills required in a function. These tests need to be administered with great care and interpretation by experts only. There has been a debate about the validity and accuracy for predicting job behaviour of these tests. But increasingly, corporations are using psychometric tests as part of their recruitment and selection process, promotions and redundancy. These psychometric tests that are used, should be a part of the comprehensive selection process, and applied in appropriate circumstances to supplement other processes, rather than making it the only tool for enabling selection of the candidate. The organisation must plan the career over a span of time for the high potential employees. Everybody has their own unique traits and capabilities, and the career plan need to be made in such a way that it gives career growth. Men and women needs to be trained and made readily available to take up the challenges arising out of the exigencies or succession.

## **Where Are We?**

Periodical review of the performance enables the employee, to know how he is performing and meeting the standards in his job, and to the organisation, how far it has achieved the business plans. Performance appraisal is not only a tool for evaluating the work, but also for developing and motivating the employee, by linking it with financial rewards and planned career progression. Some of the employees, however, see the tool as an event to point out the mistakes while reviewing. A formal system would ensure periodical assessment, highlight individual potential to carry out higher responsibilities and identify the training and development needs. The tool brings both the appraisee and the Reporting Officer to mutually agreed upon performance standards and they periodically evaluate the strengths and weaknesses. Factors that foster and hinder the work are identified and a feedback on the present performance and the scope for the future improvement is discussed. This brings in open communication considering how the appraisee is performing and to express his ideas and expectations for the improvement.

The effectiveness of the appraisal depends upon the sincerity of the HR, the seriousness of both the superior and subordinate and the impact it has on the rewards and punishments. The appraisal must take both the quantitative and the qualitative aspects through which the organisational goals have been achieved. If the goals are met, but with the means which are not acceptable as per the values and ethics of the organisation, it may have an effect on the organisation in the long run and need to be curtailed.

Performance appraisal must bring in the new initiative taken up by the subordinate and what value it adds to the organisation. Organisation needs to be agile in experimenting new things in the process so that it can bring in creativity and innovation. The appraisal process should stay away from the numerical jugglery. It must bring in those aspects that really assess the qualities of the employees. The numerical and grading system has an impact of rationalisation, where the superior and subordinate, during the review would not like to strain the relationship and end up at rationalising the performance. This will undermine the company's future of filling up with mediocre employees rather than star performers.

It has been criticised that the performance review is an annual event and everyone forgets it after the event. The process has to be interwoven in such a way that the periodical review depends upon the KRAs (Key Result Areas) defined in the beginning of the year. If no appraisal is planned, the employee will lose interest, as there is no mechanism to recognise his performance. Without performance appraisal, it is difficult to assess whether an individual is adding any value or not. Many of the organisations use this tool very seriously to upgrade the quality of their people, find the best and weed out non-performers so that everyone develops faith in the system. The process of seriousness in performance appraisal will bring in a working environment free of redundancy that breeds mediocrity and a demoralising effect. Performance appraisal needs to bring out the best efforts the employees have put in to drive the business results.

## Enable SHR-Technology Key to Success

This chapter brings in the following Strategic HR Technologies:

SHR Technology-21    Job Design—*Carving the Architecture of Corporations through Job Design.*

SHR Technology-22    HR Planning—*Optimising Human Resource through Human Resource Planning.*

SHR Technology-23    Job Analysis—*Matching Individual and Job through Job Analysis.*

SHR Technology-24    Recruitment—*Effective Hiring and Placement through Recruitment Process.*

SHR Technology-25    Psychometric Testing—*Avoiding Subjectivity through Psychometric Tests.*

SHR Technology-26    Career and Succession Planning—*Prospects of Growth in Organisations through Career and Succession Planning.*

SHR Technology-27    Role Clarity—*Avoiding Ambiguity of Roles through Role Clarity.*

SHR Technology-28    Performance Management System—*Developing Competencies through Performance Management System (PMS).*

An organisation's process is made around the various jobs that the individual in the organisation performs to achieve the desired results. The jobs are designed in such a way that it contributes directly or indirectly in the product and services that the organisation is delivering to the customers. No jobs should exist in the company which does not contribute directly or indirectly to form a value addition towards customer satisfaction. Over a period of time, organisations design more and more roles since one job is divided among many jobs and organisations land up creating more jobs and its related job holders. An organisation realises these extra fats, when appropriate job evaluation is done and redesigns the jobs suiting the current deliverables that is being expected by the organisation from the customers.

The employment market is a vast and profound place from which an employer has to select the right kind of talent to build a competent employees' pool in the organisation. Each wrong recruitment not only generates imbalance but losses to the company which is irreparable in the long run. Many organisations are striving hard to bring in more and more scientific methods for the selection of the right kind of people for hiring and placement. Besides conventional techniques of interviewing and selecting the advance processes of using psychometric tools, assessment centres are being used in these days for bringing in an error-free recruitment process. The aspiration of employees to grow in the organisation ladder is something which every organisation confronts. No organisation can sustain the right kind of people if they do not provide an opportunity to grow within the organisational hierarchies. Job description and job specification becomes a job profile for an individual stating what an individual is supposed to perform and what kind of person he should be to perform a specific job. Job analysis is a technique, which determines the job description and job specification in a given role in an organisational set-up. It helps in making role clarity and also in the recruitment process.

# Conclusion

- Every individual employee in the Organisation works in team and has a distinctive role to play vis-à-vis the boss and the subordinate. This leads to defining proper organisation design effective span of control and optimum size.
- In today's business, competency of an employee is of utmost importance. At the same time, right attitude towards job and performance is critical. It is possible to provide an input of skill but it is difficult to bring in an attitudinal change. The buzzword is 'hire for attitude, develop for skill'.
- Employees have aspiration to grow and it is the organisational responsibility to provide with the right kind of platform for individual employees to perform and grow higher. Every employee recruited must visualise that he or she can reach to an apex level of the company, i.e., be the CEO.

- Organisational complexity can be managed well if the performer of various roles in the company has complete clarity. The performance management tool is the most common technique used in every organisation for evaluating individual perform- ance on the job.
- To bring in competitiveness and enhancing productivity standards, downsizing has become the mantra of the corporate world.

# 'JOB DESIGN'
# CARVING THE ARCHITECTURE OF
# CORPORATIONS THROUGH JOB DESIGN

*Without work, all life is rotten. But when work is soulless, life stifles and dies.*

—Albert Camus

## Intent

- To understand the job and job design process in the organisation.
- To establish interdependence between each job defined.
- To design job based on modern day work practices—balancing work and family life.

## Expression

Job is a set of specified work and task activities that engage an individual in an organisation. Job design is structuring a job with the assigned work within the organisation. Job design is concerned with the relationship between workers and the nature and content of the jobs and their task functions.

## Comprehension

Task and authority relationships define an organisation's structure. Jobs are the basic building blocks of this task authority structure and are considered the micro-structural element to which employees most directly relate. Job design contains the content of the job in terms of duties and responsibilities, the methods of carrying on the job, systems and procedures, and the relationships that should exist between the job holder and the superiors, subordinates and peers. Job design means the integration of the individual into the organisational structure. The importance of job design is that it details the requirements of the job irrespective of the incumbent. This is being done to bring in clarity of thought to the job holder so that he may use his skills to the maximum extent and take up the responsibility for the discharge of his duties.

Jobs in organisations are interdependent and design to make a contribution to the organisation's overall mission and goals. For salesperson to be successful, the production people must be effective. These interdependencies require careful planning and design so that all the piece of work fit together into a whole.

Job design involves differentiation, subdividing and departmentalising the work of an organisation. Jobs result from differentiation, which is necessary because no one person can do all the work. Even a small organisation must divide work so that each person is able to accomplish a manageable piece of the whole. At the same time, the organisation divides up the work; it must also integrate those pieces back into a whole.

Traditionally, four approaches to job design were developed—scientific management, job enlargement/job rotation, job enrichment and job characteristic theory. It allows the manager to consider trade off alternatives among the approaches based on desired outcomes.

There are contemporary issues that emerge in current days with respect to job design. Telecommuting, alternative work pattern, techno-stress, task revision, home office, flexi-time, etc., are the approaches being used in organisations to manage a growing business while contributing to a better balance of work and family life for the employees.

The job is a set of task that is being performed by an individual employee in a given role. Tasks implies the performances that are being expected to be fulfilled for the achievement of the set goals. The organisation's activities are a combination of all tasks and targets. For the achievement of the organisation's goals, tasks are created and are distributed to employees for performance. Goals of the company are long-term and short-term in nature and therefore, the tasks also reflect short-term and long-term activities. The organisation has to design the jobs in such a way that all the goals are achieved with the help of all the required employees and each of them perform at the highest of their potential and competence. Wrong job design would generate redundancy and ambiguity amongst the employees. It is necessary and strategic that the organisation gives a thoughtful insight into job design prior to assigning any task to any individual.

# Experiential Application

## A. Prerequisite

- Companies should not take the particular configuration of jobs that exists at a specific point of time as unchangeable. With the change in technology, the business process changes and hence there is a change in job design and structure.

Think of how much the robotic process used in auto assembly today differs from the hand welding of earlier days. Computer assisted design/computer assisted manufacturing (CAD/CAM) had a major impact on employment in some industries. Therefore, jobs must be examined in the light of new technological changes. This greatly affects staffing, training, hiring and other aspects of overall HR planning. The HR manager needs to carefully monitor the interaction between employees and jobs in the organisations to ensure that a productive relationship is achieved and maintained.

- Job design or redesign should be undertaken only after careful consideration is given to environmental, organisational, cost and behavioural factors.
- After job redesign, managers need to update job descriptions, specifications and performance evaluation criteria.
- The reward system in the organisation should reflect the new roles and responsibilities caused by job design or redesign.
- The employees' growth need strength and their desire for job redesign should be given at least as much consideration as the cost and technical aspects of efficiency before developing and implementing a job design and redesign programme.

## B. Process Steps

| Step | Process |
|------|---------|
| Step – I | Define the scope of the project and the priorities within it. |
| Step – II | Adequate training to be provided to make job design team with tools and techniques or by their own problem solving methods. |
| Step – III | Collect existing data identifying ways to collect additional data, and map out existing work flow and patterns. |
| Step – IV | Analyse the data, identifying the problems and opportunities, and share it with the management. |
| Step – V | Decide on the nature of job redesign and make an action plan for implementation. |
| Step – VI | Initiate proper communication across the organisation and get the approvals from the heads. |
| Step – VII | Implement and review periodically. A sample size can be made to look at efficiency of the model. |

# Potential Gains and Areas of Concern

- Job design is fundamental to the organisation on which the organisational structure rests.

- A properly designed job leads to higher productivity and optimum utilisation of manpower.
- Jobs are the basic building blocks of task-authority structure of the organisation and are considered to be the micro-structural element to which employees most directly relate.
- Jobs are usually designed to complement and support other jobs in the organisation so that the overall organisational activities take place smoothly and effectively.
- Wrongly designed jobs would lead to role ambiguity and conflict of interest.
- Jobs not planned properly could be less productive and unnecessary cost to the organisation.

# Measurability

## Try It Out

(1: not at all done, 2: moderately done, 3: to some extent done, 4: to a great extent done, 5: excellently done)

- My organisation has job design document. ☐
- All the departments/functions are involved in job design for better integration of jobs. ☐
- Teams are given adequate training before taking up job design assignments. ☐
- Jobs are designed to achieve the organisational goals. ☐
- Job design is reviewed periodically to adapt to changes. ☐

Analysis: the average score would determine the extent to which job design process exists in your organisation.

## Score Card

(*: 25% achieved, **: 50% achieved, ***: 75% achieved, ****: 100% achieved)

| Technology | Objective Elements | Unit | Historical | Last Year | Current Year | Stretch Target | Status |
|---|---|---|---|---|---|---|---|
| Job Design | Strategy Document on Job Design | Doc | Nil | No | Yes | NA | ** |
| Job Design | Job Design Document | Doc | Nil | No | Yes | NA | ** |

# Proven Track Record

## Track One

### Lloyds Bank

Lloyds Bank reviewed its strategies for becoming more competitive in the early 1990s. They discovered that they were not taking full advantage of the abilities of its non-managerial employees. Therefore, it was decided to explore ways of encouraging the staff to put forward and implement solutions to problems such as improving customer service and introducing more flexible working practice. *A job design—a structure systematic and managed process'* in which the people in the workplace are required to analyse and redesign the work in a way which caters to the needs of the customer, processes and staff. In pilot project, participation at every level was voluntary. The job design team was set with different objectives depending upon the issues faced by the individual branches. These included amalgamating the working and service delivery methods of previously two competing branches making more staff available for customer services, improving the sales and marketing efforts and setting up a multi-skilled team. The project revealed under utilisation of staff, some inappropriate procedures and poorly designed job. Based on the pilot project on the job design, Lloyd's Bank redefined the work processes and redesigned it completely at various units.

## Track Two

### Toyota

Toyota's Production System (TPS) is legendary and this applies not just to manufacturing but to almost every aspect of the business. Toyota's production system has a simple concept—*maximise flow, eliminate waste and respect people*. The company designed the work to flow from process to process without picks or valley and expects its product to arrive in just the right quantity for customers. The result is a smooth running plant with little or no wastes. Toyota has sought to make work less strenuous and less tedious. Innovations have included job rotation, cross training and assembly line improvements. Job rotation has not only eliminated stress injuries and has reduced fatigue, but it has also boosted productivity. Company discovered that workers could easily move from one job to another, provided that they had the necessary skills. So Toyota has placed dummy cars on some factory floors where workers practice different assembly tasks. Applying the principle of TPS requires leadership, teamwork and communication among workers. In addition, the supportive organisation culture encourages employees to learn from their mistakes and from the success and failure of each other. Nearly all of Toyota's future growth needs to come from overseas and the company is headed in that direction. So, as Toyota evolves from multinational company into one that is truly global, TPS will have to continue to change too.

# Applied HR Case

## Smith Refineries Limited

Smith Refineries Limited functions from three locations and the central office controls the activities of the three locations. The company is dependent upon the import of oil, which it refines and sells in the domestic market through retail chain. It has three refineries in the north, south and central regions so as to build economies of scale in production process. Ben is the Head of HR and is in the department from the date of starting the plant and has grown from HR Executive to the Head of HR. He is considered as one of the senior employees and is known for his calibre. The organogram, or organisation chart of HR in Smith Refineries is as follows:

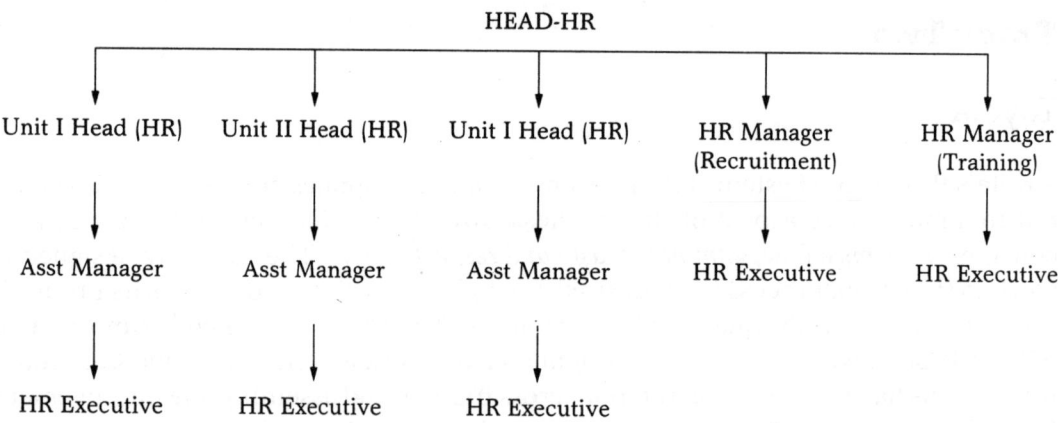

Ben has deliberately made a lean structure at the corporate office and has given independence to the unit to take decisions locally. The corporate office used to deal with critical recruitments and training plans. However, the Unit Heads are empowered to take the decision at local level. The HR in the field used to take care of the organisation design, manpower planning, Training and Development and Health, Safety, Environment and Welfare (HSEW).

During the last one year Ben has been facing problems of lack of team efforts, inter-personal relations and communication gap which concerns him. This had impact on the production and there were a series of disturbances in the plants, Plant III, and Plant I, which is the cause of concern. He has given a serious thought to planning some HR interventions to bring in organisational renewal. He has decided to appoint an HR Manager exclusively for the purpose of Organisation Design at the corporate office. He told Richard, Manager Recruitment, to make the Job Design so as to bring in clarity of role to avoid any confusion between the managers at the corporate office and as also giving clarity to the unit heads.

## Questions

1. Is Ben justified in having an exclusive Manager for Organisation Design?
2. Is Ben right at arriving at his conclusion that the problems in the plants are attributed to behavioural aspects?
3. If you were Richard, how will you plan the job Design of Manager-Organisation Design and his coordination role with the Unit Heads?

## References and Further Readings

Aadmodt, Michael G. 1991. *Applied Industrial/Organizational Psychology*, California: Wordsworth Publishing Company.

Bernardin, John H. 2003. *Human Resource Management*, New Delhi: Tata McGraw-Hill Publishing Company Limited.

Davis, Louis E. and James C. Taylor (eds). 1972. *Design of Jobs, Selected Readings*, England: Penguin Books.

Dessler, Gary. 2001. *Human Resource Management*, 7th edn, New Delhi: Prentice-Hall of India Pvt Ltd.

Dunnette, Marvin D. and Leaetta M. Hough. 1998. *Handbook of Industrial and Organizational Psychology*, Mumbai: Jaico Publishing House.

# 'HR PLANNING'
# OPTIMISING HUMAN RESOURCE
# THROUGH HUMAN RESOURCE
# PLANNING

*If I put a person into a job and she or he does not perform, I have made a mistake.*
*I have no business blaming that person, no business invoking the 'Peter Principle',*
*no business complaining. I have made a mistake.*

—Peter Drucker

## Intent

- To forecast the present and the future manpower requirement based on the business strategy.
- To take into consideration various demand and supply difficulties in HR forecasting and making availability of competent HR for the company.
- To maximise the productivity of HR by ensuring appropriate utilisation through HR planning. It helps in providing the right kind of manpower at the right time and right place.
- To evaluate HR competencies required to perform the specific job, which is built in HR planning process.

## Expression

Human resource planning is defined as 'a strategy for the acquisition, utilisation, improvement and retention of an enterprise's human resource.'

# Comprehension

Human Resource planning was previously described as manpower planning. Whatever be the nature of the organisation, HR planning should not be regarded in isolation but as an integral part of the broader process of corporate planning. Human Resource planning is linked to the development of the organisation as a whole and should be related to corporate objectives and to the organisation structure capable of achieving these objectives. Human Resource planning is a process whereby the organisation's manpower requirement is maintained by deliberate and systematic action to mobilise in reasonable balance with the demands. Since it is difficult to plan the right kind of people at the right time, proper planning will ensure that the expectations are met to a large extent.

Human Resource planning means different things to different people, general agreement exists on its ultimate objective, the most effective use of scarce talent. Human Resource planning is not the tendency to play with the numbers and norms but the skill set required to handle jobs as per the business strategy. Human Resource planning looks at the requirement of the business strategy and ensures placing manpower in achieving organisational objectives.

Human Resource planning has attained utmost importance due to the technological changes and the scarcity of skilled manpower. Manpower replacement is not like removing the damaged spare part and replacing with another, since no two humans are similar. The new enterprises require people with specialised skills and HR should know in advance the requirement of the nature of manpower so that the right kind of person can be selected for the post.

Human Resources planning involves considerable uncertainty and it's not a science and mistakes are bound to occur. However, the use of HR planning assist the organisation to foresee changes and identify the trends in staffing resource and to adopt HR policies to avoid major HR problems. Human Resources planning provides the trigger for HR management action programme aimed at reconciling differences in supply and demand. It provides a framework in which action can be taken to help overcoming the staffing difficulties faced by the organisation. Human Resources planning is a continuous process, which seek to ensure flexible researching related to internal and external environmental influences.

It is HR planning and recruitment that to an extent determines the speed and direction of the organisation. History has proved that the organisation that does not change to customer requirement slowly vanish from the corporate scenario. Manpower is thus concerned more with the management of culture and creativity who can adapt to the system and ensure the growth of the organisation with vigour and enthusiasm.

Human Resource is an asset similar to other assets which a corporation deploy for the achievement of goals. Carefully planned deployment of HR is essential because people resources are tangible and living unlike other resources of the company. There lies a commitment for a long-term association from both employees as well as from corporation. Overstaffing and excessive staffing or understaffing could create productivity issues and can be difficult to manage. Uncertainty and dynamism in business demands quick response from the organisation. Since HR is a cost as well as an asset, minute planning is very important. Strategic planning in business lays great emphasis on HR planning as one of the important parameters of the strategic planning process. Human Resource planning is a strategic technology and is the beginning of all HR processes.

# Experiential Application

## A. Prerequisite

- Human Resource planning itself can be a strategic or tactical. It may be done organisation wide or can be restricted to departments, divisions or any common employee groups.
- It may be carried out on a recurring basis annually or sporadically, e.g., while launching a new product line or at the outset of capital expansion project.
- At the level of strategic planning HR planning is concerned with such issues as assessing the management implication of the future business needs, assessing factors external to the firms and gauging the internal supply of manpower over the long run.
- At the level of operational and tactical planning HR planning is concerned with the detailed forecast of employee supply and employee demand. Based on the forecast, specific HR plan can be undertaken. These may involve recruitment, changing incentives, promotion, training or transfers.

## B. Process Steps

| Step | Process |
| --- | --- |
| Step – I | An analysis of existing staffing resources through records and inventory. |
| Step – II | To carry out a talent inventory to assess the current HR and how they are currently being utilised. |
| Step – III | To forecast the staffing requirement necessary to achieve the goals that demand forecast, including loss due to attrition. |
| Step – IV | Measures to ensure that the required staffing resources are available as and when required. |
| Step – V | To fill the projected vacancies through recruitment, training, transfers, promotion and development. |
| Step – VI | Periodical review of the status of manpower planning. |
| Step – VII | Effective monitoring of the HR planning system by the degree of attainment of HR objectives. |

# Potential Gains and Areas of Concern

- Effective HR planning can help to anticipate the potential future difficulties while there is still a choice of action.
- Human Resource planning should enable the organisation to develop effective HR strategies related to such activities, such as recruitment and selection, training and retraining, management development and career progression, transfers and redeployment, early retirement, wage and salary levels, anticipated redundancies and accommodation requirement.
- Human Resource planning helps to provide a framework for the effective management of people.
- Human Resource planning is to be genuinely effective. It must be linked with different levels of general business planning not as an end or a goal in itself but rather as a means to an end of building a more competitive organisation.
- Progressive firms regard HR issues as people related business issues that will have powerful impact on their strategic business and HR planning.
- Non-existence of HR planning would lead to faulty manpower placement.
- Improper HR planning could either lead to excess manpower or shortage of manpower, both harmful to the organisation's productivity.
- HR planning is the planning of the valuable resources, the so-called human assets of the company. Since human asset is the only asset, which requires retention, improper planning could jeopardise the retention efforts.
- Everything comes back to people at last. If you don't appoint with the right ability, temperament and willingness, all these fancy theories on motivation empowerment and commitment are not likely to be of much use.

# Measurability

## Try It Out

(1: not at all done, 2: moderately done, 3: to some extent done, 4: to a great extent done, 5: excellently done)

- My organisation has HR planning norms.                                    ☐
- All the departments/functions participate in the HR planning process.     ☐

- Human Resource Department is trained to plan the HR planning process. ☐
- Human Resource planning is reviewed periodically to adapt to the ☐
  changing environment.
- One of the parameters of measurement of performance of HR function is ☐
  adherence to HR planning norms.

Analysis: the average score would determine the extent to which HR planning process exists in your organisation.

## Score Card

(*: 25% achieved, **: 50% achieved, ***: 75% achieved, ****: 100% achieved)

| Technology | Objective Elements | Unit | Historical | Last Year | Current Year | Stretch Target | Status |
|---|---|---|---|---|---|---|---|
| HR Planning | HR Planning Norms | Doc | Doc | Doc | June | April | ** |

# Proven Track Record

## Track One

## Amazon.com

Human Resource Planning means forecasting HR needs in the context of strategic business planning. Many of the organisations have adopted a long-term perspective and have integrated human resource planning with strategic business planning centred on consideration of core business competencies. Sometimes companies forecast reduction in sales and profits and by reducing the labour costs through downsizing, achieve reduced costs and turnaround. Amazon.com downsizing in 2001 is an example of strategic HR planning involving business forecasting, customer demand, and labour force needs and options. Amazon.com, the Internet retailer, had sales of $972 millions during the fourth quarter of 2000, 40 per cent higher than in 1999. It had over $1 billion in cash on hand. Despite its rosy scenario, it cut over 1,300 jobs in 2001 which was 15 per cent of its workforce. The cuts were a function of new sales projections that were half of earlier projections and a thorough study of their overhead and alternative strategies of delivering goods and service to their customers. The cut in return, paid off. Amazon made profit in 2002.

(Source: Bernardin, 2003: 81–83)

## Track Two

## Hindustan Lever Limited (HLL)

Hindustan Lever Limited (HLL) is India's largest fast moving consumer goods company manufacturing home and personal care products, foods and beverages, etc. In HLL people are first and everything is next, and hence adequate care is taken to recruit quality manpower. Hindustan Lever Limited emphasises on HR planning and development of manpower to align with business strategy.

Management trainees are being taken to fill in the future managerial positions and a formal management programme is planned for graduates, selected without formal management education, called Business Education programme covering all the functions of management, so that they can become the future managers. Recruitment and promotions in the organisation are based on assessments. To bring in the right kind of people, the managers in the selection board are being trained in selection and interviewing skills. The resourcing process is related to a specific life stage in which various businesses in the company are placed, e.g., a new/nascent business, a business in growth stage; mature or stable business, etc. Approach to HR planning varies at which level the business is in. With the right kind of manpower being provided for HLL ensures retaining its leadership position in the industry.

(Source: Nair, 1998: 24.)

# Applied HR Case

## Excel Computer Incorporation

Excel Computer is a large computer manufacturing company located in rapidly growing areas in the southeastern part of the capital city. Over the past several years Excel computers experienced a significant expansion in size and operations and a rapid influx of new personnel at all organisational levels. The company has realised the pressing need for talented and knowledgeable personnel. Over the past several years learned men had been hired from outside the company, but top management had become convinced that in the long run the health of the company depended upon being able to manage the talent internally.

Kiran Saini had recently been hired to develop and install a new HR planning system at Excel computers. She had previous experience both in computer software and hardware industry in the HR process. So, she seemed like a logical choice for the job. On the basis of her prior experience Kiran Saini knew that many functions with cross-divisional lines exist in the company and required broad exposure to computer manufacturing. Further she knew that division heads of the computer peripheral with a high degree of autonomy and the divisional and corporate objectives are not directly aligned. Therefore, Kiran Saini knew that the new HR planning process would have to be corporate-wide in scope. Only from that perspective would a planner assess company-wide HR need.

When Kiran Saini arrived at her new job her boss had informed her that the focus of HR planning system should be on management development and succession planning. To emphasise that focus she was given the title of Director of Management Development and HR planning. The position had corporate-wide staff authority over all presently existing activities that related to management development and HR planning. Today Kiran Saini is thinking about the briefing that she is to give the executive officers of the company next week. They have asked her to provide them with a statement of objectives of the new HR planning systems as she sees it as an outline of the potential benefit that might accrue to Excel Computers, and the list of the suggested steps in the implementation of the HR planning systems.

## Questions

1. If you were Kiran Saini, what would you be prepared to say to the executive officers in terms of:

   A. Objectives of HR planning?
   B. Potential benefit of HR planning?
   C. Important steps in the implementation of HR planning systems?

## References and Further Readings

Bernardin, H. John. 2003. *Human Resource Management—An Experiential Approach*, New Delhi: Tata McGraw-Hill.

Bernardin, H. John and Joyce Russell. 1998. *Human Resource Management—An Experiential Approach*, Boston: Irwin/McGraw-Hill.

Bramham, John. 1998. *Human Resource Planning*, 2nd edn, Mumbai: Jaico Publishing House.

Flippo, Edwin B. 1984. *Personnel Management*, 6th edn, New York: McGraw-Hill Book Company.

Heisler, William J., W. David Jones and Philip O. Benham. 1988. *Managing Human Resources Issues*, San Francisco: Jossey-Bass Publishers.

Rothwell, R.J. and Kazannas, H.C. 1988. *Strategic Human Resource Planning and Management*, New Jersey: Prentice Hall.

Nair, R.R. 1998. 'Aligning HR with Business Strategy—HLL Experience' in *Business Led HR Strategies*, All India Management Association, New Delhi: Excel Books.

Schuler S. Randell and Huber Vandra. 1989. *Personnel and Human Resource Management*, St Paul: West Publishing Company.

Werther, William B., Keith Davis and William Werther Jr. 1996. *Human Resources and Personnel Management*, Boston: Irwin/McGraw Hill.

# 'JOB ANALYSIS'
# MATCHING INDIVIDUAL AND JOB
# THROUGH JOB ANALYSIS

*It is your Work in life that is the ultimate seduction.*

—Pablo Picasso

## Intent

- To discuss the nature of job analysis including what it is and how it is used.
- To understand the various methods of collecting job analysis information and based on that making descriptions and job specifications.
- To explain job analysis in an organisational situation including what it means and how it is done in practice.

## Expression

Job analysis is a procedure for determining the duties and skills requirements of a job and the kind of person who should be hired for it. The job analysis is useful for writing job description, i.e., a list of job duties, responsibilities, reporting relationships, working condition and supervisory responsibilities as one product of job analysis. Another product of job analysis is job specification, i.e., a list of human requirement for a job such as requisite education, skills, personality, and so on.

## Comprehension

Simply stated a job analysis involves collecting data from the jobholder, the jobholder's manager, jobholder's colleagues or team members about the job performed in an organisation. However, this definition is probably too simplistic when all of the different types of information collected are considered, e.g., the data collected must describe exactly what is required to perform a specific job. This includes the knowledge, skills and ability that the incumbent must possess. In simple terms, it is not what actually happens and why, not what people would like to think happens, or what they feel people should be like to make it to happen. Knowledge is defined as a degree to which a job-holder is required to know about the specific material. Skill is defined as an adequate performance on task requiring the use of tools, equipment and machinery. Ability refers to the physical and mental capabilities needed to perform task. Job analysis is the process of determining the knowledge and skill required for an incumbent who should be recruited to handle the role.

The data collected from the job analysis can be used for a variety of purposes. One of the most important is writing job descriptions and job specifications. The job analysis data can be applied to a variety of HR functions. It can be useful as input for the organisation's job evaluation system, determining the worth of the job in an organisation. A good job analysis should provide information useful in planning for recruitment, selections and placement. Job analysis can help both the labour and management. The management also understands what should be expected from each job incumbent and how much employees should be compensated for performing a particular job. The information would also be helpful to classify the jobs, determining the worth against each job and to provide sufficient authority and responsibility in the discharge of the duties.

Job analysis sets the tone for performance appraisal as the standards of the performance are being derived to review whether the incumbent has performed the job as per the expectations. Training can be provided by designing appropriate programmes basing on the details available on knowledge and skills of the employees.

Job analysis provides managers with clear descriptions and specifications about the jobs. It is possible to determine which jobs are most critical for a particular organisational strategy or objectives. For example, if management decides to downsize an organisation, the information provided by the job analysis should prove invaluable once a company decides which jobs to retain, change or eliminate. Similarly, an organisation with a growth strategy can use this information to identify the areas that need expansions or development.

De-jobbing is gradually picking up due to the rapid changes in technology and business. Organisations are facing immense competition due to globalisation, technological changes and the demands of the customer. The role of specific jobs are gradually getting eroded especially in the service industry, where the sole aim is to serve the customer. The concepts of work teams, boundary-less organisation and re-engineering are some of the examples. Though the new initiatives revolve employing the people around the task to be accomplished, the analysis of the knowledge and skills would always be useful in preparing the team.

It is observed that over a period of time overlapping and role ambiguity develops. Also at the time of allocation of a new job to role holder, defining the role and its detailed activities are required. A systematic approach to define job in terms of activities involved in it and the skills required to be performed is job analysis and this process determines all future jobs and the task orientation of those job holders hence, it is strategic in nature. Periodic job analysis is a must since it helps in refining the job holders' skills and competencies and also helps in defining all activities under the same.

# Experiential Application

## A. Prerequisite

- The reason for conducting job analysis should be clearly specified to help ensure that all relevant information is examined.
- The purpose of conducting job analysis should serve as input for the type of information collected.
- The purpose of job analysis, the type of information required, the extent of employee involvement and the level of detailed desire should be specified before choosing one or more method of data collection.
- The job analysis should be designed so that job description and job specification can be derived easily.
- Managers should communicate all relevant information to employees concerning the job analysis to prevent uncertainty and anxiety.
- If major organisational changes have taken place, the manager should consider conducting job analysis.
- If major organisational changes are anticipated the manager should consider conducting a job-oriented analysis for the future.

## B. Process Steps

| Step | Process |
|------|---------|
| Step – I | Determining the purpose for conducting job analysis in line with the strategy of organisation. |
| Step – II | Identify the jobs to be analysed. |
| Step – III | Extensive communication required and involves the employee so that the right kind of information is being obtained. |
| Step – IV | Method or combination of method to be used and how to collect the information. |
| Step – V | Process the job analysis information. Standardised reporting format can also be used to collect data. |
| Step – VI | Review and update frequently in line with corporate strategy. |

# Potential Gains and Areas of Concern

- Job analysis provides clear descriptions and specifications about the jobs to all the employees of the organisation.
- With the help of job analysis, it is possible to determine which jobs are most critical for a particular organisational strategy or objectives.
- Job analysis provides detail information of the job, which is useful in planning for recruitment, selections and placement.
- Job analysis can help understand employee and management about expectation from each job incumbent and helps to determine compensation for performing a particular job.
- Job analysis determines the job description and job specification for a given job. Due to this the flexibility in the job gets lost.
- The business scenario warrants employees to work beyond the boundaries of the job, hence job analysis hinders the performance of an employee if though in a watertight compartment.
- Though for each job there could have been the right job analysis, but as per the job description as well as job specification, it is difficult to get the right placement of employees as stated in it.

# Measurability

## Try It Out

(1: not at all done, 2: moderately done, 3: to some extent done, 4: to a great extent done, 5: excellently done)

- My organisation has laid down job analysis process. ☐
- Job analysis is used in the Performance Management System as a standard ☐ of tool of the job to be performed.
- Job analysis is used in recruitment, selection, placement, transfers, etc. ☐
- My organisation carries out periodic review of job analysis. ☐

Analysis: the average score would determine the extent to which Job Analysis process exists in your organisation.

## Score Card

(*: 25% achieved, **: 50% achieved, ***: 75% achieved, ****: 100% achieved)

| Technology | Objective Elements | Unit | Historical | Last Year | Current Year | Stretch Target | Status |
|---|---|---|---|---|---|---|---|
| Job Analysis | Document on Job Analysis | Doc | Nil | No | Dec. | Nov. | * |

# Proven Track Record

## Track One

### Allstate Insurance

Allstate Insurance is the second personal lines insurance company in the United States, as well as a major life insurer. It insures 1 of every 8 homes and automobiles in the country and has over 15,000 agents and 39,000 non-agent employees. Attract, select and retain highly skilled and motivational people is the key for survival of Allstate Insurance, where the sector is highly competitive. Agents interact everyday with the existing and potential customers. Allstate has embraced the use of technology to improve the company's selection process, which is based on job analysis and other research of what defines 'star' performer. Data was collected on the following methods:

1. Work/job analysis interviews with current agents at different performance level.
2. Interviews with agency managers.
3. Benchmarking.
4. Analysis of longitudinal data files of test responses and business results.
5. Analysis of data from application forms.

Based on the detailed analysis, the dimensions were identified that were critical for success and that distinguished 'stars' from lower performers. Interviews were also conducted with vendors and consultants to determine the gap between Allstate's needs and their products. Through job analysis method, Allstate was able to devise a selection process for recruiting future agents.

(*Source*: Cochrane and Ellen, 2001: 337–55.)

## Track Two

### Bull UK

Bull UK has developed software, which provides for skill profiling for generic and specific jobs. The profiles are built up through structured question and answer sessions, where the user is asked to describe the responsibilities and functions of the job in question. The software draws interfaces from the responses and produces a job profile in terms of essential and desirable skill attributes within its skill knowledge database. They have been tailored and modified to suit Bull's requirements. The HR has allied its activity to the very heart of business and need to be responsive to the customer.

(*Source*: Matthewman, 1993: 118.)

# Applied HR Case

## Clara Forgings Inc.

When the organisation was achieving an all-time high in production, sales, profit growth, etc., Mr Phillips, Managing Director of M/s Clara Forgings Inc. has decided to sell the unit to a multinational, which is into the similar business. The unit was manufacturing the rare alloys, which are used in the defense industry and was running very well. Mr Phillips, a metallurgical engineer by profession has got a dream of making big and since the job will not make his dreams come true, started the firm with another colleague and four employees manufacturing rare alloys. Phillips used to look after the production, and his partner the marketing. The unit has tremendously grown to 135 employees and was running extremely well. Unfortunately, the partner died in a car accident and Phillips was not in a position to concentrate on both production and marketing. Meanwhile, an offer has come for takeover with a good price of four times the market capitalisation, which Phillips does not want to lose. Since, he has a lot of attachment towards the unit, after retaining only 5 per cent of the shares he sold the rest.

Mr Daniel, HR Manager was assigned for the smooth takeover of the unit. He found that since the firm is small there is no designated HR person and the function is taken care by the Finance Department. Except the technical personnel, the work is divided among the employees by convenience and skills rather than designation. Daniel in order to integrate the unit with the larger unit need to do Job Analysis, since he has to submit a report about the action plan on integration.

## Questions

1. What is the agenda with Daniel on Job Analysis?
2. If you were Daniel, how you will go about doing Job Analysis?

## References and Further Readings

Bernardin, H. John and Joyce Russell. 1998. *Human Resource Management—An Experiential Approach*, Boston: Irwin/McGraw-Hill.

Cascio, Wayne F. 1998. *Managing Human Resources—Productivity, Quality of Work Life, Profits*, USA: Irwin/McGraw-Hill.

Cochrane, A. Alice and Papper M. Ellen. 2001. 'Allstate Insurance' in Carter Louis, Giber David and Goldsmith Marshall (eds), *Best Practices in Organization Development and Change*, CA: Jossey-Bass/Pfeiffer.

Cushway, Barry. 1994. *Human Resource Management*, London: Kogan Page.

Dale, Margaret and Paul Iles. 1998. *Assessing Management Skills—A Guide to Competencies and Evaluation Techniques*, Mumbai: Jaico Publishing House.

Dunnette, Marvin D. and Leaetta M. Hough. 1998. *Handbook of Industrial and Organisational Psychology*, Mumbai: Jaico Publishing House.

Gael, Sidney. 1983. *Job Analysis—A Guide to Assessing Work Activities*, San Francisco: Jossey-Bass Publishers.

Matthewman, Jim. 1993. *HR Effectiveness*, London: Institute of Personnel and Development.

Pearn, M. and R. Kandola. 1993. *Job Analysis: A Manager's Guide*, London: IPM.

Schuler S. Randell and Huber Vandra. 1989. *Personnel and Human Resource Management*, St Paul: West Publishing Company.

# 'RECRUITMENT'
# EFFECTIVE HIRING AND PLACEMENT
# THROUGH RECRUITMENT PROCESS

*No matter how good or successful you are or how clever or crafty, your business and its future are in the hands of the people you hire.*

—Akio Morita, Co-founder and CEO of Sony

## Intent

- To understand how the process of recruitment takes place in a scientific manner.
- To learn recruitment and selection process as a support to the business process of the company.
- To know the process of goodwill generation of the company by way of recruitment from the masses of the society.
- To make recruitment as a highly motivated culture within the company by recruiting motivated incumbents.

## Expression

The first stage in selection is to make the vacancies known to a large number of people and the opportunity that the organisation offers. In response to this knowledge, potential applicants would write to the organisation. The process of attracting people to apply is called recruitment.

# Comprehension

In today's competitive business scenario, choice of the right personnel has far-reaching implications for an organisation's functioning. Employees well selected with the right kind of skills, knowledge and potentials and well placed would not only contribute to the efficient running of the organisation but also offer significant potential for future replacement. Efficient recruitment does not entail maintaining the status quo and perpetuating the moribund culture, but shall have the radical changes in thinking about the competencies required for the future to achieve sustainable growth and cultural change. Recruitment does not end in placing the person but the retention of right kind of people is vital and hence the process is called as 'Planning with people in mind' (Quinn Mills, 1985). Whatever changes and shifts has occurred in the HR effective recruitment is the critical component of the HR department, since a firm operating in a local area or a multinational operating in various countries needs to recruit talented people.

Recruitment is a form of business competition. Just as corporations compete to develop, manufacture and market the best product or service, so they must also compete to identify, attract and hire the most qualified people. It demands serious attention from management, for any business strategy will falter without the talent to execute it. The recruitment strategy need to integrate with the business strategy by way of understanding the projection of required manpower as per the strategy and selecting the best talent available, understanding the organisational strategy towards the decentralisation, mergers and acquisitions, delayering, introduction of new technology, etc., and planning the recruitment strategy and finally to bring in the cultural changes by way of performance orientation, quality, customer service, teamwork, attitudes, beliefs, etc. Bad recruitment will result in high turnover, poor performance and low motivation, which will be detrimental to the interests of the organisation.

Recruitment is done basing on the requirement of the organisation, which may arise due to expansion of the business, diversification, expansion, replacement, transfer, etc. Basing on the job description a search brief is prepared detailing the essential skills and knowledge required to handle the role, essential and desirable qualification and experience. The main advantage of search brief is that it avoids the ambiguity on part of the interviewer and the incumbent. The search brief is then released for recruitment.

Recruitment is generally done with internal and external process. Job posting, employee referrals, head hunting, temporary worker pools, etc., are the internal process. Campus recruitment, executive search firms, employment agencies, trade and professional associations, recruitment advertising, etc., are the external recruitment processes. Taking advantage of the technology, e-recruitment has picked up and many companies recruit people by posting the vacancies in their Websites and certain exclusive job sites available. This method is cost-effective and quick.

Another method of recruitment, which is soon gaining ground, is the Assessment Centre method. This technology is explained in this book (see SHR Technology 35). This method is increasingly used to get the candidate with the right kind of knowledge and skill and avoid any subjectivity. In Assessment Centres there has been an increasing use of psychometric tools like Thomas Profiling, 16PF, MBTI, etc.

However, the HR must not attempt to look at recruitment as one stop solution for acquiring the skills but can also look at the possibility of job enrichment, job enlargement, training, career management, downsizing, etc. The recruitment process must ensure that adequate reference check is being carried out from the previous employer and also references given by the candidate, but the reference given by one must not be taken as depicting the characteristic of the candidate since the referee may give a biased judgement.

Probably most neglected process in HR is recruitment. Anybody and everybody involved in the recruitment process and subsequently in the organisation wonder always how to approach the right man for the right job. Human Resources problems including attitude, skills and productivity issues are all begun at the stage of recruiting. With wrong recruitment, the company has to pay heavily in terms of low productivity, low competency and wrong fitment. The Organisation suffers heavily in beating competition, bringing innovation, if proper recruitment is not done and the right kind of manpower is not deployed in the organisation. Recruitment cannot be done in isolation. It has a great strategic importance and has to be done in line with business and HR strategy of the company.

# Experiential Application

## A. Prerequisite

- The process of recruitment begins with defining various jobs that are going to be performed by the potential new recruits. These jobs are then converted into appropriate job profiles comprising job description and job specification, which are made public.
- The organisation must ensure that the job opportunity must be publicised widely so that it generates interest in a wide cross-section of society.
- Recruitment has no meaning if the applicants available for vacancies are of the same kind in terms of their education, socio-economic status, and experience.

In such a case, an organisation does not have to select but choose at random from the applicants.

- The entire recruitment process must be planned properly. Objectivity, reliability and validity ensures better choice of employees.

## B. Process Steps

| Step | Process |
|------|---------|
| Step – I | Identifying the need for recruitment, find out the positions, make the search brief for recruitment. |
| Step – II | Dissemination of information through all modes about the vacancies in the organisation to a large number of people. |
| Step – III | Potential candidates would apply for the positions. |
| Step – IV | Short-listing of candidates to be made from all the applications received. |
| Step – V | The candidates short-listed are asked to fill applications for greater detail of the candidates. |
| Step – VI | Conduct psychometric test (optional), group discussions and two-tier interviews to look into the skills. |
| Step – VII | Selected candidates informed about their selection and compensation offering discussed and decided. |
| Step – VIII | The letter of appointment handed over to the selected candidates. |

# Potential Gains and Areas of Concern

- Recruitment helps generating only relevant application through a self-selection process on the part of the potential candidates.
- Proper recruitment ensures high degree of satisfaction among employees since they would appreciate that their potentials were identified and hence selected. This helps improving the morale of other employees too.
- The department wanting to fill new vacancies will have high morale due to prompt recruitment of critical vacancies.
- The data generated bring tremendous help to the Human Resource Information System (HRIS) of the company for future utility.
- There could be chance of selecting the wrong person in the recruitment process and could be chance of loosing the right person as well. Both are equally costly to the organisation.
- Recruitment is not a one-time affair. If objectivity and meritorious selection process is not followed, the company lands up with more 'dead wood' than performers.

# Measurability

## Try It Out

(1: not at all done, 2: moderately done, 3: to some extent done, 4: to a great extent done, 5: excellently done)

- My organisation has laid down recruitment strategy. ☐
- Recruitment strategy and plan attracts the best talent in the industry. ☐
- We have assessment centre method for recruitment. ☐
- Recruitment team is well trained to look out for the competencies required for the jobs. ☐
- All the departments/functions are involved in the recruitment process. ☐
- My organisation has perspective recruitment strategy. ☐

Analysis: the average score would determine the extent to which scientific recruitment process exists in your organisation.

## Score Card

(*: 25% achieved, **: 50% achieved, ***: 75% achieved, ****: 100% achieved)

| Technology | Objective Elements | Unit | Historical | Last Year | Current Year | Stretch Target | Status |
|---|---|---|---|---|---|---|---|
| Recruitment | Recruitment Strategy | Doc | Yes | Yes | June | April | ** |
| Recruitment | Campus Recruitment | Nos | 50 | 30 | 60 | 75 | ** |
| Recruitment | Lead Time for Recruitment | Days | 40 | 38 | 32 | 30 | ** |
| Recruitment | Cost Per Hire | $ | $200 | $220 | $180 | $175 | ** |

# Proven Track Record

## Track One

## McDonalds

Every three to four hours a new outlet of McDonalds opens for business. As a result, the chain has now over 23,000 restaurants in more than 90 countries around the world.

The organisational philosophy is evident in the company's hiring strategies. McDonald's is one of the largest US employers of young people, and half of its employees are students. But if students' grades start to suffer, often the first answer is to quit work. So to retain their employees many outlets of McDonalds offer extra pay for good grades, reimbursement for schoolbooks and paid study hours.

Another recruitment strategy that give an edge over the competition is its REHIREMENT programme, which provides part time jobs for more than 40,000 older workers many of whom are retired. Older workers have proven to be very loyal, which lowers the company's turnover cost. Flexible scheduling allows those retired previously to set the number of hours they work each week so that their social security benefits are not jeopardised.

(*Source*: Mescon, Bovee and Thill, 1996.)

## Track Two

## Marks & Spencer Plc.

Over the years, Marks & Spencer have developed rigorous and sophisticated selection process to handle the thousands of applications they receive each year for a commensurately small number of vacancies. All candidates are assessed against seven criteria, which are a range of personal skills and which they have identified as being essential for effective performance on the job. These are planning and organising, assertiveness, leadership, job motivation, analytical consideration, awareness and teamwork and adaptability. The application forms provide the first view of the candidates, which goes through a screening through a bespoke computer programme with built-in management controls and the main objective is to select those candidates who should have an interview. Candidates at the initial interview are assessed against four of the seven criteria. Tests are administered and the final evaluation and decision reflects both on the quality of the information gathered against the criteria and an awareness of what candidates will face at the next stage.

The assessment centre is a group evaluation where eight candidates come together to perform a series of management exercises, designed to reflect activities they are likely to face on the job. Candidates at the centre are assessed for all the seven criteria in each exercise. Finally, the candidate will go through the final board interview, and if successful, will be expected to be at the operational level and then at the managerial level within a far shorter time-scale. They, therefore, must have relevant transferable skills.

(*Source*: Mullins, 1999.)

# Applied HR Case 'Fredrick's First Day in Office'

## Carter Publishing

Mr Fredrick was recruited as HR Head of M/s Carter Publishing House, which has pioneered in publishing good quality textbooks at the primary school level. The unit started about four years ago and gradually expanded to 12 units with the turnover increasing at 50 per cent per annum. The Managing Director, Mr Mumford, was a retired school principal and the whole unit is his brainchild. With increasing business, it was becoming very difficult to handle the manpower which has increased from four to 198 including the field staff and the marketing personnel. At the same time, during last year he was not able to meet the demand of the market since he was not able to supply the required numbers, though the units have the capacity to supply. The constant complaint was the non-availability of manpower and the breakdowns. Mr Mumford decided to recruit a HR Manager who can take care of the HR activities of the firm and the outcome was Mr Fredrick. Mr Fredrick has his masters degree in HR Management and about nine years of experience in the industry. The MD on assumption of the charge on the first day advised him to visit the units, assess the situation and plan his strategy to streamline the operations.

Mr Fredrick went around the unit, which is attached to the office. He was first introduced to Mr John, he was curious to know about the nature of the work he was doing. Mr John replied that he was working on a machine that he does not know but was operating it since two months. He had newly joined after completion of his graduation and was slowly picking up the skills. He then moved on to the packing section, where he was introduced to Mr Nath, the supervisor. Mr Nath told that though the work was going as per the schedule, but it was not as per the workflow. There was severe shortage of manpower and he had to depend upon other departments. Last one month two employees had left and there was no replacement.

Fredrick went to the billing section and saw Mr Jagannath looking at the invoices and making the entries and another person sitting in front of him watching. He just smiled and was on his job. When enquired about his work, he replied that he was in the organisation for the last two years and since two of his colleagues had resigned in the last two months, he was not in a position to train the newcomers, and since he needed to submit the bills he had to perform the job on his own.

Finally, Mr Fredrick met Mr Akilesh, who is the head of the unit. He enquired about the performance of the unit and the processes related to HR. Mr Akilesh said that the unit was reaching the targets, but due to attrition the performance was not up to the mark and sometimes they are getting complaints from the customers. The recruitment is left to the unit heads who decide their nature of work and pay. The situation in the other units is also the same.

Mr Fredrick understood the whole situation and was trying to analyse what strategy to be planned and the action plan anchored. He needed to submit the report to the MD during the following week.

## Questions

1. What do you think are the problems of Carter Publishing?
2. Do you think that the HR Manager can add value to streamline the business?
3. If you were Mr Fredrick what strategy and action plan you would present to the MD?

## References and Further Readings

Aadmodt, Michael G. 1991. *Applied Industrial/Organisational Psychology*, California: Wordsworth Publishing Company.
Bernardin, H. John and Joyce Russell. 1998. *Human Resource Management—An Experiential Approach*, Boston: Irwin/McGraw-Hill.
Bird, Malcom. 1989. *The Best Person for the Job*, London: Piatkus.
Cascio, Wayne F. 1998. *Managing Human Resources—Productivity, Quality of Work Life Profits*, New York: Irwin/McGraw-Hill Book Company.
Dunnette, Marvin D. and Leaetta M. Hough. 1998. *Handbook of Industrial and Organisational Psychology*, Mumbai: Jaico Publishing House.
Maitland, Lain. 2001. *Handbook of Recruiting, Interviewing, Testing and Starting Work*, New Delhi: Infinity Books.
Mescon, Michael H., Courtland L. Bovee and John Thill. 1996. *Business Today*, New Jersey: Prentice Hall.
Mukherjee, Ashok. 2004. 'Smart Enough to be Global', *Human Capital*, vol. 7, no. 8, January.
Mullins, Laurie J. 1999. 'Management and Organisational Behavior', UK: Prentice Hall.
Quinn, Mills D. 1985. *Planning With People in Mind*, Harvard Business Review Article.
Werther, William B., Keith Davis and William Werther Jr. 1996. *Human Resources and Personnel Management*, Boston: Irwin/McGraw-Hill.

# 'PSYCHOMETRIC TESTING' AVOIDING SUBJECTIVITY THROUGH PSYCHOMETRIC TESTS

*Your legacy should be that you made it better than it was when you got it.*

—Lee Lacocca

## Intent

- To understand the underlying assumption of psychology testing.
- To review different sorts of psychology tests and their purposes for which their tests are used.
- To define how the test course are interpreted and to find out more about this testing.
- To generate information which helps in making decisions in a rationale way relatively efficient in terms of time and money?

## Expression

A psychological test is a systematic procedure for observing behaviour and describing with the aid of numerical skills or fixed categories. A psychological test is essentially an objective and standardised measure of a sample of behaviour.

## Comprehension

People are all different and the uniqueness among the people is something to celebrate. To study the difference between the people, psychologists have developed the psychological tests. Development and use of psychological test is probably what psychology is best known for the world at large and tests are being used in for selecting people for jobs, employment setting, and also for promotions within. Over the last 10 years the impact of testing in the organisations has increased considerably and more people are affected than testing than ever before. The main advantage of using these tests is their objectivity and standards of tests. However, it requires uniform procedure for administration and scoring and also proper training to the one who is administering the test.

According to the British Psychological Society, 'psychological tests refer to a procedure for the evaluation of psychological functions. Psychological tests involve those being tested in solving problems, performing skilled tasks or making judgements. Psychological test procedures are characterised by standard methods of administration and scoring. Results are usually quantified by means of normative or other scaling procedures but they may also be interpreted qualitatively by reference to psychological theory'.

Psychology tests have been developed as measurement procedures, which means producing the results that are quantifiable. Test scores are typically given as numbers, which facilitates their analyses by mathematical and statistical needs. Psychology tests are distinguished in two broad categories, one—*test for maximum performance*—where the person taking the test is asked to perform to the best of their ability having right or wrong answer, second—*test of typical response*—it is designed to measure typical behaviour of a person where there are no right or wrong answers. The sum of psychological tests for performance measurement is the test of general mental ability for individual and group and test for measurement of special abilities. The measures for special abilities are observation method, self-report, projective techniques, etc. Since these techniques are objective and the scorer's judgement does not lead to variations in the score, instrument needs to be validated and sufficient proof needs to be maintained about the validity of the tests. The tests can be used to know the intellectual abilities, aptitude, perception, personality, interests, values, preferences, etc.

Complete details need to be maintained about the test and the consistency of the test in ensuring the right analysis. If the test results and the behaviour of the incumbent are different then the validity of the test needs to be looked into. Utmost care needs to be taken while choosing the test, validating the results with the behaviour, administration and periodical review. Tests need to be administered with the trained staff, results to be interpreted accurately and necessary care taken as per the advice of the designer's recommendation.

With the advent of the information technology, the usage of these tests has widely increased. The jobs have become highly technical and the organisation need to take utmost care of looking at the incumbent's culture, perception, values, personality, etc. Mere interview for a couple of hours or a series of interviews will not give the complete and objective picture, and hence the increasing usage of the computers in the area of tests, wherein the aspirant needs to take the test in the computer and the system will automatically give the result. The data can be used for the objective it is meant for.

For selecting people for the job and to generate self-insight, many organisations use certain personality questionnaires. Some of the tests, which are widely used, are Cattle's 16 PF, Myers-Briggs Type Indicator (MBTI), Thomas profiling, Saville and Holdsworth's (SHL) occupational personality, etc. Getting insight into how an individual's behavioural preferences compare with those of other people is likely to be helpful in many counselling situations, especially where the counselling is concerned with helping people to deal with typical day-to-day problems. Feedback need to be given to him so that the incumbent knows where he stands and where he can improve upon and he also gets satisfied because he knows where he is lacking. While giving the feedback the organisation not only is enabling to give an opportunity to correct but helps the individual to improve upon.

More than the skill, in the present business context, right kind of attitude is a must. People are hired not for the skill but for the attitude. The attitude plays a vital and important role in business success. The psychometric tests are such tools through which attitude and aptitude of the individual towards the job, people and the organisation can be evaluated. A small instance of interview no matter conducted by best experts could still be a misnomer. The psychometric tools help understanding the inner self of the individual through a variety of time tested tools so that the organisation can take the best decision while recruiting. These tests are equally applicable at the time of other important decision making such as promotion, transfer, project deployment, etc. Strategic utility of psychometric test are widely accepted in the corporations.

# Experiential Application

## A. Prerequisite

- More and more advancement in testing techniques of human beings for perspective jobs is invented and it is the organisation who has to make a right kind of choice of what technique is necessary to implement while undertaking the recruitment process. Psychometric tests are of a variety of types.

- All have different purposes and meanings and each test leads to different results. The HR must choose appropriate psychometric tools depending upon the need of the organisation, level of the candidate and the function.
- The results of the tests are scientific however the results could be skewed if there is a variation in administration as well as variation due to evaluation techniques.
- At the same time if the candidate has the knowledge of the tests like a typical HR person he can easily make it through the test and the whole purpose of tests is vitiated.

## B. Process Steps

| Step | Process |
|------|---------|
| Step – I | Map the purpose, target population and the situations requiring administering psychometric test. |
| Step – II | Derive information on the development and the design of the test including scientific validity. |
| Step – III | The test questionnaire need to be test administered and the scores are being described. |
| Step – IV | The tests need to be standardised giving the details of sample size and its representativeness. |
| Step – V | The test needs to be administered for the purpose it has been chosen. |
| Step – VI | To collect the data of the test being administered and validate. |
| Step – VII | Review periodically of its impact and usefulness for the purpose of it being designed. |

# Potential Gains and Areas of Concern

- Psychological testing is used for job analysis, which includes selection and placement of new recruits, training and development of new activities, performance appraisal, human resource planning and pay and reward.
- The psychology test generates information to help in making decisions in rationale way relatively efficient in terms of time and money.
- Psychological tests are fairer than traditional impressionistic techniques, which are vulnerable to prejudice and bias.
- The test cannot measure unique characteristics, background or context in which the test is taken and the dynamic nature of human personality.
- The tests must meet the recognised standards; if not, the whole purpose of the tool goes waste.

- The tests must not be administered for the test sake, but it should be designed to suit to the objective, if not, there is a scope for getting the diagonally opposite analysis of the personality.
- The results would be skewed, if administering and proper management of tools were not taken care.

# Measurability

## Try It Out

(1: not at all done, 2: moderately done, 3: to some extent done, 4: to a great extent done, 5: excellently done)

- My organisation uses psychometric tools for objective evaluation.  ☐
- Objectives are determined for evaluating competencies and related psychometric tests.  ☐
- My organisation has trained evaluators of psychometric tests.  ☐
- Feedback is given to the employees/candidates about the strengths and scope for development.  ☐

Analysis: the average score would determine the extent to which psychometric test are used in your organisation.

## Score Card

(*: 25% achieved, **: 50% achieved, ***: 75% achieved, ****: 100% achieved)

| Technology | Objective Elements | Unit | Historical | Last Year | Current Year | Stretch Target | Status |
|---|---|---|---|---|---|---|---|
| Psychometric Testing | Strategy Document on Psychometric Testing | Doc | Nil | No | Yes | NA | ** |
| Psychometric Testing | Usage of Psychometric Tests for Job Interviews | Nos | Nil | Nil | 01 | 01 | ** |
| Psychometric Testing | Usage of Psychometric Tests during Assessment Centre | Nos | 01 | 01 | 02 | 02 | ** |

# Proven Track Record

## Track One

### Bristol–Myers

Attracting and retaining employees was a perennial issue with Bristol–Myers. This was because there was a mismatch between selection criteria and actual recruitment practices. This resulted in dissimilarities in the candidates that the company was looking for, and the ones that they actually ended up hiring. The company thus, started using psychological testing when they found that outsiders who were hired tended to leave the organisation because they did not fit into the company's culture in terms of its values. However, psychological testing is being criticised for the reason that management style cannot be measured.

After using psychological testing, the right kind of candidates through psychological assessments is recruited and thus retention rate among those hired from outside the company has increased by 25 per cent.

(*Source*: Nelson and Quick, 2003: 552.)

## Track Two

### City Garage

City Garage was using the simple method of recruitment by way of paper and pencil and a plain interview, which was sufficient for a small enterprise. As the organisation is growing and the customer interface with the mechanics increased, City Garage was facing difficulty to handle.

City Garage has purchased a Personality Profile Analysis (PPA) from Thomas International. A simple 10-minute test is administered with 24-question PPA. This test shows whether the applicant is high or low in four personality characteristics; it also produces follow-up questions. If the candidates answer satisfactorily, they're backed by all-day interviews after which the hiring decisions were made. Company expects to improve its process substantially.

(*Source*: Dessler, 2003: 154.)

# Applied HR Case

## 'Crescendo Technologies Limited'

Crescendo Technologies Limited is in the manufacture of precision instruments and UPS. On assumption of the charge, Owens wanted to bring in an intervention that will be able to give value to the function and benefit to the organisation. Owens was going through the HR planning data given by his subordinate. When he analysed the distribution of manpower, he found that they are divided into production, marketing, finance and accounts, HR, stores, administration and customer service. Owens analysed the data on the recruitment and attrition rate and was surprised to find out that the rate is 18 per cent and 21 per cent respectively which is high in all respects pertaining to the nature of the industry. He soon realised that there is no coordination among the departments and each department is working as silo and work independently. The main concern for each department is their interest rather than their customers.

The immediate requirement that came across was recruitment of 10 customer service executives for the call centre since the attrition rate is as high as 40 per cent. At the same time Owens analysed that the team and customer orientation is not there even to the desired extent. Mr Owens wanted to go to the MD to seek permission to make certain changes so that the problems can be plugged. He would like to take some concrete data to prove his point and also to ensure that the new entrants who enter the organisation have those characteristics. Owens decided to use the psychometric tool to analyse the competencies and apply the same to the employees with the consent from the MD.

## Questions

1. Do you think Owens has taken a right decision to introduce the psychometric tests?
2. If you think that Owens is right in his decision, suggest those competencies that need to be analysed and what kind of tests will help him to get the details.

## References and Further Readings

Barrett, Jim. 2000. *Test Yourself*, New Delhi: Kogan Page India Pvt. Ltd.

Davidson, Mark. 2002. *How to Master Personality Questionnaire*, 2nd edn, New Delhi: Kogan Page India Pvt Ltd.

Dessler, Gary. 2003. *Human Resource Management*, 9th edn, New Delhi: Prentice-Hall of India Private Limited.

Dunnette, Marvin D. and Leaetta M. Hough. 1998. *Handbook of Industrial and Organizational Psychology*, Mumbai: Jaico Publishing House.

Jackson, Charles. 2001. *Understanding Psychological Testing*, Mumbai: Jaico Publishing House.

Nelson and Quick. 2003. *Organizational Behavior*, Ohio: Thomson Learning.

Pestonjee, D.M. (ed.). 1997. *Third Handbook of Psychological and Social Instruments*, New Delhi: Concept Publishing Company.

Pfeiffer, William J. and Bellew Anlette C. 1993. *Using Instruments in Human Resource Development*, New Delhi: Aditya Books Pvt Ltd.

Toplis, John, Victor Dulewicz and Clive Fletcher. 1998. *Psychological Testing*, Mumbai: Jaico Publishing House.

# 'CAREER AND SUCCESSION PLANNING' PROSPECTS OF GROWTH IN ORGANISATIONS THROUGH CAREER AND SUCCESSION PLANNING

*Plans get you into things but you got to work your way out.*

—Will Rogers (1949)

## Intent

- To understand the process of career planning in an organisation.
- To provide an opportunity to potential high performing employees for career enhancement.

## Expression

The pattern of work related experience that spans the course of a person's life is called career. A life long process of learning about self, jobs and organisations, setting personal career goals developing strategies for achieving the goals and revising the goals based on work and life experiences is career management.

## Comprehension

Career planning is the primary responsibility of the employee, but the organisation plays a complimentary role. The responsibility lies with the company to show the career path if an employee would like to go up in the ladder. Career means the series of world related positions that help the employee to grow through exhibiting his competencies in job skills, success and fulfilment of the targets. Career planning is the process where the employee is aware of the skills, knowledge, achievements, etc., that are required to act each level up in the organisation ladder and the opportunities available to him to attain his personal goals.

Career plans shape the progression of the individual within an organisation in accordance with the assessments of organisational needs and performance and the potential of the individual members. The career plans give the organisation the requisite manpower for the managerial succession, for the individual the training and experience that will give them competencies to take up higher responsibilities and the path to those who have the potential to grow and achieve successful careers.

Individuals who were hoping to make a quick scramble to the top have to re-imagine their goals, rethink their strategies, and re-evaluate what they think is important. Many individuals and organisations both don't know how to start and manage the careers. The career ladder is a structured series of job positions, through which an individual progresses in an organisation. With re-engineering and restructuring the balance between individuals and organisations in terms of managing careers has shifted in different times. The corporate ladder has fallen down. Now questions are asked on an employee's expectations; what an employee will get from the organisation if he is not guaranteed lifelong employment and time-bound automated promotion; and similarly the organisation is asked about its expectations from their employees. The employees do recognise that they must manage their own career development. A discrete exchange occurs when an organisation gains productivity while a person gains work experience.

In a short-term arrangement which recognises such job skill changes value and re-negotiations must occur for conditional change. This contrast is sharply with the manual loyalty contract of the old career paradigm in which employee loyalty was exchanged for job security. A common view of understanding this is that this is a series of stages through which an individual passes during their working lives. This is that this is also called career paths.

Management succession planning aims to ensure that a sufficient supply of appropriately qualified and capable men and women are available to meet the future needs of the organisation. Such men and women should be available readily to fill vacancies caused through retirement, death, resignation, promotion or transfer of staff or through the establishment of new positions. Despite the influence of delayering, changes to the traditional hierarchical structure and less opportunity of job for life, there is still an important need for effective succession planning to develop internal talent and help maintain loyalty and commitment to the organisation. In succession planning, key positions are identified and analysed, candidates are assessed against job and personal requirements, individual development plans are created, and people are selected. Succession planning is position specific in that it focuses on replacements for positions even if the current candidate may not match the position requirements well. Therefore usually, just the top positions have successors identified.

Growth is everybody's need. From the organisation to an individual, upward progress is always desired. Career Planning process is a complex process. It is difficult and quite uncertain since no one can predict the future accurately and the future role and job.

Career planning made in haste and without strategic input is merely a paperwork, will not serve any purpose. Employees will not be happy if the career does not move with the planned process as determined before. Thus, career planning is a strategic move and a must for all HR functionaries in an organisation.

# Experiential Application

## A. Prerequisite

- Career planning/replacement planning is an important process in the organisation since it concerns every employee of the organisation. The organisation must create a bottom up approach where managers at the lower levels make initial recommendations as to who can be the replacements for their direct reports.
- Consider the top three management levels in an organisation as an appropriate number for positions to include.
- In a highly technical, detailed and stable organisation, competencies may need to identify themselves with all key positions through a formal job analysis process.
- The tool of assessment centre is the best formal method because the employees are evaluated on job-sample exercise, which closely resemble the actual job. It provides extremely accurate measures of performance and capabilities.
- Some specific strategies are:

  - avoid reality shock;
  - provide challenging initial job;
  - provide realistic job preview in recruiting;
  - improve personal planning and forecasting;
  - assign new recruit to demanding, specially trained first bosses; and
  - provide periodic job rotation and job pathing.

## B. Process Steps

| Step | Process |
| --- | --- |
| Step – I | Projection of manpower is made basing on the factors like plant expansion, contraction, attrition, etc. |
| Step – II | Human Resource department to review its management skill inventory to identify the management talent now employed. |
| Step – III | Using multiple review method, an inventory of permutable employee to be found out. |
| Step – IV | Define and determine high potential employees with their availability. |

*(Continued)*

(*Continued*)

| Step | Process |
|------|---------|
| Step – V | Management replacement charts are drawn to fill the management and individual development needs. |
| Step – VI | Each higher level management reviews the recommendations and makes revisions. |
| Step – VII | Assess candidates against competencies and criteria. |

# Potential Gains and Areas of Concern

- Career planning can provide employees with information to enable them to make better career decisions.
- Every individual needs to continuously reassess his or her life goals and assess the progress towards them. Career planning is usually done at some crisis point, where the individual is faced with possible alternative career pattern.
- Career planning of an individual keeps changing because an individual's objectives and opportunities will probably change during his/her lifetime.
- Though an organisation makes plan for the career development of an individual, with changing business environment, an organisation may not be able to fulfil the planned career as worked out for an individual.
- The career once planned may not yield desire results since with the rising career an employee may not develop the requisite competencies to effectively manage the higher level job.

# Measurability

## Try It Out

(1: not at all done, 2: moderately done, 3: to some extent done, 4: to a great extent done, 5: excellently done)

- My organisation has career and development plan for employees.  ☐
- My organisation has a cross-functional team to deliberate and release  ☐
  career plan.
- My organisation has Management Succession Plan.  ☐
- Various training programmes and mentoring processes are planned to  ☐
  develop the competencies of employees to grow in their career.

Analysis: the average score would determine the extent to which career and succession planning exist in your organisation.

## Score Card

(*: 25% achieved, **: 50% achieved, ***: 75% achieved, ****: 100% achieved)

| Technology | Objective Elements | Unit | Historical | Last Year | Current Year | Stretch Target | Status |
|---|---|---|---|---|---|---|---|
| Career and Succession Planning | Strategy Document on Career and Succession Planning | Doc | Nil | No | Yes | NA | ** |

# Proven Track Record

## Track One

### Hewlett-Packard

Three months course on personal career management was developed at Hewlett-Packard (HP) Colorado spring division. The two methods used in the course were self-assessment and subsequent application of finding the workplace to chart a career path for each employee. The idea of self-assessment towards career planning is certainly not new.

Hewlett-Packard uses six devises to generate data for self-assessment. These include: a written self-interview, strong vocational interest inventory, Allport Vernon–Lindsey study of values, twenty-four hours' diaries, interview with two 'significant others', and lifestyle representation. The key ingredient of this programme is its emphasis on an inductive approach. Following the self-assessment, the department manager interviews their subordinates to learn about their career objectives. Career development objectives for each employee are incorporated into the performance objectives for future performance appraisal. The department head monitors the employee's career progress as part of the review process and sees himself responsible for offering all possible support.

(*Source*: Cascio 1998: 345.)

## Track Two

### Borroughs Welcome Company

Borroughs Welcome Company provides aid to individual employee's self-assessment and career development planning. It is the responsibility of every employee, manager and the organisation itself to provide the opportunities for career planning. Career development will enhance retention, mobility, or development of the needed talent in the tight labour market.

The employee has to take the responsibility of career development; self-assessment, meet the objectives, take the feedback and communicate the interests and developmental needs with the manager. He needs to follow the development plans as decided.

The manager supports the employee in career development including communicating career information to others as needed. He has to communicate job requirements and responsibilities, open and honest performance feedback, conduct career development discussions and encourage and support the employee in his development plans. The organisation needs to communicate its mission, vision and goals so that a realistic career plan can be made. The organisation needs to provide information on career requirements, opportunities and developmental systems, design and implement effective superior–subordinate career development discussions, train managers to be coach and mentor, integrate career plans into comprehensive system and evaluate and recognise managers for their success in employee career development. This process has enabled the organisation to put in strong career planning which helped in retention and bringing in competencies as required by the organisation.

(*Source*: Walker, 1992: 209.)

# Applied HR Case

## Moon Textures Limited

If one can think of fast growth and try to equate the name that symbolises it, it is Moon Textures Limited. The firm which started as Moon Tailors with a small establishment has made it to Moon Textures Limited within a span of eight years with the turnover growing at a very fast pace. The main feature of the firm is that they have designed an unique shirt and trouser that gives an executive look though they are purely casual in nature. The design was an instant hit and soon they started getting orders from all over the country. The firm that had started with one worker soon became a big establishment of 300 employees and there is no looking back. They moved on to other garments for ladies and children.

In order to go international, the firm has thought of hiring management graduates who has specialisation in international markets and also marketing. The HR and Personnel Manager recruited about 15 trainees and also managers who have experience in international selling. The HR and Personnel Manager has confirmed two of them looking at the performance in the executive cadre. Later on due to the work pressure another two were taken as managers and were sent for the assignments abroad. Time has passed and the balance 11 trainees are worried about their future in the organisation. They have approached the Personnel Manager about the career plan and he answered that depending upon the requirement they will be absorbed into the company. Within a span of two months ten out of the 11 have left the organisation and the two executives who were confirmed also left, since they were not given the confirmation in the managerial cadre.

When the MD was reviewing the performance with the Head-International Marketing, he saw a gradual fall in the sales in the international market and the cause was attributed to the leaving of the trainees. The HR and Personnel Manager was summoned to the review and during the discussion he told the discussion that he had with the 11 trainees and the subsequent attrition. Immediately the MD asked the HR and Personnel Manager to look into the causes of the attrition and asked him to ensure a plan that will retain majority of the trainees in the firm since it is running very well and there is no problem pertaining to the cash flow and profitability.

## Questions

1. What are the problems faced by Moon Textures Limited?
2. Can you find a way out in ensuring that the trainees can be retained?
3. If you were the HR and Personnel Manager what do you suggest to the Management?

## References and Further Readings

Bernardin H. John and Joyce Russell, 1998. *Human Resource Management—An Experiential Approach*, Boston: Irwin/McGraw-Hill.

Bernardin, H. John. 2003. *Human Resource Management*, New Delhi: Tata McGraw-Hill Publishing Company Limited.

Cascio, Wayne F. 1998. *Managing Human Resources*, USA: Irwin/McGraw-Hill.

Rothwell, William J. 2001. *Effective Succession Planning: Ensuring Leadership Continuity and Building Talent from Within*, New York: AMACOM.

Griffin, Ricky W. 2000. *Fundamentals of Management*, Chennai: All India Publishers and Distributors.

Schuler S. Randell and Huber Vandra. 1989. *Personnel and Human Resource Management*, St Paul: West Publishing Company.

Singh, P.N. 1993. *Developing and Managing Human Resources*, 2nd edn, Bombay: Suchandra Publications.

Walker, James W. 1992. *Human Resource Strategy*, New York: McGraw-Hill/International Editions.

# 'ROLE CLARITY'
# AVOIDING AMBIGUITY OF ROLES
# THROUGH ROLE CLARITY

*Whatever their job is, people see their role as not just to be doing things the way they're designed today, but to figure out the way they ought to be done tomorrow.*

—Anonymous

## Intent

- To examine the ambiguity of the role between different jobholders.
- To understand the process of making role clarity through role negotiation process.
- To generate the clarity of role among the employees by using role clarity exercise and making balance of job for what to do or what not to do.

## Expression

A 'role' is the expected pattern of behaviour associated with members occupying a particular position within the structure of the organisation. Role clarity is an exercise to clarify the roles amongst the group of role players and to remove role ambiguity persisting amongst the role players.

## Comprehension

The concept of role is important to the functioning of groups and for an understanding of group processes and behaviour and helps to clarify the structure and to define the pattern of complex relationship within the group. It is through role differentiation that the structure of the work group and relationship among its members is established. The development of group entails the identification of distinct roles for each of its members.

In an organisation role incongruence take place when a member of the staff is perceived as having a high and responsible position in one respect but a slow standing in another respect. Difficulties with role incongruence can arise from the nature of groupings and formal relationship within the structure of the organisation.

The need for role clarity takes place when there is a role conflict. Role conflict arises when there is a gap between behavioural aspects of a particular role vis-à-vis the personality of the individual who is performing that role. Role conflicts include role incompatibility, role ambiguity, role overload and role underload. There are a number of ways through which the management might attempt to avoid or reduce role conflicts and bring in role clarity. Role non-clarity may result from a lack of formally prescribed expectation. It is likely to arise in large, diverse groups or at times of constant change. Role clarity exercise deals with increased specification and clarity of prescribed role expectations, for example, through written statements of objectives and policy, use of manuals and set procedures, introduction of appropriate rules and detail job descriptions.

Uncertainty often relates to such matters as the method of performing tasks, the extent of the person's authority and responsibilities, standards of work and the evaluation and appraisal of the performance.

Role is a casting that each employee is asked to perform on the centre stage of an organisation. The casting and performance can only go well if the cast member and the director of the role-play define the role clearly well in advance. A thorough rehearsal is made so that everyone knows what to perform. Even slightest ambiguity in this would deter the performance and one would not be able to deliver as per the expectation of the role. The organisation scenario is even more complex and demands sometimes multiple roles and casting from each employee. It is imperative that HR must clearly define all the roles to its greatest extent so that each one of them could perform the role diligently and to the best of their capability. Role clarity is a process and is required substantial input. It needs to be managed strategically in the organisation's context.

# Experiential Application

## A. Prerequisite

- Role clarity is directed at work relationship among the group members. The techniques basically involve a series of controlled negotiations between participants.
- In the course of role clarity process, the manager frankly discusses what they want from each other and explains why.
- Many companies teach its managers the art of negotiations with one another in a workshop mode in off-site setting.

## B. Process Steps

| Step | Process |
|------|---------|
| Step - I | Employee prepares a list for each member three things—things to do more, things to do less and things to do the same. |
| Step - II | Each member writes out a master list combining the list written about him/her, and the list is circulated among all. |
| Step - III | After feedback the role occupant lists duties and behaviour. |
| Step - IV | Role negotiation is being done to arrive at the correct duties and behaviour through a process of discussion. |
| Step - V | Role set reaches consensus on role occupants' expectations. |
| Step - VI | Written role negotiation agreement lays down the additions and concessions given regarding one's role. |
| Step - VII | Periodic review of the role agreement in line with the changing business strategy. |

# Potential Gains and Areas of Concern

- The concept of role is important to the functioning of individual and groups and for an understanding of group processes and behaviour.
- Through role clarity, the exercise group entails the identifications of distinct roles for each of its members and defines the pattern of complex relationship within the group.
- Difficulties with role incongruence can arise from the nature of groupings and formal relationship within the structure of the organisation.
- In an organisation role incongruence takes place when a member of the staff is perceived as having a high and responsible position in one respect but a slow standing in another respect.

# Measurability

## Try It Out

(1: not at all done, 2: moderately done, 3: to some extent done, 4: to a great extent done, 5: excellently done)

- My organisation has laid down role directory and employees derive their ☐ roles from this directory.

- Role conflict is addressed on top priority through discussions and          □
  deliberations.
- Role clarity exercises are conducted periodically to bring in congruence      □
  of roles.

Analysis: the average score would determine the extent to which role clarity process exists in your organisation.

## Score Card

(*: 25% achieved, **: 50% achieved, ***: 75% achieved, ****: 100% achieved)

| Technology | Objective Elements | Unit | Historical | Last Year | Current Year | Stretch Target | Status |
|---|---|---|---|---|---|---|---|
| Role Clarity | Role Directory | Doc | Yes | Yes | Dec | Nov | ** |
| Role Clarity | Role Clarity Workshops | Nos | 2 | 1 | 12 | 16 | ** |

# Proven Track Record

## Track One

### Escorts

Escorts Group ranks among India's top engineering conglomerates having associates and group subsidiaries. The total business of Escorts was restructured in the early 1990s to face the liberalised economy, to garner business opportunities and become a member of the global village. Restructuring exercise led to delineation of the role of HR professionals in the group.

Human Resource professionals in the Escorts group like any other group operate at the unit level or at the headquarter level. During the course of restructuring Group HR–SBU-HR, HR interface was deliberated and clarified. The roles have been laid down to bring in clarity and to attain the goals of the business strategy. The corporate HR is the policy making body while the SBU (Strategic Business Unit) was to propose and implement the policies. This has helped the company to overcome the gaps in restructuring and enabled the company to become a global player.

(*Source*: Shukla, 1998: 71.)

## Track Two

## Indian Organic Chemicals Limited

Indian Organic Chemicals Limited (IOCL) was incorporated as Public Limited Company manufacturing diverse products. To bring in the change it has been decided to introduce assessment centres for middle and upper middle management groups to zero in high performers, chalk out retention plans and reward systems and make each member a change agent. As part of the process role clarity exercises were conducted to bring in clarity of each other's role in the business process.

Role clarity exercises brought in a lot of issues regarding structure, responsibility, authority, which the panel members have noted. It has also helped individuals to have a clear position of role clarity and know one's strength and weakness. The organisation took steps to bring in more clarity about the various roles thus bringing in transparency.

(*Source*: Sahu, 1994: 421.)

# Applied HR Case

## Haari Computers

Suresh, Head of HR of Haari Computers has about five years of professional experience and is considered as an young, energetic and team player. He used to treat employees of other departments as internal customers and trained all his subordinates to act as one stop solution for grievance of any sort that the employee had. The total strength of the function was four members and they comprised a good team that has created a niche among all the departments.

Haari Computers acquired Amar Computer Components Pvt Limited to forwardly integrate the capability to the assembly unit. In order to bring in goodwill among the employees and to drive the company forward, it was decided that the company will take care of the employees during mergers and acquisitions. The strength of the HR increased to 10 members. Amar Computers had a small accommodation and in order to integrate the machine, material and employees, it had to move to Haari Computers. Initially there was a great deal of resistance from both sides. However, with firm commitment from the top management, the employees started responding positively towards the management.

After the unit became large Suresh was constantly being pressurised by the employees and the heads that they were not getting the right kind of response from the HR and a lot of issues needed to be resolved until the process got smoothened. During the half yearly appraisal process Suresh was appraising the half yearly performance and found that his team is utterly failing in meeting the targets. Suresh had reprimanded all the HR personnel for their non-performance, which was reflecting during the meetings.

All the HR personnel gathered and decided to tell that Suresh was wrong in his judgement since they were working as per the style suggested by him. Suresh was surprised to hear all the HR personnel when they started responding to the issue of non-performance by stating that it was his style of functioning which had resulted in low performance. They further stated that they were only doing what they were asked to do without going into the depth of the task and were only looking to resolve their personal grievances. A lot of time was getting wasted in knowing and learning about the process and helping the internal customers. Since there was no focus of what they were intending to do, their performance was not up to the desired level. Suresh was very upset since if this was the scenario within his department, what would happen with the other departments?

## Questions

1. Was Suresh right in his approach towards the functioning of his department?
2. Was Suresh correct in extrapolating his department's functioning with other departments?
3. If you were in the place of Suresh what action plan would you make to ensure that every HR person knows what he is doing and is expected to do?

## References and Further Readings

Dunnette, Marvin D. and Leaetta M. Hough, 1998. *Handbook of Industrial and Organizational Psychology*, Mumbai: Jaico Publishing House.

Pareek, Udai. 1993. *Making Organizational Roles Effective*, New Delhi: Tata McGraw-Hill Publishing Company Limited.

Sahu, Bhabatosh. 1994. 'Assessment Centre Approach for Organization Development: Sharing Practical Experience', in Uddesh Kohli, Dharni P. Sinha (eds), *HRD Global Changes and Strategies in 2000 AD*, New Delhi: Allied Publishers Ltd.

Sarangi, P.K. 1988. 'A Descriptive Note on Role Analysis, Experience of Indian Oil Corporation Limited', in T.V. Rao, K.K. Verma, Anil Khandelwal and Abraham (eds), *Alternative Approaches and Strategies of HRD*, Jaipur: Rawat Publications.

Shukla, P.N. 1998. 'Aligning HR Interventions with Corporate Goals—Escorts Experience', in *Business Led HR Strategies*, All India Management Association, New Delhi: Excel Books.

Singh, P.N. 1993. *Developing and Managing Human Resources*, 2nd edn. Bombay: Suchandra Publications.

# 'PERFORMANCE MANAGEMENT SYSTEM' DEVELOPING COMPETENCIES THROUGH PERFORMANCE MANAGEMENT SYSTEM (PMS)

*Management by objectives works if you first think through your objectives. Ninety per cent of the time you haven't.*

—Peter Drucker

## Intent

- To understand PMS and its importance to an individual and the organisations.
- To bring in the improvement in the individual performance and in turn the unit and the organisational performance.
- To define key result areas (KRA)/ key performance indicators (KPI) of an employee to establish work goals for a specific period in an open atmosphere. It also provides an avenue for the employee and his manager to plan the training and development activities.
- To review individual performance based on the set target.
- To arrive at certain personnel decisions based on the results of PMS.
- To evaluate the organisational performance vis-à-vis individual performance.

## Expression

Performance management is defined as a process for establishing a shared understanding about what is to be achieved, and how it is to be achieved, and an approach to managing people that increases the probability of success which can be achieved in the long-term or short-term.

# Comprehension

Many attempts have been made by many companies to project performance management as the developmental tool. The tool aims at establishing the performance culture which both the individuals and the groups take responsibility for continuous improvement of business process, their own skill and contributions to the achievement of business goals. The process can also be used to communicate down the line the organisation's strategies and norms, and integrate the individual goals with that of the organisation.

Performance appraisal is a key evaluation system for evaluating individual performance of the employee on the job and over a period of time. Performance Management System has undergone sea change from a closed confidential system to an open and transparent system. In the past, generally, the process was adopted for gathering performance data for compensation and reward-related support but however, in these days, the performance appraisal is used for developmental orientation. However, at the end, experience shows that the end result of performance appraisal tends to decide the compensation and reward management and some part of the developmental area. Though the system is being viewed more on the outcome of the appraisal, i.e., the rewards, development orientation need to be reoriented to bring in performance driven culture rather than the financial aspect. While setting the tone for the PMS, some of the organisations besides giving due weightage to the achievement of the key result areas, also look into the areas of improvement in the performance standards and the development of the individual. With this not only the performance is being taken care but also the way the KRA are being achieved and how the individual has improved over time are being addressed.

Performance management is the system approach in which the individuals, teams, their supervisors and organisations are first to plan the performance, set targets and build the KRAs. In the words of McGregor, PMS should be founded on the principle of *Management of objectives and self-control* rather than management of command. On a specific time frame these KRAs are reviewed through discussion mode and subsequently ratings are given on performance areas as well as certain defined behavioural areas. Rating is normally given on a scale ranging from four points to seven points depending upon the organisational suitability.

Traditionally, performance appraisal is an appraisal process between the employee and the boss and now, this has further developed to performance management wherein other employees such as bosse's boss and the employee's peers, also play an important role in determining the performance of the employee. The HR department serves the policy making and advisory role. It provides the system with support not only by way of forms and formats but also ensures the process is followed properly while performance appraisal is being implemented between the employee and their bosses. The HR department facilitates the results of PMS and uses it scientifically for various personnel decisions.

The story of performance management does not end with the declaring of the rewards and the related compensation, but giving the feedback so that they can monitor their performance and take corrective action. The rapid development in the area of information technology enables the individual to be given qualitative and quantitative feedback to improve further.

Review and rewarding performance is an issue all HR professionals confront with since the organisations have started realising HR processes. Finding ways through a variety of performance measuring tools and performance management systems in different forms came into existence. Varying with the organisational requirement and maturity of the culture, different kinds of performance appraisal processes are put in right from completely close and confidential kind of appraisals to open appraisals including 360-degree feedback processes. In all such cases, the central theme remains that the organisation is in constant look for the best way to appraise their employee so that the performers get appropriate rewards and the non-performers are given inputs for the areas that they require improvements. Performance Management System is a strategic technology since this is the only tool that is being used in the organisation for performance management of all employees.

# Experiential Application

## A. Prerequisite

- The important prerequisite is to have a thorough job analysis prior to implementing a performance management system. Job analysis is approached through job description and job specification for each job. Performance standard should be developed from the job analysis as input into the performance appraisal.
- Performance management should evaluate a number of specific behaviours as opposed to evaluating overall job performance using one or a few global measures. Performance review discussion should be a two-way communication between the evaluator and the employee.
- It should not be used only as a means of evaluating performance but also a means of motivating and developing the employees. The purpose of performance management and the objective of the organisation must be considered carefully before deciding on a performance management method.
- A proper training programme must be given to all concerned and a link between performance appraisal system and the organisation's long-term strategic plan should be clearly defined.
- A successful PMS should be build around clear objective, have the support of both management and employee, be flexible enough to adapt to organisational changes and foster open discussion between supervisor and employees.

- The validity of the PMS should be examined at regular intervals.

## B. Process Steps

| Step | Process |
|---|---|
| Step - I | At the beginning of the year, the business plan to be communicated to all employees through workshop, brochures, Intranet, etc. |
| Step - II | Employees to fill their KRAs for the year in line with the business plan in consultation with the Reporting Officer. |
| Step - III | Employee and the Reporting Officer to have continuous dialogue about achievement and non-achievement of KRAs. |
| Step - IV | Reporting Officer to give feedback to the employee on his performance in discussion with the Reviewing Officer. |
| Step - V | Employee would take the feedback and work on improvements for the next year. |
| Step - VI | The HR department to consolidate the results of PMS ratings for compensation, reward and other personnel decisions. |
| Step - VII | The HR Department to maintain the database of PMS of all employees and repeat the cycle every year. |

# Potential Gains and Areas of Concern

- Well-planned KRAs would lead to achievement of set organisational goals.
- The objectivity of the review would reflect through performance review discussions and employees will get an opportunity to express his or her view over the performance.
- The PMS brings in a sense of ownership and a mutual agreement between the parties to the performance management, which ultimately bring in a collaborative approach.
- Since the entire appraisal process is open, it will bring in transparency and openness in the culture of the organisation.
- The organisational decisions for compensation, reward, etc., will be based on scientific derivatives of PMS rather than ad hoc decisions.
- The top management needs to drive the process of building objectives and cascading down to the individual level. Lack of support of the top management means the whole PMS is a farce. At the same time, the role of the line managers is also important in the success of the PMS.
- No matter how objectively the system is planned, there are chances that the appraisal process will have subjectivity during appraisal. This is due to the human processes involved in it.

- Since performance management is generally linked to compensation and reward decisions, the PMS results are normally skewed looking at the financial gain/loss of individual employees by the reporting officers.
- Too many forms and formats are time-consuming in nature.

# Measurability

## Try It Out

(1: not at all done, 2: moderately done, 3: to some extent done, 4: to a great extent done, 5: excellently done)

- My organisation has an objective PMS. ☐
- Management, officers and employees are sincere in filling up appraisal forms and they adhere to the schedules. ☐
- Organisational goals are cascaded down the line and all employees derive their KRAs. ☐
- My organisation gives importance to the behavioural aspects besides the performance parameters. ☐
- Performance Appraisals follow with compensation revision and employees' CTC (cost to company) is revised as per the performance. ☐

Analysis: the average score would determine the extent to which Performance Management process exists in your organisation.

## Score Card

(*: 25% achieved, **: 50% achieved, ***: 75% achieved, ****: 100% achieved)

| Technology | Objective Elements | Unit | Historical | Last Year | Current Year | Stretch Target | Status |
|---|---|---|---|---|---|---|---|
| Performance Management System | Strategy Document on Performance Management System | Doc | Yes | Yes | Yes | Nov | ** |
| Performance Management System | 100% coverage of all employees | % | 98% | 99% | 100% | 100% | ** |
| Performance Management System | Workbook on the implementation of PMS | Doc | Yes | Yes | May | April | * |

# Proven Track Record

## Track One

## Federal Express

Federal Express has an upward appraisal system called Survey Feedback Action (SFA). It has three phases. First, the survey itself is given each year to every employee. It contains items designed to gather information about those things that help and hinder employees in their work environment. Results of the survey for a workgroup are then compiled and returned to the manager.

A feedback session between the manager and his or her workgroup is the second phase. The session's goal is to identify specific concerns or problems, examine specific causes for these problems and devise action plan to correct the problems. As a result managers are trained to ask probing questions. The feedback meeting should lead to a third action plan phase. The plan itself is a list of actions that the manager will take to address the employees' concern and boost the results.

(*Source*: Dessler, 1997.)

## Track Two

## Xerox Corporation

Rather than attempting to fix the old appraisal system, Xerox found a task force to create a new system from scratch. The task force was made up of senior human resource executives and other middle management employees. The task force designed and developed a new performance management system altogether different from the old one. The new system has three stages as opposed to the one step process of the old system.

The first stage occurs at the beginning of the year where the manager and employees together work out written agreement on the employees' goals, objectives, plans and tasks for the year. Standards of satisfactory performance are explicitly spelled out in measurable, attainable and specific terms. The second stage is mid-year where the mandatory feedback and discussion session takes place to review the progress. And the third stage in the process is the formal performance review that takes place at the year end. They can meet and discuss the performance of the employees resolving any discrepancies between the perceptions among each other and these emphasise more on feedback and improvement. This stage also includes a developmental planning session in which training, education or developmental experiences that can help employees.

(*Source*: Anthony, Kacmar and Perrewe, 2002: 386.)

# Applied HR Case

## Performance Appraisal at Electra Appliances Limited

Electra Appliances Limited has established itself as an upcoming appliance industry that has grown from 12 employees to 245 employees with the annual growth rate of more than 30 per cent. The most important aspect of the company is its quality and after sales service. The unit was always used to run with the required manpower and employees used to share the responsibility. The compensation though was not matching with the market, but the operational freedom and flexible hours has led to retention of some of the good performers. The employees are not satisfied because at the time of joining their salaries were good but when it has come to the annual increments, there is no objective method of assessment and employees were given as per the decision taken by the MD. There was no full-fledged HR manager and the function is being taken care by the Accounts Department. The performance was being measured on a form that has only certain subjective qualities and does not focus on the factual performance. The rating depends upon the value judgement of the supervisors and the managers.

The following format gives the Performance Appraisal Format of Electra Appliances Limited:

*Confidential*

**ELECTRA APPLIANCES LIMITED**

**Performance Appraisal Form**

| | |
|---|---|
| Name: | Employment No: |
| Designation: | Grade: |
| Department: | Qualification: |
| Reporting Officer: | Reviewing Officer: |

Instructions for filling up of the Appraisal Form:

The assessment of skills is made on the performance during the review period and you are required to assess for the whole year taking the data of what the employee has performed. Please take the signature of the employee after appraising him. Send the form to the HR department after completion in confidence. The interpretation of the scale enables you to mark basing on the judgement of the performance. You need to just mark in the appropriate box as given under:

1. Excellent: exceeding the expectations.
2. Very Good: beyond the expectations.

3. Good: Meeting the expectations.

4. Satisfactory: Not meeting the expectations.

| Sl. No. | Performance Parameter | Excellent | Very Good | Good | Satisfactory |
|---|---|---|---|---|---|
| 1. | Target achievement | | | | |
| 2. | Product knowledge | | | | |
| 3. | Adherence to quality | | | | |
| 4. | Customer orientation | | | | |
| 5. | Loyalty to organisation | | | | |
| 6. | Initiative and drive | | | | |
| 7. | Communication | | | | |
| 8. | Potential to grow | | | | |
| 9. | Leadership skills | | | | |
| 10. | Acceptance of responsibility | | | | |

Reporting Officer's Signature:

Employee's Signature:

Reviewing Officer's Signature:

HR Dept. use:
Overall rating:
Increment to be given:
Remarks:

The performance rating of the employees are being maintained in the database. Promotion depends upon the discretion of the Managing Director. Increments are given basing on the ratings and the judgement of the MD. The employees take the whole process with utmost sarcasm since the manager does the review within two minutes by just ticking the appropriate box and depending upon his mood to give the marks. He may or may not discuss the performance for the year. The employees feel that it is just a ritual since the MD decides the increment to be given and the promotions and the HR has no role to play, but to display and keep the records that the appraisal is being done.

But during the last one year, there had been problem of attrition since there is no proper recognition of the performance and the efforts put in throughout the year are not being rewarded. The attrition starts after announcing the rewards. The MD was worried about the attrition since the competitors are picking up the employees and also the clients. He decided to hire a consultant to advise him on changing the process.

## Questions

1. Do you think that the problem is with the appraisal process for attrition? If not, mention the other reasons.
2. Do you think the MD can intervene in the process and try to contain the subjective element in the process?
3. If you are taken as a consultant to the company, how do you strategise and design the new appraisal process?

## References and Further Readings

Anderson, Gordon, C. 1993. *Managing Performance Appraisal Systems*, UK: Blackwell Publishers.

Anthony, William P., K. Michelle Kacmar, and Pamela L. Perrewe. 2002. *Human Resource Management— A Strategic Approach*, Florida, USA: Harcourt Inc.

Carter, Louis, David Giber and Marshall Goldsmith (eds). 2001. *Best Practices in Organisation Development and Change*, MA: Linkage Incorporated and Jossey-Bass/Pfeiffer.

Dessler, Gary. 1997. *Human Resource Management*, New Jersey: Prentice Hall.

Fisher, Martin. 1996. *Performance Appraisals*, London: Kogan Page.

Macdonald R. Charles. 1982. *MBO Can Work*, New York: McGraw-Hill.

Maddux, Robert B. 1993. *Effective Performance Appraisals*, California: Crisp Publications Inc.

Murphy, Kevin R. and Jeanette N. Cleaveland. 1995. *Understanding Performance Appraisal*, California: Sage Publications.

Rao, T.V. 2004. *Performance Management and Appraisal System*, New Delhi: Response Books.

Rao T.V., Gopal Mahapatra, Raju Rao and Nandini Chawla. 2002. *360 Degree Feedback and Performance Management System*, New Delhi: TVRLS/Excel Books.

Thompson, Roy Lecky. 1999. *Constructive Appraisals*, New York: American Management Association.

Weihrich, Heinz and Harold Koontz. 1994. *Management—A Global Perspective*, New York: McGraw-Hill.

# 7 PAY FOR PERFORMANCE

## Contents

## Learning Objectives

- To take a holistic view of the compensation scenario in the business organisations.
- To determine relative worth of a job in terms of compensation and rewards for a given job. To understand the current trends of fixed versus variable pay in the organisations.
- To understand the various motivational techniques through incentives and non-monetary reward mechanism.
- To define Employee Stock Option Plan (ESOP) for partnering profit for employees.

# Compensation Scenario in Modern Corporations

Compensation strategy plays a dominant role in the achievement of the business plans of the organisation. A strategic compensation influences the performance; innovation and creativity of the employee would influence the productivity thereby increasing the organisational productivity. It may be difficult to measure exactly the extent of influence of the compensation strategy on the productivity of HR but can enhance productivity. Organisation is an open system having the influence of the outside environment and hence the compensation shall have a balance of the external competitiveness, employee satisfaction, equity within the organisation and the paying capacity of the organisation.

Research has proved that the money is not the sole criteria of performance, but it is one of the important factors, which can influence the performance in relation to other factors. The employees in terms of their fairness always evaluate the compensation given by the employer and unless the same are being acceptable to them, they will breed in demotivation and lack of commitment. Compensation and other benefits when strategised and implemented can reinforce the overall corporate objective, achievement motivation and team efforts as they effect every single employee from a workman to that of the CEO. Thus, the compensation strategy aims at attracting the talent, retain them and motivate them to perform better.

Further, the compensation is decided by the employer whereas the components are being decided by the employee. The employee fixes the cost to the company that how much it can pay the employee and the employee in turn decides under what components the amount is to be decided taking into consideration the benefits according to the Income Tax Act. The independence given to the employee gives them an opportunity to participate in their compensation structure and thus moving away from a paternalistic organisation to that of participate organisation.

The significant factors in modern organisations are first, the compensation given is valued; second, the compensation is based on the performance of an individual and third, the compensation is moving from fixed salary to variable salary depending upon the performance. The compensation is based on the competencies and the value addition an employee brings in the organisation. The traditional way of rewarding the employee by way of their seniority, hike due to inflation, loyalty etc., is paving the way for 'pay for performance'. It does not necessarily mean that seniority will be paid below the organisational capacity, but will be paid as per eligibility. It is the performance that counts while paying the compensation and good performers are always rewarded positively. 'Pay for Performance' can be at the time of joining, but to maintain the performance orientation the payment should depend on the achievements by the employee.

In the macro level, the trend of management is to do more with less number of people, i.e., a lean organisation. The demand from the line functions is to have people who perform and have sufficient competencies, but not large in number. Every organisation would like to cut down their fad. The employers would like to leverage the compensation at a higher side than the competitors to attract good talent. Companies can pay only when it has sufficient profits and the enhanced profits can be shared among the employees.

Ultimately the compensation strategy must be linked with the business strategy, and should take care of the vision and mission. Inferior performance by a firm can be associated with a lack of parity between its pay policy and its business strategy.

## Pay as Per the Worth of the Job

The compensation for the individual employee is determined by his worth and the organisation's capacity to pay. This is done by way of job evaluation method wherein the value of the job of the incumbent is evaluated against the roles and the position of other employees directly or against any standard. This method is considered as one of the best methods of fixing up the pay structure of a person.

In an interesting article Gubman (2004) suggests that as employee 'carry more responsibility for the sales, assets, and equity of their companies,', the management might do well to consider aligning its people strategies to its business strategies. This is specially the firm's basic value proposition using three 'value disciplines'—product leadership, operational excellence and customer intimacy. Gubman suggests that each need is to be supported by a different array of people practices.

- Companies that drive for product leadership (Nike, Motorola, 3M and Johnson and Johnson) should work to provide a 'positive, comfortable, creative environment'. Rewards should be kept neutral. This means that basic salaries and benefits should be competitive or above market. Profit sharing should be broad based or shared equally. There should be many lifestyle services, but benefits, choices should be kept at a minimum.
- Among companies that strive for operational excellence (Whirlpool, Wal-Mart, American Airlines and Federal Express), the objective is to emphasise motivation and corporate spirit. Rewards should be used as a strategic tool. Basic pay maybe below market, but there are multiple incentives based on organisation, unit or team results. Benefits packages are competitive with other companies and allows a moderate amount of choice.
- For those companies, driving for customer intimacy (GM, Home Depot), the guiding principle is that 'satisfied employees will satisfy customers'. In this environment, rewards are based on 'behavioural, subjective assessments'. There maybe some differentiation in individual pay, and profit sharing will be differentiated based on the individual's contributions. Choices in benefits will be plentiful, and job structure may be broad-banded.

# Fixed to Variable Compensation Strategy

Developing compensation strategy that can channel incentives with fewer fixed salaries will enable better performance. Any pay procedure that is linked directly to the performance leads to increased performance when compared with no performance-linked pay. If the incentive systems are anchored whether it is individual or group performance it would enable the organisation to perform orientation. If the company is able to do good business and earns profits, the employee is benefited by way of better salaries and the profits will be high at the same cost. This makes the employee to be part of global competitiveness and hence can work smart to earn smart. The whole strategy must be derived from an assessment of what can motivate and retain the right people, what an organisation can afford and what will be required to meet the organisation's strategic goals.

A structure will have two components, first, the fixed component and second, the variable component. The fixed component is fixed in such a way that it takes care of the basic necessities of the employees at that level, whereas the variable part the employee needs to achieve targets and the payments are being made monthly, quarterly or any period that is decided by the management. Thus while the fixed component serves as the basic wages, the variable component tries to energise the employee to achieve the stretch targets.

The incentives must have the characteristics of **SMASH**.

**Simple** means the scheme has to be very simple so that everyone can participate in the process.

**Measurable** means that the employee while working can measure his own performance and can determine whether he can get the incentive or not.

**Achievable** means that the targets given are achievable and can motivate the employees to achieve the stretch targets.

**Specific** means that at the starting of the incentive scheme all those concerned shall be intimated about the scheme and the targets given shall be specific in nature.

**Holistic** means that the targets shall be fixed in such a way that it is linked to the individual key performance areas and the organisational business plans. This enables an employee to chase his targets to get his incentive and at the same time ensuring that the goals of the organisation have been achieved.

Effective use of incentives can lead to efficient use of existing assets and achievement of the long-term plans. The incentives shall never be aimed at achieving the short-term goals as it may prove disastrous during the long run. The production manager in order to show less of expenses in the production can do away with the maintenance of the machinery. During the short-term the firm may show profits, but if the machines are run without proper maintenance it may cost the company dearer. Long-terms plans are thus for strategic gains.

# Partnering Profit

The organisations in their endeavour to encourage employees to participate in the business have embarked upon paying a part of their profits and gains. In gain sharing the belief is that when the employee becomes a part and parcel of the business the cost of the production reduces and their method of thinking to ensure that the organisation grows both in long-term and short-term receives encouragement. It can also produce greater results like the employee giving ideas about the improvement of business processes; participation in production plans, drastic reduction in the rejections, etc.

On the other hand, profit sharing is to ensure group incentive for increased productivity, to institute a flexible reward structure that reflects a company's actual economic position. The money is payable only when the organisation makes profit. The main emphasis of these plans are to retain workers more easily or to educate individuals about the factors that underlies business success and the capability system. This would also promote the interest of the employees in the financial health of the organisation. The reward need to be announced and given promptly, if not, it may prove to be a demotivating factor. However, from the employee's point of view these incentives would only value them when these plans are transparent and the method of evaluation is not cumbersome. The employee needs to be very strong in achieving the targets and the organisation to have the strategic plan about the peak performing levels. This can bring in an environment of cooperation in the organisational culture. There should be mutual trust and harmonious relationship with the top management.

# Enable SHR Technology—Key to Success

This chapter brings in the following Strategic HR technologies:

SHR Technology–29   Job Evaluation—*Examining Relative Worth of a Job through Job Evaluation.*

SHR Technology–30   Compensation Strategy—*Organisation Growth versus Compensation Strategy.*

SHR Technology–31   Incentive Plans—*Work Smart Earn Smart through Incentive Plans.*
SHR Technology–32   Motivational Techniques—*Charge up the Employees through Motivational Techniques.*

Relative worth of a job is important to know when it is a matter of rewarding back to the employees for which an employee works in the organisation. Every job has its relative importance right from the car driver to a MD and is appropriately needed to be compensated in the form of salary and rewards. This is being done through job evaluation technique.

In the future the centrally determined compensation plans may not motivate the employees to outperform. The future pay would be payment for each individual employee and his contribution in improving results rather than the levels. There will be a dramatic shift from creating order and directing behaviour to encouraging involvement and commitment. The payment structure would be competency-based pay with customised incentives and better gain sharing.

Fixed components of compensation become a hygiene factor over a period of time. In order to motivate employees to achieve stretch target and the output that is beyond the normal limit, incentive is the right kind of a tool universally adapted in all kinds of product and service industry. The incentives are normally linked to performance and are so flexible that an employee can earn more and more if he stretch beyond usual standards. Every job and function must add value to the business process of the company which ultimately will reach to the customer in the form of product or services. Economic value added is a tool through which the company can evaluate the value addition that the HR has provided in the business directly or indirectly.

Another mode of profiting the employee is to provide the stock options, where in the employee is given the option to buy the company stock. The health of an organisation is determined through market capitalisation that an organisation makes. The share price of a company determines the relative worth of an organisation in the marketplace. It also gives an indirect boost to employees for taking pride in working with a company, which is highly regarded in the stock market. The partnership of employees in such pride is reflected through making employees partner in holding shares of the company. This brings in a sense of ownership that if employees work toward betterment of the company, the company flourishes and they flourish and similarly if they don't perform, company shrinks so as they. ESOP is a tool through which employees are made partners in the business ownership.

Great behavioural scientists like Maslow and McGregor, have emphasised in great depth the need for motivation in the workplace for employees to make them perform. These theories have given ways for organisations to think that merely a flat compensation is not the only source of keeping employees motivated, there is something beyond the compensation. Various motivational techniques are being used in the industry depending upon the needs of the individuals working with the company.

# Conclusion

- Research has proved that money is not the sole criteria for performance. Beside compensation there are various needs through which motivation level of an employee could be enhanced.
- Every individual has different competencies and hence different levels of performance. With the level at which one performs, the compensation criteria is determined.
- The fixed compensation has now moved towards variable compensation strategy. 'Pay for performance' is a buzzword in the industry.
- Employees are no more to be treated as merely the employment seeker and is satisfied with compensation. All employees are now offered partnership in the ownership of the company through employee stock option plan.
- There are various processes through which motivation of an individual can be enhanced. Various theories of motivational techniques provide an understanding on the ways in which the employee's motivational issues can be addressed.

## Reference

Gubman, Edward L. 2004. *Compensation and Benefit Review*, USA: Hewitt Associates.

# 'JOB EVALUATION' EXAMINING RELATIVE WORTH OF A JOB THROUGH JOB EVALUATION

*What I want is for people to have greater ambitions, but also to understand how to de-risk those ambitions.*

—Anonymous

## Intent

- To evolve a comparable worth of each job in a scientific and proven way.
- To remove the inequalities in the existing structure of compensation.
- To provide equitable wage/salary opportunities to all employees based on the skill that one has acquired and the requirement of the job.
- To draw appropriate compensation plan and pay grades using job evaluation as an input.
- To design individual compensation vis-à-vis the job one is handling in comparison to other jobs.
- To demonstrate that organisational processes recognises their contribution and needs and pays them accordingly without any discrimination.

## Expression

Job evaluation as an art is a systematic comparison of the jobs done in order to determine the worth of one job relative to another.

# Comprehension

Job evaluation is a formal and systematic comparison of jobs to determine the worth of one job related to another and eventually makes a rational basis for determination and management of internal relativities between jobs and design of pay structures. The comparison is by way of knowledge, skills required, level of responsibility, level of decision making and impact on end results with the incidence of the same factors with the other jobs. The purpose of job evaluation is to ensure internal equity in the eyes of the members of the organisation. The basic concept is to compare the variety of jobs in relation to one another.

While working on internal and external data there is no standard method for dealing with job evaluation. A wage structure is generally developed from job evaluation. While undertaking job evaluation various factors are taken into consideration such as training and experience required, efforts, the difficulty, responsibility and hazards of the job, the value or contribution of the job to the organisation and the organisation traditions of internal job relationships. Since job evaluation is based on the analysis of the relevant facts about a job, the information collected in job evaluation exercise can be used for other purposes like making an organogram, HR planning, training and development.

There are four basic methods of job evaluation. One, *Ranking*—where the ranking jobs in relation to another job in terms of significant factors in the job. Two, *Classification*—where jobs are classified into grades and levels, which has the most closely corresponding description. Three, *Point Method*—where four or more factors common to the jobs are being evaluated and then to rate each of the job a numerical scale relating to each factor. Four, *Factor Comparison*—where benchmark jobs are ranked in relation to each other on the basis of each factor at the outset of the process.

Many believe that there is a high correlation between experience and productivity. People believe that long-term employees should be rewarded for their faithful services, even though their performance may not justify it. Occasionally, people are paid higher than average salaries because they appear to have outstanding potential. Achievement motivated people like to know that they will receive extra pay or benefits for performance above the minimum level. A common justification for paying a person more is that he or she has more experience than others in the same type of positions. Being in a right place at the right time is an old cliché that should not be ignored in relation to individual wages. Luck often encountered when one applicant is hired over another and when establishing a starting wage. Politics, we know are part of reality.

The job evaluation methods give clear comparison among the jobs in terms of their relative worth. Key benchmark jobs are priced and the method of job evaluation used to evaluate the worth of all the other jobs in the firm in relation to these key jobs. Then we are well on our way to being able to equitably price all the jobs in our organisation. Job evaluation helps in determining the end results, since there is an emphasis on the output and can support on any programme on change management, which entails performance culture. Job evaluation exercise can also help in encouraging employees to acquire additional skills or to improve the levels of competence.

Is an individual's capacity to bargain due to market demand or job requirement a determinant for job compensation? This question is worth examining. The differences in compensation and anomalies observed is the result of these factors leading to dissatisfaction amongst the employees. An organisation confronting with this scenario chooses to carry out job evaluation processes periodically in order to eliminate such differences and anomalies. Job evaluation helps finding out the relative worth of a job in the context of the marketplace, other jobs and the content of the job. A strategic investment in carrying out job evaluation time to time is an important process. Hays' online job evaluation process is one such job evaluation process available to all organisations for specific jobs.

# Experiential Application

## A. Prerequisite

- The purpose of job evaluation is to create a hierarchy of jobs based on their value, or worth, to the company. Managers are usually persuaded to accept a job evaluation programme when they examine the cost of their employee's turnover.
- Both management and the employees must work cooperatively to develop a good job evaluation programme. Job evaluation must be done through a committee typically composed of five members. This committee must have access to the written job description of the employees.
- The job description should describe each job accurately and employees holding those positions should examine their own job description to see if the descriptions are correct and complete.
- With use of various tools, benchmarks are to be decided with each job positions with low or high value in the organisation.
- Try to select positions that are rather clearly defined, and are non-controversial, and have a minimum of errors. The job of non-controversial positions and placing them within the wage programme is easier to develop after the wage structure has been established.
- Frequently, there is some difference in wage rates for benchmark positions because of seniority or merit. So an average or an entry level wage rate is used for each job.

## B. Process Steps

| Step | Process |
|------|---------|
| Step – I | Defining the objectives of job evaluation. |
| Step – II | A committee is formed comprising five members, two from management two from employees and one from both. |
| Step – III | Team to deliberate on job evaluation to be used. |
| Step – IV | The committee to benchmark positions used to establish the foundation of the wage structure programme. |
| Step – V | The benchmark positions are allocated wages close to current area wages so as to assure acceptance by all. |

# Potential Gains and Areas of Concern

- Job evaluation helps in bring out a reward system that seems equitable to both the employer and the employee.
- It helps in motivating employees to continue to work more effectively for the compensation received.
- It helps differentiating compensation for different levels of hierarchy since each job is different from the other job.
- If the employee perceives that the exchange is inequitable, they will seek to increase their pay, to reduce their contribution in terms of efforts or to form a union.
- Absence of scientific job evaluation study would generate imbalance in the organisation in terms of job vis-à-vis its compensation structure.
- Job evaluation oversimplifies, whereas in reality it is always difficult to compare. For example, one cannot compare an apple with a pear. The quantification of the subjective judgements does not make them objective.
- Though the method of job evaluation claims objectivity, but subjectivity creeps in while interpreting the varying standards among evaluators. There is also scope for manipulation by vested interests.

# Measurability

## Try It Out

(1: not at all done, 2: moderately done, 3: to some extent done, 4: to a great extent done, 5: excellently done)

- Compensation is fixed as per the job evaluation method. ☐

- My organisation has equitable pay structure as per the skills one has and ☐ the requirement of the job.
- Top management and employees are committed to implementation of job ☐ evaluation-based pay.
- My organisation used online job evaluations available to know the relative ☐ worth of jobs and then fixes the compensation.

Analysis: the average score would determine the extent to which job evaluation process exists in your organisation.

## Score Card

(*: 25% achieved, **: 50% achieved, ***: 75% achieved, ****: 100% achieved)

| Technology | Objective Elements | Unit | Historical | Last Year | Current Year | Stretch Target | Status |
|---|---|---|---|---|---|---|---|
| Job Evaluation | Strategy Document on Job Evaluation | Doc | Nil | No | Yes | Jan | ** |
| Job Evaluation | Job Evaluation Document | Doc | Nil | No | Yes | Mar | * |

# Proven Track Record

## Track One

### IBM

It is a classic example of organisational renewal. In the 1980s it dominated the industry, but by 1990s it became sluggish. To revive Mr Louis Gerstner was hired and his priority was to transform the culture and the job evaluation. The existing compensation plan was based on decades-old point-factor method.

The inherent problem was to maintain point rating for 100,000 employees and which was preoccupied with internal equity rather than the market and competitive rates of pay. The first step was to shift to different salary structures and merit budgets for different jobs and hence the compensation is tuned towards the market oriented way. The second step was broad banding the jobs into 10 leading to a flatter organisation, which responds to the market needs. Third, linkage of the performance appraisal with the compensation increase. The new method enabled managers to rank employees by way of critical skills, results, etc., which are more useful in evaluation. Fourth, the implementation of pay for performance, wherein 10 per cent of the salary is being tied to performance. The company used the compensation to support its strategic plans.

*(Source*: Dessler, 2003: 325.)

## Track Two

## Aquatec Chemical International

One of the problems that encountered during the merger is the disparity of pay systems. Aquatec Chemical International recognised this as a potential problem when the company was created through the merger of three separate companies. WMS and Company, Pennsylvania, helped to design a suitable compensation system. After developing accurate job descriptions, WMS and Company used point system of job evaluation to measure all jobs in the organisation. It measured a total of 33 exempt and 23 non-exempt jobs.

All the jobs were evaluated using a set of four or five readily understood criteria such as experience, education/skills, job impact and working conditions. The jobs ranged from 101 points for a receptionist to 2,463 points of vice-president. By involving employees in the development of the new compensation system and using a simple and easily understood point method, Aquatec was able to avoid the loss of its brightest and best employees when the company was created.

*(Source*: Byars and Rue, 339.)

# Applied HR Case

## Goodwill Bank

Goodwill Bank was in the business since three years and was operating in the four main important cities of the country. Its financial results were encouraging and have a good clientele base. The bank has growth from one branch to four branches and has grown over the years. The recruitment was done depending upon the requirement and the prevailing market rate. Since the number of employees was large no HR Head was able to take a decision on reviving the compensation to bring in parity in line with the skills. Some of the newly joined clerks were being paid at par with the officers, since they were not able to get the right kind of people. John, new HR Head has observed the growing discontent among the employees and wanted to bring the salaries based on the skills and jobs handled rather than the market demands. John proposed to the management to implement the job evaluation method of compensation revision and has shows statistics that such a method has proved fruitful for many companies and is possible.

The Chairman was optimistic about the new method, however there was resentment among some of his colleagues. Finance Head expressed his opinion that his job cannot be rated on the scale used for his subordinates. Accounts Head has strongly objected expressing that others cannot appreciate their work and their work is unique, though looks simplistic. The qualities of the managers and the nature of jobs they handle are quite different and one cannot rate the horse and zebra, as both are different species.

Chairman and Board were convinced that the bank requires such an exercise and has given approval to prepare the report.

## Questions

1. Do you consider job evaluation as the correct method of fixing the pay? Explain?
2. By what methods do you think that John can convince the heads who are opposed to the job evaluation?
3. If you were John, prepare a project report giving the justification for the method used, modalities to arrive at the job evaluation and the fixation of pay taking into consideration the laws of the land?

## References and Further Readings

Admodt, Michael G. and Whitcoms J. Alan. 1991. *I/O Psychology in Action*, California: Wordsworth Publishing Company.

Armstrong, Michael and Angela Baron. 1997. *The Job Evaluation Handbook*, Mumbai: Jaico Publishing House.

British Institute of Management. 1971. *Job Evaluation*, London: Management Publications Limited.

Byars, Llyod L. and Leslie W. Rue. 2004. *Human Resource Management*, US: Irwin.

Dessler, Gary. 2003. *Human Resource Management*, 9th edn, New Delhi: Prentice-Hall of India Private Limited.

Schuster, Fredrick E. 1985. *Human Resource Management—Concepts, Cases and Readings*, Virginia: Reston Publishing Company, Inc.

Thompson F. George, 1987. *Job Evaluation and Work Measurement*, England: Gower Publishing Company Limited.

Tyson, Shaun and Alfred York. 1996. *Human Resource Management (Made Simple)*, 3rd edn, UK: Oxford.

# 'COMPENSATION STRATEGY' ORGANISATION GROWTH VERSUS COMPENSATION STRATEGY

*The goal is not to save money but to make money.*
—Goldratt M. Eliyahu, *The Goal* (2004)

## Intent

- To support the achievement of the organisation's strategic objectives by ensuring that skilled, competent, motivated and committed employees are recruited.
- To determine the value for the services provided by the employee and provide compensation which is competitive in the employment market to attract and retain the talent.
- To evolve organisational compensation plan based on market compensation status of other progressing companies.
- To provide equitable compensation based on job evaluations for employee retention and motivation.

## Expression

Compensation means the benefits and services paid to the employees in return of their services in terms of money. Employee compensation means all forms of pay or rewards going to employees and arising from their employment.

## Comprehension

Compensation plays an important role though it is not the only motivating factor to the employees. In fact people use compensation as a yardstick for measuring their success in the world of employment. Money has always been the universal reward for an employee. In return for their services, employees receive compensation, a combination of payments, benefits and employer services. Compensation is made of many factors, wage or salary, incentive programmes, bonuses and commission, profit sharing and gain sharing, knowledge-based pay and broadbanding, employee benefit and services, pension plank, employees stock options, etc. An effective compensation system requires more than an absolute level of compensation that compares favourably with other organisations. Compensation also enables appropriate organisational culture, increasing the motivation and the commitment of the employees.

Although money is clearly important to people to work, research in the behavioural science has demonstrated that most people are not motivated solely by financial reward, other needs are also important. For at least a few these other needs may be more important than pay. Thus an effective reward system provides both financial and non-financial rewards. The organisation needs to recognise that compensation is determined by the business need, but the underlying fact is that the employees are stakeholders and their needs need to be addressed and views sought. In addition, the compensation must be divided among the organisation employees in a way that they are considered to be equitable.

The compensation in an organisation is proportionate to the profit generated by the organisation. Compensation is more or less fixed in nature however it's variable subject to the organisation's performance. The incremental rise in compensation considering inflation and profitability depends upon how the organisation is performing. It is observed that organisations pay well when it makes profit and do not when there is decline in profit.

Compensation is also worked out based on extrinsic and intrinsic rewards. A fairly recent development in compensation is flexible compensation called Cafeteria Compensation. This system gives every individual a number of options as to the form and the timing of his or her total compensation package. An extrinsic reward refers to both financial and non-financial but is external to the job itself. For example, in response to the quality and quantity employees' performance reward is being paid in cash and in kind while intrinsic reward comes from the individual response to the work itself.

The concept of the Cost to the Company (CTC) is gradually gaining ground which includes payment made to the employee including pensions, health insurance, death in service, gratuity, company car or own the car scheme, child-care provisions, subsidised meals, etc. The CTC includes all the investment made by the employer to the employee including the monetary and the non-monetary benefits.

The trend today is for employers to reduce their salary grades ranging from 10 to three to five, and the process is called broadbanding. Broadbanding means collapsing salary grades and ranges into just a few wide level or bands, each of which then contain a relatively wide range of jobs and salary level. Broadbanding's basic advantage is that it injects greater flexibility into the employee's compensation. It is sensible where firms flatter their hierarchies and organise around self-managing teams.

Finally, in the words of Flannery and Platten (1996):

> Organisations are beginning to understand that pay should no longer be considered only in terms of specific jobs and current financial results. Compensation must inextricably be tied to people, their performance and the organisational vision and values that their performance supports. It is an important tool for communicating and reinforcing new values and behaviors, supporting accountability of results and rewarding the achievement of new performance goals.

When we examine about what motivates employees in the organisation one common factor that gains highest attention is compensation. It's a hygiene factor for all employees to be on the job and work. Compensation is the most important reason for productivity and for the standard of work performance. Looking at the importance of compensation, the design of the compensation is very critical. Many factors go in designing and managing compensation in the organisation such as capacity to pay, market pay variables, the regulation pertaining to tax structure, bargaining capacity, importance and criticality of the job, etc. All these factors need attention while implementing the compensation strategy in the organisation. The strategic compensation management is thus, a technology which has long lasting impact on the organisation performance.

# Experiential Application

## A. Prerequisite

- A good compensation programme allows the average employees to be paid no higher than the midpoint of the salary range for the position. Only the outstanding performer should be able to rise to the top of the pay range.
- The most popular pay for performance method is the merit plan. Merit pay increases are relevant to all jobs which pay a fixed wage. Performance evaluation becomes an even more important tool under a merit plan because wage increases are based on the outcome of evaluation.
- The HR department must clarify the increase in compensation between an average employee and an outstanding performer.
- There are three major compensation programmes and each one requires a different programme.

  - the blue and white collar workers,
  - the professionals, and
  - the supervisors, managers and executives.

- The last two groups have great difference between their starting salary and their final maximum salary.

## B. Process Steps

| Step | Process |
| --- | --- |
| Step – I | Defining the need for compensation strategy and survey. |
| Step – II | Analyse the current compensation of the company vis-à-vis the market, through compensation survey. |
| Step – III | Proposal to the management to adopt a strategy based on the findings of the survey. |
| Step – IV | Compensation plan made based on the acceptance of the management. |
| Step – V | Individual compensation package is made and communicated to each employee. |
| Step – VI | Changes incorporated in payroll and the expenditure monitored vis-à-vis the budget sanctioned. |

# Potential Gains and Areas of Concern

- Compensation strategy helps attracting and retaining talents in the organisation as it is the first motivator for an employee to be in the job.
- Market driven compensation keeps the balancing between the current compensation level of the organisation vis-à-vis other organisations.
- Mix of fixed and variable compensation helps all those employees earn more with the high level of performance.
- The market driven compensation strategy brings additional burden on the organisation in terms of cost. The companies compared do neither necessarily reveal the right data nor compared in absolute terms of business.
- Compensation is only one of the motivation for the employees. In the absence of other motivation processes, it alone can sustain its importance.

# Measurability

## Try it Out

(1: not at all done, 2: moderately done, 3: to some extent done, 4: to a great extent done, 5: excellently done)

- My organisation believes in 'Pay for Performance'.	☐

- My organisation has flexi compensation plan giving independence to the ☐
employees to determine the structure and plan his tax savings.
- Compensation is fixed as per the industry standard and through the ☐
survey of industries.
- Compensation attracts the best of the talent available in the industry. ☐
- Organisation fixes the compensation as per job evaluation method. ☐
- Organisation has yearly performance review compensation revision. ☐
- Human Resource makes various analysis to measure compensation trends ☐
and various ratios like CTC versus Sales, CTC versus Revenue, etc.

Analysis: the average score would determine the extent to which compensation strategy process exists in your organisation.

## Score Card

(*: 25% achieved, **: 50% achieved, ***: 75% achieved, ****: 100% achieved)

| Technology | Objective Elements | Unit | Historical | Last Year | Current Year | Stretch Target | Status |
|---|---|---|---|---|---|---|---|
| Compensation Strategy | Strategy Document on Compensation | Doc | Yes | Yes | Yes | Feb | ** |
| Compensation Strategy | Compensation Survey | Doc | Once in 3 Years | No | Yes | Jan | ** |

# Proven Track Record

## Track One

## Sonoco

Sonoco is a 100-year old packaging company accounting for sales worth $2.6 billion, having 16,500 employees spread over 250 different locations across 31 countries in 5 continents. Sonoco has SPMS (Sonoco Performance Management System) to help employees understand their role within the organisation and align their goals with business organisation. The compensation system is deliberately not linked to SPMS. Compensation decisions are based on many factors, including judgements of individual performance and the performance of the organisation as a whole. Meetings on performance occur early in the year, and meetings on pay occur towards the middle of the year. The separation of these meetings is intentional. This way the developmental focus of SPMS is not lost, and ratings are less likely to be inflated by managers trying to increase the pay of employees. To be more objective, Sonoco has recently switched to a broadband system that pays employees based on their value to the organisation (even if it is above market value), as opposed to the old system that paid employees in relation to the mid point of their position. Sonoco realised that linking compensation with SPMS may inflate the ratings and hence moved away performance review with compensation and therefore created a separate method of revising the compensation mid-year. Later it switched on to evaluating their value to the organisation.

(*Source*: Maloney and Derek, 2001: 419–37.)

## Track Two

## Polaroid Corporation

Polaroid initiated of late a companywide competency based pay system. Polaroid employees are encouraged to form work teams and to redesign their work function in order to make them more efficient. Although Polaroid systems include everyone from the mail room clerk to the CEO, it has been more effective in the manufacturing part of the business.

Polaroid manufacturing employees have learnt skills in a number of different areas, rather than focusing on a single job. Employees who have succeeded in the new jobs have received more money. The focus of Polaroid white-collar employees has been on learning new technologies, but here the process has not worked as smoothly. Part of the problem is that skills and competencies are not so easy to measure in managerial jobs. But, that will not stop companies to apply these schemes for their while collar workforce as well. Slowly but surely this is also going in the while collar workforce as well.

(*Source*: Cascio, 1998: 401–2.)

## Applied HR Case

## Jetspeed Couriers Limited

The company is in the business of catering to the courier needs of the customers within the city. Due to its conscious strategy of not expanding and only catering to the needs of the city, the local firms depend upon Jetspeed since the courier given for delivery is delivered by noon next day and the service level is 100 per cent. The firm has become the favourite of the city and soon the major players started using the services of Jetspeed for local deliveries.

Managing Director, Khanna in order to expand the business has started accepting courier for other cities and while booking the consignment, the company used to clarify to the customer that they are routing through another major player and they will always provide the best of service as they did for local service. The decision to expand the business has been a boon and at the same time a problem since the manpower has increased drastically and there were some service failures due to the shortage of manpower. Khanna used to pay as per the market rate and in the peak season 10 per cent above the market rate on a weekly basis. Khanna used to recruit the unemployed youth who is from the area so that it will be easy to identify and cither book or deliver the consignment. The problems got aggrieved since the part-timers started to go for secured jobs and where they have some more benefits. Khanna soon made about 50 per cent of them as the permanent employees with all the benefits to retain service levels and commitment to the customers. They are made permanent depending upon their experience and proximity to Khanna. In spite of providing them the secure employment the attrition rate is growing and Khanna is not in a position to control. Instead of concentrating on the expansion of the business and visiting the customers for more business, he has to concentrate more on interviewing and recruiting part-time and full-time employees in a piecemeal manner.

During the discussion with those who were leaving the organisation many of them felt that they are discriminated while fixing the pay or the pay is not sufficient or pay is not commensurate with their experience. The firm is at its peak growth and Khanna does not want to lose the opportunity. He has taken the help of his friend Khader who is a consultant in HR.

## Questions

1. What are the problems facing Jetspeed Couriers?
2. Do you attribute the attrition due to lack of a compensation strategy?
3. If you were Khader how you will go about suggesting a solution to Khanna?

## References and Further Readings

Armstrong, M. and H. Murils. 1988. *Reward Management*, London: Kogan Page.
———. 1999. *The Art of HRD, Reward Management*, vol. 9, India: Crest Publishing House.
Bernardin, H. John and Russel Joyce. 1993. *Human Resource Management—An Experiential Approach*, Boston: Irwin/McGraw-Hill.

Bower, Joseph L. (ed.). 1991. *The Craft of General Management*, Boston: Harvard Business School Publications.

Cascio, Wayne F. 1998. *Managing Human Resources*, USA: Irwin/McGraw-Hill.

Chandra, Apoorva. 2004. 'The Way the World Pays', *Human Capital*, vol. 7, no. 11, April.

Flannery, T., D. Hofrichter and P. Platten. 1996. *People, Performance and Pay*, New York: The Free Press.

Maloney, Rick and Smith A. Derek. 2001. 'SONCO' in Carter Louis, Giber David and Goldsmith Marshall (eds), *Best Practices in Organization Development and Change*, CA: Jossey-Bass/Pfeiffer.

Milkovich, George and John Boudreau. 1997. *Human Resource Management*, Chicago: Irwin.

Mitchell, Daniel J.B. 1989. *Human Resource Management—An Economic Approach*, Boston: PWS-Kent Publishing Company.

# 'INCENTIVE PLANS'
# WORK SMART EARN SMART THROUGH INCENTIVE PLANS

*Compensation and incentives are important, but for very different reasons in good-to great companies. The purpose of a compensation system should not be to get the right behavior from the wrong people, but to get the right people on the bus in the first place, and to keep them there.*

—Jim Collins, *Good to Great*

## Intent

- To understand the different forms of incentives.
- The usefulness of incentives in the workplace.
- To understand the cost benefits in relation to the total cost of compensation package.
- To operationalise an effective incentive programme in the company to improve productivity in the organisation.

## Expression

An incentive means cash payments to employees who produce at a desired level or whose unit (often the company as a whole) produces at a desired level.

## Comprehension

Many companies around the world are concerned with productivity. Incentives are associated with the achievement of the company's goals and profitability targets, and in some cases, is also linked to the achievement of the individual targets and accountabilities. Incentive is the reward in cash or kind received by the employee over his agreed salary who meets the specific individual performance parameters. Incentives are more common now that companies are becoming team oriented. Today's emphasis on quality improvement teams and commitment building programmes are creating a renaissance for financial incentives or pay for performance plans. To encourage the employees' innovativeness and commitment to their work, to perform the stretch targets, companies often provide their employees with incentives i.e., cash payments or in kind. In other words, achievements are made the basis for payment. Incentive schemes are also associated with unmotivated performance or routine functions, and any reward which is more flexible is likely to motivate than sitting around and waiting for the next automatic increments.

The motivator behind the urge to perform is the money. However, it has been proved that the money is not the only motivator and there are other factors, which makes an employee motivate. Incentive schemes need to be given only for realising the stretch targets and they must be used judiciously, if not, the scheme need to be given to achieve the normal targets. If motivation is the problem in performance, incentive scheme is a short-term measure, but organisations need to diagnose and plan OD (Organisation Development) interventions. If incentive schemes can be used to leverage performance, it would bring about a cultural change in the direction of accountability for results and orientation towards high performance. It ensures that everyone in the organisation understands the performance imperatives of the organisation. Besides the basic salary, the pay to individuals and teams are based on their achieving the quality and quantity goals, which is 30 to 40 per cent of their compensation as an incentive. Thus traditional pay plans are giving way to skill based plan, and to spot awards, team incentives, etc.

Developing a workable individual incentive plan requires both job evaluation and industrial engineering. Job evaluation enables you to assign an hourly wage rate to the job in question. Industrial engineering provides production standards in terms of standard number of minute/hour per unit predications. Group incentives are a standard of output of each member in a team. Members in the group are then paid based on various formulas such as all members receive the pay earned by the higher producer or the lower producer or in equal weightage. Team incentives are always advantageous since several jobs are interrelated. Here incentives are based not on one worker's performance but on the co-workers as well. Thus team incentives make sense.

To bring in motivation and performance culture, the organisations are resorting to variable pay scale where the employee is paid as per the commitment given and the balance is paid if he achieves his targets. The targets are fixed with mutual consent in such a way that the employee needs to put in extra efforts to achieve the stretch targets to get the amount. The firm is also in a position to attract good talent since the pay scale is high.

Pay for performance is a common notion in every job. This helps employees to fulfil the job commitment associated with it. In the environment of competitiveness and demanding output, stretching beyond the normal is the order of the day. How can one be motivated to perform beyond the normal and stretch for the enhanced output? One such form of motivation is associated with appropriate incentive programme. Incentives are variable financial gains applicable with the productivity parameters and hence it ensures an output beyond normal. In an organisation, these days almost for all functions incentive programmes are designed which brings in a healthy competitive environment within and employees are encouraged to perform beyond the normal capacity. This technology is critical in designing since, it has long-term impact on the bottomline of the company.

# Experiential Application

## A. Prerequisite

- People have to be motivated to work, either because of the financial rewards or because they enjoy the work. Once an employee's basic needs are met through adequate wages, fringe benefits can add most welcome incentives.
- The pay an employee receives is for the time they work and the incentives are addition to the wages that has been fixed for a given job performed in a given time.
- While formulating an incentives plan for the company the following strategy is to be adapted:

  - incentives are to be linked with enhanced performance of the employee to reach the stretch target;
  - incentives can be either for an individual or for a group for completion of a task or for a process;
  - the amount allocated should be attractive in nature, so that it can generate an enthusiasm and drive for employees to achieve higher goals to receive the incentives;
  - the incentives declared should be supported with higher performance achieved by the employees and to be paid timely; and
  - the amount of incentives fixed for a specific period must enhance for the next specific period since the money value degrades over a period of time with inflation.

## B. Process Steps

| Step | Process |
| --- | --- |
| Step – I | Defining the achievement criteria of business process. |
| Step – II | To decide about the stretch targets and the criteria for performance. |
| Step – III | Quantification of the incentives to be fixed. |

*(Continued)*

*(Continued)*

| Step | Process |
|------|---------|
| Step – IV | Communicating to all the employees about the incentive scheme. |
| Step – V | Based on the achievement criteria the achievers are identified and the incentives calculated and disbursed. |
| Step – VI | Based on the feedback and popularity the incentive programme needs to be reevaluated. |

# Potential Gains and Areas of Concern

- It enhances the productivity and performance orientation among the employees.
- It focus attention and endeavour on the key performance issues.
- It gives an opportunity for an employee to earn additional wages over and above the basic fixed salary.
- It generates a sense of competition among the employees. It differentiates rewards to people consistently and equitably according to their contribution and competence.
- It benefits the organisation for achieving higher business results.
- It helps to change the culture towards more performance, targets, quality and customer service orientations.
- It becomes a chronic performance issue since incentives would only drive the performance and the base salary would remain unproductive.
- Incentives over a period of time also become unattractive unless it is periodically enhanced to the higher side.
- Incentives after some time would lose the charm since money is not the only motivator.
- There is also a trap of a universal incentive scheme that only promotes narrow thinking of performance of a job and may not benefit the innovativeness, long-term issues and quality.
- Incentive schemes if not prudently leveraged would lead to rise of pay and CTC but not the performance since the performance is only linked to the pay but not any other factor.

# Measurability

## Try it Out

(1: not at all done, 2: moderately done, 3: to some extent done, 4: to a great extent done, 5: excellently done)

- My organisation has an incentive strategy and is part of the compensation ☐
  strategy which is linked to business strategy.
- Incentive plans are laid down and communicated across the organisation. ☐
- Incentive plans are designed to achieve the stretch targets. ☐
- My organisation emphasises on team orientation and on achievement of ☐
  stretch targets than individual performance.
- Incentive plans are devised to bring in healthy competition among various ☐
  departments functions.

Analysis: the average score would determine the extent to which incentive plan
exists in your organisation.

## Score Card

(*: 25% achieved, **: 50% achieved, ***: 75% achieved, ****: 100% achieved)

| Technology | Objective Elements | Unit | Historical | Last Year | Current Year | Stretch Target | Status |
|---|---|---|---|---|---|---|---|
| Incentive Plan | Strategy Document on Incentive Schemes | Doc | Yes | Yes | Yes | NA | ** |
| Incentive Plan | 4 Incentive Schemes | Nos | 2 | 2 | 4 | – | ** |

# Proven Track Record

## Track One

### Ameri Steel

Ameri Steel's new incentive plan is 'Partners in Performance'. The firm's strategy is to address a three-year-trend of losses and a declining market share by reorienting the firm to focus on productivity and competitiveness by designing an incentive plan signalling the employees to be more productive. It has four mini steel plants each having 250 employees.

As per the plan, from the CEO to down-the-line employee there was 15 per cent cut in the basic and the amount used with a gain sharing incentive plan. For every 1 per cent additional productivity of the 70 per cent production capacity, employees would earn 0.5 per cent of their basic pay. If they produce 100 per cent their compensation will be whole. The employees would get an additional 5 per cent of improvement over 100 per cent, which means that the company is ready to share 33 per cent of the gains from improved productivity with the employees. By various support programmes the management has set aside 7.5 per cent of company's stock for non-management employees. The plan became a success. The firm's production rose by 20 per cent and profits rose from $22 million to $38 million per year. Ameri Steel has achieved its strategic aims with the HR based partners in performance.

(*Source*: Dessler, 2003: 354.)

## Track Two

## Lincoln Electric

Lincoln Electric, maker of welding machinery, is a Fortune 500 company based at Ohio. It is considered to be one of the corporate America's greatest success stories using piece-rate system of incentive plans. The company pays its 3,000 employees according to the piece-rate. Workers are simply paid for what they have produced except a two-week vacation and a pension scheme.

As per the statistics each worker earns over $50,000 based on piece-rate system, which is considered as the highest salary for a factory worker in the world. The company also provides a lifetime employment policy, never laid off any worker, provides substantial bonuses to workers based on the performance and the difference between a workman and the CEO is only seven times. His bonus is also linked to the bonus of other workmen. Though there has been criticism of absence of basic pay, the workers love the company and the money they earn. An average of over 40 per cent of Lincoln's pre-tax income goes to the employees. Lincoln also uses performance appraisal that reveal a letter grade for each worker's dependability, quality, output and cooperation.

(*Source*: Bernardin and Russell 1998: 321.)

# Applied HR Case

## Highsteel Inc.

Highsteel has started its production last year and reached 60 per cent of its capacity utilisation. The market is responsive to the product and being well received. The pricing strategy was cost above 15 per cent as the profit and the rates were very competitive. Mohan realised that sustaining at this rate will be difficult and hence planned to increase the capacity to 70 per cent while controlling the variable cost. Rakesh a close friend of Mohan has advised him to devise an incentive plan that will enhance the productivity without raising the manpower.

The following are the various types of the employees working in the steel plant:

- managers who are heading the departments and other roles who constitute 2 per cent;
- supervisors who are in charge of the sections and constitute 10 per cent of the manpower;
- workmen who are in the routine operations and constitute 30 per cent;
- daily wage workers who are taken as per the production schedules and constitute 25 per cent; and
- piece-rated workers who constitute the major part and the balance.

An executive who is a relative and is not aware much about the systems and procedures handles the HR activities. At a pilot level he has introduced the incentive scheme to the piece-rated workers, which was successful. Mohan is determined to implement the scheme across the organisation to bring in performance orientation and also to achieve the goals. Mohan hired the services of a consultant who is an expert in the area of compensation management.

## Questions

1. Was Mohan right in introducing the incentive scheme only to the piece-rated workers?
2. Do you attribute the increase in the production due to the new incentive scheme announced by Mohan?
3. If you were a consultant how do you devise an incentive scheme across the organisation.

## References and Further Readings

Bernardin H. John and Joyce Russell. 1998. *Human Resource Management—An Experiential Approach*, Boston: Irwin/McGraw-Hill.

Bernardin, H. John. 2003. *Human Resource Management*. New Delhi: Tata McGraw-Hill Publishing Company Limited.

Cascio, Wayne. 1986. *Managing Human Resources—Productivity, Quality of Work Life Profits*, New York: McGraw-Hill Book Company.

Dessler, Gary. 2003. *Human Resource Management*, 9th edn, New Delhi: Prentice-Hall of India Private Limited.

Mitchell, Daniel J.B. 1989. *Human Resource Management—An Economic Approach*, Boston: PWS-Kent Publishing Company.

Smith, Ian. 1987. 'Incentive Schemes', in Sally Harper (ed.), *Personnel Management Hand Book*, England: Gower Publishing Company Limited.

Werther, William B. Jr and Keith Davis. 1996. *Human Resources and Personnel Management*, Boston: Irwin/McGraw-Hill.

# 'MOTIVATIONAL TECHNIQUES' CHARGE UP THE EMPLOYEES THROUGH MOTIVATIONAL TECHNIQUES

*When people work in a place that cares about them, they contribute a lot more than duty.*

—Dennis Hayes

## Intent

- To analyse the factors effecting the employees motivation in the organisation.
- To develop the tools and mechanism through which employees' motivation can be maintained and enhanced.
- To introduce various motivational techniques in real life situations for achieving organisational objectives.
- To provide equity and fairness at all levels of pay and to cover all the employees.
- To analyse the implications of demotivated employees and its effect on the morale and performance of the organisation.

## Expression

Motivation is a process which starts with physiological or psychological deficiency or need that activates a behaviour or a drive that is aimed at a goal or incentive. Motivation is the force that moves individuals to take actions.

## Comprehension

Motivation has been a topic of interest to managers for more than a hundred years. Robert Owen, a nineteenth century Scottish industrialist first time thought of linking between employees' morale and motivation. He reduced working hours, provided meal facilities, improved employees housing and introduced other innovations. This remained anonymous for long. Frederick Taylor developed scientific management, a management approach that seeks to improve employees' efficiency through the scientific study of work. In his view, people were motivated almost exclusively by money, so he set up pay systems that rewarded employees when they were productive.

Besides Taylor's scientific management, Maslow's 'Hierarchy of Needs', McGregor's theory X and theory Y, and theory Z of W. Ouchi, etc., have propounded various research base motivation theory. Technically the word motivation can be traced to the Latin word *movere*, which means *'to move'*. Motivation is about getting the people to move in the direction you want them to go in order to achieve the task. Motivation is a goal-directed behaviour and the barometer of motivation is when people take course of action, which is likely to lead to the attainment of the goal and also value their success as achievement of their goals.

Humans are motivated by many factors. Everyone has a need and expectation and only when the goals are being satisfied the needs gets satisfied. The achievement of the goals reinforces the success behaviour. The organisation can provide the motivators by way of incentives, rewards and opportunities, but the scope is very limited. The real challenge lies with the managers who will inspire employees to give their best and use the benefits given by the organisation to achieve their goals and in turn organisational goals. As we can see today's employees are motivated by more than just good pay; satisfaction of higher level needs is equally important. To motivate people, employees must go beyond traditional incentives. Many now boost motivation and morale through goal setting, behaviour modification, investment in employees, better quality of work life, flexible schedules, telecommuting and work and job sharing. In the words of McClelland the major three factors that motivate a person are achievement, power and affiliation. The need for achievement is defined as the need for competitive success measured against a personal standard of excellence.

Motivation at work can be of two ways:

- *Intrinsic Motivation.* It is a process where the motivation is derived from the work itself wherein it leads them to expect that their goals will be achieved. It is self-generated in those people who would like to seek the type of work, which satisfies their goals, and the organisation can enhance the process by way of empowerment, development, job design, policies and practices.
- *Extrinsic Motivation.* Motivation arrives when the organisation provides the rewards as increased pay, promotion, etc.

Extrinsic motivators are only powerful and immediate tools which do not last for long. Organisations need to focus more on the intrinsic motivation, which have a deeper and longer effect.

Employee empowerment can also be a powerful motivational tool because it gives employees more say in the actual working of the company, usually by offering them greater decision making power. At the same time empowerment places more value on employee ideas, which gives employees greater responsibilities and greater account-ability for the companies' performance. This type of involvement leads towards a deeper sense of satisfaction when employees' ideas and work contributions help achieve the companies' goals. Another powerful motivator is teamwork. As teamwork becomes the norm in business worldwide, increasing numbers of companies are realising productiv-ity and quality gains even as costs decrease. Once teamwork becomes embedded in the organisation culture, management finds that motivating employees is easier because they are more committed to the goals of the organisation.

The motivation techniques usually considered for employee motivations are:

- hygiene factors through appropriate structure;
- safety factors through social security measures;
- degree of satisfaction through job satisfaction and enhanced role;
- esteem factor through growth of hierarchies in the corporate ladder, authority and responsibilities;
- equity approach for equal treatment to all; and
- achievement orientation through goal setting and rewards on achievement.

What motivates one most is a million dollar question that all HR professionals are trying to find answer since decades. There are different schools of thought on motivation and with various theories propounded on motivation, this question have become more complex. If we look at the simple hierarchy of need motivational theory, we find that the level of motivation grows with the fulfilment of basic needs and to the extent of reaching one's self-actualisation level. The motivation techniques in the organisation set-up goes from basic needs to ego and self-actualisation level. Each of the organisation cadre and level, get motivated by satisfying different levels of their needs. It is presumed that at the lowest level of the organisation hierarchy, basic need fulfilment is the focus. However, at the top management level self-esteem and actualisation are the motiv-ational needs. Therefore, managing motivation in the complex hierarchy of the organ-isation is a strategic technology.

# Experiential Application

## A. Prerequisite

- Rewards should be tied to performance. Motivation is the greatest when obtaining the reward depends on performance. For those tasks and people for whom the pay is the most obvious reward, this suggests an emphasis on incentive bonuses and piece rate plans. For all jobs it suggests tying to non-financial rewards.

- Rewards should be equitable. Employees who are paid on straight salary basis but who feel they are underpaid will reduce the quality or quantity of their performance, while those who believe they are being overpaid will improve their performance.
- A person should have the ability to accomplish the task to be motivated. If a person believes there is little or no chance of successfully completing a task, that person would probably not be motivated to accomplish it.
- Distinguish between lower level needs and higher level needs.

  - Lower level needs are those needs that people have for food, clothing, shelter and security.
  - Higher level needs are those needs that people have for recognition, achievement and self-actualisation.

- Wherever possible try to elicit motivation by appealing to the relatively infinite higher level needs. Before doing so, however, make sure the lower level needs are adequately satisfied.

## B. Process Steps

| Step | Process |
|------|---------|
| Step – I | Analyse the performance orientation of the organisation and whether the targets are being achieved. |
| Step – II | Analyse whether the processes are in place and the employees are performing as per the organisational objectives. |
| Step – III | If there is any gap, identify the areas where the gap needs to be filled. |
| Step – IV | Devise an action plan to motivate the employees to perform the task and submit the proposal to the top management. |
| Step – V | The plan is to be discussed with the line managers or the managers where the plan is going to be implemented. |
| Step – VI | Implement the plan after due discussion and approval and analyse the results. |
| Step – VII | Evaluate the results against the objectives of the scheme and basing on the feedback make the changes in the scheme. |

# Potential Gains and Areas of Concern

- A person's motivation reflects his or her drive to achieve some purpose.
- Motivation involves all the management functions—from developing all the appropriate plans and hiring the right people for right jobs to ensuring that the organisation structure fits the tasks.

- Money can act as a motivator only to a certain extent. The Manager needs to plan the periodicity of motivating through other factors. Right kind of motivation will recognise the accomplishments of the employees and satisfies their esteem needs.
- The motivators need to be designed to be potential motivators like flexi pay, paid holidays, etc.
- Human needs are the main springs of motivation. All motivation ultimately derives from a tension that results when one or more of our important needs are unsatisfied.
- Mere making of motivational plans will not bring in the desired change if realistic performance goals are not established. Periodic feedback is important to constantly guide them towards performance.

# Measurability

## Try It Out

(1: not at all done, 2: moderately done, 3: to some extent done, 4: to a great extent done, 5: excellently done)

- My organisation believes in 'performance through people'. □
- My organisation has various extrinsic methods to motivate employees. □
- Managers/Top Management emphasises and also gives inputs to motivation □ employees intrinsically.

Analysis: the average score would determine the extent to which motivational techniques exist in your organisation.

## Score Card

(*: 25% achieved, **: 50% achieved, ***: 75% achieved, ****: 100% achieved)

| Technology | Objective Elements | Unit | Historical | Last Year | Current Year | Stretch Target | Status |
|---|---|---|---|---|---|---|---|
| Motivational Techniques | Strategy Document on Motivating Employees | Doc | Nil | No | Yes | NA | ** |
| Motivational Techniques | Motivational Programmes | Nos | 2 | 1 | 3 | 4 | ** |

# Proven Track Record

## Track One

### Southwest Airlines

Southwest Airlines is the only low fare airline to achieve long-term success and become the nation's largest airline with 63.7 million passengers and earnings topping $ 625 million in 2000. Herv Kelleher became the much studied celebrity CEO of the Southwest who was able to generate fierce loyalty from his employees with his wild management style and who became widely known for his wide jinks approach to motivating employees.

Southwest employees accept responsibility and challenge while Kelleher creates space for growth and achievements. This is true for Southwest's executives, managers, pilots, secretaries and airport ramp employees. The transition at Southwest was an exceedingly orderly one, which saw the internal advancement of employees in contrast to external recruitment of executives. This approach is consistent with Southwest's culture of nurturing and developing employees to achieve their full potentials. The company has ensured that all employees are recognised for their contribution, and often Herv write a note to the baggage handler or a ticket agent who did something special.

(*Source*: Nelson and Quick, 2003: 156.)

## Track Two

### Xerox

Xerox believes firmly that one of the factors for the employees' motivation is excellent reward and recognition policies of the company. This helps in bringing in any organisational change initiative. Strong reinforcement of reward and recognition system is the key for reinforcing the virtue of new management systems.

Reward and recognition system recognises individuals who contribute to team performance rewards empowered teams based on performance results, both being essential factors to the long-term success of empowerment efforts. Other key attributes of Xerox's reward and recognition system include: recognition for demonstrated desired habits, continuous improvement and skill development. Rewards are earned and are contingent upon team performance. Reward provides a clear link between the work group as well as team, and organisational performance. Rewards should be timely and tied to the events that warranted it. Rewards should be based on both results and continuous improvement.

(*Source*: Carter, Giber and Goldsmith, 2001.)

## Track Three

## Bobcart Construction Company, Kentucky

Recognising goes a long way towards motivating employees to do their best and stay with the company and it doesn't necessarily take a tremendous amount of money to provide a positive work environment. Bobcart, a construction equipment dealership in Kentucky has almost no turnover in any industry with thousands of vacant jobs. A few of its less traditional and less tangible benefits that keep Bobcart workers from leaving are:

- twice a year employees children receive a fifty dollar savings bond when they bring in all 'A's' report card;
- every Friday, employees rotate jobs for one hour to help combat the we–they syndrome; and
- employees celebrate their work anniversaries with a cake and receive hundred dollars for each year employed.

(*Source*: Greg Smith)

# Applied HR Case—'Motivating to Improve'

## Shop and Save

Mr De'Souza has worked as Marketing Manager of a retail chain for about 12 years and he had a dream to set up his own business. He along with his friend Mr Xavier who is in the back end operations had made a plan to set up the retail chain starting with two branches in the city and it materialised. Mr De'Souza felt that he could realise his dreams since it's cost-effective and also can quickly establish himself. Since both of them were in similar business it did not take much time to penetrate into the market and within a span of four years the two branches became 10 branches. There was consistent growth in the sales and each branch used to compete with other companies and also with their respective units.

The main strength of the firm were the employees who were given adequate training to make the customers happy. To avoid any distinction among the employees everyone was given the uniform and unless a person was known by name and designation, it was difficult to know who was the boss and who the worker. The employees used to help the customers by giving the details of the various schemes available and the new arrivals.

Shop and Save has invested 10 per cent of their amount in the information technology and it is one of their strengths. The billing is being done through bar code scanners and computers. The bills were made in the name of the customer taking his personal details and contact numbers. This has helped the firm to understand the nature of requirement of each individual and whenever a customer comes to the store he is being given special treatment and is given the details of the schemes and arrivals pertaining to his tastes. The customer is given the feedback form to identify any person who has helped him during making the purchases and the employee who gets the maximum nominations is declared the *'employee of the month'* and one month's salary is given to him to further work towards customer satisfaction.

The employees are given special prize when any of their suggestion is being accepted and changes made in the establishment. Every week a contest is conducted where the employee judges the sales for the week. Each salesman has special incentives for promoting certain products. In order to bring in healthy competition among the branches the best branch is given the *'simply the best'* award for outstanding contribution to the growth of the business during the quarter.

The measures were able to keep the employees motivated and since the work is taken in a very sportive manner the organisation is soon competing with the established brands.

## Questions

1. How does 'Shop and Save' motivate its employees?
2. How effective do you think can the various methods used by 'Shop and Save' be used in your organisation?
3. If you were Mr De'Souza what other strategies will you use for a faster growth?
4. Can you administer any of these motivational plans in your firm? If not, what are the limitations?

## References and Further Readings

Bernardin, John H. 2003. *Human Resource Management*, New Delhi: Tata McGraw-Hill Publishing Company Limited.

Carter L., D. Giber, R.E. Beckhard and M. Goldsmith. 2001. *Best Practices in Organisation Development and Change: Culture. Leadership. Retention, Performance, Coaching*, CA: Jossey-Bass.

Gordon, Judith R. 1999. *Organizational Behaviour: A Diagnostic Approach*, 6th edn, NJ: Prentice Hall International Inc.

Green, Thad. 2001. *Motivation Management*, Mumbai: Jaico Publishing House.
Hagemann, Gisela. 1992. *The Motivation Manual*, England: Gower Press.
Kreitner, Robert. 1999. *Management*, Delhi: AITBS Publishers & Distributors.
Maslow, Abraham H. 1998. *Maslow on Management*, New York: John Wiley and Sons Inc.
McClelland, David C. 1987. *Human Motivation*, Cambridge: Cambridge University Press.
Nelson D.L. and J.C. Quick. 2003. *Organizational Behavior*, USA: Thompson Learning.
Ouchi, William G. 2005 (originally 1981). 'The Z Organization' in J.M. Shafritz, J.S. Ott and Y.S. Jang (eds) *In Classics of Organizational Theory*, pp. 424–35, Belmont CA: Wadsworth.
Smith, Greg. *The Navigator*, Newsletter, www.charthouse.com.
Steers, Richard M., Lyman W. Porter and Gregory A. Bigley. (eds) 1996. *Motivation and Leadership at Work*, New York: McGraw-Hill/Irwin.
Weihrich, Heinz and Harold Koontz. 1994. *Management—A Global Perspective*, New York: McGraw-Hill.

# 8 ESSENCE OF COMPETENCY BUILDING

## Content

→ Learning Objectives
→ Measuring and Building Competencies of Employees
→ Handling Complex Behavioural Concerns through Organisation Behaviour and Organisation Development
→ Building KSA through Training
→ Enable SHR Technology—Key to Success

→ Conclusion

## Learning Objectives

- To understand the process of measuring competencies of employees and provide input for building competencies.
- To know the method of assessment centre.
- To analyse the process of building skill knowledge and attitude through training and development approach.
- To define the competency mapping process and understand its bridging programme.

# Measuring and Building Competencies of Employees

The number of people recruited to manage the growth of business has increased enormously, making the diseconomies appalling. Inflexibility, unresponsiveness, the absence of customer focus, obsession with activity rather than result, bureaucratic paralysis, lack of innovation, are the common problems stemming out of this number legacy. The need of the hour is to constantly refine the manpower that is competent to handle the job, upgrade the quality by training those men to excel, find the best people through performance management system and cull out the redundant. Human Resource needs to identify those competencies, which are required in future for effective performance rather than the number of heads.

The important component that gives competitive advantage to the organisations is the 'competencies'. In the organisation these competencies need to be nurtured to attain the competitive advantage. The role of each individual is very important in the organisation and the competency of each need is to be assessed and developed. Competency consists of knowledge, skill and attitude. Competency refers to abilities based on behaviour. For example, the competency of a manager to take a decision depends upon the nature and content of the information available. It is the competency, which determines the effectiveness of such decisions. As the competencies are observable, the skills need to be demonstrated to show the performance. The performance must be accompanied by the success of accomplishing a task. Such competencies can be demonstrated in any area given an opportunity to perform. Building the organisation on competencies has a paradigm shift on the way organisations are functioning. Earlier organisations are based on the tasks where the people fill the roles to accomplish the tasks; whereas in the changing scenario it depends upon the competency of the people. These competencies need to be distinguished for high performance and the practices of HR need to demonstrate and reinforce building these competencies.

Competencies are those critical behaviours, skills, attributes and proficiencies that every organisation member is expected to possess and display. Organisation must give those competencies which are critical and futuristic for the organisation's success. All the employees must maintain consistent, demanding standards for every one and keep raising those standards. This would give an opportunity to identify high potential managers and professionals and their development.

Competency mapping is a process narrating the gap between job competencies existing and required in an employee for a specific role or similar roles. The job analysis method is largely being used, and while doing so it is important to differentiate between routine and practised behaviour and the competencies in handling the job successfully. Data is being gathered from employees, peers, superiors and subordinates of the critical attributes like knowledge, skills, etc., pertaining to the job. This can be done by way of interviewing for evidence on the success of the job. The interviewer must enlist all the critical incidents through which one can arrive at the effective and ineffective performers. Promoting the employees in the organisation is heavily dependent on the job tenure in the company, KRA and the performance review. The results are based on the present performance rather than the future performance and this method does not ensure whether the employees have necessary knowledge and skills to handle the jobs of higher level. To build the organisations on the competencies, an objective method of evaluation—Assessment Centre is designed.

The Assessment Centre is a technique to measure the competencies of the candidates and to determine whether they can be selected or not, placed under potential appraisal. This tool is also increasingly used to recruit people so that they match with the competencies of the existing employees. Assessment Centre is designed in such a way that it has multiple competencies to be assessed using multiple techniques, and in order to reduce the subjectivity, multiple assessors are engaged. It is a better method of observing the competencies as it has various simulation exercises and role-plays which can demonstrate the ability of the candidate to handle the roles. A battery of tests can help in mapping the person's competencies for the personnel requirements of the organisation.

Competencies can also be nurtured and build through mentoring, training, job rotation, management development programmes, etc. Mentoring is a process where one experienced person assists another person to grow and learn. A mentor guides the mentee through examples and provides opportunities to practise new found behaviours, so that the mentee can learn from them. Standards of technical performance, unique competencies of trade, etc., can be developed by a mentee by observing and learning when demonstrated. Job rotation provides opportunity to develop new competencies required to perform well in the new position. Training programmes with faculty from outside and within help in building or strengthening the competencies. Organisations shall also build a conducive atmosphere for learning. If there is no atmosphere in which an employee can learn, then the efforts made towards competency-based organisation may be futile. The concept of competencies and the existence of a framework to assess, measure and build can provide invaluable basis for integrating the key activities and achieving a strategic approach to managing the people.

# Handling Complex Behavioural Concerns through Organisation Behaviour and Organisation Development

Organisation Development (OD) and Organisation Behaviour (OB) have one common focus, i.e., human factor in an organisation setting. Though both have to deal with people in the organisation, their focus is different. Organisation Behaviour concerns itself with the study and understanding of the individual and group behaviour and patterns of structure in order to improve organisational effectiveness and performance. Organisation Behaviour is more concerned about the behaviour of people, people in-groups, people in the organisations and the impact of the external environment on the people.

Organisation Development is a long-term effort, led and supported by top management, to improve an organisation's visioning, empowerment, learning and problem-solving processes through an ongoing, collaborative management of organisation culture with special emphasis on the culture of intact work teams and other team configurations using consultant–facilitator role and the theory and technology of applied behavioural science, including action research. For OD the commitment of the top management is vital and they need to be an integral part and participate effectively in the change management. Also they should have an insight of the applied behavioural sciences approach in understanding the behaviour of people for bringing in the desired result. Organisation Development focuses on culture and processes team building, system changes and enabling the organisation to solve its problems in its own by way of continual support from the consultants.

Organisation Development concentrates mainly on individuals, dyads and triads, teams and groups, inter group relations and the total organisation. The main emphasis is to bring in better interpersonal relations and change the orientation to improve the overall performance and effectiveness of the organisation. It is a clinical way of examination of organisational health and implementation of change. Role of the HR is to bring in OB and OD interventions to appreciate the complex nature of behaviour of people and organisation renewal.

# Building KSA through Training

Training helps the individuals in understanding what to do and how to perform effectively. Training aims at planned programmes designed to improve upon the competencies of the individuals, groups and the organisation. In fact, it is a very good tool to enhance the competencies wherein the measures can be evaluated from the angle of knowledge, skill and attitude. The most important part in the training is to identify the needs of the training and what will be the likely outcome of the training. For an employee who has joined new, for him to build the competencies he can be trained in all aspects, but for an employee who is already serving the organisation for him to bring in focused improvement in his performance, it is difficult. The performance appraisal would bring out the requirements of training.

There are various methods of training—traditional methods like on-the-job training where people will be asked to perform a job directly under a supervisor and learn while performing the job, or apprenticeship training given by combining classroom training and on-the-job training. The most widely used method of training is the classroom method of training wherein an expert trainer or facilitator would impart subject/subjects to the participants using audit visual aids and simulations. The new method that has evolved with the growth of information technology are computer-based training which enables the employee to sit on a system and learn through an interactive mode of teaching and also give constant feedbacks on the learning. Vast amount of data is available on the Internet and through these sites employee can develop his competencies by learning and implementation.

Experimental or situational learning is a new method wherein the employee are exposed to a situation away from the classrooms and are being taught various concepts like team building or any identified training objectives through various games and exercises. This is a method, which involves learning through fun. People enjoy moving out and do a group of exercises and the learning and facilitator debriefs the learning. As the objectives can be fulfilled in a more interesting method of playing and learning it ensures better participation of employees and helps the learners to remember what they have learnt.

Three aspects can guide the self-directed learning process and the implementation on the job, first learning through job instructions and implementing on the job; second, learning through observation and imbibing skills; and finally, learning through various tools available on improvement of self; like self-motivation techniques, etc.

The post-training evaluation and action plan would ensure right kind of participation and imbibing of skills. Training is actually an investment, which an organisation makes to enhance the knowledge and skills of the employees for present and future performance. It is an investment of human capital and hence it should not be accounted in expenses part, as the deliverables would take time to fill the gap. The following measures can enhance the training process: (a) training needs to be part of the corporate culture; (b) training should be part of the business strategy objectives and linked to the bottom line; a comprehensive approach of training and retraining need to be there; and there should be a commitment to invest in resources.

Training is to mean competitive strategies, which will enable one to gain competitive advantage from the competitive market. All the training must be related to the specific competitive strategies. More of workshops are needed than training. Training material is to be provided to reinforce that these terms and concepts be learnt.

If an organisation would like to innovate and be competitive, the consequence would be to get highly skilled manpower, provide better empowerment, exercise minimal controls and make greater investment in HR processes, reward successes and allow failures to happen. However, this process depends heavily on individual expertise and creativity. Hence, long-term training programmes are needed to bring in the right motivation and to look at enhancing the competencies.

# Enable SHR Technology—Key to Success

This chapter brings in the following Strategic HR technologies:

SHR Technology-33    Training and Development—*Brushing of Knowledge and Skills through Training and Development.*

SHR Technology-34    Outbound Training—*Learning through Fun by Adventure and Situation Training Programme.*

SHR Technology-35    Assessment Centre—*Gauging and Building Competencies through Assessment Centre.*

SHR Technology-36    Competency Mapping—*Assessing Individual Competencies through Competency Mapping.*

To remain competitive for an individual it is needless to mention that an employee has to upgrade his/her competencies with changing time. It is solely the responsibility of an individual to advance their competency levels. However, an organisation is equally responsible for providing opportunity and platform for all those individuals to improve their skill level. The training and development efforts of the company gives employees a path to build their knowledge, skills and attitude towards the desired level for better performance in the company.

Many a time organisations make mistakes of employing or deploying an employee on the job which does not fit with his or her competency. This makes the employee as well as the organisation to suffer. Assessment Centre is a scientific tool through which individual competency for a given job or performance can be assessed so that appropriate competency matching can take place. It helps in evolving a database on individual competency. An organisation must also evolve an inventory of competency required for a given job to perform their best. The gap between the existing competency of an individual and the requisite competency of the company in a given job needs to be bridged through various processes. This process is a competency mapping process for both the individual and the company.

# Conclusion

- Competencies have always been a matter of live debate in every organisation. Since jobs demands different competency levels from the job holder, it is necessary that the job holder must possess relevant competencies to perform.
- The problem of performance arises when there exists a gap between available competency and the desired competencies.

- Assessment Centre is a powerful tool to evaluate individual competency of a person for a given job and it helps identifying the gap as well as the areas requiring improvements. It is universally used for bridging the competency gap as well as taking promotions and progression decisions.
- Competency enhancement is usually done through training and development efforts. Constant upgradation of skills and knowledge through training input is necessary for a learning organisation.
- Training has now travelled beyond the classroom and more and more innovations are seen in imparting training. The latest approach to training is outbound and an adventure simulated training process which has broken the barriers of the four-walled classroom type training process.

# 'TRAINING AND DEVELOPMENT' BRUSHING OF KNOWLEDGE AND SKILLS THROUGH TRAINING AND DEVELOPMENT

*Give a man a fish, and you feed him for a day. Teach him to fish, and you feed him for a lifetime.*

—Chinese Proverb

## Intent

- To equip employees to assume a level of responsibility compatible with their ability through training.
- To continuously improve the performance of the employee in the current and the future role.
- To provide an opportunity to sharpen skill, knowledge and attitude of an employee.
- To provide an opportunity to an employee to gain knowledge and competencies in current performance area as well as newly developed roles through multi-skilling.

## Expression

Training means a session or a procedure, which helps in acclimatising a new employee or an existing employee to the organisation. Primarily it is for enhancement of the skill, knowledge and attitude of an employee for the present and future performance.

## Comprehension

In one way or another new employees as well as the existing employees in the company needs training. Training is a planned method of imparting competencies so that the employees, groups and the organisation as a whole improve the performance. Each company has its own way of doing even routine procedures to make sure that all the new employees understand the company's goal, policies and procedures. Most large organisations and many small ones have well-defined orientation programmes. Although they vary, such programmes usually include information about the company background and structure, equal employment opportunity and practice of safety regulations, standard of employee conduct, employee compensation and benefit plans, work timings and other topics that newly hired employees might have questions about.

Most companies also offer training because employee competence has a direct effect on productivity and profits. Management development also requires combination of on-the-job training, for example, through delegation, project work, self-analysis, trail period and simulation and off-the-job learning, for example, through external short courses, study for a diploma in management studies or MBA qualification, This training and learning should be aimed at providing and blending technological competence, social and human skill and conceptual ability.

A particular and increasingly popular approach to management development course is through action learning. Action learning involves a small self-selecting team undertaking a practical, real life and organisation-based project. It is a learner driven process.

Employee training may also involve a self-study component using training manuals and taste. Many companies are using computer-based training (CBT) in which employees access a series of multimedia training modules on CD-ROM at the computer terminal. Many companies in these days are now distributing training and orientation material via their Intranet. Electronic formats that can be accessed by employees are being used for training documents such as product direction, diversity information and sales tips.

An important part of the process of improving the performance of the manager is training but it is a self-development process. It is the extent to which individual managers take advantage of development opportunities around them. It is self-initiated.

Unfortunately, the organisations are more interested in the training programmes and the methods used, but not on the feedback of the programme. The feedback is being taken for the head count rather than analysis and improvement of the training intervention. The focus also gets lost of what the employee desires to learn and the areas, which he is lacking by not looking at the training needs and the organisational requirements. The important feature of the training is to know whether the training imparted has the impact on the performance and a study needs to be conducted on the feedback of the impact of the training in the performance. The process is called 'transfer of learning', which indicates the extent up to which the employee, who has undergone training, has been able to use the same in his job and improve upon his performance.

The three common factors: ASK, i.e., Attitude, Skill and Knowledge are the ingredients of success for any individual. These factors are not the birth right but are ingrained over a period of time with efforts and commitment in an individual. Besides many ways to bring about change in attitude, enhancement of knowledge and upgrading skills, training is the most effective technique. With the input of effective training process, these ASK factors can definitely be strengthened to a great extent. The changing business environment and need for bringing in positive attitude and knowledge and competency building through skill development is perennial and training is one of the powerful technology through which this is possible. Companies are investing sizeable money for imparting training including investment in training centres and training resources. Achievement of a certain number of training man days generally reflects in the business strategy of the company. Thus, training is a strategic technology in modern HR management.

# Experiential Application

## A. Prerequisite

- An effective training programme needs to be integrated with a comprehensive development to reinforce the concept and practices stressed in training on-the-job.
- Effective training also requires a commitment to self-development from all employees, top management support, a comprehensive on-the-job training programme supplemented with off-the-job training and support from first line supervisor.
- The responsibility for effective training is shared by the organisation's top management, HR department and the employee.
- The greatest responsibility lies with the employee who needs to learn and transfer the learning.
- Method for training and development involves various on-the-jobs' technique. The programme includes outside short courses and seminars.
- An effective training and development programme achieves a unique blend of on-the-job and off-the-job methods suitable for the individual. Lectures, lecture discussion, multimedia presentation, job coaching, programme instruction, case analysis, role playing and gaming are the instructional techniques that are used in recent days.
- It is important that an organisation chooses resources that best meet its needs for training and development. The real success of training and programme can be assessed ultimately on the base of success and health of the organisation.
- The ideal assessment framework involves a cost-benefit analysis of the skills or knowledge possessed by a group who has attended a training or programme compared with a group who has not received training.

- The following are important for the training:

  - trainee must be motivated to learn;
  - information must be meaningful;
  - learning must be reinforced;
  - both rewards and punishment to be used;
  - immediate feedback on learning to be provided; and
  - organisation of appropriate training materials to be made.

## B. Process Steps

| Step | Process |
|------|---------|
| Step – I | Determine the specific training and development needs of the company through performance appraisal/training needs identifications (TNI). |
| Step – II | Design the specific performance objective that the training is to accomplish. |
| Step – III | Identify the employees who need the training. |
| Step – IV | Design the training programme including topics, instructors, media, cases, exercises, handouts, and so on. |
| Step – V | Conduct the training programme for the employees to be trained. |
| Step – VI | Compare the performance measure of the employees who went through the programme with those who did not. |
| Step – VII | Compare the benefits as measured as improvement in performance measures for the trained group with the cost of the programme. |

# Potential Gains and Areas of Concern

- Training promotes good human relations. It helps gaining self-confidence and security, which in turn promote cooperation and respect.
- Training helps enhancing the career. As people expand their abilities, the supervisors' role will also grow. As individual increases their efficiency, the group benefits.
- Time can be used more advantageously in learning through training.
- Training promotes health and safety. By emphasising health and safety rules, violations and accidents are less likely.
- If the training planned is not effective, the money spent is wasted.
- Truly wasteful expenditure occurs when people are promoted and then never trained in their new duties. Peter Principle states that the employees are raised to their highest levels of incompetence.

# Measurability

## Try It Out

(1: not at all done, 2: moderately done, 3: to some extent done, 4: to a great extent done, 5: excellently done)

- Organisation has laid down Training and Development Strategy.  ☐
- Organisation has structured methods of TNI (Training Needs Identification) and TNA (Training Needs Analysis) and designing a yearly training calendar.  ☐
- Organisation allows the participants to develop their competencies by allowing them to attend the training programme as per the schedule.  ☐
- Organisation has post-training feedback mechanism for reviewing the objectives.  ☐
- Organisation has a methodology to assess the quality of faculty, facilities provided, training material provided and the training itself.  ☐
- Feedback is communicated to the participants and also the faculty on the performance during the programme.  ☐

Analysis: the average score would determine the extent to which training and development process exist in your organisation.

## Score Card

(*: 25% achieved, **: 50% achieved, ***: 75% achieved, ****: 100% achieved)

| Technology | Objective Elements | Unit | Historical | Last Year | Current Year | Stretch Target | Status |
|---|---|---|---|---|---|---|---|
| Training and Development | Strategy Document on Training and Development | Doc | Nil | No | Yes | Jan | ** |
| Training and Development | Training Need Identification and Analysis | Doc | Nil | No | Yes | Feb | ** |
| Training and Development | Training Calendar | Doc | Nil | No | Yes | Mar | * |
| Training and Development | Post-Training Feedback | 5 point Scale | 3 | 3 | 3.5 | 3.7 | *** |
| Training and Development | Survey on Training Effectiveness | Doc | Nil | Nil | 1 | Dec | * |

# Proven Track Record

## Track One

## Anderson Consulting

Anderson Consulting uses a multi-media CBT programme to dramatically reduce the six weeks of training most new consultants received before their first consulting assignment. The new system known as BPC—Business Practices Course is a self-placed, interactive computer based training programme. The BPC consists of 15 modular computerised components that stimulates a business situation that the staff of Anderson might encounter in a consulting engagement at a hypothetical printing and book publishing company.

Using audit and video clips stored on CD-ROM the consultant trainee interviews the company's personnel, receives phone calls, gets advice from senior Anderson consultants, reviews internal Anderson memos, and attends meeting with senior members of the client management staff. At the end of the CBT programme the consultant-trainee delivers a presentation outlining the kinds of findings and recommendation that would normally be delivered to a client.

(*Source*: Dessler, 1997.)

## Track Two

## Boeing Corporation

Boeing is the largest commercial jet airline producing company in the world. When Boeing wanted to install the largest computing system it had ever developed in its commercial spare parts department, the manager at Boeing knew that the installation of new system would require extensive retraining of its employees. It would effect almost all of the seven hundred people in the spare parts department not only in terms of technical aspect of using the new computer system, but also because the department offices would become virtually paperless. Perhaps more scary to the employees was the fact that they would have to spend much more of the day working at their computer terminal.

Given functional diversity of the group Boeing knew the challenge ahead. Before deciding whether the training programme would be managed internally or by a consulting firm, Boeing knew that it had to be clearer about the actual training objectives. For instance, in addition to the purely technical aspects of the training, there was the need to make the employees to use the system in a manner that is more customer friendly. Employee communication and assertiveness skills possibly had to be developed so that they could make their needs known if there was any particular information they wanted from the system that was not being provided by the employees who would now input the data.

(*Source*: Dessler, 1997.)

## Track Three

## Core Healthcare

Core Healthcare grew as an international pharmaceutical and healthcare company in a span of a decade. One of the key strengths of the Core Healthcare is the information sharing and cross-functional innovative training. The company in an year invests about 35 man hours of training to each employee including the employees at the corporate office and the field sales. Besides driven by technology and research and to keep itself in touch with the latest developments globally, the organisation invests in the knowledge base of the employees through participation in international conferences and seminars. The 'Core Healthcare way' is the induction training given for the fresh recruits to groom them to take up responsibilities at a young age, which enabled the company to create a bank of officials to take up higher challenges.

Out of many training programmes, which the organisation conducts, one such programme is called '*Maradona*'. Through this training programme, the organisation envisages each employee to be a multi-skilled, dynamic player having the ability to work at any place and function. *Maradona* was at ease as a defender, sharp-shooter, midfielder and has the vision and intuition to find out open spaces, create opportunities and tactically send the ball through dribbling dodging, kicking or passing as the need arose. Like *Maradona* every employee is groomed to start with a humble beginning and achieve his status through sheer hard work, determination and commitment to excel.

(*Source*: Jain, 2000.)

# Applied HR Case

## Beacon Elmac Systems Limited

The rapid changes in technology have brought in many changes to improvise the production process and also the problems of adoption to the new technology. The firm was manufacturing unique and customised technical equipment in the country and for export, which are electromechanical in nature. Since the firm was set up more than 10 years back, the technology used was old. It was designed to replace all the new machines, which had state of art technology and used computers and microprocessors. The new technology demanded new knowledge and skills, which were lacking with 70 per cent of the employees.

Mr Raman Rao, Head HR of the unit was called by the MD and was told to revamp the total machinery to ensure that the plant dispatches quality products and be able to match the time schedules with the international standards. He was asked to plan the VRS (Voluntary Retirement Scheme) so that new employees with requisite skills could be recruited. The machinery was going to arrive within two months and they would be commissioned in another two months. The plant needed at least 10 employees to be recruited immediately who had the requisite skills. Raman had opposed the suggestion to declare the VRS and said that since they were just in their 30s and were young, a VRS would lead them to nowhere. The MD was also of the same opinion, but since the machinery needed to be changed and production schedules to be maintained, he did not have any option. He advised Raman to prepare an alternative action plan, if any, in three days.

## Questions

1. Can you assess where Raman was wrong in designing his HR systems?
2. Was the MD right in asking Raman to declare the VRS for employees?
3. If you are Raman what alternative strategy will you propose and how are you going to address the issues of the MD and employees.

## References and Further Readings

Barrington, Harry and Margaret A. Reid. 2001. *Training Interventions—Managing Employee Development*, Mumbai: Jaico Publishing House.
Dessler, Gary. 1997. *Human Resource Management*, New Jersey: Prentice Hall.
Jain, Arun Kumar. 2000. *Competitive Excellence*, New Delhi: Vikas Publishing House Pvt Ltd.
Lawrence J. Peter and Raymond Hull. 1969. *The Peter Principle: Why Things Always Go Wrong*, New York: William Morrow and Company Inc.
Mager, Robert F. and Peter Pipe. 1998. *HRD Training and Development*, Mumbai: Jaico Publishing House.
Pfeiffer, J. William and Arlette C. Ballew. 1993. *Using Lecturettes, Theory and Models in HRD*, New Delhi: Aditya Books Pvt Ltd.
Phillips, Jack J. and Drew Stone. 2002. *How to Measure Training Results*, New York: McGraw-Hill.
Rae, Leslie. 1996. *Using Activities in Training and Development*, London: Kogan Page.
———. 2002. *The Art of Training and Development in Management*, New Delhi: Crest Publishing House.
Shandler, Donald. 1996. *Reengineering the Training Function*, Florida: St Lucie Press.
Singh, P.N. 2001. *Training for Management Development*, Mumbai: Suchandra Publications/ISTD.

# 'OUTBOUND TRAINING' LEARNING THROUGH FUN BY ADVENTURE AND SITUATION TRAINING PROGRAMME

*Reflection is the capacity to 'notice oneself noticing'; that is, to step back and see one's mind working in relation to it's projects.*

—Peter B. Vaill

## Intent

- The participation of all the participants on equal footing without any barriers of hierarchy, department, etc., which ensures fulfilment of the objectives of learning.
- The programme provides an opportunity for the participants to learn each other's role and perspective providing with a better bondage. For example, the team building exercise may bring in the Production Manager and the Marketing Manager together who are erstwhile banking upon silos.
- If the exercise is built with relevant experience of process along with an analogy of a real work situation, it will reinforce the learning and would enable fulfilment of learning objectives of the organisation.

## Expression

Outdoor learning is a training that moves away from the theoretical, classroom and parrot-fashion learning methods of traditional learning. It challenges the assumptions of traditional learning and provides direct and personal learning, providing individual commitment and great responsibility for learners to learn.

# Comprehension

The traditional learning method of training depends upon the classroom learning where the flip charts replace the chalkboards, handouts replaced the textbooks and the training rooms are like typical classrooms. It is often viewed as activity divorced from the real world, dealing with abstract concepts with a predictable end point. Outdoor learning has challenged the traditional learning and the main emphasis is on learning by experience. For example, driving a car can be done by practically learning rather than through classroom. At the same time, learning is with fun and enjoyment and participants are emotionally attached and have a sense of success and accomplishment of learning. When an employee is on the job he learns with daily experiences and his interactions with his external environment, i.e., peers, culture, customers, etc.

Learning depends upon the continuity and interaction. Every experience is learning and each experiential learning reinforces the other. An experience is always through the interaction of the person with others or the environment, i.e., a book, person, game, location, etc. Through this framework the human impulse enable every individual to learn, have a sense of purpose and meaning. The principles of continuity and interaction in experience and the inevitable march to a sense of purpose are central to the dynamics of outdoor learning.

Outdoor learning is a four step method. First, the personal experience of every participant, second, observation and reflection of one's experiences, third the formation of generalisations and abstract concepts and fourth, the hypothesis to be tested on future actions. The role of a facilitator needs to be limited as far as possible to provide effective design, and a focus and reflection, and the drawing of conclusions need to be done from the participants.

When we talk of training, the general picture emerges is that a classroom with training aids, a faculty and a training module materials. It means a host of lectures and theories to understand and deal with. The outbound training is something different than this usual picture. There is no classroom but the setting of training in nature like hills, a valley, a forest or in a playground. The conventional set-up of the classroom has limitations and sometimes end up in a few case discussions. Unlike this the outbound programme are so designed that it practically gives an opportunity to explore the managerial competencies of each participant. The outbound set-up gives challenges and obstacles like real life situations which participants have to learn to overcome. Thus outbound training brings more closeness to organisational situations and solving those issues in such circumstances gives better learning processes and hence it has become very popular with the training professionals. Today's business environment demands training which is close to reality and thus outbound training processes have taken a strategic role in the HRD initiatives.

# Experiential Application

## A. Prerequisite

- Outbound training has in-built physical activities hence it could lead to—accidents and injuries, especially when delegates go for a task too far; resentment and rejection of potential learning.
- It is recommended that every course contain must have 50:50 ratio of physical tasks to non-physical activity such as review and input. Circumstances may alter cases, for example, it maybe that people need to learn lessons about handling pressure and hence, the 50:50 ratio is merely a guideline.
- Trainers often feel a pressure to stuff outdoor programme with activities in ways, which they would never do on indoor courses. One very negative result is the propagation of myths by participants, who often talk at great length about the activities but not much about the review. The resulting folklore tends to be about people dangling upside down over cliffs or in caves, or suffering exhaustion from a hard walk in the forest, all of which can have a very negative effect on subsequent participants.
- Car parking or field exercise, equipment, safety precautions, first aids, navigation instruments, water and eatables, extra clothing, protective gears, boots and rain-coats, etc., are important elements to plan before undertaking the outbound programme.

## B. Process Steps

| Step | Process |
| --- | --- |
| Step – I | Design the outbound programme based on the organisation needs and the kind of participants' profile. |
| Step – II | Choose exercises for outbound programme, which are full of relevant process experience. |
| Step – III | Initiate and conduct outbound programme at the specific location with the measures. |
| Step – IV | Review the processes underlying the exercises to articulate the learning that took place. |
| Step – V | Provide input to participants to make sense to their learning and put it within a legitimate framework. |
| Step – VI | Give participants the opportunity to plan how they will use the new ideas in future situations. |

# Potential Gains and Areas of Concern

- The responsibility of learning lies with the participant, who needs to be active and assertive to learn and make a strategy for implementation.
- Outdoor learning has strong memories of experience, weather, environment and the learning itself. Recall of events lead to recall of learning which is absent in the classroom programme.
- The programme can be devised to impart behavioural and skill training to all the employees irrespective of their organisational hierarchy, physical abilities, etc.
- The programme can bring in shared experience and the bonds of companionship may outlast the course itself. If the delegates are from the same organisation the bonds become much stronger.
- Objects need to be spelt properly, without which the programme may lead to haphazard and ineffective learning and sometimes maybe counter-productive.
- Experience without reflection does not help learning. Theory without the scope to implement will only lead to wastage of resources.
- Outdoor programme needs to be done with utmost caution and care with experts only. For example, rafting in high-speed waters is dangerous, and if not done properly, may take the life of participants.
- The facilitator should reinforce the learning process during the programme as it may happen that the participants may become more interested in enjoying the outdoor exercise rather than learning.

# Measurability

## Try It Out

(1: not at all done, 2: moderately done, 3: to some extent done, 4: to a great extent done, 5: excellently done)

- My organisation has a strategy for imparting learning through learning outbound activities.  ☐
- Top management views outbound learning as an important tool for imparting management concepts and a method of learning.  ☐
- Organisation has a structured training calender including outbound training and the participants are chosen as per the identified training needs.  ☐

- Activities are structured to achieve the objectives of the programme rather ☐ than providing entertainment to the participants.
- Debriefing and feedback is given to all the participants. ☐
- Post-training evaluation is obtained from the participants on the ☐ effectiveness of the training programme.

Analysis: the average score would determine the extent to which outbound training process exists in your organisation.

## Score Card

(*: 25% achieved, **: 50% achieved, ***: 75% achieved, ****: 100% achieved)

| Technology | Objective Elements | Unit | Historical | Last Year | Current Year | Stretch Target | Status |
|---|---|---|---|---|---|---|---|
| Outbound Training | Outbound Learning Programmes | Nos | 2 | 2 | 6 | 8 | ** |
| Outbound Training | Training Feedback | 5 Point Scale | 3.5 | 3.5 | 4.0 | 4.30 | * |

# Proven Track Record

## Track One

## Knight-Ridder Inc.

Knight-Ridder is a global communications company involved in information services, newspaper publishing, cable television, etc. The company conducts Organisation Development (OD) exercise for team building to enhance the cohesiveness of the departments by helping members to function as a team, through an outbound learning programme. The employees spend two days in the Florida Keys participating in intergroup and team building activities, such as building rafts and race across a swamp.

The organisation uses these programmes to build trust, cooperation and team spirit among the managers. Since the media in which the company is running is highly competitive, such programmes help managers to adapt better to massive changes.

(*Source*: Daft, 1997: 402.)

## Track Two

## Mercury Communications

Mike Harris, Chief Executive of Mercury Communications of UK has instituted the process of empowerment and has changed the culture in an unique way. The employees had to undergo 'ignition' sessions in huge canvas igloos located in a car park at Birmingham's National Exhibition Centre. The training programme lasted for 10 hours, which includes intense debate, self-disclosure, and much applause, all interspersed with a sound and light show. The technique was highly effective and an enriching experience that motivated employees toward an exciting experience.

The sole aim is to introduce the staff to the culture of empowerment and putting the employee first and the customer second. During the process the employees are encouraged to come up with suggestions improving all parts of the organisation, from small details of working methods to whole new product ideas, and are often financially rewarded for doing so. The organisation had hundreds of workable ideas and many new products were introduced in record time as a direct result of these *'ignition'* sessions.

(*Source*: Shackleton, 1995: 134.)

# Applied HR Case

## Fresh Learning Systems

Dorothy is the Head of the Marketing department and the seniormost of all the Heads of the Department. The other departments of the company, which is into the printing of textbooks and other printing material, are Production, Quality, Research and Development, Accounts and Finance, Logistics and HR. Susan has just joined as the HR Head and is also the least experienced in comparison with others.

Susan observes that Dorothy is almost like next to MD and she takes all decisions on behalf of him. If things goes well, she claims the credit but when something goes wrong she throws the responsibility on others. Since, Dorothy is the seniormost among all and very close to MD, none is able to say anything against her.

Susan wants to bring in change among all the Heads so that they can discharge their duties. She always believes and works in teams rather than working under another colleague. During the monthly meeting Susan proposes to train all the Heads in the interpersonal skills and wants everyone's time on next Saturday, since the faculty has available dates only for next Saturday. She does not want to waste the Sunday of all the Heads. The session is planned in a hotel and everyone is asked to come without mobiles as one needs to forget the office and start concentrating on the training. Katherine, the Head of Finance suggests that since it's a weekend and they can go for an outbound programme wherein they can have learning and fun. Susan was about to propose, but since the idea has come from her colleague, she thought she can sell the concept to her and responded that she knows a classmate who is into outbound training and would be ready to take the assignment. Susan was of the opinion that the real time learning may bring the team culture among the Heads. However, Dorothy is suspicious about the whole adventure and is against the proposal. The MD decides that it is a long time that they had a party and this gives them a good opportunity for learning and also partying.

## Questions

1. Do you think Susan was right in choosing the outbound learning to bring in team spirit?
2. If you were the trainer for the programme how will you plan the programme? Please explain with the objectives, content, scheduling, exercise and debriefing.

## References and Further Readings

Daft, Richard L. 1997. *Management*, Fort Worth: The Dryden Press.
Kirby, Andy. 1992. *Games for Trainer*, England: Gower Publishing Company.
Krouwell, Bill and Steve Goodwill. 1999. *Outdoor Training*, New Delhi: Viva Books Pvt Ltd.
Shackleton, Viv. 1995. *Business Leadership*, London: Routledge.
Sloman, Martyn. 2001. *A Handbook on Training Strategy*, Mumbai: Jaico Publishing House.

# 'ASSESSMENT CENTRE'
# GAUGING AND BUILDING COMPETENCIES
# THROUGH ASSESSMENT CENTRE

*It's not enough to imagine the future—you also have to build it.*

—Anonymous

## Intent

- To evaluate the competency of the individuals vis-à-vis the present and future capabilities.
- To evaluate the competency gaps in an individual so that suitable developmental plan can be prepared.
- To generate a database on the skill set of the employee for taking organisational decisions such as promotions, transfers, job rotations and succession planning.
- To provide a platform for analysing critical situations in a simulated way for problem solving and decision making.

## Expression

Assessment Centre consists of standardised evaluation of behaviour based on multiple input. Multiple trained observers and techniques are used. Judgements about behaviour are made in part from specially developed assessment simulations. These judgements are pulled by the assessors at an evaluation meeting during which all relevant data are reported and discussed and the assessors agree on the evaluation of the dimensions and any overall evaluation that is made.

# Comprehension

The Assessment Centre method, which was originally made to identify the potential officers, was a British innovation during the World War II by the Armed Forces, which was followed by the Civil Services. Later on American Telephone & Telegraph Company (AT&T) applied it for their recruitment process. Over the past few years, the Assessment Centre method has become increasingly popular. The term may suggest a specific building or institute or some form of training. However, it has nothing to do with it. Assessment Centre consists of the observation of candidates carrying out a variety of assignments, individually or in a group, over a stipulated period. Assessment centres were widely used because of the problems found with the alternative methods of selection like appraisals, committees, etc. There are certain positions, which require completely different set of skills from what the incumbents possess. The Assessment Centre method is the best method to assess the competencies in an objective manner.

An Assessment Centre is an evaluation process, which can be used to identify the future potential of employees and job candidates. The method is systematic, effective and reliable. It is designed to enable HR managers, career advisors, and especially line managers to determine which qualities are essential for successful job performance, to evaluate people and identify future potential. Mainly the Assessment Centre is used (a) in simulation and role-play, (b) for selection, assessment and training purpose, (c) for actual evaluation, and (d) as the basis for dealing with personal issues.

Initially the term, Assessment Centre refers to a set of simulations of real work. However this core is frequently combined with other assessment instruments, such as intelligence tests, personality questionnaires and interviews. As one item cannot project the personality or the Competencies (Attitude, Skill and Knowledge), batteries of tests are administered. Use of psychometric tests have been found increasing among the companies, which have the assessment centre to find the intellectual capabilities, personality and motivation. Since this term is not protected by copyright, every assessment procedure can be called by that name.

There has been a shift in the process of Assessment Centre wherein, the primary focus was to find the potential of the candidate for the next job and these were run primarily for the purpose of the organisation. The individual was not gaining any or little feedback apart from knowing whether he gets the job/promotion. A candidate who has extremely done well in one competency may not have performed in another competency, for example, he may have done extremely well in written exercise but fared poorly in the in-basket exercise. This data will be extremely useful for the participant to improve upon the required competencies.

The emphasis has been increasingly being placed on the development of the participants. Feedback is given to the participants who will have a lengthy discussion on the areas of the strength and the areas for improvement and action planning. The process of identification of the gaps in the performance and efforts to bridge the gap is now being called as the Development Centre. Various organisations use these two modules combined or separately. A combined module of the assessment, if any gaps are found, conduct the Development Centre which is called the ADC (Assessment and Development Centre).

Performance appraisal and potential appraisal has vast differentiation but generally they are understood as being the same and therefore, similar HR tools are used to evaluate the performance as well as potential of individual employees. Assessment Centre is a technology to evaluate the potentials of an employee for a future job and future performance. It brings out the potentials of the employee to perform in a given situation since different kinds of situations are simulated during the evaluation processes of Assessment Centre. Assessment Centre is a systematic process comprising of various psychological tools and tests conducted in a pre-defined set-up with the help of experienced assessors. A simulated environment gives proper setting and this helps bringing out the true potential of an individual. In a large number of companies, all promotion, transfer and job rotation decisions are based on the Assessment Centre outcome and therefore, it has become a strategic technology.

# Experiential Application

## A. Prerequisite

- In planning the assessment process the following must be considered:
  - list of competencies or other qualities to be assessed and the procedures for scoring and rating.
  - the weightage to be assigned to each element and exercise.
  - to ensure consistency of judgement and the prevention of any bias, the various forms of assessments to be done for a competency.

- Assessment Centres need to be properly designed and implemented to achieve the desire results without any bias. It is necessary to decide as to what to include in the assessment battery, which largely determine the duration of the assessment centre.

- A typical Assessment Centre usually involves 1–2 days. It includes a sufficient range of exercises involving challenging tasks in realistic settings, with a focus on assess-ing behaviour in simulated work setting.

- A balance between individual and group activities is kept considering the nature of the job, and the target level performance for which the assessment is to be carried out.

- These needs proper staffing. If the organisation does not have proper expertise, a consultant may be hired initially to train the staff and to undertake the responsibility of running the Assessment Centre after the expiry of the contract.
- If the organisation cannot allocate large resources for the Assessment Centre, it may focus on factors/competencies that have proven links with the business. The Assessment Centre will add value if it can identify and select people who demonstrate competencies that drive outstanding performance.

## B. Process Steps

| Step | Process |
|------|---------|
| Step – I | The top management to be convinced on the benefit of the Assessment Centre and the need established. |
| Step – II | An appropriate communication to be given to all the employees about the Assessment Centre and get the feedback. |
| Step – III | Designing the appropriate Assessment Centre suiting the jobs. |
| Step – IV | Define job analysis and competencies for all the jobs and roles which are to be assessed. |
| Step – V | Designing the tools of the Assessment Centre and make a pilot application if required. |
| Step – VI | Identify and train the assessors either through external consultants or through internal expertise. |
| Step – VII | Intimate the candidates who are to be assessed and communicate to them the whole purpose and process. |
| Step – VIII | Conduct the Assessment Centre and communicate the outcome and the developmental plans. |
| Step – IX | Prepare a report on the Assessment Centre and the process for future reference. |

# Potential Gains and Areas of Concern

- It gives an accurate and objective assessment of the competency of each candidate appearing for Assessment Centre.
- Assessment Centre being a multi rated system, the bias of an assessor towards one candidate is eliminated since the outcome is on averaging all the assessors. This is more valid since the assessor's evaluation is done independently not jointly.
- Clear evidences of the competencies of an individual vis-à-vis the area requiring improvement in competencies when visible, employees could be told to work on those areas.

- Organisational decisions such as job rotation, promotions and transfers can be done based on this result since the mechanism is objective and is acceptable by all.
- A greater amount of transparency can be achieved in the organisation system, which helps building the culture of performance orientations.
- While Assessment Centre can provide a very effective platform for an objective and fair assessment, they can also result in a traumatic experience with frightful consequences of increased attrition, lower employee morale, etc.
- If the organisation's preparedness for Assessment Centre is poor, the results of the Assessment Centre may not be effective to all participants as well as subsequently to the organisation.
- The tests need to be validated in terms of the objectives for which the Assessment Centre is being conducted, if not, the assessment centre becomes counter productive.
- The Assessment Centre needs to be conducted with the analysis of the required competencies and the batteries of tests, if not it will become an extension of the psychometric test.

# Measurability

## Try It Out

(1: not at all done, 2: moderately done, 3: to some extent done, 4: to a great extent done, 5: excellently done)

- Human Resources has approved Assessment Centre strategy document.  ☐
- Human Resources has identified all the competencies required for the roles for which Assessment Centre is to be conducted.  ☐
- The tests are designed to assess the competencies and these tests are validated for their reliability.  ☐
- Organisation provides for training for all the assessors for objectivity and coherence.  ☐
- Feedback is given to all the participants about their level of competencies and the organisational/role requirement.  ☐

Analysis: the average score would determine the extent to which Assessment Centre process exists in your organisation.

## Score Card

(*: 25% achieved, **: 50% achieved, ***: 75% achieved, ****: 100% achieved)

| Technology | Objective Elements | Unit | Historical | Last Year | Current Year | Stretch Target | Status |
|---|---|---|---|---|---|---|---|
| Assessment Centre | Strategy Document on Assessment Centre | Doc | Nil | No | Yes | NA | ** |
| Assessment Centre | Assessment Centre for Top Management | Nos | Nil | No | 01 | 01 | * |
| Assessment Centre | Assessment Centre for Middle Management | Nos | Nil | No | 04 | 06 | ** |

# Proven Track Record

## Track One

## Pricewaterhouse Coopers

Pricewaterhouse Cooper's approach for Assessment Centres aims to balance the aspects of technical correctness by ensuring validity and feasibility of implementation. Each competency, that needs to be assessed is defined in terms of its behavioural indicators.

To make the definitions and hence the assessment more precise, each of the competencies coupled be separately defined at various levels. A rating scale is also defined so as to facilitate measurement/assessment. If an organisation already has a competency framework then obviously those definitions and levels are used at the Assessment Centre. Pricewaterhouse Coopers has conducted both broad-based and customised Assessment Centres.

(*Source*: Sharma, 2002.)

## Track Two

## Various Companies, USA

Assessment is a commonly shared element. These assessments range from KRAFT Foods organisations assessment to Boeings' team/project assessment process, where individuals receive feedback about themselves in a non-threatening environment. The assessment delivered to both individuals and the team helps in improving performance.

Assessment centres have become the norm for business and companies are using them to drive the change in the business processes. SmithKline Beecham, Sun Microsystems, Media one and others are using various assessment centre techniques. Individual coaching is very important in assessment centres. This coaching has been extremely successful for firms such as DowCorning, Media One, Johnson & Johnson and others.

(*Source*: Carter, Gider and Goldsmith, 2001: xvi.)

# Applied HR Case

## SN Pharmaceuticals

Michael, Head of Production is having serious problem with his managers who are losing their interest in work or attrition. Since two years he has been only training the managers and once the training is over, and has put in one year of working, either they are losing the interest or they are leaving the job. The managers who worked with him also started leaving for better prospects. Michael was surprised at this phenomena as he had 24 years of experience in this industry. He was of the opinion that the discontent may be either because of his talent or the leadership style. Michael went to Arun who is the Head of HR and explained him about the whole episode of losing people and after two decades of experience he started questioning the fundamentals of his beliefs and his skills.

Arun listened patiently and he had similar discussion with the Finance and Administration heads also. Three years back, the company had recruited young and bright students from the premier management institute as management trainees in all the departments, which has helped bring change in the company culture. The intervention was successful and they are able to perform well since they have lesser learning curve. Arun convinced Michael that the attrition is not due to his skills but the problems arising in the organisation and he is very good at his subject and also in the managerial skills.

Arun has made a detailed study of those people who are leaving and found the following:

- Among the management trainees who were taken in batches and confirmed as Assistant Managers, those who were placed in the marketing got promotion as Deputy Manager after completion of one year of service since the Head of

Marketing, Paul, who had considerable influence with the MD was able to get the promotions based on their performances.

- Managers who had put in about four to six years of service who are also from good schools, were frustrated since the management trainees by virtue of being educated from premier schools were getting promotions within two years while others in spite of their best performance were not getting promotions. In spite of their experience and knowledge sometimes they even have to report to these managers.

The best talents were leaving the company, which was the cause of concern, and if the trend continued for another two years the company would lose the best talents and would be run by the mediocre.

Arun was worried about the development and remembered that during his university education in management, he studied the Assessment and Development Centre. He went to the library and read about the whole concept and convinced himself that the organisation needs to have an objective way of assessing the competencies of the people so that the best of the talent goes up the ladder and every one has equal opportunity to compete for the future posts.

## Questions

1. Do you subscribe to Arun that Assessment Centre is the only way to come out of the problems faced by the company? If so please justify.
2. If you were Arun, please design an Assessment Centre suiting the culture of the company?
3. Prepare an action plan of how you are going to sell the concept to the HODs, Unions, Officers' Association and implement the same in the company?

## References and Further Readings

Bhatnagar, Jyotsna and L. D'Souza, 2002. 'Bridging the HR Strategy Gap with Assessment Centres', *Indian Journal of Training and Development*, April–June.

Carter Louis, David Giber and Marshall Goldsmith. 2001. *Best Practices in Organization Development and Change: Culture, Leadership, Retention, Performance, Coaching*, CA: Joseey-Bass.

Dale, Margaret and Paul Iles. 1998. *Assessing Management Skills—A Guide to Competencies and Evaluation Techniques*, Mumbai: Jaico Publishing House.

Kandula, Srinivas R. and B. Hari Bapuji (eds). 2000. *Perspectives on HRD & OD in Indian Organizations*, Ahmedabad: Academy of HRD.

Moses, J.L. and W.C. Byham (eds). 1977. *Applying the Assessment Centre Method*, New York: Pergamon.

Paul, Jansen. 1997. *Assessment Centers—A Practical Handbook*, NY: John Wiley & Sons.

Sawardekar, Nitin. 2002. *Assessment Centre*, New Delhi: Response Books.

Sharma, Radha R. 2002. *360 Degree Feedback, Competency Mapping and Assessment Center*, New Delhi: Tata McGraw-Hill Publishing Company Limited.

Woodruffe, C. 1990. *Assessment Centres: Identifying and Developing Competence*, London: IPM.

———. 1992. 'What is Meant by Competency?' in R. Boam and P. Sparrow (eds), *Designing and Achieving Competency: A Competency Based Approach to Developing People and Organizations*, Maidenhead: McGraw-Hill.

# 'COMPETENCY MAPPING'
# ASSESSING INDIVIDUAL COMPETENCIES
# THROUGH COMPETENCY MAPPING

*Competing for the future is not merely about having foresight.*

—Anonymous

## Intent

- To observe what an employee does rather than relying on the assumption pertaining to traits and intelligence.
- To measure and predict performance is to assess whether the people have performance as the key aspect of competencies.
- To derive a linkage as to how people should perform in the real world.

## Expression

Competency means ability of an employee to respond to demands placed on him by the organisational environment. It is an underlined characteristic of a person that results in efficient work performance by the individual. The process of evaluating current and the future competencies required for an individual to perform is called competency mapping.

## Comprehension

The central component of human capital is competence. Competence is one of the key elements of performance. People must have desire, knowledge, skills and abilities to perform their tasks. Individual competencies interacting with the organisation's technological and behavioural processes generate organisational performance.

Competency forms the basis of an individual's consistent thinking and behaviour in a variety of situations. The following are the steps involved in identifying the competencies:

- The first and foremost step in identifying the competency or a set of competencies is to clearly establish the performance criteria.
- Select samples of average and outstanding performers. The idea is to have two contrasting groups selected on the basis of the performance criteria.
- Collect the data about the nature of competencies, which can be done through nature of survey, expert panel and behavioural event interviews.
- Data collection is followed by analysis for building a competency model. The analysis involves a thematic analysis of the interview content and a statistical analysis of the differences between the star and the average performer. The analysis may finally be presented in the form of a competency dictionary with behaviour description as per the requirement of the organisation.

The identification of competencies and the subsequent development of competency model constitute a specialised task. If an organisation is aware of its competency requirements for various level jobs, it can straightaway adopt the Assessment Centre approach; otherwise running an Assessment Centre without the knowledge of the requisite competencies will be like an exercise without a definite goal.

'Right man for the right job' is the quotation that is being talked about widespread in HR and the right fit is something which has become the major task for recruitment professionals. The next step to this is competency. Right man is possible only if the competency of an individual matches with the performance of the job. How is it possible to examine competency of an individual. The potential and capabilities leading to competency for managing a job is a complex subject to deal with. The management in corporate world has become very conscious about individual competencies vis-à-vis job competencies. Mapping the gap between the two and dealing with bridging those gaps through proper Organisation Development interventions is necessary. For the success of business and to have competent employees, competency mapping is the strategic tool and it can bring about desire results from the individual employees.

# Experiential Application

## A. Prerequisite

- Before taking up competency mapping the needs should be clearly established and accepted by the top management.

- A framework should be built on what exists rather than offering something totally new.
- It is very important to begin with organisational values because no framework can succeed if it contradicts them.
- Competencies should be defined for a role and not for a job, since owing to the dynamic environment of today, jobs keep changing. Competencies should be defined for all roles in given functions for a business. This is because people at a lower level want to find out what will take them to the next level. And after knowing, they need time to develop these competencies.
- First the competencies should be defined and then one must look for measuring instruments. There are so many measuring instruments which might confuse the employee on what is being measured and why.
- Assessment Centre and development centres should be planned after the competencies are fully soaked into the organisation, otherwise there is a danger that the output of these programmes may not be reinforced.

## B. Process Steps

| Step | Process |
|------|---------|
| Step – I | Defining the need for competency mapping and the objectives to be defined. |
| Step – II | Best practice companies need to be examined and the consent of the top management needs to be obtained. |
| Step – III | Formation of a team consisting of line managers of the business units. |
| Step – IV | Using various techniques of competency mapping, define competencies for a given role as well as role above and below. |
| Step – V | Extensive interviews are held for assessment. |
| Step – VI | Consolidate all competencies that are mapped on to various functional roles and different levels in the organisations. |
| Step – VII | New selection and training incorporate the competencies that are identified. |

# Potential Gains and Areas of Concern

- It not only addresses the key issue of the quality of the available managerial resources, but also reinforce the organisational belief and faith in the competencies of in-house resources.
- Competency methods provide the HR with a toolkit for capturing and communicating actionable learning, in clear behavioural terms that can be easily understood and implemented.

- Competencies identified for each position helps in job evaluation and further developing Assessment Centres.
- Competency model focuses on individual, which needed to understand and improve team, including cross-functional and virtual teams and process performance.
- It depends on open information environment, therefore less precise definition of competencies.
- It focuses on past behaviour and therefore difficult to focus on future performance requirements.

# Measurability

## Try It Out

(1: not at all done, 2: moderately done, 3: to some extent done, 4: to a great extent done, 5: excellently done)

- My organisation has laid down the role directory. □
- My organisation has a competency model. □
- My organisation identified all the competencies required for all roles. □
- My organisation periodically reviews the competencies mapped. □
- My organisation maps the competencies of all the new incumbents vis-à-vis the role. □

Analysis: the average score would determine the extent to which competency mapping process exists in your organisation.

## Score Card

(*: 25% achieved, **: 50% achieved, ***: 75% achieved, ****: 100% achieved)

| Technology | Objective Elements | Unit | Historical | Last Year | Current Year | Stretch Target | Status |
|---|---|---|---|---|---|---|---|
| Competency Mapping | Strategy Document | Doc | Nil | No | Yes | NA | ** |
| Competency Mapping | Competency Mapping Process | % | 70% | 70% | 100% | Dec | ** |

# Proven Track Record

## Track One

## Wipro

Wipro has created its own niche in the software industry in India and has its own products like lights and other domestic products. The success of Wipro is due to its emphasis on developing success through competencies. In Wipro the vision is 'people come first' emphasising the importance of the people. Competencies are defined to enable employees to know what is expected from them. Having reached level 5 of PCMM (People Capability Maturity Model) and to proceed to level 3, requires people process based on competencies.

The competencies are mapped using various techniques like critical incident method, repertory grid, structured interviews, observation, etc. Once the competencies are mapped Wipro has taken the help of Saville and Handsworth, an internationally renowned organisation for measuring the competencies. Wipro at the end has come out with 24 competencies, which are being used for various purposes like training and development, Assessment Centre, etc.

(*Source*: Acharya and Mazumdar, 2002: 139.)

## Track Two

## Larsen & Toubro Limited

L&T Limited is one of the largest engineering industry having more than 26,000 employees in manufacturing units at 20 locations and sales offices at 25 locations, covering core sector of economy: power, infrastructure, oil and gas, refinery, cement, etc. Business Process Re-engineering is being done to align the business process with people and organisation and information technology in a phased manner. To bring the HR process in line with the business process, competency mapping is being done to focus on career development. Competency is being defined by L&T as 'a cluster of related knowledge, skills and attitudes (KSA) that affects a person's performance in his role at different levels. It can be measured against well accepted standards and can be improved by training and development'. The company has identified five levels of managerial competencies into four heads:

- communication related competencies;
- task effectiveness related competencies;

- people oriented competencies; and
- strategic and conceptual competencies.

The competencies identified under the above groups have been defined and the knowledge, skills and attitudes required to achieve the competency has also been defined. The behavioural manifestation for each of these competencies has also been listed to bring in clarity at all locations. The process of competency mapping has helped to bring in uniformity of HR process at all locations to bring in standards of performance to be a world leader.

(*Source*: Srivastava and Kumar, 1998: 142.)

# Applied HR Case

## Grower Electronics Limited

Grower is a well-known name for its white goods and has grown over the past 10 years from a city-based firm to a niche product of the country. Grower has entered into the manufacturing by change and there is no looking back. Grower has a small departmental store and has been selling almost everything, from chocolates to televisions. One of the suppliers of automatic washing machines had asked him whether he would take the option of opening a service centre in the store and later on he will provide CKD (Completely Knocked Down) kits which he can assemble and sell, which will give him greater margin. Grower immediately accepted the proposal and thus his success story started with assembling CKD kits to a full-fledged manufacturer of white goods.

Grower was always of the opinion that commitment is important for every person to grow in life and if he is committed, it will lead the path to success. His method of recruitment was to see whether he has the commitment to take up the responsibility and perform.

Gerald, General Manager HR, was a Management Graduate and though himself and Grower have similar thoughts about the business, they used to differ on aspects of commitment and competency. Gerald is of the opinion that a person should have competency to handle the job and any commitment will bring him up in the life.

Over the last six months Grower was facing the problem of service failures and the design problem of new washing machine, which was launched. Customers are complaining of technical problems and the service centre is flooded with complaints. Grower is struck with the problem and he has to take the help of the technical expert to rectify and repair all the machines, but the damage has already been caused. Grower realising that competency is equally important asks Gerald to prepare a plan and submit a report by next week.

## Questions

1. Is Grower right in his conclusion that competencies are equally important to that of commitment?
2. What is the difference between competency and commitment? Are they supplementary or contradictory?
3. If you were Gerald, prepare a report on competency mapping and competency development for the company.

# References and Further Readings

Acharya, R. and T. Mazumdar. 2002. 'Building a Competency-Centred Organization: The Wipro Story', in Radha R. Sharma (ed.), *360 Degree Feedback, Comepetency Mapping and Assessment Centres*, New Delhi: Tata McGraw-Hill.

Misra, Shishir and Nandini Chawla. 2003. 'Identifying Competency Enhancement Needs Through 360 Degree Feedback', *HRD News Letter*, vol. 19, Issue 3, June.

Moses J.L. and W.C. Byham (eds). 1977. *Applying the Assessment Centre Method*, New York: Pergamon.

Rao T.V., A. Gangopadyay and R.S.S. Mani (eds). 2002. *HR @ Heart of Business*, New Delhi: Excel Books.

Sanghi, Seema. 2004. *The Handbook of Competency Mapping*, New Delhi: Response Books.

Spencer, Lyle M. and Signe Spencer. 1993. *Competence at Work*, US: John Wiley & Sons Inc.

Srivastava, Kaul and Shiva Kumar. 1998. 'Strategies for Change for Building a World Class Company—Larsen & Toubro Limited Experience' in All India Management Association's *Business Led HR Strategies*, New Delhi: Excel Books.

Woodruffe, C. 1990. *Assessment Centres: Identifying and Developing Competence*, London: IPM.

# Spectrum IV
## HR Technologies for Rethinking the Future

Today as we look to the future, there is no certainty at all where we are going and how we get there. We no longer see a long, straight free way stretching into the horizon. Instead, we find ourselves starting at the end of the road. The close of the 20th century might be said to represent the end of the whole order of things; the end of the industrial paradigm; the end of the post-War world; the end of US predominance; the end of welfare state; the end of communism and of post-War capitalism; and perhaps, even the end of history. In place of certainty there is a sense that our industrial society is in deep trouble, as we drive collectively towards what scientists called the age of chaos—a period of violent transition when the old order of things finally give ways to the new. Yet at the same time, there is also a sense of tremendous adventure and opportunity for all.

The organisational dilemma is moving in the same paradise shift. It becomes clear that the organisation requires a new set of skills and attitude with a very different kind of driving skill and a whole new sense of direction. In short, the organisational energy should be focused more towards rethinking the future. But since the future is so encompassing, it is a million dollar question of how do we go about rethinking the future.

The spectrum emphasises on how HR technology supports organisational strive and drive towards rethinking the future beating all odds. Human Resource technologies such as operating through virtual teams, exploring the information technology and the explosion of knowledge management are all keys towards the rethinking of the future. Four such technologies are brought herein in this spectrum under the chapter 'Responding to Future Needs'.

# 9 RESPONDING TO FUTURE NEEDS

## Learning Objectives

- To know about the technological evolution affecting HR systems.
- To understand the latest buzzword of Employee Self-Services (ESS) exploiting technology.
- To break the boundaries through virtual team approach.
- To create a learning organisation through knowledge management.

# Future of Change Management

Major changes, both major threats and major opportunities, will dominate the executive task for the next 10 to 15 years or even may be much longer. It is necessary that in the futuristic change management, the leader's job is to set a clear direction of what their organisation mean by results. The leader needs to provide a clear understanding of when it is time to push here and push back there and when it is time to abandon something and exit. Those days are gone when charisma was supporting the leadership. Tomorrow's leader would not be able to lead by charisma; they will need to think through the fundamentals so that other people can work productively. The speed of change will demand this. The new workforce expectation and the increasingly competitive world economy call for change at a higher speed.

A leader's job is becoming more and more complex like running an opera in which you have your stars wherein you cannot give orders. You have the supporting casts and orchestra, you have the people who are behind the scenes and you have your audience. Each group is completely different but the opera conductor has a score and everybody has a same score. Similarly, in business, tomorrow's leader has to make sure that the entire group produces the desired result. Many knowledge workers of present days are less productive than they could be because their schedules are filled with operational activities that do not reflect training and talent. The intellectual capital with the company expects continuous learning and training and also desires want of respect. With the growing phase of the company a corporation will need a top management, separate, powerful and accountable. Top management's responsibility will cover the organisation direction, planning, strategy, value and principles, its structure and relationship between its various members, its alliances, its partnership and joint venture and its research, design and innovation. An equally important task for the top management will be to balance the three dimensions of corporation as economic organisation, as a human organisation and as an important social organisation.

Change management's first need is for a people policy that covers all those who work for an enterprise, whether they are employed by it or not. After all, the performance of every single one of them matters. Second, all those who are not going to work with the enterprise in the near future such as those who have reached their official term and age of retirement. These people would be a great change agent for the organisation in the larger organisation environment. The most effective way to manage successfully is to create change. The enterprise has to become a change agent. This requires the organised abandonment of things that have been shown to be unsuccessful and the organised and continuous improvement of every product and services and process within the enterprise. Change management requires the exploitation of success, especially unexpected and unplanned and it requires systematic innovation. Organisation can become change agent provided it changes the mindset of the whole organisation; instead of seeing change as a threat, the people of the organisation must see change as an opportunity.

# Human Resources Information System (HRIS)

The basis for a good HR function and the decisions it takes depends upon the information it generates not only for itself but for all those who are involved in the business process. The business decisions depend upon how fast data is retrieved and the accuracy of such information. Human Resource stores the information in files and information folders and retrieves as and when required. Much of the time of HR is being spent in handling the administrative work.

The world witnessed the way the business was revolutionised with the advent of e-commerce. The economies of scale, changing operations, business process outsourcing, etc., has put the pressure on the organisations to excel in their field and produce the products and services to the utmost satisfaction of the customer. This has put an increasing pressure on HR to change management, to bring up the competencies and have sustained competitive advantage. The senior management wants HR to play a dominant and strategic role beyond the administrative function and the deliverables.

This has put an increasing pressure on HR to change and build those competencies for a sustained competitive advantage. The new information technology revolution has enabled HR to have electronic database and creation of paperless office. The HRIS gathers data and helps to analyse the data to enable HR to do the job more perfectly. It is meant for making better decisions and solving problems, which were earlier difficult to do, and hence the decisions taken after computerisation can bring in those changes like timely, accurate and better solutions that gives customer satisfaction. With the knowledge creating a value edge to the organisations, its enhancement and managing it become the most important factor for the organisation. It is vital to have the complete and accurate history of the employees and their competencies to take the right kind of decisions. However, it should be noted that the HRIS per se will not be a problem solver, but would enable HR to function effectively by giving high quality information.

The computerised database of all the employees and all the systems, policies and procedures of the HR has simplified the nature of role the HR used to play. Routine administrative functions are being handled by the HRIS and HR has ample time to look at enhancing the competencies of the employees and also the development activities.

The HR was basically a supporting function to support the business process rather than taking a lead and driving the business. But the new technologies had enabled HR to become a partner in the business strategy by taking up challenges of the business and adding value rather than to be a support function. The costs involved in the installation of the HRIS are high and it requires lot of man-hours to be invested in designing, feeding the information, processing and retrieving the information, but the benefits are multiple.

The HRIS acts as a valuable tool for strategic planning and implementation. It would help the decision makers understand how HR management can be valuable as a competitive tool. The systems can give the information from various variables in relation to the production process. With the information one can work out the placement of the manpower resources vis-à-vis their utilisation. Cost of the employment is one of the variables in the factors of the production and the HRIS can evolve a strategy to reduce the costs or else enhance the productivity by way of effective management of manpower resources.

The HRIS is being designed in such a way that the manpower planning can be planned. Especially in large organisations where the monitoring of manpower and business process involves critical competencies, fast changing technologies and the requirement of critical manpower are vital. The HRIS can provide the valuable database of the present status of manpower and the future requirement. E-recruitment has enabled the organisations to attract manpower and can create its own database for future requirement. An amalgamation of manpower requirement and database will shorten the supply time of the manpower and also the money involved. The increased response time in data management will enable HR to plan manpower in advance so that they can concentrate more on developmental activities. It has been a misconception that computerisation is the answer to manage business. But it is a fact that the HRIS can speeden up the process which means that human skills remain the same and the systems have taken up the those functions which are data base management, paving the way for HR to look at constructive human relations.

## HRIS and Intranet

Intranet has given unlimited advantage to the organisations by way of disseminating the information and also obtaining the feedback. Intranet is an internal Website containing the details of the organisation as a whole. The Intranet can not only boosts the productivity but also encourages the employees to brainstorm their ideas.

The Intranet can enhance the internal customer value by providing quick information. The technology has enabled the employee to raise various queries and get the answers online so that he need not go to HR for simple doubts. This is being called as 'Employee Self-Service'. This can also save time and money. Various papers need to be printed by way of forms for claiming leaves, filling up of appraisals, etc. Electronic data does away with the paperwork and everything can be connected online. The information provided is accurate and changes can be informed by way of making the changes in the software, and at a single stroke the changes can be incorporated and intimated to all the employees across the organisation.

Organisation vide surveys can be conducted like the Employee Satisfaction Survey which gives the details of how the employees would rate their satisfaction as per the pay, performance, treatment with dignity, etc. The result can also be instantaneous as the programme is made in such a way that the results are processed and the HR Manager can have the feedback immediately after the employee had filled in. Both the employer and the employee can mutually exchange their information and viewpoints so that the information flows both top down and bottom up.

## Integrating the Teams

The boom in the information technology and the automation has enabled building teams to work, which was impossible earlier. The technology revolution has paved the way to connect the teams worldwide without moving from their desks thus building virtual teams. The facilities like e-mail, online chat, voicemail, net phone, video conferencing, etc., has build the teams spanning across the nations. Managing these teams is the task of every HR manager as to build, keeping their morale high, and managing the diversity requires different skills as the existing systems and premises of human relations management may not be suitable or may even be unproductive.

Virtual teams are not bound by the typical hierarchies and workflow methods; they are designed to ensure the goals are accomplished and once they are achieved the team may be disbanded or given another project. Second, the team members are interrelated and interdependent with specialist roles and requiring specialist competencies. This requires different kinds of skills to manage the teams. To manage complex problems, technological systems help; however, to integrate behavioural issues of each group, it is necessary to resort to different behavioural tools to effectively manage these high performing teams. This can also be compounded by the mobility of manpower due to attrition or transfer and building cohesiveness once again is the task. The challenges of the HR are to integrate these teams in new and imaginative ways, strengthening the communication process, building and sustaining the work cultures like building the team identity, fostering the process of team maturity, empowering and enabling the key members of the projects, etc.

# Value Addition through Knowledge Management

Knowledge and information are not the same thing, but the boundary between them is fuzzy and shifting. What one person treats, as information may in fact be knowledge to another. Knowledge includes information, but put it in a context of judgements and understanding. Developed through experience overtime, knowledge has depth and complexity. Whether it is knowledge, know-how or expertise, it means a rich understanding of a subject and an ability to use what is already known to evaluate new information. Knowledge is deeply human. It often works at intuitive level, allowing people to understand situations and make good decisions quickly without always being fully aware of their own thought processes. The complex power of knowledge both makes it valuable and its management complex because the richest knowledge is not easily captured in documents and information technology systems.

The information revolution has opened up the gates of knowledge available all over the world and it is every organisation's endeavour to capture this widely available knowledge to obtain the competitive advantage. Knowledge is not only available at the outside world but the accumulated knowledge of all the employees of the company when shared would also bring in learning in the organisation. This use of precious knowledge and experience can improve control and efficiency. It is not necessary to reinvent the wheel again and again as it has been already invented and one needs to have access to it. The organisations have understood the need for building the knowledge and hence the endeavour of every organisation to build knowledge management. Knowledge is of two kinds, i.e., tacit and explicit. Tacit knowledge is derived from experiences of the people whereas explicit knowledge is the knowledge available around us.

There are various methods through which knowledge is being shared among various employees in the organisation and one of the best methods of doing so is by way of usage of information technology and the Intranet. The HR can not only act as an anchor for acquiring, updating, maintaining and disseminating knowledge but also by changing the culture of the organisation. The change in culture is required to make the employees understand the need for sharing the information, openness, trust and the whole benefits of the knowledge management itself. This requires that the systems need to align to facilitate the knowledge management. Sharing and creating knowledge has to be everybody's job, but it is difficult to make the employees share the knowledge as they feel that it is important for them in the organisation structure and this applies more in an organisation where information play a crucial role. An important factor remains that employees must start learning and it is the responsibility of the organisation to create an environment to make the organisation a knowledge based organisation.

In the most information-oriented companies we studied, people were least likely to share information freely.... As people's jobs and roles become defined by the unique information they hold, they may be less likely to share information—viewing it as a source of power and indispensability rather than more so. When information is primary unit of organisational currency, we should not expect its owners to give it away.

(*Source*: Devenport, Eccles and Prusak, 1992.)

The benefits of knowledge management can be reaped when all the employees are hooked electronically by way of Intranet/e-mail, etc., but the human systems must be made to share the information. Effective management of knowledge management can only possible with the synergy of technology and the people. The interest in knowledge management has grown along with advances in computers, networks and data systems. Sharing and collaborating with thousands of people scattered around the globe depends on the technology of connection and organised electronic storage of content, and many knowledge projects have focused on building systems to connect people and capture knowledge.

# Enable SHR Technology—Key to Success

This chapter brings in following Strategic HR technologies:

SHR Technology–37    Human Resource Information System (HRIS)—*Employee Self-Service through HRIS.*

SHR Technology–38    Virtual Teams—*Integrating Organisation through Virtual Teams.*

SHR Technology–39    Knowledge Management—*Creating Learning Organisation through Knowledge Management.*

SHR Technology–40    Change Management—*Creating Competitive Organisation through Change Management.*

Computer technology has taken place in every business process of the company such as manufacturing, product designing, finance, human resource, purchase, etc. The technological advancements have also helped HR function to be computer savvy through developing HRIS. The HRIS is a comprehensive information tool which can provide details of each employee merely by clicking a button in computer and the organisations can take appropriate immediate decision best suited for the organisations. The employees seeking help to know about their legitimate right and understanding the benefit schemes and the rules and regulations can avail such information directly from computer through employee self-service techniques under advanced HRIS programmes.

The Internet has changed the ways of doing businesses. Physical and geographical boundaries have collapsed and the employee can now function smoothly without the barrier of being physically present at one location or in front of each other. Other technologies such as video conferencing are widely used for bringing employees together and forming virtual teams.

Intellectual capital is the source of competitive advantage of any organisation. This capital lies in the mind of individual employees. The intellectual capital which an employee has gathered over a period of time in the organisation is knowledge and the organisation has to learn how to manage this knowledge since association of an employee with the organisation could be of a limited period while knowledge is the only source for the organisation's existence.

Knowledge is the organisational asset that must be systematically valued, nourished, shared and used. Effective knowledge management is essential for success in an increasingly and rapidly changing global economy. Because knowledge is rooted in human experience and social context, managing it well means paying attention to people, culture and the organisational structure, as well as to the technology that is an essential tool for knowledge sharing and is used in large organisations. Successful knowledge management may require fundamental and lasting changes in the way organisations operate internally and how they do business with their customers and partners.

The intellectual capital management system of IBM gives its practitioners in the consulting and systems integration groups ready access to existing intellectual content and tools to work collaboratively with their peers. Discussion databases proposals, technical documents, engagement summaries and other materials are available via a Lotus Notes worldwide network to members of competency groups who work in more than 100 countries and spend much of their time at client sites. The number of users is expected to grow in the coming years.

At the end of all the technologies that we have described we found the underlined theme for all that an organisation does is managing change to keep up pace with the ever changing world. It is necessary therefore to recognise this important aspect and build a case on how change management initiatives can be implemented in the company. Though change management is top management and managers are involved in strategic planning affairs, the HR cannot remain aloof in participating and driving the process of change in the company. As we all know, change management is not only to do with change in processes and structure of the company, but it has all the things to do with people processes. No change management initiatives are successful unless and until the people process are taken care of. Therefore, we believe that change management is an integral part of the human resource process and is the most important technology to deal with.

# Conclusion

* With the advent of e-technology has the way in which business is done today has completely changed. Business speed is parallel to the communication that flows along with it.
* The HRIS has become a source for decision making for managers in companies and employees too can avail all benefit-related information of their own from computer through Employee Self-Services (ESS).
* Integrated HRIS is helpful for all HR-related decisions, and has comprehensive data about each and every employee. This supports right from organisation design, job design, job evaluation and other HR systems.
* The intellectual capital is the essence of an organisation. Holding Intellectual capital and developing knowledge management process is a key to success for any organisation.
* Change management is inevitable for every organisation to survive and the organisations, which adapt to change, can thrive in the competitive environment.

# References

Devenport T.H., R.G. Eccles and L. Prusak. 1992. 'Information Politics', *Sloan Management Review*. 53–65.

Conference Board:report number 1194–97.

# 'HUMAN RESOURCE INFORMATION SYSTEM (HRIS)' EMPLOYEE SELF-SERVICE THROUGH HRIS

*Imagination is more important than knowledge.*

—Albert Einstein

## Intent

- A common database of information on jobs, people and organisation variables that is shared by many HR functions and that provides a common language and integrates all HR services.
- A knowledge base of algorithms or decision rules that can assist management in making professional HR choices, e.g., whom to select for a job; the most cost-effective training available to improve an employee's productivity, etc.
- An administrative system that supports maintenance and security, which protects against excess to sensitive employees or organisational data.
- To provide a platform for employee self-services through accessibility of HRIS by all.

## Expression

The HRIS means management of human resource information of a company through computerised systems using latest technologies. The HRIS includes information on employees' history, compensation details, learning and development data, competency details, past historical benefit schemes available, etc., for each employee of the company.

# Comprehension

Information Technology is transforming HR management. Its impact includes: Outsourcing—80 per cent of major organisations are considering outsourcing most HR functions and services; Automation—most HR services will be provided by personal computers and interactive voice response systems; Integration—HR functions such as staffing, performance management, training and development, compensation and so on will be integrated by Integrated HRIS. These systems will be used directly by employee end-users to get bundles of multiple services to solve problems or to achieve personal objectives. Top line management will have instant access to comprehensive HR balance sheets and profit and loss statements for strategic planning; line managers will have HR professional services through decentralised processes; and individual employees will have access to their HR policies through 'Employees Self-Service' system directly from their workstation.

The HRIS are evolving from databases, used primarily from salary, benefits and administrative record keeping, to expert system knowledge bases that integrate HR functions and help HR professionals make decisions. The HRIS contains shared databases of information about jobs, people and the organisation with artificial intelligence decision support capabilities that can improve HR management.

The HRIS is crossing the boundaries and is now entering into the hands of all the employees of the company by releasing all controls that historically lay in the hands of HR people only. The master key of HRIS usually remains in the hands of HR people and other employees generally do not have access to HRIS. The HRIS helps in making HR people adding more value and leaving away from the mundane and routine task of responding to each and every employee of their queries on minute details such as payroll issues, eligibility of benefits, avail of benefit schemes, deduction of statutory payments, blood group, etc. With the HRIS becoming easy to operate, employees can access to it from any part of the world by simply logging on to access password and interactively resolving all their queries. This latest process is named as 'Employee Self-Services'. This would reduce tremendous amount of routine task from the HR and employees will also be satisfied with computers getting the answers for their queries.

Each employee is different from others in terms of competency, personal needs, level of motivation, attitude, knowledge and skills. The HRD function has the primary role to identify these and work towards the betterment of each employee. For example, training and development needs if known properly then suitable training inputs can be provided to individual employees and they can be developed. While working with these specific individuals and collective needs, the information about all employees in great detail is required. This is possible thorough maintaining proper record. As the organisation grows and strength of employees becomes large, database and record management of all these employees becomes difficult. Computerisation is the only handy solution available. Proven software specifically developed to maintain employees' database right from personal history, social security details, training, performance management, compensation and reward details, etc., is necessary to take prompt decision. This system is Human Resource Information System. It is essential and strategic in today's computer-based business environment.

# Experiential Application

## A. Prerequisite

- The HRIS must include the following four elements:
    - a database of such variables as employee id, job code and salary level;
    - data entry/edit, i.e., an efficient method for creating and updating data;
    - data retrieval and report generating; and
    - an administrative system that supports maintenance security which protects against access to sensitive employees on organisational data.

- The HRIS should be used for the purpose of scientific HR decision-making systems. Report format should be so designed to act on specific questions.
- The HRIS must be multi-user and it should have integration features so that data generated or used by one function can be accessed and used in other functions.
- The system should have easy accessibility and user friendliness. The HRIS should not be purely for information management and reporting but primarily aimed at decision support.
- The issues in the HRIS such as fragmentation of systems by using different and often conflicting language and systems at various locations of one unit, inefficient use of resources de-staffing and decentralisation should be taken care of while designing appropriate HRIS.
- In real sense, the emphasis should be made to work on advance HRIS that is Integrated Human Resource Management System (IHRMS).
- The architecture integrated HR Information System should have mainly seven basic HR elements, and they are; organisation design; staffing; performance management; training and development; compensation; organisation development; and health, safety, environment and welfare (HSEW).

    - The HR plan should be integrated with the overall organisation plan especially with the firm's growth objective.

- Outside influence of economic condition, technology, labour market, and so on should be adequately considered when developing the HRIS.
- The specific operational objectives of each functional area in HR function should be integrated with overall HRIS.
- The HRIS should be used as a decision support system and should alert managers to problems and opportunity.
- The HRIS should involve significant line management input at all points in the process.

## B. Process Steps

| Step | Process |
|------|---------|
| Step – I | The employee information, company policy and procedures and other HR related information must be compiled. |
| Step – II | Transformation of data and programming instruction that tell the computer what to do, how to do it and when to do it. |
| Step – III | Proper design of HRIS with proper support system to provide high quality information to make good decision. |
| Step – IV | User manuals and communication throughout organisation to be made to bring in awareness of HRIS. |

# Potential Gains and Areas of Concern

- Internal customers of the company, i.e., employees will be served hassle free on their HR related issues through self-service.
- The HR function will be able to operate efficiently and effectively since the database will be updated online and would be away from routine and mundane activities.
- Uniformity in HR services since the HRIS will have multiple entry and user access.
- Quick and quality decision support on every HR matter.
- Proper database management using latest technology would help the HR function in the organisation to take correct decisions and make development plans for a competent workforce.
- The HRIS would enable the internal customers more happy and can bring in achievement motivation among the employees.
- The HRIS with futuristic thought would enable the organisation to have sustained competitive advantage.
- With changing office automation scenario, elimination of paperwork is must, sooner or later, HRIS has to replace individuals operations.

- There is a likely chance that with the HRIS and the employee self-services, HR loses personal touch with the employees of the organisation.
- The computerisation not necessarily make the system effective, it might generate overhead cost and possibe redundancies, which could lead to dissatisfaction and low morale of affected ones.

# Measurability

## Try It Out

(1: not at all done, 2: moderately done, 3: to some extent done, 4: to a great extent done, 5: excellently done)

- The HR has all laid down policies, processes and good practices.                                   □
- The HR uses Information Technology extensively as a tool for Employee            □
  Self-Service (ESS).
- Suggestions/improvements are elicited through continual feedback                 □
  mechanism and HR changes its HRIS/policies/processes accordingly.
- The HR Department utilises the time for development of employees.                 □
- The HRIS has brought in transparency and trust in the HR processes.               □
- The HRIS is being used beyond payroll and e-mail.                                 □
- The HR analyses the response time and always tends to beat the                    □
  benchmarks.

Analysis: the average score would determine the extent at which HRIS system exists in your organisation.

## Score Card

(*: 25% achieved, **: 50% achieved, ***: 75% achieved, ****: 100% achieved)

| Technology | Objective Elements | Unit | Historical | Last Year | Current Year | Stretch Target | Status |
|---|---|---|---|---|---|---|---|
| HRIS | HRIS Strategy Document | Doc | Nil | No | | | ** |
| HRIS | HRIS | Software | Nil | No | | | ** |
| HRIS | HR on Intranet | IT Infrastructure | Nil | No | | | ** |
| HRIS | IVR for ESS | Software | Nil | No | | | * |

# Proven Track Record

## Track One

## KLM Royal Dutch Airlines

KLM Royal Dutch Airlines was one of the first passenger airlines with a tradition on quality service. Way back they decided to computerise personnel information which was vital if the function was to provide information of sufficient quality and at an acceptable speed for line managers. The roles of staff within the department were reorganised to ensure smooth process. Bringing in new blood has helped in bringing about change in both operation and image of the department. The system is build in a way that it is easy-to-use, providing sufficient flexibility to add or tailor records and allowing import and export of information to other packages. It is a multi-user system which allows each member to access both input and output across the entire departmental network.

Sufficient checks and balances are provided to ensure that the data is not tampered with. The system takes care of identity care renewals, industrial accident record, medical and travel insurance information, test results, training, payroll, organisation charts, electronic timing, pensions, recruitment, etc. This enabled KLM to have quick and accurate information. It also enabled the company to provide better benefits to the staff and the important fact is saving time of the personnel department.

(*Source*: Matthewman, 1993: 79.)

## Track Two

## Polaroid

Polaroid prevents the loss of talented staff by monitoring wage and labour issues and talent availability for promotion on its HRIS. They analyse internal pay and compensation data in relation to surveys of pay scales in comparable companies, using an IBM personal computer. They also review job categories to monitor which ones may become obsolete and use their system when they are going to have forced reductions in the workplace.

Scenarios can be worked through the computer, using compensation and benefits costs, seniority and age, and so forth in order to choose the most advantageous approach to use in a lay-off. Polaroid also developed a model to use on merit increase based on what they know of the past history, how often their people were given merit increase, and what their projected costs would be.

(Source: Cook, 1987: 250.)

# Applied HR Case

## Seamless Technologies Limited

Mr Narang, Head of HR was newly recruited in the organisation and his first day encounter with the Director was a very bad experience. Mr Agarwal, Director has asked for a personal file of Mr Kalyan, Head Marketing and the details about his compensation. Mr Narang immediately checked with the department and found that the files were under the control of Mr Narayana, HR Executive who was on leave. When he enquired about the details of the CTC, he got an answer that the salaries are being paid through payroll, reimbursements and through claims.

Since it would be time consuming to get all the details and the personal file only had details of the payments made to Mr Kalyan, based on the compensation revision letter, Mr Narang had to go empty handed, and felt very awkward to face the Director. Mr Agarwal knew of the present scenario of the HR department and asked him to design a system, which could store personal details and the compensation details of all the employees in soft copy that could be obtained in a short span of time.

Since it is an IT company, Mr Narang entrusted the work to Mr Narayana to prepare a module of HRIS which is user-friendly and at the same time contains the details of all the employees in all respects. This would not only reduce the paperwork but also save time and accurate information, which could be compared, and analysed for various HR policies. The HRIS would also be useful in Employee Self-Service and need to be operational within two months.

Mr Narayana has taken about three month's time to prepare the module on HR processes of file maintenance, personal and compensation details of employees. He has not consulted Mr Narang about the module, since he assumed that as he is senior and that he knows the requirement of the managing director and the system to be designed to fulfil his expectations. Whenever Narang used to ask him the status, he just used to answer that the module is in the making. Mr Narang was very angry with Mr Narayana of not comprehending the scope and use of the HRIS and how it can add value to HR in the organisation.

## Questions

1. What is your analysis of the situation?
2. How do you think Mr Narang would manage the scenario?
3. Do you think the HRIS needs to exist? How can it be managed?

## References and Further Readings

Cook, Mary F. 1987. *New Directions in HR: A Handbook*, NJ: Prentice Hall Inc.
Dudeja, V.D. 2000. *Management Information System in the New Millennium*, New Delhi: Commonwealth.
Matthewman, Jim. 1993. *HR Effectiveness*, London: Institute of Personnel and Development.
Schultheis, Robert and Mary Summer. 1999. *Management Information Systems—The Managers View*, New Delhi: Tata McGraw-Hill Publishing Company Limited.
Schuster, Fredrick E. 1985. *Human Resource Management—Concepts, Cases and Readings*, Virginia: Reston Publishing Company, Inc.

# 'VIRTUAL TEAMS'
# INTEGRATING ORGANISATION
# THROUGH VIRTUAL TEAMS

*We must all lean the same way to get around corners.*

—Dando-Collins (1996)

## Intent

- Members who come together tentatively are able to recognise one another's work habits, bond as a group, challenge one another and eventually focus on accomplishing the goal.
- To resolve the cultural boundaries, solve conflicts, interpret outside influences and decide on consensus method with virtual team approach.
- To operate cultural differences which range from unique communication style to complex value systems; complicated by language barriers can be worked out with virtual team.

## Expression

A group of people geographically different but brought together by a common goal that uses communication technology to achieve a common goal.

## Comprehension

Training is an accepted method to improve skills and process work combined that may be disbursed throughout the organisation. But with globalisation of organisations and telecommunications employees performing their job in different shifts and different time zones, teaming is often difficult. The virtual team is a new type of team to meet the requirements of the changing environment and the organisation shall respond to it if they want to remain competitive. At the same time to bring the organisation closer to the customer and face the immense competition, it is inevitable that the organisation spread.

Virtual teams allow corporate entities to continue the work of a team 24 hours a day by crossing the traditional time barriers. For example, a document that begins in New York is passed to his counterpart after the New York employee retires for the day, and the worker in New Delhi, in turn passes the document to an employee in Taipei. When the New York employee returns to work the next morning, the document arrives electronically from Taipei. The advantages of these teams are that the expertise can be brought in without much disturbance. But, there are certain challenges these teams face like culture, language, style, communication, etc., which need to be addressed with appropriate solutions.

Most virtual teams have 25 people as its limit. When more than 25 people form teams, even with completely electronic and virtual communication, subgroups begin to form and hence the size of the group should be considered at the planning stage itself but not after the group has been formed. Members are chosen based on the skills but not proximity. Virtual teams may be separated by time zones or by an entire day. Team members may work at the same location, but work at different hours. In some cases team members come from different organisations but are chosen on the basis of their skills. Virtual teams are a reality, but not better than the conventional teams since they face challenges as they carry out the tasks. The role of the leader is important since he needs to handle and overcome all the obstacles and knit the team around the goals.

Virtual teams are not a phenomenon but rather a permanent off-shoot of the creation of technology that supports them. As the technology expands, the role of virtual team will increase. New technologies and electronic commerce are here to stay and are changing the work environment virtually in some cases. As forces of change, new technologies are a double-edged sword that can be used to improve job performance or to create stress. On the positive side, modern technologies are revolutionising jobs and are designed in a way to get work done. Virtual offices are mobile platforms of computer, and the telecommunications services allow mobile workforce members to conduct business virtually anywhere, any time globally.

Global village and crossing the boundaries of the nations is becoming true in the case of large corporations. Even companies are spreading within the countries and establishing existence at various locations. Decision making in such circumstances is difficult unless the collective approach is not taken. It is not possible for the decision makers to meet frequently due to distance and logistics issue. With the advent of enhance communication facilities it is now possible to form teams and interact via Internet, video conferencing, etc. This helps taking decisions and sharing business information without physically moving away from the base location. This is a great process through which a team of like-minded people can be established and they can share their point of view. Without physically moving, this helps in virtual presence; hence, virtual team technology is the modern day's important HR technology.

# Experiential Application

## A. Prerequisite

- The virtual project teams are drawn together because each participant has a specific skill to reach the common goal. Each member must have the roles assigned based on his or her specific skill acquired and team members must recognise the contribution from the other team members also.
- Since the time and distance differences exist, it is often difficult to maintain the commitment for the span of the project. Methods of commitment must be addressed and put in the project plan.
- The virtual team project leader must spend time in working closely with the individual team members as well as building those individuals into a team. Communication with individuals and the group must be refined and supervised electronically.
- The trust factor and measure of accountability must be monitored more closely. The most widely used electronic method for virtual team includes video conferencing, teleconference, Group Ware (software applications that allow shared document typed conversation and voting), e-mail, shared database, message board, online chatting application and voice mail.
- Establish a clear large organisation involved with the team.

## B. Process Steps

| Step | Process |
| --- | --- |
| Step – I | Building the trust within the virtual team greatly influences and enhances productivity, collaborations and success. |
| Step – II | Responsibilities and decision-making authority should be specified in the early stage to bring in clarity of roles. |
| Step – III | Team leader has to help in establishing processes and strategies to stay on task. |
| Step – IV | Collaboration culture needs to be brought in as the virtual team functions autonomously and the roles are independent. |
| Step – V | Continuous communication is a must and all the team members must have continuous communication. |

# Potential Gains and Areas of Concern

- Goal accomplishment despite cultural differences and diversity.
- Decision making in different time zones with the help of communication technology which is cost- and time-effective.
- Competing in the global environment when the organisation is scattered and present across the globe and operating on different dimensions.
- Virtual team is the invention of modern day's electronic revolutions.
- Unlike traditional teams where team members face each other, in virtual teams the members are scattered and therefore, it is required to deal with softer issues of team management to keep the team together.
- Virtual teams that have been brought together for a specific duration such as a project should incorporate some adjournment process into the structure.
- Monitoring and control in a virtual team is difficult, except through project schedules.
- Poor integration could cause irrecoverable damage to the project.
- One of the biggest mistakes of a virtual team leader can make is to underestimate the power of trust.
- Conflict within virtual team is inevitable and can threaten and even erode the resultant and the team can become dysfunctional.

# Measurability

## Try It Out

(1: not at all done, 2: moderately done, 3: to some extent done, 4: to a great extent done, 5: excellently done)

- My organisation has art of technology to connect the team members. ☐
- Organisation uses diversity as a strategic tool for competitive advantage ☐ while designing and developing the team.
- Top management supports the team leader and the team in the pursuit ☐ of goals.
- Organisation takes an active part in reducing the communication barriers ☐ among the team members.

Analysis: the average score would determine the extent to which virtual team process exists in your organisation.

## Score Card

(*: 25% achieved, **: 50% achieved, ***: 75% achieved, ****: 100% achieved)

| Technology | Objective Elements | Unit | Historical | Last Year | Current Year | Stretch Target | Status |
|---|---|---|---|---|---|---|---|
| Virtual Teams | Teams | Nos | 01 | 01 | Yes | 03 | ** |
| Virtual Teams | Training Programmes on Effective Communication | Nos | 03 | 03 | 06 | 08 | * |

# Proven Track Record

## Track One

### IBM

IBM's experience of creating virtual teams is a good example of well-balanced cost-benefit ratios. It began piloting various alternative workplace (AW) options in 1989 to reduce the real estate costs and explore the use of technology to support the sales force. In 1993 the initiative was transformed into mainstream initiative in the North American sales and service organisation—an initiative designed to improve customer responsiveness, reduce costs and increase the productivity. With the implementation of AW, the travel time of the employees was reduced since they need not attend the office and could spend time with the customers and also the dedicated workplace at the office. As a result, 12,500 employees have given up their workspaces and another 13,000 are capable of mobile operation.

The initiative was also implemented in Asia, Europe and Latin America. Hence, 17 per cent of IBM's total worldwide workforce is equipped and trained to work in AW formats and one-third of all the company's departments have at least some mobile employees. The company was able to reduce the cost per person from $15,900 to $9,800 and combined ratio of occupancy and voice-IT expenses to revenues dropped from 8.8 per cent to 4.2 per cent.

(*Source*: Apgar, 1999.)

## Track Two

### British Petroleum

The IT infrastructure has enabled British Petroleum (BP) to build virtual team thereby saving the time, efforts and also solving the problems. It enabled the organisation to cope up with the complex and difficult problems and challenges. The infrastructure gave relevant, rich, timely and accurate information to every employee who may need and use it. Each member of BP's top management team, and each general manager of the business units, has at least one virtual teamwork station. The network enables the firm to engage in continuous conversation about competitive dynamics and performance.

Virtual team network was able to reduce the manhours needed to solve problems as a result of improved interaction between land-based drilling engineers and off-shore rig crews; decrease the number of helicopter trips to off-shore oil platforms; and reduce rework during construction projects because designers, fabricators, construction workers and operations people could collaborate more effectively. The refinery shut down was avoided as technical experts at another location could examine the corrosion problem remotely. The company has saved substantially with the virtual teams network.

(*Source*: Rastogi, 1999.)

## Track Three

### Gati Limited

An integrated supply chain and logistics company has created many virtual teams across the levels and functions and is operating on a regular basis through online chat provided under company's in-house Intranet. Different groups under different leadership log on specific time given and establish connectivity for various decisions making and passing on information down the line.

These help the organisation to foster team building and collaborative decision making process since its customer base is widespread across the Indian subcontinent and has a complex geographical presence. It also has explored the usage of Internet Protocol phoning (IP Phone) mechanism to keep all the work units spread across the country on line with each other surpassing the traditional ground telephoning provided by the government machinery.

(*Source*: Author's self-experience.)

## Applied HR Case

### Brenda Telecom Inc.

Brenda Telecom Inc. is the software provider for the mobile companies and has its branches in all the 10 states in the country. Managing Director Richard has started the unit in the memory of his mother who had helped him in his graduation and also in setting up the company. With one unit he has expanded to the other nine branches all over the country. The strength of the company was in the quality of software and after-sales service. The problems get resolved within one day and the customers are happy. There are three mobile companies and he works for all three of them. The three companies have also their offices in the states and the branches are given enough authority to handle the customers for sales and technical support services. The design team sits at the Corporate Office and software design and training is given to the employees who are at the field to take care of after-sales services. Each unit works as an independent profit centre and there is healthy competition among the different branches. The usual point of contact between the teams is the communication from the corporate office; however, the amount of contact between the units is less since there is not much interaction between them for any technical or service support.

With the breakthrough and the latest technological changes, the demands from the customers have vastly increased. Richard had tough time in changing to the techno-logical changes. The mobile companies have started complaining about the poor ser-vice provided by some of the branches and at the same time there is gap in the rates and also the quality of the service provided.

To overcome the problem Richard has decided to implement the latest technology connecting all the branches for the branch managers so that there is no communication gap and also they work as a team.

## Questions

1. What kind of new technology can be introduced to bring in the concept of team?
2. Do you think that with the existing structure can bring in the team spirit among the branch managers?
3. If you were Richard and intend to bring in team spirit what actions will you take to ensure that there is team spirit among the branch managers? Elaborate.

## References and Further Readings

Apgar, Mahlon. 1999. 'Alternative Workplace', Harvard Business Review on Managing People, USA: Harvard Business School Press.

Herb, Dreo, Pat Kunkel and Thomas Mitchell. 2003. *Virtual Teams Guide Book for Managers*, Wisconsin: ASQ Quality Press.

Fischer, Kimball and Mareen Duncan. 2000. *The Distance Manager—A Hands-on Guide to Managing Off-Site Employees and Virtual Teams*, New York: McGraw-Hill.

Henry, Jane E. and Meg Hartzler. 1997. *Tools for Virtual Teams*, Wisconsin: ASQ Quality Press.

Lipnack, Jessica, and Jeffrey Stamps. 2000. *Virtual Teams*, New York: John Wiley and Sons.

Rastogi, P.N. 1999. 'The Nature and Dimension of Knowledge Management', in Udai Pareek and Sisodia (eds), *HRD in the New Millennium*, New Delhi: Tata McGraw-Hill Publishing Company Limited.

Stephen Dando-Collins. 1996. *The Customer Care Revolution*, Melbourne: Pitman.

# 'KNOWLEDGE MANAGEMENT' CREATING LEARNING ORGANISATION THROUGH KNOWLEDGE MANAGEMENT

*More and more, the productivity of knowledge is going to become for a country and industry or a company, the determining competitive factor. In the matter of knowledge no one country, no one industry, no one company has a natural advantage or disadvantage. The only advantage that it can ensure to itself is to be able to draw more from the knowledge available to all than the others are able to do.*

—Drucker (1993)

## Intent

- To identify preserve and retrieve the organisational knowledge from individuals of the organisations for the organisational competitive advantage.
- To provide a strategic and systematic approach to manage the vast explicit and tacit knowledge of the organisations through the knowledge management processes.
- To create successful knowledge strategies for building competitive advantage over others.
- To provide a direction to the knowledge managers for their roles and responsibility as managers within the organisations.

## Expression

Knowledge Management is a discipline that promotes an integrated approach to identifying, managing and sharing the enterprise's complete information assets, including database, documents, policies and procedures, as well as the unarticulated expertise and experience of the resident individual workers.

# Comprehension

In the current business context across the globe organisational knowledge is recognised as the significant source of competitive advantage. Information about products and services, vendors and suppliers, customers and competitors did exist within the organisation both in explicit and tacit forms for a long time. Organisations do invest considerable efforts and energies to collect and use this information. What significantly add value and contributes to the competitive advantage in the information and technology age is the ability to manage 'knowledge' within the organisations. The organisations continue to value the knowledge of the employees to provide a sustained competitive advantage in the competitive environment. The knowledge needs to be disseminated so that its purview widens and everyone learns from experience, making knowledge a leveraging factor. In the words of Prahlad and Hamel 'An organisation's capacity to improve existing skills and learn new ones offers the most defensible competitive advantage of all'.

Knowledge by definition resides within people. People must identify, interpret and internalise knowledge. Knowledge management is the explicit and systematic management of vital knowledge in the organisation and the associated processes of creating, gathering, diffusing, uasage and exploitation within the organisation. It requires turning personal knowledge into organisational knowledge that can be widely shared throughout the organisation and appropriately applied. The basic premise on which knowledge management is built is the recognition that organisational knowledge resides in the minds of the individual, both within and outside the organisation.

Effective implementation of knowledge management requires contributions from many parts of the organisation. It needs the support of top management in the form of commitment and espousing knowledge values. Contribution of HRD is critical in creating knowledge roles and human systems for knowledge management, and promoting a knowledge family culture, that is, a culture where knowledge is shared as it happens in a family environment. The role of technologist in setting up and maintaining it is central because explicit knowledge is stored and retrieved with the help of technology. The knowledge managers, who take on various knowledge roles, need to read from the front. At the end, the organisations at large must support knowledge management and make knowledge creation as part of a new way of life.

The study of the field of knowledge management is akin to the pursuit of the 'elusive intangible'. Academicians and practitioners recognise the tacit nature of organisational knowledge. Knowledge management is conceptualised from numerous disciplines making the field a mosaic of perspectives. Accountants are interested in how to measure it on the balance sheet, information technologist quantify it on systems, sociologist wants to balance power with it, psychologists want to develop minds because of it, human resource managers want to calculate an ROI on it, and training and development officers want to make sure that they can build it. Explicit knowledge can be expressed in words and numbers and shared in the form of data formulas while tacit knowledge includes subjective insight, intuitions and is highly personal and hard to formularise and thus difficult to communicate and share with others. Effective management of knowledge requires hybrid solutions of technology and people. Therefore, HRD plays an important role in knowledge management. Today, the nature and the performance consequences of the strategies used by the organisations to develop, maintain, and exploit knowledge for innovation constitute an important topic in business strategy.

Intellectual capital for an organisation is worth bigger than the total value of an organisation. Intellectual capital is the learning of experiences that each employee possesses in an organisation on which the organisation's success depends, for example, intellectual capabilities like the tricks of marketing, formulation technique of medicine, product design capabilities, service excellence mechanism. These properties go away with the brain of an individual when he leaves the organisation for any reason. Employee's attrition is a common phenomenon in the business world. Managing this intellectual property within the company and retaining it is knowledge management. If proper knowledge management is not done, then these intellectual property would drain out from the organisation and would suffer a heavy loss which can be recovered immediately. Therefore, technology to manage intellectual property in the form of knowledge management is strategic for the company.

# Experiential Application

## A. Prerequisite

- One of the most overlooked aspects of building intellectual capital is the fact that different types of knowledge are interdependent and impact each other's value and performance in an organisation.
- Just as executives are careful about choosing in what market and products they will invest their financial resources, so too are they careful in choosing where and how to invest in different types of intellectual capital.

  - Avoid focusing on only one element of intellectual capital.
  - Anticipate the changes in the relationship between the elements of intellectual capital.
  - Look for indirect investment.
  - Understand the core business process and define key business drives.
  - Focus on knowledge that will support critical formal and informal decision-making.

- Complexities of decisions will determine focus on intellectual capital.
- Type of decisions will also determine the tools and techniques of knowledge management.

• There are clear and explicit links to business strategy—Is knowledge strategy something separate or is it simply another layer or view of existing business strategy? How does knowledge or know-how add value to your business strategy?

• Be knowledgeable about knowledge—How much knowledge is discussed in your organisation? How well is it understood? Where are the experts on knowledge management?

• A compelling vision and architecture drives the knowledge agenda—Is the knowledge facet of business well articulated? Is there a coherent framework that guides management decisions? Would an innovator give you millions of dollars to exploit your intangible ideas?

• Information and knowledge processes are both systematic and chaotic—Do you have systematic process for capturing knowledge, organising it and sharing it throughout the organisation? Do you have processes that enhance knowledge creation and innovation?

• A well-developed technological infrastructure—Are people and information readily accessible through your computer and communication networks anywhere in the world, 24 hours a day, 365 days a year? Does this network extend outside the organisations?

• A knowledge enriching culture—Are mistakes viewed as learning opportunities or harshly punished? Are your personnel systems geared to recognise and reward individuals and team knowledge contributions?

• Knowledge leadership and champions—Is knowledge enthusiastically talked about throughout your business? Is there an obvious network of knowledge practitioners? Does your CEO visibly reiterates the importance of your organisational knowledge to your business success?

## B. Process Steps

| Step | Process |
|------|---------|
| Step – I | Specifying knowledge goals of the organisation. |
| Step – II | Identifying the knowledge that the organisation is seeking. |
| Step – III | Identification of the source and means of knowledge. |
| Step – IV | Processing and representation of the acquired knowledge. |
| Step – V | Transfer of knowledge—across individuals, with and among the organisations. |
| Step – VI | Application of knowledge through proper utilisation of this knowledge generated for value addition. |
| Step – VII | Preservation of knowledge through a proper mechanism within the organisation. |
| Step – VIII | The evaluation of the implementation for feedback. |

# Potential Gains and Areas of Concern

- It results in building and preserving the explicit and tacit knowledge of all the employees, which are vital for gaining the competitive advantage.
- In the dawning of the knowledge era the future performance of firms will be determined by 'knowledge capital'. Firms that create and leverage this unique source of competitive advantage most effectively will be the winner in tomorrow's business climate.
- Making the right strategic investment to build the firm's intangible assets means taking a comprehensive approach to the problem by understanding the relationship between structural, human and social capital.
- Knowledge management is inextricably linked to practice, and creating values for the firm means improving how knowledge is actually used in activities critical to the business.
- Knowledge management is a valuable proposition for the company. Wrongly managed could take away this precious asset of the company to other competitors.
- Knowledge by definition resides within employees of the organisation. With attrition of the knowledge worker, the gained and acquired knowledge drains out from the organisation.
- If the organisation failed to give opportunity to individual, the transmission of knowledge for the organisation cannot take place.

# Measurability

## Try It Out

(1: not at all done, 2: moderately done, 3: to some extent done, 4: to a great extent done, 5: excellently done)

- My organisation has centralised knowledge storage and dissemination ☐ facilities.
- All the employees in the organisation voluntarily share their experiences ☐ and knowledge.
- An organisation allows employees access to all kinds of information ☐ available in the Central database.

- An organisation has an incentive/reward scheme for contribution to knowledge management. ☐
- All the departments/functions take an active part in knowledge management implementation. ☐

Analysis: the average score would determine the extent to which knowledge management process exists in your organisation.

## Score Card

(*: 25% achieved, **: 50% achieved, ***: 75% achieved, ****: 100% achieved)

| Technology | Objective Elements | Unit | Historical | Last Year | Current Year | Stretch Target | Status |
|---|---|---|---|---|---|---|---|
| Knowledge Management | Strategy Document | Doc | Nil | No | Yes | NA | ** |
| Knowledge Management | Intranet | IT Infrastructure | Nil | No | Yes | | ** |

# Proven Track Record

## Track One

### McKinsey

Every learning organisation knows how to capture the learnings whether they are successes or heart-wrenching failures, through various methods of knowledge management. For McKinsey knowledge-based strategies must begin with a strategy, which is linked to organisational performance and success rather than knowledge or technology. Executing a knowledge-based strategy is not about managing knowledge, but nurturing people with knowledge and leverage knowledge through networks of people who collaborate, but not through the networks of technology. At McKinsey every employee is rewarded for putting their learning into database within the practice information centres. The organisation created a position, Director of Knowledge Management. Transfer of knowledge is seen as a professional responsibility and part of everyone's job and is made part of the evaluation process. Every employee has to make a two-page report of how and what he has learnt from the project so as to enable him to get his reimbursements.

An online information system called the 'Practice Development Network' (PDNet) is updated weekly. A bulletin appears two to three times per week for each of the practice areas, featuring new ideas and information that a particular area wants to 'parade' in front of the company's staff.

(*Source*: Schwandt and Marquardt, 2000.)

## Track Two

## Motorola Corporation, USA

Motorola has had one of the finest reputation of quality for any American Company. By the turn of the century, Motorola executives reckon their rival companies completely on quality. Few companies approach organisational learning with greater fervor than Motorola. The company already spends near four times the American industrial average on training, and hopes to quadruple that figure in the coming years. Like any good learning organisations, Motorola learns from its mistakes, a new customised 16-hour training module on competitive awareness was developed and given over to 2,500 Motorola managers. The second hallmark of organisational learning at Motorola is the way it extends throughout the company's entire value change. Motorola tries to inculcate skills and values such as teamwork, problem solving and communication and interdisciplinary learning, which it considers as the critical success factors for the workforce of the future.

(*Source*: Kiernan, 1996: 193.)

# Applied HR Case

## Silver Maritime Company

Stanley has inherited the company and being a marine and electronics engineer he was able to bring in a lot of changes in the company. The company had 12 cargo ships, which used to go around the world. Since the company has a long standing in the business, Stanley used to get regular business and has no problem. The company was recognised for its ethics and values and they never used to bribe for any business.

Stanley's cause of concern is capacity utilisation and increase in profitability so that he can venture into building of cruise ships. The profit from existing ships is sufficient for him to run the business. He has convened the Heads of the Departments and the Country Heads who are in six different countries. This is the first time in the history of the company that the Heads and the Country Heads were meeting to discuss a serious issue concerning the company. Earlier the HODs used to go to the countries or the Country Heads used to come as per the convenience.

When the meeting started Stanley observed that there is no good interaction between the HODs and the Country Heads and even among the country heads. Everyone has given their opinion of increasing the capacity utilisation and the necessity to increase the profits. They were also very positive about the company's vision to venture into the building of cruise ships.

Stanley after the meeting has found out that there is lack of information flowing among the branches, which is the cause for lack of capacity utilisation and communication gap. He has thought of establishing a network through which all the employees of the company can share their knowledge and the local information so that the company works as a unit rather than as a corporate office with its branches. The new technology can also enable them to have a cheaper mode of communication between the units and also the ships. Stanley was ready to invest in this kind of infrastructure, which will be helpful to him not only in the present but also the future business.

## Questions

1. Do you think that the company needs investment in knowledge dissemination among the employees and units?
2. Can you visualise and design a knowledge management system for Stanley?
3. What are the advantages which Stanley accrues by implementing the new system?

## References and Further Readings

Bukowitz, Wendi R. and Ruth L. Williams. 1999. *The Knowledge Management Fieldbook*, London: Financial Times/Prentice Hall.

Honeywell, Jerry. 2001. *Knowledge Management Strategies*, New Delhi: Prentice Hall of India Pvt Ltd.

Kiernan, Mathew J. 1996. *Get Innovative or Get Dead*, Malaysia: Synergy Books.

Morey, et al. 2001. *Knowledge Management*, Hyderabad: University Press.

Prahlad, C.K. and Gary Hamel. 1996. *Competing for the Future*, UK: Harvard Business School Press.

Schwandt, David R. and Michael J. Marquardt, 2000. *Organizational Learning*, Boca Raton, Florida: St Lucie Press.

Tiwana, Amrit. 2000. *The Knowledge Management Toolkit*, Singapore: Pearson Education Asia Pte Ltd.

# 'CHANGE MANAGEMENT'
# CREATING COMPETITIVE ORGANISATION
# THROUGH CHANGE MANAGEMENT

*A revolutionary confluence of technological change has set the stage for*
*a new environment that will empower individuals as never before.*

—John Naisbitt, American Social Forecaster, New York (1994)

## Intent

- To understand the change management principles.
- To develop strategy for effective management of change in the complex business environment.
- To hold the gains of change process with consolidation and stabilisation process in the organisation.

## Expression

It is a process of metamorphoses that happens with time in the organisation's system, processes, products, culture, etc., and the effective management of such processes for organisational excellence.

## Comprehension

Every organisation no matter how small or big, ought to have clear cut goals and objectives predefined apart from the pursuit of profit, that justify its existence among the society. These goals are the secular mission for the company. If the CEO of the company has the sense of mission, he can tell his employees what it is that the company seeks to accomplish and explain the ideology. Craig Weatherup, President of Pepsi Cola gave his managers a model train to symbolise the message 'Change or get run over', and he made every manager to be alert to the problems that threaten future success. If the employees understand that they are not working for bread alone, they will be motivated to work harder together towards the realisation of a common goal. Those who does not respond to the changes or fail to change when required find themselves out of the business.

What makes an organisation change? The difficulty is that many organisations view the concept of change as a highly programmed process which starts with having something to rectify. Further it is believed that change has to be broken down into various constituent parts, analyse possible alternatives, select the prefer solutions and then apply these solutions in a relentless pursuit with problem recognition, diagnosis and resolution. But change management is not these. There are a number of specific even obvious factors that need to be examined and considered while managing change in the organisation.

Sometimes attributing change entirely to the environment would be a denial of extreme magnitude. Change management is internal reason; it could be environmental or internal processes which the company would like to re-do. Thus, if the concept of change is examined from internal, external or proactive set of view points, then the response of the managers has to be equally widespread. The nature of change influences our reaction to it. In a purely technical nature change, such as a component or machine upgradation, a normal mechanistic manner is applied for implementation of change. However, if the change is related to system-based technical problem which calls upon the application of knowledge of a highly structural and mechanistic nature, then it might make change difficult. And therefore, when it affects the people and the structure, the change process needs to be handled with the right perspective.

A Tropic test can be applied to understand the impact and magnitude of a change, which is occurring in an organisation. Tropic stands for time scale, resources, objectives, perception, interest, control and source (Paton and McCalman 2000). Managing change is a multidisciplinary activity and each one involved must have necessary skill, resources, support and knowledge to implement the change. The process of change may include the resistance to change, low stability, high levels of stress, misdirected energy, conflict and losing momentum, and hence every step and likely impediments to the smooth introduction of change need to be anticipated. The employees need to be educated on the necessity for change, involve them during various stages, and reward the constructive behaviours and creating a learning organisation.

In managing the change the role of a leader is very important since he creates the vision and strategy in the changed scenario and articulates how the goals can be achieved. By doing so he enlists the support of the team members in ensuring that the people carry out the tasks as envisaged. If the management of change has failed, it attributes to the human resources who did not appreciate the change, since they do not want to deviate from the practicing behaviour. Change can be possible with the right kind of information and the purpose of such change being given to him.

Change is a way of life for each one of us. No one can deny change. Organisation in the present business environment has to cope with the all-round changes that are occurring in product, services, customer orientation, etc. How an organisation can manage change is a question that every organisation is trying to find out. Dealing with the change has no unique solution. It has to be managed differently depending on the situation. Every organisation manages changes according to its own perspective. However, there is a way to manage changes in a certain way which makes it less difficult while dealing with changes. The technology of managing change is an HR tool through which any organisation can deal with change management.

# Experiential Application

## A. Prerequisite

- The consent of the top management and support of business functions are very essential.
- One of the most fundamental steps in achieving the successful implementation of change is that of obtaining a shared perception amongst those affected, concerning their viewpoints regarding the issue and implication associated with the change.
- If the problem owner can reach a point at which all those parties with a vested interest in change view it in such a way as to see common objectives and mutual benefits, then a great deal of progress in change management can take place.
- Another factor associated with the successful implementation of change is the ability of the problem owner to overcome any personal prejudices regarding the change.
- However, they also need to ensure that the views and indeed prejudice exhibited by all the other affected parties are taken on board. These needs to be understood, countered and incorporated where appropriate.
- Recognise that not all the suggestions offered and views expressed can be totally wrong, just as the problem owners are unlikely to be totally correct at all times.
- Ensure that they are seen to be actively encouraging collaboration. Change management of all but the simplest projects is a multidisciplinary group activity. Everyone must be pulling in the same direction.
- Be seen to have as much support and authority as possible. Senior management must be clearly identified with the project.

# B. Process Steps

| Step | Process |
|------|---------|
| Step - I | Problem/System specification and description to isolate and determine the system interactions, relationships and cultures. |
| Step - II | Formulation of success criteria by setting objectives and constrains, and generating options to the original objectives. |
| Step - III | Identification of performance quantifiable measures, such as cost, saving, volume, labour and time. |
| Step - IV | Generation of options to solutions. |
| Step - V | Options are evaluated against the previously determined change objectives. |
| Step - VI | Development of implementation strategy. |
| Step - VII | Package the findings into a coherent whole and introduce the change to the system. |
| Step - VIII | Consolidation of the changes with the right kind of support of communication. |

# Potential Gains and Areas of Concern

- Change is a way of life. Organisation and their employees must recognise the need to adopt strategic approaches when facing transformation situations.
- Change started at one point can lead to somewhere else; hence understanding the complexity through change management concept is important.
- Organisation and the managers must recognise that the change, in itself, is not necessarily a problem. The problem often lies in an inability to effectively manage change.
- Sometime not only the adopted process may be wrong, but also the conceptual framework may lack vision and understanding.
- Change initiatives fail in the organisation due to the growing inability of managers to appropriately develop and reinforce their role and purpose within complex, dynamic and challenging organisations.

# Measurability

## Try It Out

(1: not at all done, 2: moderately done, 3: to some extent done, 4: to a great extent done, 5: excellently done)

- My organisation is agile and can take up any challenge.                    ☐

- Change initiatives in the organisation are accepted without much resistance. □
- Top management perceive change as dynamic and takes measures to adapt □ to change.
- Employees are communicated about the need for change and the benefits □ going to be derived from adapting the change process.
- Employees across all levels and all functions participated in the change □ management process.

Analysis: the average score would determine the extent to which change management process exists in your organisation.

## Score Card

(*: 25% achieved, **: 50% achieved, ***: 75% achieved, ****: 100% achieved)

| Technology | Objective Elements | Unit | Historical | Last Year | Current Year | Stretch Target | Status |
|---|---|---|---|---|---|---|---|
| Change Management | Strategy Document | Doc | Nil | No | Yes | NA | ** |
| | Change Management Programme – 01 | Nos | – | – | Yes | – | ** |

# Proven Track Record

## Track One

## SmithKline Beecham, USA

The rate of introduction of change had accelerated in SKB Irvine, since the merger of SmithKline with Beecham. The tried and tested activity driven processes which had been the main experience at SKB had been found wanting in respect of the resource requirements to complete implementation. Frustration and disillusionment can be the order of the day as limited progress is achieved inside the design team, whilst outside the organisation struggle to maintain the status quo remains.

On the other hand, a BPR (Business Process Re-engineering) approach would have been completely inappropriate if the need of the workforce were to bypass to deliver reduced cost with fewer but less motivated and more highly stressed employees. To deliver the required change process, the critical role is of the change agent, who must be suitably equipped with the appropriate skills and the necessary charisma to tackle the complex issues hand on. SKB started off with external change agents and then developed, with limited success, its own team of internal facilitators.

(*Source*: Paton and McCalman, 2000: 245.)

## Track Two

### Nortel Networks

Nortel Networks is a leading multinational data and voice telecommunication company employing over 80,000 people worldwide. It supplies much of the world's voice and data communication equipment including optical network systems. At one point of time it was critical to get the organisation to move from being 'unconsciously unaware' to being 'consciously unaware' of the need to address the people's side of this large organisation because of its highly technical and tool-focused culture.

The company developed the Change Capability Evaluation Programme. It was designed as a self assessment and monitoring device to assist the organisation in preparing the people for the significant changes tailored under the supply chain management initiative. The Change Capability Evaluation (CCE) is a three volume series that included a guide, a tool kit with the tools and specific instructions on their use, a resource manual to give background and theoretical underpinnings, and to link the CCE clearly into monitoring process for the total initiative.

(*Source*: Carter, Giber and Goldsmith, 2001: 40.)

# Applied HR Case

## Republic Bank

Pramod has joined as the Manager of the Credit Control Division and he had the previous experience in the finance company and he has consistently performed in recovering the money from the defaulters. Looking at this performance, Republic Bank has selected him giving him salary higher than other Managers of the same rank. The bank was facing problem with the recovery and the credits are piling up and there was audit objections regarding the non-recovery.

Pramod is being assisted by three supervisors taking care of credit analysis, credit sales and credit collections. Pramod started with looking at the function of credit analysis of how the money is being sanctioned to the customers and the basis on which the amount is arrived at. Robert who is the seniormost of all had good experience and is handling the role since three years. But since three months his performance has gone down significantly because of his domestic problems. He is being warned for not coming to the office regularly and keeping the files pending for a long time. The main contention is that Robert used to handle the role of Pramod before he was recruited and was performing to the best of his abilities. After Pramod was recruited he did not show any interest in the department, which has stunned the total branch itself. He is considered to be one of the senior and hardworking employees.

Pramod in order to assist Robert has given him one trainee so that he gets some relief and at the same time train somebody in analysis so that the files can be moved faster. Pramod tried to tell Robert that if he has any attitude problem with him, he will recommend the General Manager to transfer him any of the function in the bank, but Robert used to tell him that he is very comfortable and he is learning a lot of things from him.

The actual problem started with the constant complaints being received from the trainee that Robert neither teaches him about the work nor allows him to work. Pramod called Robert and asked him about the indifferent attitude, but Robert replied that he is training the new recruit on all matters and he is slow at learning.

The problems started increasing with the complaints being directly received from the customer and Pramod is in a fix of how to handle Robert.

## Questions

1. Do you think that change can be brought about in Robert?
2. Please give your plan to change him with the time schedule?
3. Do you think that Robert will change after administering him the plan?

## References and Further Readings

Chanda, Ashok and Shilpa Kabra. 2000. *Human Resource Strategy—Architecture for Change*, New Delhi: Response Books.

Carter, L., David Giber, Marshall Goldsmith, Richard F. Beckhard, W. Walner Bulke, Edward L. Lawler III, Beverley L. Kaye and Jay Alden Conger. 2001. *Best Practices in Organizational Development and Change: Culture, Leadership, Retention, Performances, Coaching*, San Francisco, CA: Pfeiffer.

Gordon, Judith R. 1999. *Organisational Behavior—A Diagnostic Approach*, New Jersey: Prentice Hall International Inc.

Johnson, Spencer. 1998. *Who Moved My Cheese*, London: Vermilion.

Newman L. Karen, Nollen D. Stanley, 1998. *Managing Radical Organisational Change*, Thousand Oaks, CA: Sage Publications.

Nilakant V. and S. Ramnarayan. 1998. *Managing Organisational Change*, New Delhi: Response Books.

Palmer, Brien. 2003. *Making Change Work: Practical Tools for Overcoming Human Resistance*, Wisconsin: ASQ Quality Press.

Paton R.A. and James McCalman. 2000. *Change Management*, New Delhi: Sage Publications.

Pettigrew Andrew and Richard Whipp. 2001. *Change Management for Competitive Success*, New Delhi: Infinity Books.

Scott, Cynthia D. and Dennis T. Jaffe. 1995. *Managing Change at Work*, California: Crisp Publications Inc.

Smith, Douglas K. 1996. *Taking Charge of Change*, Reading, MA: Addison-Wesley Publishing Company.

Weihrich, Heinz and Harold Koontz. 1994. *Management—A Global Perspective*, New York: McGraw-Hill Inc.

Wilson Patrica. 1996. *Managing through Change*, England: Gower Publishing Limited.

# Part 3

## Branding of HR Technologies

# 10    HR BRANDING

## Learning Objectives

- To learn the concept of branding and its impact in theme promotion within the organisation.
- To define branding for HR technologies and through which making movement for a desire change.
- To pave a way for creativity and innovation in branding HR technologies in making it unique in its expression and presentation.
- To learn about various brands that are being used creatively in many world class companies across the globe.

## The Concept of Branding

Everything in the world is named. For everything, a word is exclusively created for identification. My name, your name, things around us is all tagged by a specific generic name. Imagine a world where there is no name for the things. How would you refer that person or item which does not have a name? As a famous poet once said, 'What is there in a name?' Name is everything. It is an expression. It gave birth to language. Languages are the medium of expression. With varied languages all things around us are identified with a specific word. The people who understand that language know the name of those things. Different people identify with the same thing with a different word. When the same thing is in the possession of different people or when a product has varied suppliers, it needs identification; then the concept of branding comes in the picture. Branding is an identity and whenever the object is thought about, the name must get reflected in the mind; that is the recall value of the product.

Every product today available in the market is branded. For example, consumer durable items such as television, cameras are all branded. Customers hesitate buying any consumer durable product which is not branded. Brand is a symbol of quality, services and reliability. Services are also branded. For example, courier services provided by FedEx is highly quality oriented and reliable. People prefer sending couriers through those companies who has earned credit on their brand.

Brand is depiction of ownership. Laws back it as well. It prevents copying. Many a times brand becomes synonymous with a product. Xerox as we all know is actually a brand. The real product is photocopying, however, we often use Xerox as a product not as a brand. Over a period of time people forget the products but the brand becomes the product. Pepsi and Coca-Cola are brands for soft drinks but gradually they are becoming products by themselves. In fast moving consumer goods, shampoos and soaps are the products attached with different brand names.

## The Current Status of HR in the Industry

Why is it that in most organisations the HR function is just treated as a function without due respect and credit? Normally, it is perceived as a cost centre and not as one adding value to the bottom line. How much can HR contribute? Is it more than a bunch of clerks processing benefit forms and keeping track of attendance and holidays? The environment today has changed phenomenally from that of ten years earlier. The organisations are pushing themselves to the highest possible level in terms of getting their products to the market quicker, making their services stand out from the crowd and beating the competition in every possible way. Employees have had pretty much to fall in line with the organisation goals and get along with the programmes.

The old employment contract of lifetime employment in exchange of loyalty has fallen by the wayside. A new employment contract of shared responsibility has emerged. Under the new employment contract, meeting the needs of both employers and employees is emphasised, which does not have long-term commitments. Many articles have been published referring to this change process worldwide. Besides very basic fundamentals of employment, many other new changes have come up with the change in business environment. Competency, productivity and value additions are the buzzwords these days that is dealt with in every organisation.

## The Art of Innovation and Branding in HR

'To exist is to change. To exist a long time is to change often' (anonymous). Change is perhaps the dominant characteristic of contemporary companies. Change, of course, can be either beneficial or detrimental, and it is often well into the process before you can even tell one from the other. There are only two things about change: it must occur, and its outcome is uncertain. Creativity and innovations are the engines of constructive change. Creativity has been heralded as the procedure for transforming problems into opportunity whereas innovations have been called as a mechanism for dealing with uncertainty. Creativity is the process by which novel ideas are generated and innovations is the process by which those novel ideas are transformed into things tangible and useful. Creativity forms something from nothing and innovations shape that something into practical products and services. Ideas and implementation go together.

Innovations and creativity are equally essential in the area of HR. Human Resource function is concerned with the creation of harmonious working relationships among the employees and to bring out individual human potential. There is a need for innovations and creativity in the field of HR. Innovations has to be made in HR practices considering the requirements of the present employees. For instance, training is considered as an investment rather than an expense by many companies. Training and development offer valuable benefits to both employees and employer. Earlier, the employees were sent outside their organisation for training but nowadays many companies arrange for the training of their employees within the company. So, this is an innovation in the area of training.

Innovation can be simply brought out by thinking innovatively. However, if a systematic process is followed then it becomes easier to bring out innovative practices. When we talk of branding of HR, we do not mean labelling of HR but the creation of an identity for the very basic HR function. The HR function has continuously evolved and undergone changes over a period of time. The erstwhile approach of industrial relations has moved from personnel management to a gradual evolution towards Human Resource Development, and further on, to Human Resource Management. The term branding in normal connotation, as well as according to the Webster's dictionary indicates 'labelling and imprinting'. We define branding of the Human Resource function as 'The identification, creation and implementation of the value of the Human Resource function so as to create a felt need and identity of the function'.

Why is HR based only on 'content', that is, human resources? Why can it not be known as 'Center of excellence?' The question is why is it not based on the 'context', that is, what it aims to do as a 'center of excellence'? Branding pertains not to the function as a whole but to each of its individual components, its nuts and bolts. So you can brand the normal interventions of reward as something or maybe your annual remuneration and compensation as something. The approach, the names, the identity are organisation specific and work in that way. Branding should be in alignment to the organisation's HR strategy as well as the future growth path of an organisation.

# Process of Innovation and Branding in HR

## Knowing the Current Practices

It involves listing of current HR practices and their features. The process involves carrying out the current HR practices, listing what has been achieved by these practices and what really needs improvements. It also involves listing the demands and requirements of the employees.

## Finding the Alternatives

After the HR practices are listed, each of them is studied to know which area requires innovation. Start an idea generation stage to know the various alternative ideas. There are various ways through which it can be done. The most common one is brainstorming. This technique is directed to generate unconventional ideas by suppressing the common tendency to criticise or reject them. In the brainstorming session, no criticism is permitted; there is freewheeling of ideas. The combinations and development of ideas are encouraged.

## Feasibility of Innovations

After the ideas are generated they are checked for their feasibility, whether they can be implemented, whether they fit well with the organisation culture and structure, and whether they will really help in fulfilling the wants of the employees.

## Selecting the Best and Implementing

After the ideas are checked for their feasibility, the best one is selected and implemented. But this is not an easy task. Innovation in HR practice is a product by itself. A product can be called innovative only when a proper distinction can be made between the features of the original and new product. There has to be an addition or upgradation of features in the new product compared to the original product and then only the new product can be called innovative.

After a proper distinction is made between original and new product, a name or an acronym has to be assigned. In short, a 'brand' is attached to the product. After the product is named, it is marketed. A proper marketing strategy for the product is made. The new product could be for any segment say, shop-floor workers, middle executives, and top management people. A single product cannot be targeted for all of these segments. The employees for whom the particular new product is, should be made aware of that product. They must know what good the product holds for them, what features the new product has. The company can publish handy manuals, put it on company's network, carry out workshops, and if necessary, also arrange for their training.

## Refine Again and Again

The product after implementing should be checked at regular intervals say three or six months to know whether it meets the requirements of the employees and what attributes are missing in the new product. Thereafter, keeping these attributes in mind, the product is refined again and again.

## Throw Unwanted and Outdated and Bring Fresh and Latest

The productivity, change and continuous striving for excellence in business have led to a widespread debate over the role of HR and its contribution to organisational performance. Though, it is one of the forces for organisation growth, it is the beleaguered reputation of HR, which has added to its woes. The competitive forces of the future demand a change in the perception of the function as well as its role. Top management in organisations doesn't seem to recognise that they badly need help in developing and maintaining a positive corporate culture, which is the heart and soul of any organisation.

Branding for the HR function and its tools can be done in a three-manner approach. First, watch the internal customers and work backwards. How do the employees and the customers view the HR function? Second, broad-base your definition as far as you can. If the internal customer views HR in one way how can we change them to think in another way? Third, make crucial refinement—the way the common consumer durables are made and branded to suit the varied tastes of consumers for different regions for different kinds of people, for different climates, so is the case for the HR tools and techniques.

Nescafe is branded and sold in a different manner in India than it is in Switzerland. Similarly, the way Coke is made, branded and marketed varies in America compared to India. The way interventions are branded in the organisation needs to be done in light of the organisation's needs, goals and its culture. Thus, if the environment in the organisation is very open and the perception of change and creativity prevails very high, weird branded names can be used otherwise standardised brand names may work better.

# Conclusion

A compilation of all different brands creatively and innovatively conceptualised and successfully implemented in many world-class companies have been given in the following pages. These are all learning experiences of branded HR products and services. The examples shared here have primarily been obtained from various literature and publications. The concept and the brand depicted are in a summarised form. The greater details would only help in understanding how the brand evolved, what was its impact and how it moved within the company. The idea here is to bring such brands to generate curiosity and learning on how innovatively the HR technologies can be interestingly implemented in the organisation with a lot of propaganda.

# 'News Scope'

## Organisational Communication

## Bell Telephone

## SHR Technology – 07 – Internal Communication

Bell Telephone of Illinois has a monthly video cast called 'News Scope'. An anchorwoman from the community relations department opens the programme giving the top headlines and interesting company news. This is being very popular with the employees. They also run surveys of their employees from time to time to find out what they want to see, which questions they want to be answered. Many corporations are putting together their own corporate video newscasts giving employees the latest information about the company. Corporate newscasts communicate anything from new products to the employee benefits. If employees can quickly grasp the employer's side of a controversial issue through in-house television, they are more likely to accept the company's position and pass the information along to other employees.

(*Source*: Cook, 1987: 353.)

# 'Ears'

## Communication and Positive Orientation

## ESSO

## SHR Technology – 07 – Internal Communication

ESSO unit at Singapore have implemented programmes on 'listening skills' so that they overcome the communication barrier and always encourage positive communication. The company has organised the programme on 'EARS'. This programme is designed for managers who are mobile and have to go places. It helps in overcoming their communication barriers and encourages two-way communication. The results have improved total quality management because of greater customer loyalty and employees have been able to learn about the ultimate results of their work.

(*Source*: Daft, 1998: 539.)

# 'Leadership Development Inventory' (LDI)

## Leadership Development through 360-Degree Feedback

## Hughes Software

## SHR Technology – 12 – 360-Degree Feedback

Hughes Software has named 360-degree feedback as '*Leadership Development Inventory*' *(LDI)*. The instrument of LDI is designed in-house. The areas of feedback is derived from '*HSS Ways*' (Hughes Software System Ways) and '*Ethics of Managers*'. The process involves senior leadership and is made applicable from their 360 respondents. It is an annual process. Target is not just those in the senior level but also those who are step away from them. The feedback forms are given and collected in a sealed docket from all respondents and then processed in a very confidential manner. The process is completely developmental and not evaluative. The experience of LDI in Hughes Software is extremely positive. It has helped managers understand their role as leaders. It has brought in a high level of top down accountability. Communication clarity has improved a lot. Its success lies in the high credibility that it enjoys as a source of honest, constructive feedback.

(*Source*: Rao, 2001: 3–15.)

# 'Standards of Leadership' (SOL)

## Leadership Building and 360-Degree Feedback

### Johnson & Johnson

### SHR Technology – 12 – 360-Degree Feedback

Johnson & Johnson is the world's most comprehensive and broadly based manufacturer of healthcare products, as well as provider of related services. Johnson & Johnson has been in the 'Fortune Top 10' list of Most Admired Companies in the world for three successive years in the 1990s. To remain successful and retain the market leadership position, they require leaders who credo values, give business results, focus on the customer and marketplace, manage complexity, innovation, organisation and people development and finally interdependent partnering. These are incorporated in a model called '*Standards of Leadership*' *(SOL)*. To emphasise the qualities of SOL, the model has been made part of the performance appraisal. Twenty to 30 per cent weightage is given to SOL and the balance to the Key Result Areas (KRA). To bring in the qualities, 360-degree feedback instrument is being implemented. The tool is being implemented in a phased manner from the top management down to the line managers. The tool was used to help the individuals to receive feedback on leadership, identify areas of improvement, make a personal development plan and seek continuous feedback on the progress of the development plan and behaviour change. Johnson & Johnson (J&J) intends to bring out leaders through the 360-degree feedback.

(*Source*: Ghosh, 2000: 100.)

# 'McJobs'

## Diversity in Jobs

## McDonalds, USA

## SHR Technology – 13 – Managing Diversity

McDonalds created *'McJobs'*; a programme that has trained and hired more then 9,000 mentally and physically challenged individuals since 1981. McJobs is a corporate plan to recruit, train and retain individuals with disabilities. Its participants include workers with visuals, hearing or orthopaedic impairments, learning disabilities and retardation. Through classroom and on-site training, the McJob programme prepares individuals with disability for the work environment. Before McJob workers go on site, sensitivity training sessions are held with store managers and crew members. These sessions help workers to deal with disability and explore the opportunities available. Some McJob workers with visual impairment prefer to work on the back line whereas others who use wheelchairs can work at the drive-throw window.

*(Source*: Debra, 2003: 48.)

# 'Working Together'

## Diversity Training Process

## Alcon Laboratories, USA

## SHR Technology – 13 – Managing Diversity

Alcon Laboratories addresses the issues of diversity through its *'Working Together'* training programme. Begun in the early 1990s, *'Working Together'* is a multi module diversity-training programme that uses case studies, self-report rating scales, role-playing and video tapes as delivery methods. The first module presents the rationale for why appreciating diversity at work is important for both individuals and the organisation. The second module explores the participants' personal attitudes and beliefs about those who are *'different'*. The third module addresses the issue of bias, and how a person's attitudes and behaviours influence his/her interactions with other peoples. The forth module makes a case for becoming a *'Diversity Change Agent'*, bringing attention to specific actions individuals may take to help create a more respectful work environment for all. The final module ask participants to make a personal commitment to become *Diversity Change Agents*, thus contributing to an organisational culture that creates a climate for the success of each and every employee by appreciating the uniqueness that each person brings to the workplace. Alcon Laboratories have found that working together contributes to stronger, healthier work environment.

(*Source*: Debra, 2003: 45.)

# 'Teamwork Day'

## Celebration for Knowledge Sharing and Teamwork

## Xerox Inc., USA

## SHR Technology – 16 – Teams

Xerox is a global corporation, a world leader in documentation business, employing around 75,000 employees worldwide. In Xerox high emphasis is given on teamwork and employees are encouraged to perform in a team. *'Teamwork Day'* is a celebration of employees of Xerox, to their commitment to knowledge sharing, teamwork and customer satisfaction. Ever since the teamwork day event started in Xerox, the event has grown into an international celebration attracting thousands of participants in many worldwide locations. Teams of empowered Xerox people, representing every organisation within the company, joins together and shares their successes and best practices with co-workers, suppliers, partners and other special guests. Learning sessions, interactive displays, colourful exhibits, in a festive-like atmosphere, team showcase their use of quality processes and tools to ensure customer and employee satisfaction and to achieve superior results. The energy and enthusiasm of participating teams are contagious as they share what they have learned with others. Each organisation within the Xerox group develops its own team selection process that best meets the needs. Team exhibits and presentations provide the people with the unique opportunity to meet co-workers from variety of Xerox locations and to learn from each other through practice sharing.

(*Source*: Carter, Giber and Goldsmith, 2001)

# 'InnovAAtions'

## Generating Ideas through Teams

### American Airlines

### SHR Technology – 16 – Teams

American Airlines is the largest commercial airline company in the world. In a de-regulated and highly competitive industry, American Airlines continues to look for ways to add value to its product and to bring its product to market in the most profitable way. The company started an innovative scheme wherein the teams could earn significant merchandise awards for approved ideas. Ideas were evaluated with minimum delay. With a strong communications campaign and solid backing from the CEO, Innov-AAtions took off with 3,428 teams from across the company. In less than four months, the programme had produced 1,660 adopted ideas, yielding in excess of $53 million in the first year net savings or revenue.

*(Source*: Mai, 1996: 117.)

# 'Gap Group'

## Overcoming the Gaps in Performance

### AT&T

### SHR Technology – 17 – Cross-Functional Task Force

AT&T has a *'Gap Group'* programme in which leaders of each group seek to identify and overcome the gaps in performance or output faced by the divisions. High potential managers bring in a key problem from their division. They then work with an action set of six to seven peers from other divisions over a period of seven days, during which each person gets one day of air time that is dedicated to working on his/her business problem. The set then wrestles with the problem and searches for agreement as to the true nature of problem. Possible alternative and solutions are proposed. A set facilitator or subject matter expert guides the process. When the group has agreed on a possible solution, the client develops an action plan for his/her problem and is accountable for producing the results in the time period designated.

*(Source*: Schwandt and Marquardt, 2000: 147.)

# 'Asset Management Team' (AMT)

## Problem Solving

## Maxus Energy

## SHR Technology – 17 – Cross-Functional Task Force

Maxus Energy is an example of a company that has risen to the challenge in bringing teams from collision to collaboration. The company is an operator of a production-sharing contract with M/s Pertamina, Indonesian government's oil company. The company by forming teams was able to retain the production levels and significant amounts of reserves were added. *Asset Management Teams* (AMT) were formed to effectively and efficienctly optimise production and reserves from producing areas and serve as a training vehicle for technical as well as leadership skills. The AMT is a multidisciplinary team, self-directed, focused by clearly generated goals and objectives that had management's input and agreement. The teams are given technical support, monetary and decision-making authority. The teams meet regularly to discuss progress and jointly work out problems, promote cross-functional solutions and input from all the members, seek technical audit from functional groups and recommend expenditures for projects based on team decisions. Maxus's team approach has been very successful.

*(Source*: Odenwald, 1996: 118.)

# 'Stretch for Success'

## Performance Improvement

## TIG Insurance

## SHR Technology – 17 – Cross-Functional Task Force

TIG Insurance formerly known as Transamerica Insurance Group has the pride of being lean at the top. It makes decisions faster, is less bureaucratic, and very agile as an organisation. TIG Insurance has worked to build such an organisation by emphasising teams, continuous improvement and feedback. Company has started an initiative called *'Stretch for Success'* and targeted work process measures to energise performance improvement of many departments. Natural workgroups at department levels—including administration and operations, underwriting, marketing and claims—focus on a specific range of corporate objectives. Measures are identified as a source of performance feedback for each work group or team. Teams are accountable for performance goals that they can impact, and for which they can receive clear and regular feedback. The team earn awards for goal achievement, with the top performing teams earning an additional, special award. The targets are derived from average performance over the last 12-month period. TIG also prepares team leaders to assist their teams in understanding both baselines and rationale, which enable the teams to know the priorities of the organisation. The process has helped to produce substantial productivity gains. It has also resulted in the workforce getting smarter about how to run the business.

(*Source*: Mai, 1996: 74–76.)

# 'Godfather'

## Mentoring

## Dow Chemical

## SHR Technology – 18 – Mentoring and Coaching

Dow Chemical pursues the selection and orientation of employees for international assignments on individual basis. Each international assignment is considered unique. Candidates are given information about the host country and an intensive two-week course in the language and culture. To encounter the emotional issues the employee is assigned a *'Godfather'* a high-ranking staff member in the person's function. They stay in touch, keeping each other informed of activities and career issues. The *Godfather* serves as a mentor and reviews compensation issues. Starting a year before the employee is to be repatriated to the home country, the *Godfather* begins to arrange for a new job position at the same or higher level at the home country. The *Godfather* helps the employee while handling overseas assignment and coming back to the home country.

(*Source*: Werther Jr. and Davis, 1996: 60.)

# 'E-mail Mentor Programme'

## Mentoring

## HP

## SHR Technology – 18 – Mentoring and Coaching

Hewlett-Packard has developed a structured, project-based programme through which HP employees' worldwide volunteer to Tele-mentor fifth to twelfth grade students in unique one-to-one relationships. E-mail mentoring is one of the many opportunities the company provides for HP people to bring their time and talents to the difficult challenges facing education today. The programme focuses on helping students excel in maths, science and professional communication skills, and developing education and career plans for life beyond high school. Participation in the programme is collaboration among the teacher, mentor and student. The programme allows employees to balance their desires to contribute to their communities with the time and place constraints imposed by their jobs.

(*Source*: Chanda, The Across Board Magazine, 1999.)

# 'Transformational Leadership Programme' (TLP)

## Transformational Leadership through Training

## Reliance Energy Limited

## SHR Technology – 19 – Transformational Leadership

Reliance Energy Limited is one of the largest corporations in India and is a part of Reliance Industries. Reliance has entered into the power sector by taking over BSES, the main electricity provider to the Mumbai City. The endeavour of the organisation is to bring in change among the employees to stretch and outperform. To build the leadership styles among the employees and to enable them to transform themselves, a series of programmes on Transformational Leadership is being conducted within the teams and units in which they work. The programmes consists of one day of outbound activities in which the participants are taken for mountaineering, rappelling, river crossing and various other exercises through which the participants are debriefed, through which they enjoy fun and learning. These outbound scenarios have bought a perceptive change in their way of thinking and the risk-taking ability for managing a situation in an uncertain environment. On the second day of the programme, input is given to strengthen their conceptual skills of understanding leadership, specifically transformational leadership, which is required to drive business processes in a competitive environment. The programmes are able to create synergy among the employees to have a perspective of the organisational goals and how they need to achieve them. A series of such programmes are conducted for all the new promotes to give them new competencies.

(*Source*: Authors' self-experience.)

# 'Chance Leadership Programme and Business Leadership Programme (CLP and BLP)

## Developing Future Managers through Training

## Crompton Greaves Limited

## SHR Technology – 19 – Transformational Leadership

Crompton Greaves Limited, pioneers in the engineering industry in India, uses training as an important tool for development of the employees. Quality training is being imparted to provide the required competencies. The training is being imparted at their full-fledged HRD centre at Pune, India. To groom the managers for the future, the organisation has planned 'BLP' (Business Leadership Programme) and CLP (Chance Leadership Programme). The programme aims at imparting the knowledge on management and change, which spreads over a period of 18 months. The main emphasis was to bring in transformational leadership qualities for the future managers and the programme was successful in achieving the objectives.

(*Source*: Nohria 1999: 101.)

# 'Job Change Applicant-Tracking System (JCATS)

## Promotion from Within

## Federal Express, USA

## SHR Technology – 24 – Recruitment

Federal Express has promotion from within policy. At Federal Express, for instance, 'open positions are filled, wherever and whenever possible by qualified candidates from within the existing work force'. Federal Express has job posting/career coordinating system called JCATS (Job Change Applicant Tracking System). Announcement of new job openings via this electronic system usually takes place each Friday. All employees applying for the position get numerical scores based on job performance and length of service. They are then advised as to whether they are chosen as candidates. Internal recruiting and promotion from within can thus be a force for creating employees' commitment.

(*Source*: Dessler, 1997)

# 'Job Match'

## Recruitment from Within

## Citibank, New York

## SHR Technology – 24 – Recruitment

At Citibank in New York City, in order to streamline and simplify the selection process computers are used to match present employees with internal openings. The Job Match selection system rests on matching a profile of candidates for a non-professional job with the task requirements of the job. The specific tasks required of the job are programmed into the computer, along with the specific abilities of employees. The employees with the highest match with a given opening are then considered for the job. One shortcoming of the Job Match system is that it does not consider non-task factors, such as whether the employee wants the job.

(*Source*: Werther and Davis, 1996: 217.)

# 'Creating Opportunities to Excel'

## Career Planning and Skill-Based Pay

### City of Englewood, Colorado

### SHR Technology – 26 – Career and Succession Planning

City of Englewood, Colorado developed a skill-based pay system called 'Creating Opportunities to Excel'. To develop the plan, the administrative service staff of Englewood first developed strategy outline that included (a) updating all job descriptions; (b) updating and verifying each job position's current salary; (c) defining the base job requirements, identifying the necessary skills, and assigning percentages to their importance; and (d) formulating career plans. Three steps were followed in implementing the strategy outline. The first step developed a new pay line by determining the skill base for jobs and then assigning monetary values to each skill category. The second step established an individualised career development programme for employees. The third step gave employees a choice as to whether or not they would participate in the plan. The programme has improved the communication between the employees and management. It has resulted in higher individual satisfaction, better defined personal and professional goals, increased employee empowerment and cost-effectiveness.

(*Source*: Byars and Leslie, 1997: 353.)

# 'Skill Development Programme'(SDP)

## Role Clarity Workshops

### Gati Limited

### SHR Technology – 27 – Role Clarity

Gati Limited is the leader in the express cargo industry in India and is a pioneer in evolving various benchmark practices in the industry for others to follow. The market has become competitive with the imitators, competitors, regional and multinational players entering into the field. The organisation has restructured from a hierarchical and matrix based organisation to that of a process-based organisation. Various initiatives have been taken to bring in the change management. To stabilise the process faster and to keep the new structure in place, the organisation has initiated Role Clarify Workshops called 'Skill Development Programmes (SDPs)'. Support of Managing Director was vital for ensuring successful conduct of the programme. The programmes were conducted at three levels to percolate down the line. During the first phase, all the Managers are covered in which the Head of the Department has initiated the role played by the department in the utility value chain. Subsequently, an interaction with the other Heads of the Departments on their expectations from the department and expectations from others is done to bring in congruence to achieve the organisational goals. The Managing Director devotes substantial time with each group to give his perspective and his expectations from the department to face the competition and achieve the organisational goals. During the later phase, the Executives who are in second line and the Associates are covered. The process is able to bring clarity of roles among the employees and can lead to stabilisation of the organisation structure faster than expected.

(*Source*: Authors' self-experience.)

# 'Performance Planning Review and Development System' (PPRDS)

## Performance Enhancement

## Gujarat Gas Ltd

## SHR Technology – 28 – Performance Management System

Gujarat Gas Limited, a pioneer in the natural gas distribution in India, part of British Gas Plc., has been innovative in many HR practices. To bring in performance orientation among the employees the MBO (Management by Objectives)-based Performance Management was introduced under the intervention PPRDS (Performance Planning Review and Development System). Earlier the system of performance appraisal was evaluation of the employee on fixed parameters. The appraisal was not able to bring in performance orientation as per the business plan. The PPRDS was introduced with the organisational goals declared across the organisation and these goals are cascaded down the line to various units and finally to the individuals. All the employees make their KRAs at the beginning of the year in mutual agreement with the Reporting Officer and the Reviewing Officer. To bring in uniformity, certain universal KRAs are being arrived at wherein the employees occupying a role need to take these KRAs. In this process the employees are given opportunity to make 40 per cent of their KRAs on their own. To bring in the objectivity, the Zonal and the Central Performance Review Committees are established to ensure that there is objectivity in the evaluation of the Reporting Officer and the Reviewing Officer. The Heads of the Departments at the Business Unit and the Corporate Office review the performance up to the executive level at the Business Unit and all the Managers at the Corporate Office. The process is able to bring in performance orientation and transparency in the Performance Appraisal.

*(Source*: Authors' self-experience)

# 'Performance Enhancement Programme' (PEP)

## Performance Orientation and Change

## Southern California Edison

## SHR Technology – 28 – Performance Management System

Southern California Edison based in California has been trying to change the corporate culture to be more adaptive to the changing needs. The HRD has realised that the performance appraisal is working against the values and in order to facilitate the right kind of appraisal, it has advised each department to design their own appraisal. A task force is created to look into the alternative forms of appraisal that comes out with the Performance Enhancement Programme (PEP) wherein the employee and supervisor discuss across the goals to be achieved. The process starts with the discussion between them about the vision, mission and goals of the company and how they can satisfy the customer needs. Then both of them decide the goals basing on the business strategy of the company. The employee can suggest any one of the employee to evaluate his performance at the end of the year. Employee and the supervisor determine the final list of reviewers who will interview about the employee's performance and come up with the list of questions to be used in the interviewing. After the review process in the follow-up session, the employee and the supervisor share the notes, ideas and define what each of them must do to work on the problem areas. The employees praise this system stating that it has given them openness and more control. With this process HR and other departments have become true partners in improving the company.

*(Source*: Daft, 1998: 435.)

# 'Benefit Bucks'

## Matching People with Benefits

### Nike

### SHR Technology – 30 – Compensation Strategy

To attract and retain skilled workers, Nike enlists current employees to help enrich its benefits offerings. It starts by probing workers' fears, needs and desires in focus groups and surveys, in which employees often express worries about not been able to buy a house, send their children to college, or care for elderly parents. Then Nike asks employees' teams to design new benefits packages that offer more choices without raising cost. Some of the choices the team comes up with include company-matching funds for college tuition, subsidised expenditure for child care or care for the elders, paid time off for family leave, group discounts on auto or home insurance, discounted mortgages, legal service and financial planning advise.

Many of the new offerings are relatively cheap for the company. To contain cost further, Nike give employees incentives to make health-benefits trade-off, such as pledging to stop smoking or using the company's physicians networks. By tailoring its benefits to those that employees really need and care deeply about, Nike is maximising the return on its 'Benefits Bucks'.

(*Source*: Cascio, 1998: 436–37.)

# 'Improshare'

## Bonus Sharing Formula

### Carrier Inc. Programmes

### SHR Technology – 31 – Incentive Plans

Programmes based on Improshare stress quality and quantity goals derived from engineering standards. The bonus formula used in these types of plans is based on productivity standards that emphasise quality and quantity in relation to total labour hours expended. Improshare plans need not include an employee involvement component, but such an element has been used successfully in conjunction with quality circles and other types of work team situations. Carrier, a subsidiary of United Technologies, introduced Improshare to its employees in 1988. In its first year, productivity increased by 24 per cent over its base year (1986), and rejects decreased dramatically. Savings in labour costs are split 50–50 between the company and its employees, with each employee receiving the same percentage bonus. In 1988, 2,500 employees shared $3 million in bonus pay. Carrier claims that its success is due to employee involvement. Plant productivity is posted daily on the bulletin board; quarterly meetings to discuss the budget, business conditions and the economy are held with all employees in groups of 70 to 80; and employees are encouraged to talk to plant managers about their ideas.

(*Source*: E.Ost, 1989: 92–96.)

# 'Brain Day'

## Motivation and Participation

## Solar Press Inc.

## SHR Technology – 32 – Motivational Techniques

Mr John Hudetz, owner of the firm Solar Press Inc. had a problem while managing team-based production activity. The production was based on the achievements based on performance, but it soon rose to an unhealthy competition between the teams. There was no regular maintenance of equipment, employees hoarded ideas from fellow employees for fear of not winning bonus, and team-based production activity caused more problems than it solved. The company has adopted another system, wherein when an individual employee does a good job, their pay increase. All the employees are also given bonuses from a pool based on the company's profits. Thus employees cooperate to help the company make more money. When the company does well, employees get a share. In order to ensure better participation, the company organises one day as 'Brain Day' on which every employee reviews sales, production goals, equipment needs, and so on for the next year. The system ensures that the employees will see how they fit in the overall plan and how their contribution affects the overall performance.

(*Source*: Daft 1998: 539.)

# 'Simply the Best'

## Motivation through Recognition

### Reliance Energy Limited

### SHR Technology – 32 – Motivational Techniques

Reliance Energy, which aims at doing its best, has initiated various measures to improve the efficiency and effectiveness. Reliance Energy is a group company, which ventured into the power sector by taking over the BSES. To motivate the teams and bring in healthy competition the organisation has started 'Simply the Best Awards', recognising the best zone in the technical and commercial functions. For each function, there is an award to be given to the zone, which was the topper, but at the same time the 'Best Zone' award goes to that zone which has scored highest points in the functions. Initially there was some hesitation about the necessity, authenticity, reluctance to participate, etc., but the commitment of the top management was vital to ensure its success. The measure has increased the benchmarks for others to follow and has created an aura of 'achievement motivation' to perform better and win the 'award'. The performance of the units and in turn the organisation has shown positive results.

(*Source*: Authors' self-experience.)

# 'Top Wrench'

## Reward Scheme(s) for Mechanics and Others

### Southwest Airlines—USA

### SHR Technology – 32 – Motivational Techniques

Southwest has very high maintenance standards and celebrates its best mechanics through the 'Top Wrench' programme, created in 1989 to reward the efforts of mechanics, whose contribution might otherwise go unrecognised. To qualify for Top Wrench Award, a mechanic must be trained to work on and taxi every aeroplane in Southwest's fleet. Daily workmanship and attitude are also taken into consideration by the selection committee, a group of former top wrench recipients. Honorees for Top Wrench are selected once a month or once a quarter, depending on the size of the location. Once a year Southwest invites monthly top wrench winners to Phoenix or Dallas for a banquet to honour the Top Wrench of the year. Other occasional and occasionally offbeat awards presented at Southwest have included the *'Luv'*, *'Most Spirited In-Law'*, *'Heart and Soul'*, *'Creativity and Guts'*, *'Training Excellence'*, *'Tell It Like It Is'*, *'Hairdresser of the Year'*, *Sense of Humour Award'*, and *'Positively Outrageous Customer Service Award'*.

(*Source*: Freiberg, 1996: 197.)

# 'Transfer of Training' (TOT)

## Strategic Management Training

## TRW

## SHR Technology – 33 – Training and Development

At TRW, systems learning help focus attention on the important concept of Transfer of Training (TOT). All training activities are designed with a built-in compatibility between what managers are expected to learn and what they are expected to do on their jobs. Here is an example. Following instructions in the concept of competitive strategy, TRW presented a three-phase strategic management seminar to natural business teams between the companies. For example, a divisional vice-president and his/her staff. In phase one, each team receives (a) more instruction in the concepts of competitive strategy and (b) a detailed assignment. The teams must apply the concept to their business and develop an action strategy. Each team must plan a maximum of six actions that it will take over the next 18 months, and it must designate responsibility to particular team members for each action. The teams then, 'go home' to work on their strategy for about eight weeks.

Phase two of the seminar is called 'Mid-term review'. Seminar faculty member visits each team to review its progress on the assignments and provides a detailed feedback on how well the team is applying the concept. Sometimes a team makes major changes at this point. As they recognise, for instance, that their competitive analysis is not thorough enough.

Towards the following eight weeks, phase three of the programme, each team prepares its final strategic presentation to be delivered in the presence of two or three other teams. After each team presents its strategy, the audience provides constructive comments and criticism. Next, the audience votes on whether to accept or reject the strategy, indicating on their ballots what they like and dislike about the strategy. The votes and comments are collected and offered to the presenting team, along with comments and concerns from the faculty members. What is happening here? A powerful peer review process.

Ensuring a tight 'fit' between training and application required that some changes be made in TRWs organisational practices, such as changing the process of developing strategic plan, modifying the compensation systems so that long-term success is rewarded, and changing the performance appraisal process to emphasise long-term thinking, planning and action. However, the biggest change of all was senior management's willingness to encourage the kind of risk taking required to implement some of the strategies. This is the essence of system learning.

(*Source*: Cascio, 1998: 276–77.)

# 'Future Mapping'

## Vision Building and Strategic Planning through Training

### International Training Service (ITS) Limited, UK

### SHR Technology – 33 – Training and Development

ITS is a consulting firm and has developed a process called 'Future Mapping', which helps the individuals, teams and the organisations to create a clear and compelling vision. The process also helps them to decide how to achieve the vision and generate motivation to act. The process has been applied in many corporations and has yielded results. The first step is to build the future plan and by what time the project is going to be completed. The second step is to project self into future and describe the success using the present sense as though it has really happened. Having experienced and enjoyed success, the next step is to look back from the base in the future and identify the key events or achievements, which were crucial to the successful outcome. These milestones will be described as if they were the past. During the process, the participants are asked to identify the new things and the changes made to achieve. The final step is to return to the present; participants are made to know what is needed to achieve the targets. It is very important to review your present situation in a very positive manner and how to drive the teams with enthusiasm to steer along the identified path of success. The main advantage of the whole process is to bring in a sense of motivation that will neutralise negative thinking. This programme also helps in sharing views up and down the organisation which will help in business planning and will lead to a vision being widely understood and accepted.

(*Source*: Conway, 1994: 115.)

# 'WorkOut'

## Problem Solving through Action Learning

## General Electric

Probably one of the most well-known and successful of all corporation action/reflection programmes is GE's WorkOut, which began in 1989. Among the key goals of WorkOut are:

- Solve critical system-wide problems.
- Develop learning capacities of employees.
- Improve responsiveness to customers.
- Minimize vertical and horizontal barriers.
- Rid the company of boundaries and needless bureaucracy.

WorkOut is also seen as an opportunity to provide GE professional with a broad array of functional experiences in organisational learning. WorkOuts generally occur over a 3-day period and involve a group of 40–100 people who meet at a conference centre or hotel. Sessions begin with a talk by CEO Jack Welch or another leader who roughs out a problem agenda for them to fix and then leaves. An outside facilitator breaks the group into action and sets to tackle various parts of the agenda. Over the next 2 days, the groups identify solutions and prepare presentations for the final day. On the third day, GE executive returns and takes a place in front of the room. One by one, the teams present their proposals. The rules of the WorkOut require the executive to make only one of the three responses: (1) agree on the spot (2) say 'no' or (3) ask for more information—in which case the person must charter a team to get it done by an agreed-upon date. Almost always, the response is a 'yes', and a 'no' answer would need great reasoning and destroy the tremendous power and value of the WorkOuts.

(*Source*: Schwandt and Marquardt, 2000: 119.)

# 'Tradition I'

## Disney's Orientation Programme

## Walt Disney Theme Park, USA

## SHR Technology – 33 – Training and Development

One of the most successful orientation programmes for US firm is the one developed by the Disney Organisation. Everyone attends Disney University and must pass 'Traditions I' before going for specialised training. Tradition I is an all-day experience, in which

Disney philosophy, tradition and culture are presented. At Disney, employees are called 'Cast members', and whenever they are working for public, they are 'on stage'. Customers are called 'guests'. Employees are told about all functions and how they relate to the 'show'. They are reminded of how important their roles are in making the show a success. Every ticket taker receive four eight-hour days of instruction in order to learn locations of restrooms when the parade starts, show schedules, and so on. In other words, they are required to know more than the ticket-taking job; they are also expected to know other information to make the guest's stay as enjoyable as possible. Disney emphasises on the 'Disney way' in orientation, training, and follow-up employee evaluation. Because of this emphasis, the company is sometimes criticised for brainwashing its employees. The firm requires the conformity to the Disney way, and employees are given little opportunity to express creativity and innovation. If one examines the success of Disney Theme Park, it is found the wide use of part-time and student recruits helps in the critical nature of their jobs in terms of customer contact. The rigid, highly formalised orientation and wide training programme are probably the best answer to this success. And of course, it is difficult to argue with a success story.

(*Source*: Peters and Waterman, Video.)

## 'Skillware'

### Skill-Based Training

### Manpower Inc., USA

### SHR Technology – 33 – Training and Development

Manpower Inc. is the world's largest supplier of temporary workers. As office automation becomes more complex, employers find it does not pay to hire temporary workers unless they have been trained to operate their specific equipment. Training is expensive and time consuming since the labour turnover of the company grew as high as 35 per cent and training through classroom and on job proved to be more costlier. A programme called Skillware system was designed which is cost-effective as well as a highly effective way of developing skilled operators. It is a disc-based computer programme. The programme leads step by step from disc insertion to document print out on the actual machinery for which he or she is being trained right in the manpower office. It also uses operator-to-operator language. It gives enough humour to offset fatigue. The programme can be mastered within six hours to two days. No instructor is needed and it has an operation manual through which one can operate. Skillware has helped to cement relations between manpower and corporate clients. Three companies, which helped to meet their unique training needs, are Miller Brewing Company, Xerox Corporation and Vista Chemical Company. The system also enables to look at the learning capacity of a person like his efficiency in handling documents, clerical skills, etc., through which the company can offer best candidates to handle the job.

*(Source*: Roscow and Zager, 1988: 138.)

# 'Tiger'

## Sales Training

## Core Healthcare

## SH Technology – 33 – Training and Development

Core Healthcare Limited has grown phenomenally since its inception and became a truly international pharmaceutical and healthcare company. The success of the organisation is because of the unique training given to its sales team. Every new salesman has to undergo a training programme called 'Tiger'. The emphasis in the module is on transforming a meek salesman into aggressive salesman. The theme is, 'in long run, tigers make more friends and close more sales, too', though the meek salesman does a fine job of prospecting and establishing the initial contact. He makes a good presentation, but is not too sharp at replying to sales objections and closing the deal. The programme trains him to view every sales objection as an opportunity for telling more about the product, and at the end, he knows how to close the deal and bag the order.

*(Source*: Jain, 2000: 187.)

# 'Leadership and Performance' (LEAP)

## Leadership Building

## Shell

## SHR Technology – 33 – Training and Development

Shell's Leadership and Performance (LEAP) project is an action-learning programme, which reaches 20,000 employees per year. The strength of Shell's learning organisation derives from the fact that action-learning focuses on business results, the engagement of senior leadership and the involvement of personnel at all levels. To improve the service station revenues along major highways, the company brought together a cross-functional team that was made up of a dealer, union trucker, and four to five marketing executives. New business model and leadership skills were developed to prepare participants to apply new tools to their local market. There were a series of teams, which went through the programme. The teams came back to the 'boot camp' (base camp) for a peer-review meeting. At the end of the third workshop each team sat in a 'fish bowl' environment to review its business plan as other teams looked on. The teams returned home for another 60 days during which they worked to put their ideas into action. At the end of the 60 days they returned to discuss not only their breakthroughs but also their breakdowns. The meetings are being chaired by the group Managing Director himself. The learning enables project teams and other units not only to solve problems and complete projects, but also to reflect on learning from each episode, and bank this learning in institutional memory. This will provide increased adaptability and ability to learn and adjust.

(*Source:* Schwandt and Marquardt, 2000: 149.)

# 'Goal Based Scenario' (GBS)

## Skill Enhancement

## Andersen Worldwide

## SHR Technology – 33 – Training and Development

Andersen worldwide has introduced GBS (Goal Based Scenario) training, which is a simulated task that makes clear to participants what skills they need and why, what problems they are likely to encounter and when; what is the most effective means of dealing with those problems; and why they are effective. Teaching and learning always take place within the context of a clearly perceived need, as part of the larger goals of the organisation. A motivational framework is provided by GBS that serves not only to facilitate the acquisition of individual skills and facts, but also to enable staff to understand how these skills and facts can solve client business problems.

(*Source*: Schwandt and Marquardt, 2000: 222.)

# 'Division Management Simulation' (DIVSIM)

## Overcoming the Downturns

HP

## SHR Technology – 33 – Training and Development

Hewlett Packard's international Headquarters has been running Divsim, for Division Management Simulation. It addresses the need among some of their functional managers for better understanding of the steps they could take to respond to the downturns in the economy. A Scottish economics had designed the simulation for HP Corporation. Four teams of seven players compete to ring up the highest marks on complicated scoring system that considers factors such as profit generation and the shape the company is in at the end of the simulated five-year period in terms of assets, hour, etc. Each team has a General Manager and several functional managers who head divisions corresponding to HPs. One of the main purposes is to teach each manager how the pieces of the company fit together and affect one another; nobody is allowed to play a real-life role. As HP has no lay-off policy, it is vital for managers to understand what to do when the economy goes sour. In Divsim the economy and the demand of HP products can go as sour as the trainer wants it to and the lessons are many. There is one about placing orders in anticipation of need versus real need. If you are backlogged on inventory when economy goes down, you can really be in trouble.

(*Source*: Cook, 1987: 232.)

# 'HR4YOU'

## A Help Desk for Employee Self-Services

Mellon Bank – USA

## SHR Technology – 37—Human Resource Information System (HRIS)

Mellon's help desk, HR generalist with expert system support, combine the benefit of 'multiskilling' and 'functioning with highest level of licensure' to provide twice as much as service at half Mellon's previous cost. Before the 'HR4YOU' help desk, HR specialist costing $28.00 an hour received 20,000 calls from Mellon employees. Calls averaged two minutes, and cost $2.00. Nine thousand of these calls were callbacks because the specialist did not have the information the employee needed and had to look it up or refer the employee to someone else. HR4YOU help desk generalist, costing $13.50 an hour, reduced calls to 11,000 by achieving 85 per cent customer satisfaction at first point of contact. Calls average 90 seconds and cost $1.00. Mellon saved 73 per cent by reducing calls by 45 per cent, using skilled generalist who cost half what specialists cost and achieve higher level of customer service.

(*Source*: Spencer, 1995: 88.)

# 'Survey, Market Analysis and Reporting Tools' (SMART)

## Decision Support System

## Liberty Mutual Insurance Group

## SHR Technology – 37 – Human Resource Information System(HRIS)

Liberty Mutual uses a Windows-based decision-support system called 'Survey, Market Analysis and Reporting Tools' (SMART). The company's need to respond to change, with more then 21,000 employees located in more then 400 offices in the United States and abroad, prompted development of the SMART system. As the company moved to a decentralised structure, it found that managers needed additional compensation information and consulting services. SMART, a multi-user system on a local area network, responds to that need. Here are several defining features of the system:

- automated access to and summarising employee and job information and market data;
- ability to input data either manually or electronically;
- standardised forms for entering and viewing information;
- standardised reports to support job evaluation and market analysis; and
- a user-friendly interface.

(*Source*: Cascio, 1998: 398.)

# 'Communities of Practice' (CoP)

## Sharing Knowledge

### Siemens

### SHR Technology – 39 – Knowledge Management

Siemens believes in the realities of 'Communities of Practice' (CoP) as a structure of communication, sharing and growth. The knowledge management initiative based its Knowledge Management Metrics on the idea that one of the primary values in knowledge management is its ability to expand support communities which the company has identified as an important communication channel.

Knowledge communities: the organisation communities, people dimensions, etc.
Knowledge marketplace: technology involved.
Key Knowledge management processes: sharing and creation.
Knowledge environment: encompasses all mentioned above.

Siemens measures quarterly the knowledge coming into and going out of various communities and the feedback coming and going out. It has different questionnaires that provide information punctually about both quality and quantity within its CoP. It also goes so far on the requirements that evidence of competency in Knowledge Management is part of the employee's formal performance evaluation.

(*Source*: Nilson, 2002: 213.)

# 'Infocosm'

## Bringing Best Practices

### Andersen Consulting

### SHR Technology – 39 – Knowledge Management

Andersen Consulting has placed high priority on developing and utilising the 'Global Best Practices' knowledge base. This knowledge base identifies and describes best practices, best companies, engagement experiences, studies and articles, performance measures, diagnostics, process definitions and process experts. The firm has created 'Infocosm' an information highway to make the process easier and faster to access. To facilitate the exchange of the firm's knowledge capital, the firm developed a team to create and implement a knowledge capital delivery system, which is considered as one of the largest knowledge exchange applications. More than 1,000 CD-ROM discs of the knowledge base have been distributed worldwide and the workshops have been conducted for Andersen staff in offices around the globe. Andersen has a deliberate strategy to gain knowledge through training, research and participation in professional and trade associations. In order to maximise the in-house transfer of conference participation, Andersen strives to have at least three staff members attending seminars or conferences identified as valuable for the firm that enables it towards quality preparation, research and learning.

(*Source*: Schwandt and Marquardt, 2000: 94.)

# Market Oriented Total Management System (MTM)

## Information Sharing and Product Development

## Matsushita Electric

## SHR Technology – 39 – Knowledge Management

Matsushita Electric Industrial is the world's largest consumer electronics market selling in more than 180 countries. The company always took the advantage of knowledge it created in various projects and spiralled that knowledge throughout Matsushita. This has enabled the organisation to identify the type of knowledge required by the changing environment and enhances the enabling conditions continuously. To further enable the dissemination of knowledge, Matsushita installed a new communication infrastructure called 'Market Oriented Total Management System' (MTM) that connected various R&D factories and retail stores online. The company realised that the greatest knowledge creation resides in the free flow and sharing of information among different functional groups. Under this system, the sales and manufacturing departments shared the same explicit knowledge. The system allowed product development teams to obtain instant feedback on how well a particular product or model sold at retail.

(*Source:* Schwandt and Marquardt, 2000: 129.)

# 'Parivartan'

## An Attitudinal Change Initiative through Training

## Indian Airlines, India

## SHR Technology – 40 – Change Management

Indian Airlines during 1996 was convinced that there was a need for attitudinal change, especially in respect of the employees in the front line. The new programme was initiated under the title 'Parivartan'. In Sanskrit 'Parivartan' means 'change'. In phase one, frontline and the operational staff of the northern and western regions were covered. In phase two of the programme the southern and eastern regions were covered. The basic objectives of the Parivartan programme were:

- to bring out the best in everyone;
- build the individual confidence, self-esteem and pride;
- solicit individual motivation to deliver excellent services; and
- develop a culture, which would encourage and support employees shouldering responsibility.

To expose the frontline staff to specific training with a view to enhance their customer relation skills, a number of programmers were organised providing for direct feedback from our customers.

(*Source:* All India Management Association, 1998: 60.)

# 'Freedom to Manage'

## Harnessing Change Management

## British Airport Authority, UK

## SHR Technology – 40 – Change Management

The British Airport Authority (BAA) plc recognised the potential benefits of harnessing creative power of the team as a means of further developing its competitive advantage and securing future success. To this end they instigated a 'freedom to manage' programme designed to stimulate change. The terminal three senior management staff at Heathrow, London, piloted the initiative. The team first identified the critical success factors for the change initiatives. The critical success factors identified were leadership, pace and patience, freedom to act, internal alignment, investment in people, communication, profitability awareness and drive, people guarantees, early results and focus on the frontline. These factors became the focus for further investigation by staff teams, led by an external consultant and with the aim of identifying what would have to be done to close the gap between the present position and the goal of achieving the freedom to manage. The pilot proved successful and was cascaded throughout BAA.

(*Source*: Paton and McCalman, 2000: 245.)

# 'High Performance Work System' (HPWS)

## Performance Orientation

## Kraft Foods Inc., USA

## SHR Technology – 40 – Change Management

Kraft Foods Inc. is a North American food business of Philip Morris Corporation Companies Inc., the largest US based package food company in the world. High Performance Work System (HPWS), a change initiative in Kraft Food has become the change management tool for creating a consistent management philosophy for the goal of operating as one company after the reorganisation. A five-stage high performance work system has been introduced to streamline processes, enhance employees' skills and align human and work systems to increase efficiency and reduce cost. High Performance Work System became a way of determining such factors as total inventory, cost of production and measurement of productivity for all of the new plans and distribution centres throughout North America. The five stages of HPWS runs as; first, organisational assessment, second, business case for change, third, design, fourth, implementation and monitoring and improvement and fifth, transition end of plan. After research and a proven track record, the operation division chose HPWS as the best way to include all that is necessary and would contribute to the vision of the undisputed leader. Kraft opened three green field plants and chose to implement an HPWS design at these locations from the beginning. This method proved to be very successful.

(*Source:* Carter, Giber and Goldsmith, 2001: 12.)

# 'Recharge, Reassure and Rejoice' (Re3)

## Internal Brand Building and Change Management

### Reliance Energy Limited

### SHR Technology – 40 – Change Management

Reliance Energy is part of the Reliance Industries, which is a Fortune 500 company. With the implementation of the power reforms, Reliance has ventured into the power sector by taking over the BSES (Bombay Suburban Electrical Services), which was the main provider of electricity to the city of Mumbai and has been in existence for the past 70 years. When the company has been taken over there were lot of apprehensions and skepticism amongst the larger mass of employees. To bring in the cultural change among the employees and bring in performance orientation, Organisation Development initiative under the banner 'Re3' was initiated. This programme was an internal brand building in which a congruence with the erstwhile culture to the culture of Reliance was the main theme. Also bringing customer orientation and meeting with the challenges of the competitive environment was its main emphasis. The Re3 message was taken across the organisation with the help of select ambassadors from the line function. They were thoroughly trained to conduct the programme and they in turn conducted a series of short duration workshop at various locations of the company inviting all sphere of the hierarchy. A survey was conducted after the programme, and the results of the survey was very encouraging which was clearly stating that due to Re3, they could understand the need for change and they have found improvement in the work atmosphere.

(*Source:* Authors' self-experience.)

TABLE 10.1
**At a Glance List of HR Brands versus Corporations**

| Sl. No. | Brand Name | Aim/Purpose | HR Technology | Organisation |
|---|---|---|---|---|
| 1. | McJobs | Diversity in jobs | Managing Diversity | McDonalds |
| 2. | Working Together | Diversity Training Process | Managing Diversity | Alcon Laboratories |
| 3. | Teamwork Day | Celebration for Knowledge Sharing and Teamwork | Teams | Xerox Inc. |
| 4. | InnovAAtions | Generating Ideas through Teams | Teams | American Airlines |
| 5. | Gap Group | Overcoming the Gaps in Performance | CFT | AT&T |

(*Table 10.1 Contd.*)

*(Table 10.1 Contd.)*

| Sl. No. | Brand Name | Aim/Purpose | HR Technology | Organisation |
|---|---|---|---|---|
| 6. | AMT | Problem Solving | CFT | Maxus Energy |
| 7. | Stretch for Success | Performance Improvement | CFT | TIG Insurance |
| 8. | LDI | Leadership Development through 360-Degree Feedback | 360-Degree Feedback | Hughes Software |
| 9. | SOL | Leadership Building and 360-Degree Feedback | 360-Degree Feedback | Johnson & Johnson |
| 10. | Godfather | Mentoring | Mentoring and Coaching | Dow Chemical |
| 11. | E-mail Mentoring Programme | Mentoring | Mentoring and Coaching | HP |
| 12. | TLP | Transformational Leader-ship through Training | TLP | Reliance Energy Limited |
| 13. | CLP and BLP | Developing Future Managers through Training | TLP | Crompton Greaves Limited |
| 14. | JCATS | Promotion from Within | Recruitment | Federal Express |
| 15. | Job Match | Recruitment from Within | Recruitment | Citibank |
| 16. | Creating Opportunities to Excel | Career Planning and Skill-Based Pay | Career and Succession Planning | City of Englewood |
| 17. | SDP | Role Clarity Workshops | Role Clarity | Gati Limited |
| 18. | PPRDS | Performance Enhancement | PMS | Gujarat Gas Ltd |
| 19. | PEP | Performance Orientation and Change | PMS | Southern California Edison |
| 20. | Benefit Bucks | Matching People with Benefits | Compensation Strategy | Nike |
| 21. | Improshare | Bonus Sharing Formula | Incentive Plans | Carrier Inc. Programmes |
| 22. | Brain Day | Motivation and Participation | Motivational Techniques | Solar Press, Inc. |
| 23. | Simply the Best | Motivation through Recognition | Motivational Techniques | Reliance Energy Limited |
| 24. | Top Wrench | Reward Scheme for Mechanics and Others | Motivational Techniques | Southwest Airline |
| 25. | TOT | Strategic Management Training | Training and Development | TRW |
| 26. | Future Mapping | Vision Building and Strategic Planning through Training | Training and Development | International Training Services Limited |
| 27. | Zen Training | Training Processes for Changing Human Behaviour | Training and Development | Laser Group |

*(Table 10.1 Contd.)*

*(Table 10.1 Contd.)*

| Sl. No. | Brand Name | Aim/Purpose | HR Technology | Organisation |
|---|---|---|---|---|
| 28. | Tradition I | Disney's Orientation Programme | Training and Development | Walt Disney Theme Park |
| 29. | Skillware | Skill-Based Training | Training and Development | Manpower Inc. |
| 30. | Tiger | Sales Training | Training and Development | Core Healthcare |
| 31. | LEAP | Leadership Building | Training and Development | Shell |
| 32. | GBS | Skill Enhancement | Training and Development | Andersen Worldwide |
| 33. | DIVSIM | Overcoming the Downturns | Training and Development | HP |
| 34. | News Scope | Organisational Communication | Internal Communication | Bell Telephone |
| 35. | Ears | Communication and Positive Orientation | Internal Communication | ESSO |
| 36. | HR4YOU | A Help Desk for Employee Self Service | HRIS | Mellon Bank |
| 37. | SMART | Decision support system | HRIS | Liberty Mutual Insurance Group |
| 38. | CoP | Sharing Knowledge | Knowledge Management | Siemens |
| 39. | Infocosm | Bringing Best Practices | Knowledge Management | Andersen Consulting |
| 40. | MTM | Information Sharing and Product Development | Knowledge Management | Matsushita Electric |
| 41. | Parivartan | An Attitudinal Change Initiative through Training | Change Management | Indian Airlines |
| 42. | Freedom to Manage | Harnessing Change Management | Change Management | British Airport Authority |
| 43. | HPWS | Performance Orientation | Change Management | Kraft Foods |
| 44. | Re3 | Internal Brand Building and Change Management | Change Management | Reliance Energy Limited |

# References and Further Readings

All India Management Association. 1998. India: Excel Book.

Byars, Llyod L. and Leslie W. Rue. 1997. *Human Resource Management*, USA: Irwin.

Carter Louis, David Giber and Marshall Goldsmith. 2001. *Best Practices in Organisation Development and Change: Culture, Leadership, Retention, Performance, Coaching*, CA: Jossey-Bass.

Cascio, Wayne F. 1998. USA: *Managing Human Resources*, Irvin/McGraw-Hill.

Conway, Tony. 1994. 'Training as a Means to Delivering Change and for Corporate Strategies', in Uddesh Kohli and Dharni P. Sinha (eds), *HRD Global Changes and Strategies in 2000 AD*, New Delhi: Allied Publishers Ltd.

Cook, Mary F. 1987. *New Directions in HR: A Handbook*, NJ: Prentice Hall Inc.

Daft, Richard L. 1998. *Management*, 4th edn, Fort Worth: The Dryden Press.

Debra, Nelson L. 2003. *Organisational Behaviour*, USA: Thomson-South Western.

Dessler, Gary. 1997. *Human Resource Management*, New Jersey: Prentice Hall.

E.Ost. 1989. 'Gain Sharing's Potential', *Personnel Administrator*, July.

Freiberg, Kevin. 1996. *Nuts*, USA: Bard Press Inc.

Ghosh, Nihar R. 2000. 'Using 360 Degree Feedback for Leadership Development', in T.V. Rao, Vijaya Lakshmi and Rao Raju (eds), *360 Degree Feedback and Performance Management System*, New Delhi: TVRLS/Excel Books.

Jain, Arun Kumar. 2000. *Competitive Excellence*, New Delhi: Vikas Publishing House Pvt Ltd.

Mai, Robert P. 1996. *Learning Partnerships*, Chicago: ASTD/Irwin Professional Publishing.

Nilson, Carolyn. 2002. *Training and Development Year Book*, NJ: Prentice Hall.

Nohria, K.K. 1999. 'Leadership and Human Resource Management', in Udai Pareek and V. Sisodia (eds), *HRD in the Millennium*, New Delhi: Tata McGraw-Hill Publishing Company Limited.

Odenwald, Sylvia B. 1996. *Global Solutions for Teams*, Chicago: Irwin Professional Publishing.

Paton and McCalman. 2000. *Change Management,* New Delhi: Sage Publications.

Peters, Tom and Robert H. Waterman, 'In Search of Excellence', Video cassette.

Rao, T.V. 2001. *360 Degree Feedback*, New Delhi: Excel Books.

Roscow, J.M. and R. Zager. 1988. *Training—the Competitive Edge*, USA: Jossey-Bass.

Schwandt, David R. and Michael J. Marquardt. 2000. *Organisational Learning*, Boca Raton: St. Lucie Press.

Spencer, Lyle M. Jr. 1995. *Reengineering Human Resources*, NY: John Wiley & Sons.

AUTHOR ? *The Across Board Magazine*. 1999. February, USA. ISSUE NO?

Werther, William B., Jr, and Keith Davis. 1996. *Human Resources and Personnel Management*, US: Irwin/McGraw-Hill.

# Part 4

## HR Word Power

# 11    HR WORD POWER

## Content

→ Learning Objectives
→ Illustration with HR Vocabulary
→ Why HR Word Power
→ Content of HR Word Power
→ Conclusion
→ HR Word Power

## Learning Objectives

- To recognise various terminologies those are being used in the discipline of human resource management, personnel management, organisation psychology, organisation behaviour, organisational development, etc.
- To understand and develop a simplified meaning through definition and explanation of all such terminologies.

## Illustration with HR Vocabulary

Imagine a world without dictionary. This means no words to express. It is always a difficult proposition. In communication, everyone uses different words or phrases depending on the context and use. Dictionary is a treasure of words and phrases. It is a methodological and codified gathering of the various meanings and definitions of the words, which are used in the process of communication.

In the world, there are various languages and within the language there are various ways of usage of words in terms of spelling, grammar, pronunciation, etc. General dictionaries are those which give the meanings, verbs, pronunciation information, word derivations, histories or etymologies, illustrations, usage guidance and examples in sentences. Dictionaries try to incorporate new words and modern slang to make them more comprehensive and at the same time omit those, which are no longer in use. However, for specific use, one has to use the single field or specialised dictionary that has been designed and compiled to cover the terms of one particular subject field to remove the ambiguity and also provide the clarity of thought like the dictionary for law, psychology, human resources, etc.

HR Word Power is a compilation of terms, definitions, acronyms and related resources, which are used in HR management. The Word Power has the terms encompassing the whole gamut of HR like training, consulting, compensation, organisation development, employment, manpower planning, benefit administration, safety, etc. Like any other dictionary, HR Word Power is for correct usage of words. However, the limitation is that this Word Power is only 'descriptive' rather than 'prescriptive' which means that it attempts to describe the way words are actually used, rather than how they should be used.

# Why HR Word Power

The HR discipline is growing in leaps and bound along with the contribution of various other disciplines such as sociology, psychology, etc. Like any other profession, HR has its own language and the terms used are unique to the profession. For example, '360-Degree Feedback', in common parlance indicates a circle but in the HR profession, it's an advanced tool used for the performance management and feedback to the employee. It is a proven technology in the HR field, which every HR professional requires to learn and implement as per the needs. Similarly, 'Effective Communication' in HR profession is also equally important as the HR's core role is to deal with the individuals. Every communication in the form of a letter that goes from HR and every word that has been used have a lot of significance. Every action that HR takes has a profound impact on all the employees of the organisation and hence every word must be used very carefully with diligence and tactfully to remove the ambiguity and also avoid any controversy.

HR professionals who are studying the subject or who are in practice might encounter with doubts since each word used in the HRM has got its own significance. For example, though the words like 'cooperation' and 'coordination' or 'effectiveness' and 'efficiency' in common parlance look similar, but they carry a lot of meaning and each word has its own significance. Many scholars have tried to bring in various terms used in the HR function for easy reference and understanding. The HR Word Power might be used to answer many quick fact questions. Definitions could include vast information which at the outset one finds it very easy to understand. For example, in the law profession, constant practicing would enrich one's knowledge and thus, one becomes a real professional. Working with HR Word Power would help in bringing professionalism in the usage of terms by way of understanding accurate meaning and clearing the doubts of many unfamiliar terms.

The main advantage of the HR Word Power is that it enables to cover many words that are used in human relations under one umbrella, if not then, one would have to keep volumes of dictionaries to get the meaning for a single word. At the same time sufficient place can be allocated for proper explanation of the terms and also the other terms that are related to that term. For example, there are different words for communication, such as Vertical Communication, Horizontal Communication, Top Down and Bottom Up, Communication Loop, Communication Process, Communication Structure, Communication Channels, etc. Linking and correlating each of these words would make for easy understanding while reading them. If one has to go through the normal dictionary it would be difficult for him to get the words and at the same time provide the meaning in relation to other similar words.

As mentioned in the previous chapter, we have in this book brought out a comprehensive perspective of all those technologies which every HR practitioner practices. While deliberating or implementing each of these technologies, one might encounter with many words which are sometimes difficult to distinguish. The user might end up using the word which he/she could use in the context rather than having command over what he/she speaks and writes. The HR Word Power is an effort to bring in some of these important words and phrases which are used quite often. This is an unending process. The HR Word Power is not exhaustive in nature with all the words but those important words that are used very often.

## Content of HR Word Power

The HR Word Power contains the terms, phrases, definitions, acronyms and related resources, which are used in HRM. It deals with various elements in it like training, consulting, compensation and benefits, organisation development, employment, manpower planning, social security, etc. Many words which are related to these words are also included and provided with meaning in the context of HRM. The Word Power contains only those terms that are in relevance to HR technologies described in this book and in the normal functioning of the HR professional. It is only a small compilation, and is not exhaustive of all the words of HRM. The terms are dealt with lucid language and given in the definition form to give the correct meaning.

# Conclusion

- Word Power contains the terms used in the HR profession and related to it. The Word Power is being included in the book to give completeness to the author's endeavour to provide the various technologies used in the profession.
- The Word Power has the terms encompassing elements of HRM to give a wider perspective and meaning.
- The Word Power is included in the book as a part, but not as a dictionary by itself. Despite the limitations, the authors have tried to bring in as many words as possible which every HR professional uses.

# Expression Potential with HR Vocabulary

- Action
- Authority and Power
- Career
- Change and Change management
- Coaching and Mentoring
- Communication
- Competencies and Skills
- Conflict and Collaboration
- Culture and Climate
- Efficiency and Effectiveness
- Environment
- Equity
- Expectancy
- Goal
- Group
- HRM
- Job
- Knowledge
- Leadership
- Management
- Motivation
- Organisation
- Organisation Behaviour
- Organisation Development

- Performance Appraisal
- Personality and Behavioural Traits
- Quality
- Research and Theory
- Reward
- Role
- Staff
- Stress
- Structure and Organisation Structure
- Task
- Team
- Training and Learning
- Value
- Work
- Commonly Used Terms in HRM

## Action

Stipulating the specific actions needed to implement a prescribed solution and overseeing their execution.

- *Action Plan*: A description of the specific steps that need to be taken to achieve an objective or bring performance back to an acceptable standard.
- *Action Research*: A database, problem-solving process of organisational character that replicates the steps involved in the scientific method. A cyclical process of identifying system problems, gathering data, taking corrective action, assessing progress, making ongoing adjustments and learning from the experience.
- *Action Research Model*: A model of the organisation development process that permits the development and assessment of original innovative interventions.

## Authority and Power

The right to act, decide, choose, give orders or institute change. Most authority comes from organisational position and is delegated downward. However, the consent of the governed is authority derived from the people and granted to leaders.

- *Authoritarian Leader*: A leader who makes almost all decisions by himself or herself, minimising the input of subordinates. Personality dimension characterised by rigid adherence to conventional values, ready obedience to recognised authority, exhibitions of a negative view of mankind, concern with power and toughness and opposition to the usual subjective feelings.

- **Autocratic Leader**: One who dictates decisions down to subordinates. Leaders who centralise power and decision making in themselves.
- **Chain of Command**: The path of authority from the lowest ranking worker to the chief executive of the organisation.
- **Controlling**: Maintaining organisational activities in conformity with plans and goals. The management functions of evaluating the performance of an organisation or organisational unit to determine whether it is progressing in the desired direction.
- **Coercive Power**: Power that is based on fear. Ability to influence derived from an individual's control over the allocation of punitive rewards. The capacity to punish other people (or to create the perceived threat to do so) so as to influence them.
- **Bottom-up View of Authority**: View that authority begins with the consent of subordinates and then flows upward in the organisation through acceptance of orders, commands and requests.
- **Decentralisation**: Low centralisation; decision making is concentrated low in the organisation. The dispersion of authority and decision making downward and outward through the hierarchy of an organisation. The opposite of centralisation.
- **Delegation**: Assigning tasks and the authority to complete those tasks. The process by which authority and work distribute assignments downward in an organisation whereby supervisors permit their subordinates to make certain decisions.
- **Direct Supervision**: The process by which a superior influences a subordinate's activities toward goal setting and goal attainment. A basic coordination mechanism in which one person takes responsibility for the work of a group of others and has the authority to decide which tasks must be performed, who will perform them, and how they will be linked together to produce the desired end result.
- **Functional Authority**: Authority of staff officials to command line workers in a limited area/issue.
- **Power**: The degree of influence an individual has over another individual or group. A capacity that A has to influence the behaviour of B so that B does something he would not otherwise do. It is the ability to influence the conduct of others and resist unwanted influence in return.
- **Autonomy**: The degree to which a job provides substantial freedom and discretion to the individual in scheduling the work and in determining the procedures to be used in carrying it out. Attribute associated with effectively designed jobs that permit the perception that the job is free from arbitrary control.
- **Responsibility**: The obligation to perform, act, carry out job assignments, meet work expectations, act on perceived needs, or take a position on a set of principles.

- *Capacity*: Superior or invulnerable position in an exchange relationship with another individual or organisation.
- *Legitimate Power*: Power or authority derived from a job title, position in organisation, status symbols, or in some societies, age. The belief by one person or group that it is rightful or desirable for another person or group to influence their actions within specific areas. Power that is delegated legitimately from higher-established authorities to others. Interpersonal power based on holding a position of formal authority.

# Career

A sequence of work-related positions occupied by a person during the course of his lifetime.

- *Career Change*: Change in type of work, organisation, level of management, or geographical location as a result of new technology, promotion, change in interests, reduction in force, termination, development of new competencies, or change in lifestyle.
- *Career Development*: All of the actions necessary to enhance career goals such as training, specialised experience, gaining expertise and skills, and learning to be self-directed. The personnel and human resource management activity that helps organisational members to plan their careers within the enterprise, to help the enterprise achieve its objectives and the employee achieve maximum self-development.
- *Career Management*: A systematic, planned approach to career development.
- *Career Planning*: The process of individuals choosing occupations, organisations, and paths that their career will follow.
- *Career Stage*: A period of time in a person's life characterised by distinctive developmental tasks, concerns, needs, values and activities.
- *Equal Employment Opportunity (EEO)*: Provision of equal opportunities to secure jobs and earn rewards in them, regardless of conditions unrelated to job performance. Having equal access to career opportunities for all individuals, whether minorities or non-minorities, on the basis of achievements and abilities. Non-discrimination in job opportunity because of race, colour, religion, natural origin, sex, or in some cases, age and physical handicap.
- *Mid-Career Crisis*: A general concern that career-minded people have between the ages of thirty-five and fifty-five about their level of career accomplishment, usually accompanied by feelings of dissatisfaction, boredom and restlessness. Usually considered to be part of the midlife crisis.

## Change and Change Management

Any alteration of events, people, circumstances, or situations. Differences that are a function of time. The process of learning new ideas and practices. To alter, vary or modify. Change is both an important impetus and a primary product of the process of organisation development.

- *Change Agent*: A person whose formal role is to bring about organisational (or, sometimes, individual) change and help make it work. Also called an OD (Organisation Development) consultant. A person who manages the organisation development process, serving both as a catalyst for change and as a source of information about organisation development.
- *Change Diffusion*: The ripple effect of change. Every change has a tendency to cause or direct other changes. This process is known as diffusion.
- *Change Resistance*: The tendency to reject change that is externally imposed or over which a person has no influence. Resistance to doing or thinking differently.
- *Internal Change*: Change that occurs within an organisation. May involve people, technology, organisational format, climate, product or service orientation and types of work.
- *Resistance to Change*: Desire not to accept a change or to accept it only partially.
- *Technological Change*: Change in organisation, jobs and society because of introduction of new technologies. Introduction of automobiles, telephones and computers are examples of technological changes affecting society at large.

## Coaching and Mentoring

The process of helping another individual to overcome a specific, immediate problem by giving him or her advice and/or encouragement.

- *Mentor*: Person who serves as a role model to help other employees gain valuable advice on roles to play and behaviours to avoid.
- *Counselling*: Discussion of a problem that usually has emotional content with an employee in order to help the employee cope with it better.
- *Directive Counselling*: Process of listening to an employee's problem, deciding with the employee what should be done, and then telling and motivating the employee to do it.

## Communication

The act of understanding and being understood. Sending, receiving, decoding and interpreting messages. The passage of information and/or messages between or among people (or animals) by use of words, letters, symbols or non-verbal communications. The exchange of information between people through a common set of symbols.

- *Communication Links*: The number of people or steps between the originator of message and its receiver. Each link weakens the probability of message accuracy. The transference and understanding of meaning.
- *Communication Loop*: Two-way flow of information from sender to receiver and back to the sender.
- *Communication Process*: Steps by which a sender reaches a receiver with a message and receives feedback on it.
- *Communication Structure*: The pattern of interactions by which group members share information.
- *Communication Channels*: Any of the verbal and non-verbal sources of communication.
- *Cross-Communication*: Communication across chains of command.
- *Direct Communication*: Face-to-face communication or voice-to-voice communication. Any communication directly between two people.
- *Body Language*: Way in which people communicate meaning to others with their bodies in interpersonal interaction.
- *Channel*: The medium through which a communication message travels.
- *Decoding*: Interpretation of either verbal or non-verbal messages. Retranslating a sender's communication message. A mental process that a receiver uses to decipher a message and make it intelligible. The translation of received messages (signals) into interpreted meanings.
- *Feedback*: A response to a signal or communication. In organisations, the reaction to a decision or communication. In communication, the reaction and response from one communicator to another. The degree to which carrying out the work activities required by a job results in the individual obtaining direct and clear information about the effectiveness of his performance. The response by the receiver to the sender's message. Also, clear and direct information about job outcomes and performances. Information that tells you how well or poorly you have performed.
- *Grapevine*: The informal communication channel. The major information communication network in an organisation, used in the transmission of both rumours and true information. Gossip chain is a grapevine in which a person contacts many others.
- *Language*: A system of shared symbols that the members of an organisation use to communicate cultural ideas and understandings.
- *Listening*: A process that integrates physical, emotional and intellectual inputs in a search for meaning and understanding.
- *Noise*: Any interference in the communication channels other than the intended message. A collective term for several factors that can distort a message as it is transmitted from one person to another.

- **Non-Verbal Communication**: Communication based on media other than spoken words or written material. All behaviours expressed consciously or unconsciously, done in the presence of another (or others) and perceived either consciously or unconsciously. Actions (or inactions) that people take which serve as a means of communication.
- **Information**: Raw facts or data presented in contextual form and that can be processed into knowledge.
- **Information Overload**: A condition in which a person is presented with more information than he or she can possibly process.
- **Information Technology**: The use of computers, software and telecommunications for a wide variety of productivity and communication applications. The use of computers, software and telecommunications for improving white-collar productivity and communications.
- **Interactions**: The verbal and non-verbal communication and contacts that actually take place between people. Refers to the fact that some unit of activity of one-person follows, or is stimulated by some unit of activity of another.
- **Verbal Ability**: A facet of mental ability that reflects the degree to which a person can understand and use written and spoken language.
- **Voice**: The formal opportunity to complain to the organisation about one's work situation.
- **Encoding**: Converting ideas, perceptions and feelings into symbols, such as words on pictures that may be used in message transmission. Converting a communication message to symbolic form. The sender's translation of 'meanings' into messages that can be transmitted.
- **Rumour**: Grapevine information that is communicated without secured standards of evidence being present.
- **Transactional Communication**: Communication that is characterised by gives and takes between two or more people. A two-way communication.

## Competencies and Skills

Areas of personal capability that allow individuals to perform successfully in their jobs by enabling them to achieve the acceptable accomplishment of outcomes or tasks. Examples of what may constitute a competency include knowledge, skills, attitudes, values or other personal characteristics. Competencies required for successful performance may or may not be formally articulated by the employer.

- **Conceptual Skills**: The ability to perceive an organisation or organisational unit as a whole, to understand how its labour is divided into tasks and reintegrated by the pursuit of common goals or objectives, and to recognise important relationships between the organisation or unit and its environment.

* *Technical Skill*: Person's knowledge and ability in any type of process or technique. Methods, procedures and techniques for performing a job. Technical skills are most important at lower managerial levels. An understanding of the specific knowledge, procedures and tools used to make the goods or services produced by an organisation or unit.
* *Assessment Centre*: The administration of a number of predictors generally including simulations assessed by the combined judgement of several experts.
* *Effectiveness*: Getting things accomplished correctly, on time, within costs. Achievement of goal.
* *Human Performance*: The accomplishment of a task in accordance with some preset standard of completeness and accuracy appropriate to evaluating the work of people.
* *Human Potential*: The belief that every person can achieve more, does more and develop their full capabilities.
* *Human Skill*: Ability to work effectively with people and to build teamwork. An ability to lead, motivate, manage conflict and encourage teamwork. The ability to work effectively as a group member and to build cooperation among the members of an organisation or unit.

## Conflict and Collaboration

A process in which an effort is purposely made by A to offset the efforts of B by some form of blocking that will result in frustrating B in attaining his goals or furthering his interests. A disagreement between two or more persons or work groups resulting from an incompatibility of goals, resources, expectations, perceptions or values.

* *Confrontation*: A process in which parties in conflict directly engage each other, openly exchange information on the issues and try to work out the differences between themselves. Bringing forth a controversial topic or contradictory material with which the other party is emotionally involved. To say 'your performance is substandard' is to initiate a confrontation.
* *Consensus*: Discovery of alternatives which are not unacceptable to either of the conflicting parties. Agreement of most of the members of a group.
* *Compromising*: A conflict-handling style that is intermediate in both assertiveness and cooperation. An attempt to 'split the difference' in terms of achieving outcomes.
* *Collaboration*: A situation where each party to a conflict desires to satisfy fully the concern of all parties. Collaborating is a conflict-handling style that is both assertive and cooperative. Concerns for one's own goals and the goals of a counterpart.

478 | Strategic Human Resource Technologies

- **Integration:** The degree of collaboration (cooperation) and mutual understanding actually achieved among the various organisation units. The meshing of individual and organisational goals and the avoidance of conflict among organisational members.
- **Interpersonal Conflict:** Conflict between two or more individuals, sometimes described as a personality clash.
- **Grievance:** A written formal complaint from an employee to a supervisor. Grievance procedure is a systematic series of steps for resolving grievances.
- **Frustration:** Reaction to a blocked need, unresolved conflict, unsolved problem or incomplete or unstated effort. Denial or thwarting of motives by obstacles that lies between the individual goals and the organisational goals.

## Culture and Climate

Social environment of human-created beliefs, customs, knowledge and practices that define conventional behaviour in a society. The shared attitudes and perceptions in an organisation that are based on a set of fundamental norms and values and help members understand the organisation.

- **Climate:** The feeling, tone, spirit or degree of voluntary cooperation found in organisations.
- **Cultural Diversity:** The recognition, acknowledgement, appreciation and positive use of the rich variety of differences among people at work.
- **Cultural Experience:** The amount of exposure a person has had working with people from different countries and cultures.
- **Cultural Shock:** Feeling of confusion, insecurity and anxiety caused by a strange new environment.
- **Organisational Climate:** A set of characteristics of the internal organisational environment as perceived by the organisation members that (a) describes the organisation, (b) distinguishes it from other organisations, (c) is relatively enduring over time, and (d) influences and directs the people within it.
- **Organisational Culture:** An organisation's personality. A relatively uniform perception held of the organisation. The set of values, beliefs and norms that is shared among its members.
- **Organisational Environment:** The objects, persons and other organisations surrounding specific organisational system, including the sources of inputs used by the organisation and the recipients of outputs produced.
- **Organisational Politics:** Any behaviour by an organisational member that is self-serving. The use of behaviours that enhance or protect a person's self-interest.

- *People-oriented Climate*: An organisational climate that emphasises the needs and development of members.

## Efficiency and Effectiveness

Getting things accomplished correctly in minimum time, minimum costs, with optimum utilisation of resources. The ratio of effective output to the input required achieving it.

- *Efficiency Perspective*: An approach to job design that focuses on the creation of jobs that economises on time, human energy, raw materials and other productive resources.
- *Organisational Effectiveness*: The degree to which an organisation is successful in achieving its goals and objectives while simultaneously ensuring its continued survival by satisfying the demands of interested parties, such as suppliers and customers.
- *Organisational Efficiency*: The ratio of outputs produced per unit of inputs consumed; minimising the raw materials and energy consumed by the production of goods and services.
- *Organisational Productivity*: The amount of goods or services produced by an organisation. Higher productivity means that more goods or services are produced.

## Environment

Anything outside the organisation itself. The totality of physical and social factors that are taken directly into consideration in the decision-making behaviour of individuals in the organisation. The context surrounding an organisation consisting of those economic, geographic and political conditions that impinge on the firm.

- *Environmental Change*: An environmental characteristic concerning the extent to which conditions in an organisation's environment change unpredictably.
- *Environmental Complexity*: An environmental characteristic referring to the degree to which an organisation's environment is complicated and therefore difficult to understand.
- *Environmental Diversity*: The degree to which an organisation's environment is varied or heterogeneous in nature.
- *Environmental Receptivity*: The degree to which an organisation's environment supports the organisation's progress towards fulfilling its purpose.

- *Environmental Turbulence*: A state in which environmental units interact in such a way that a new environmental force is created that is more powerful than the units acting separately. The speed and scope of change that occurs in the environment surrounding an organisation.
- *Environmental Uncertainty*: An organisational environment that is perceived as being uncertain due to (a) its large number of environmental units, (b) the complexity of its environmental units to interact, and (c) the rate of change among its environmental units. An environmental characteristic formed by the combination of change and complexity that reflects a lack of information about environmental factors, activities and events.

## Equity

System of rules and principles based on fairness and justice. When the ratio of a person's outcomes to inputs equals the ratio of others' outcomes to inputs.

- *Equity Theory*: A theory of motivation based on the assumptions that people compare their situation with others and expects their return on investment to be equal. A theory of work motivation based on the idea that people compare their input–output ratio to other people doing comparable work or having comparable backgrounds.

## Expectancy

The perceived probability that a particular act will be followed by a particular outcome, e.g., studying hard is highly related to receiving a good grade (outcome). Strength of belief that work related effort will result in successful completion of a task (performance). A person's beliefs regarding the link between that individual's efforts and his or her performance.

- *Expectancy Model*: Theory that motivation is a product of three factors: valence, expectancy and instrumentality.
- *Expectancy Theory*: The theory that behaviour is directed by the value of a potential outcome and the anticipated consequence of the action. Any theory of human motivation that centres on the idea that people will expend effort if they believe that effort will lead to a desired outcome, and whether or not that outcome will lead to a reward. The strength of a tendency to act in a certain way depends on the strength of an expectation that the act will be followed by a given outcome and on the attractiveness of that outcome to the individual.

# Goal

A desired outcome of a planned series of actions. A desired state of affairs. Desired end states. Concrete formulations of achievements that the organisation aims for within set periods of time.

- *Goal Clarity*: Goals must be clear if they are to be useful for directing effort. If they are clear and specific, the employee will have clear knowledge of the expectations of the boss.
- *Goal Orientation*: Behaviour that is consistently directed towards well-defined goals. A distinction drawn between people who approach a task with the goal of learning how to improve themselves (learning orientation) from those whose goals are strictly to perform at a certain level (performance orientation).
- *Goal Setting*: Managerial process associated with formulating, revising and implementing organisation goals, both long-run and short-run. The process of developing, negotiating, and formalising targets or objectives that an employee is responsible for accomplishing.
- *Goal Succession*: Introduction of new goals when the old ones have been accomplished or discarded.
- *Short-range Goals*: Goals with a time frame of completion of less than two years.
- *Superordinate Goal*: Goal that integrates the efforts of individuals or groups.
- *Vision*: A challenging and crystallised long-range portrait of what the organisation and its members can and should be—a possible (and desirable) image of the future.
- *Mission*: An organisation's purpose or reason for being.

# Group

More than two people gathered together with coordinated efforts to achieve common goals. Two or more individuals, interacting and interdependent, who come together to achieve particular objectives. A number of persons who communicate with one another often over a span of time, and who are few enough so that each person is able to communicate with all the others, not at second hand, through other people, but face to face.

- *Group Cohesiveness*: The attractiveness of the group to its members, which leads to a feeling of unity and 'stick-togetherness'.
- *Group Decision Support System*: The use of computers, decision models and technological advances to remove communication barriers, structure the decision process and generally direct the group's discussion.
- *Group Dynamics*: Social process by which people interact fact to face in small groups. The everchanging relationships among group members. Interaction among

group members. The study of the internal workings and processes of formal and informal groups; small-group psychology.

- *Group Effectiveness*: An assessment of the extent to which a group is accomplishing its task in the most productive and satisfactory manner.
- *Group Pressure*: Unwritten, informal pressures by group members to force individual members to conform to group norms.
- *Group Structure*: How a group is organised or the patterns of differentiation and interrelationships among roles.
- *Inner Circle*: A group within the dominant coalition that meets and actually maps out the salient features of the goals and strategies when the dominant coalition is too large or conflicting.
- *Integrated Work Team*: A group that decides the specific allocation of the tasks assigned to it. Implementing job enlargement in a group of interdependent employees.
- *Autonomous Groups*: Work groups that are self-managing in terms of planning the work, controlling their pace and quality, and making many of the decisions traditionally reserved for management. Implementing job enrichment to a group of interdependent employees.
- *Autonomous Work Team*: A group that is free to determine how the goal assigned to it is to be accomplished and how tasks are to be allocated.
- *Networks*: Group of people who develop and maintain contact to informally exchange information, usually about a shared interest.
- *Networking*: Being active on a network.
- *Norm*: Informal group requirement for the behaviour of its members. Expected (normal) behaviour of a group. Acceptable standards of behaviour within a group that are shared by the group's members. Generally agreed upon standards of member and group behaviour that has emerged as a result of member interaction over time. A strong set of expectations that members of a role set have for the role occupant.
- *Self-contained Work Groups*: Organisational groups that can function independently.
- *Semi-Autonomous Groups*: Groups that must follow the management direction needed to ensure adherence to organisational policies but otherwise manage themselves.
- *T-Group*: A popular form of encounter group that is highly unstructured. T-groups, as part of sensitivity training, were originally developed for training managers to become more open and honest with people but now are used widely in non-work settings.
- *Formal Group*: For official use. Usually refers to policies, procedures and signed memoranda. Formal group is a designated work group defined by organisation's structure. Groups established by the organisations that have a public identity and goal to achieve.

- **Participation**: Involvement by all members of organisations in key decision process. Sharing of power between managers and employees. Supervisory behaviours characterised by allowing subordinates' influence in the supervisor's decision-making process. Mental and emotional involvement of persons in group situations that encourage them to contribute to group goals and share responsibility with them.
- **Cohesiveness**: Degree to which group members are attracted to each other, rely on one another and share common goals. The strength of the members desires to remain in the group and their commitment to the group. A measure of the interpersonal attraction among members of a group and their attraction to the group as a whole.
- **Collectivism**: The process of placing heavy emphasis on the group and valuing harmony among its members.
- **Constituency Groups**: Groups such as employees, customers and suppliers upon whom the survival of an organisation depends. Constituency groups make demands that they expect will be fulfilled in return for their support of the organisation.
- **Differentiation**: The second stage of group development, characterised by conflicts that erupt as members seek agreement on the purpose, goals and objectives of the group and the roles of its members.
- **Coalition**: Any formal or informal group that engages in united actions to promote their own interests. Two or more individuals who combine their power to push for or support their demands. A group that forms so as to allow its members to combine their political strength and thereby pursue interests they hold in common.

# HRM

A set of distinctive activities, functions and processes that are directed at attracting, directing and maintaining an organisation's human resources.

- **Human Capital**: The knowledge, skills and competencies that reside within employees. Unlike structural capital, human capital is always 'owned' by the individual employees who possess it. Nevertheless, human capital is the source of considerable value to organisations as the renewable portion of intellectual capital which is the constant source of creativity and innovation, and has the ability to change within an organisation.
- **Human Relations**: Term applied to organisational behaviour early in its history and especially applied to practices that were less sophisticated, shallow and faddish. The art and practice of using systematic knowledge about human behaviour to achieve organisation and/or personal objectives.
- **Human Resource Cost Accounting**: The activity of assigning, budgeting for and reporting the costs of human resources incurred by an organisation. Ideally, human

resources accounting also assigns, budgets for, and reports on the income derived from the same human resources, relating the costs and income together. In practice, identifying the costs of human resources (such as salaries and training costs) has been fairly straightforward while attributing income to human resources has been more difficult.

- *Human Resource Forecasting*: Estimating the size and make-up of the future workforce necessary to accomplish the goals of the firm (Formerly referred to as manpower planning).
- *Human Resources Valuation*: The assignment of value to employees in their positions within an organisation based on the future economic services those employees are expected to render. In economic terms, employees are valued as the present worth of the services expected to be rendered to the organisation throughout the individual's life. This formulation takes into account the likelihood that an individual will stay with the organisation for a particular period of time.
- *Human Behaviour*: Any actions or activities engaged in by people including both external (such as movement) and internal activities (such as thinking and feeling).
- *Industrial Humanism*: Series of ideas about human resource management, which grew in popularity during the early 1960s and was based on optimistic assumptions about man and the viability or organisational means to humane ends. Industrial humanists are those who believe that organisations will not survive in the future unless they make significant investments in utilising the untapped potential of their employees.
- *Human Factors Engineering*: A type of methods engineering in which experts design machines, operations and work environments so that they better match human capacities and limitations.

# Job

A series of tasks that has been assigned to an individual to perform.

- *Job Content*: Conditions that relate directly to the job itself and the employee's performance of it, rather than conditions in the environment external to the job.
- *Job Context*: Job conditions in the environment surrounding the job, rather than those directly related to job performance.
- *Job Depth*: The degree of influence the employees have over their job environment. The amount of discretion that a jobholder has in choosing job activities and outcomes.
- *Job Descriptions*: Detailed statements of the activities, duties and responsibility of each position.

- *Job Design*: The way that tasks are combined to form complete jobs. The assignments of task activity duties and responsibilities to organisational members so as to accomplish organisational goals. The deliberate, purposeful planning of positions, including all its structural and social aspects and their effect on the employee.
- *Comprehensive Job Enrichment*: A type of job design that combines both horizontal and vertical improvements to stimulate employee motivation and satisfaction.
- *Job Engineering*: Job design techniques primarily concerned with product design, process design, tool design, plant layout, work measurement and operator methods.
- *Job Enlargement*: Policy of giving workers a wider variety of duties in order to reduce monotony. The horizontal expansion of jobs. Increasing the scope of a job, usually with the intention of increasing both satisfaction and performance. Increasing the scope of an employee's job. The expansion in the number of different tasks performed by an individual.
- *Job Enrichment*: A technique popularised by Frederick Herzberg for improving performance by providing greater employee control and responsibility for all aspects of assigned tasks. The vertical expansion of jobs. The addition of tasks that allows the employee to assume more responsibility for planning, organising, controlling and evaluating his/her own work. Policy of adding motivators to a job to make it more rewarding. Increasing the depth of an employee's job.
- *Job Involvement*: Degrees to which employees immerse themselves in their jobs, invest time and energy in them, and view work as a central part of their overall lives. The degree, to which a person identified with his job, actively participates in it, and considers his performance important to his sense of self-worth.
- *Job Overload*: Increasing the number of tasks, amount of work, or level of responsibility beyond an employee's ability to perform.
- *Job Performance*: The output of a job activity; how well a person does in meeting the demands of his or her job.
- *Job Range*: The number of tasks that a jobholder performs to complete the job.
- *Job Redesign*: The changing of job tasks.
- *Job Rotation*: The periodic shifting of a worker from one task to another. Periodically shifting an employee from one job to another. The movement of the employee between different tasks over time. It is closely related to job enlargement. A process whereby an individual systematically moves from one job to another over the course of time. A job rotation can also be a type of horizontal job enlargement in which workers are rotated among several jobs in a structured, predefined manner.
- *Job Satisfaction*: An attitude toward work; how one feels towards his or her job. Set of favourable or unfavourable feelings with which employees view their work. The perception that one's job enables one to fulfil important job values.

- *Job Specification*: Detailed statements of the skill requirements associated with a job.
- *Job Scope*: The number and variety of tasks included in any job.
- *Job-Oriented Behaviour*: Leadership behaviour that focuses on careful supervision of employees' work methods and performance level.
- *Vertical Job Enrichment*: A type of job design based on the idea that gives jobholders the discretion to choose job activities and outcomes will improve their satisfaction.

## Knowledge

Wisdom and attitude that an individual attains by a self-learning process over a period of time.

- *Knowledge as Power*: The ability of individuals, groups or departments to control or possess knowledge critical to the attainment of the organisation's goals.
- *Knowledge of Results*: Providing feedback to people so that they know how well they are performing an assigned task. This process is a key principle of learning.
- *Knowledge Society*: Society in which the use of knowledge and information dominates work and employs the largest proportion of the labour force.
- *Knowledge Worker*: A person whose work involves primarily conceptual skill-managers, professionals, technicians and sales representatives.

## Leadership

Process of encouraging and helping others to work enthusiastically toward achieving objectives. The act of obtaining voluntary compliance from others. Influencing others because they want to be influenced or because they believe and support the leader's perceived power. The ability to influence a group towards the achievement of goals. The ability of one person to influence the behaviour of another. The use of non-coercive influence to direct and coordinate the activities of the members of an organised group towards the accomplishment of group objectives.

- *Leader*: The person who is in charge of planning, organising and controlling in a group.
- *Leadership Style*: The characteristic manner or typical approach a particular person uses in leading people. Many different leadership styles are possible including

participatory style, production-oriented, i.e., task oriented style, etc. Total pattern of a leader's actions, as perceived by the leader's employees.

- *Achievement Oriented Leadership*: Leadership that is goal directed rather than based on personal power or survival needs. A type of leader behaviour, which encourages and supports improvement of subordinates, high standards of performance, excellence in performance.
- *Democratic Leader*: One who shares decision making with subordinates. A leader who works to ensure that all subordinates have a voice in making decisions.
- *Directive Leadership*: Leadership style based on giving orders, directing activities of others, or setting goals for others to achieve. A type of leader behaviour, which specifies expectations, rules and regulations, scheduling and standards of performance.
- *Informal Leader*: An individual who emerges over time with relatively high influence in the group. Persons who have the largest amount of status in the informal organisation, and emerge to exhibit influence on informal group members.
- *Laissez-Faire Leader*: A leader who lets a group run itself with minimal intervention from upper levels of the organisational hierarchy.
- *LPC*: Stands for least-preferred co-worker. A measure of leadership style.
- *Path-Goal Leadership*: Model that states that the leader's job is to create a work environment through structure, support and rewards that help employees reach the organisation's goals. Emphasises the influence of the leader on subordinate goals and the paths to these goals.
- *Charisma*: A leadership characteristic that inspires and influences employees to take early and sustained action to carry out one's vision.
- *Charismatic Leadership*: Creating a new vision of an organisation and getting group members to commit themselves enthusiastically to the new mission, structure and culture embodied in the vision. Encouraging members to transcend self-interests on behalf of the organisation as a whole.
- *Positive Leadership*: Leaders who emphasise rewards to motivate people.
- *Self-Leadership*: The act of leading oneself to perform naturally motivating tasks and managing one to do work that is required but not naturally rewarding.
- *Situational Approach to Leadership*: Approach to leadership research that focuses on those relationships between leader behaviours and situational characteristics that result in leader performance. Leadership style and skills determined by situation rather than by personal characteristics.
- *Situational Leadership Theory*: A leadership model based on the idea that the leader must take into account the maturity of the followers in choosing the right blend of task and relationship.
- *Emergent Leader*: A leader who, although not given the formal title of a leader, emerges from the group to assume a leadership role.

- *Social Leader*: Person who helps restore and maintain group relationships.
- *Transformational Leaders*: Managers who initiate bold strategic changes to position the organisation for its future.

## Management

A field of study devoted to determining how best to attain goals in organisations. The integration of both human and material resources toward common organisational goals. A process of planning, organising, directing and controlling organisational behaviours so as to accomplish a mission through the division of labour.

- *Manager*: A person who is responsible for planning, organising, directing and controlling behaviour in organisations.
- *Management Development*: Any planned effort to improve current or future manager performance.
- *Management Assessment Centre*: A method for evaluating managerial ability and motivation in an off-the-job situation. Managers participate in a variety of situational exercises that elicit behaviour crucial to managerial performance.
- *Management by Walking Around (MBWA)*: Communication and learning that occurs when managers take the initiative to systematically make contact with a large number of employees.
- *Management Information System (MIS)*: Computer based system designed to give timely and relevant information to managers.
- *Multiple Management*: Middle-management committees to improve the participation of managers below top organisational levels.
- *Consultative Management*: Systems of management in which employees are encouraged to think about issues and contribute their own ideas before decisions are made.
- *Directing*: Defining and implementing an internal organisational environment conducive to utilising human resources for goal attainment. The management functions of encouraging and guiding employees' efforts toward the attainment of organisational goals and objectives.
- *Japanese Management*: A management philosophy that consists of the basic orientation towards quality and standards with focus on people in which people are the most important assets of an organisation.
- *Managing by Exception*: The focus on novel and unexpected problems by management. Only significant deviations from standards are brought to the attention of the next higher level of management.

- *Organising*: The management functions of developing a structure of interrelated tasks and allocating people and resources within this structure.
- *Planning*: The specification of the means necessary for the accomplishment of goals and objectives before action toward those goals has begun. The management function of deciding what to do in the future—that is, setting goals and establishing the means to attain those goals.
- *Span of Management*: Number of people a manager directly oversees.
- *Scientific Management*: A body of literature developed in the early 1900s concerned with incentives, selection, training and the design of jobs to eliminate time and motion waste. Early management that sought to effect efficient cooperation, minute work analysis, time-and-motion study, incentive pay, job isolation, scientific selection training and managerial indoctrination. A school of management thought that emphasises maximising production from people through such means as proper selection, efficient job design and financial incentives.

## Motivation

Internal causes of behaviour. Drives, needs, desires that precede and cause activities. The willingness to do something conditioned by this action's ability to satisfy some need for the individual. A predisposition to act in a specific goal-directed manner. Strength of the drive toward an action. The factors that initiate, direct and sustain human behaviour over time.

- *Motivator Factors*: Characteristics of the job that influence the amount of satisfaction experienced at work.
- *Motivators*: It is associated with positive feelings about work. Typical motivators include the work itself, a challenging job, personal recognition and responsibility.
- *Achievement Motivation*: The need to get things accomplished. Usually the need to be part of an organisation that excels or to gain personal goals. Drive to overcome challenges and obstacles in the pursuit of goals.
- *Need Hierarchy*: There are different levels of need associated with an individual. Starting from the basic needs of food, clothing and shelter, the second level includes the physiological and safety needs; the third are social and psychological needs. The fourth need is esteem, followed lastly, by need for self-actualisation. The lower order needs must be partially satisfied before higher level needs become operational.
- *Needs, Primary*: Basic physical needs.
- *Needs, Secondary*: Social and psychological needs.

- *Hygiene*: Extrinsic factors associated with an individual's negative feelings about the work. Hygiene factors are the characteristics of the job that, according to Frederick Herzberg, influence the amount of dissatisfaction experienced at work.
- *Intrinsic Motivators*: Internal rewards that a person feels when performing a job, so that there is a direct and immediate connection between work and reward. The pleasure or value associated with the content of a work task.
- *Need*: Some internal state that makes certain outcomes appears attractive.
- *Self-Actualisation*: Self-fulfilment. Defining and doing those things that are personally satisfying. According to Maslow this is the highest need. The drive to become what one is capable of becoming. A need relating to self-fulfilment or attaining one's actual potential.
- *Empowerment*: The process of identifying and removing the conditions that causes powerlessness while enhancing feelings of self-efficacy.

# Organisation

The planned coordination of the activities of two or more people in order to achieve some common and explicit goal through division of labour and a hierarchy of authority. A relatively permanent social entity characterised by its goal-oriented nature, specialisation and structure. An assembly of people and materials brought together to accomplish a purpose that would not be achievable through the efforts of individuals working alone.

- *Organisation Chart*: A schematic representation of the formal structural relationships in an organisation.
- *Organisation Design*: The process of diagnosing the situation that confronts a particular organisation, then selecting and implementing the organisation structure most appropriate for that situation. The prescribed relationships by which jobs are related to each other in order to achieve a balance between specialisation and coordination.
- *Organisation Size*: The number of members in an organisation; its volume of sales, clients or profits; its physical capacity (for example, a hospital's number of beds or a hotel's number of rooms); or the total financial assets that it controls.

# Organisation Behaviour

A field of study that investigates the impact that individuals, groups and structure have on behaviour within organisations for the purpose of applying such knowledge toward improving an organisation's effectiveness. Study and application of knowledge about how people as individuals and groups act within organisations. A field of study that endeavours to understand, explain, predict and change human behaviour as it occurs in the organisational context. Integrated framework of elements that portrays how behaviour is guided toward achievement of organisational goals.

- *Behaviour*: Any act by a person either overt (visible) or covert (hidden). All behaviours are a response to some internal or external stimuli.
- *Behavioural Sciences*: The body of knowledge from sociology, psychology, economics and anthropology pertaining to why and how people behave as they do. According to Joe Kelly, behavioural science is the study of human behaviour that uses whatever body of knowledge is most relevant.
- *Models of Organisational Behaviour*: Underlying theories or frameworks that act as conscious or unconscious but powerful guides to managerial thought and behaviour. Also known as paradigms.
- *Perception*: Interpretation of sensory awareness. The act of interpreting what is seen, heard, smelled, tasted, felt, or sensed in other ways such as anticipation based on past events. A process by which individuals organise and interpret their sensory impressions in order to give meaning to their environment. Individual's own view of the world.
- *Adaptability*: The ability of a person to display flexibility and versatility in his or her behaviour at different times and in different situations.
- *Adaptation*: Tendency, over a period of time, to become accustomed to repeated events, sensations, styles or rules. For example, a person may become adapted to background noise at work and learn to ignore it.
- *Aggression*: Usually 'attack' behaviour; expressions of hostility, or in some cases intense determination to achieve a particular goal.
- *Assertiveness*: A power tactic; setting deadlines, giving orders and demanding compliance with requests. Assertiveness training teaches people to be more direct, honest and expressive as a means of dealing with anxiety-producing situations.
- *Empathy*: Understanding another person from that person's point of view. Understanding feelings and ideas from another's frame of reference.
- *Morale*: The general satisfaction level of an individual or group. It is the composite of feelings, attitudes and sentiments that contribute to a general feeling of satisfaction. Level of job satisfaction within a group.
- *Negative Reinforcement*: Termination of a pre-existing unpleasant event when the desired target behaviour occurs in order to increase the frequency of that behaviour. The increase in response that occurs when engaging in the response leads to the removal of an aversive stimulus. Removing something negative (such as a penalty

or uncomfortable situation) when somebody makes the desired response. Part of behaviour modification and instrumental learning. Removal of an unfavourable consequence that accompanies behaviour.

- **Positive Reinforcement**: The increase in response that occurs when engaging in the response leads to receipt of a pleasurable stimulus. Favourable consequence that accompanies behaviour and encourages repetition of the behaviour. Feedback and rewards for correct or desired behaviour. A reward that strengthens a desired behaviour. A reward for making a particular response such as receiving approval from a boss for being prompt.
- **Contingency Approach**: A view of organisations similar to a systems perspective but which focuses more sharply on specific relationships in well-defined situations. An approach to management that states that effective structure, leadership, motivation, design, etc., depends upon situational factors. The view that no single theory, procedure or set of rules is useful in every situation. Contingency approach to Organisation Behaviour describes the philosophy that different environments require different behavioural practices for effectiveness.
- **Contingency Model of Leadership**: Model, which states that the most appropriate leadership style, depends on the favourableness of the situation, especially in relation to leader–member relations, task structure and position power.
- **Ego:** The conscious mind that consists of feelings, thoughts, perceptions and memories of which we are aware and can express to others and ourselves.
- **Ego States:** Psychological positions of parent, adult and child that form the basis for social transactions.

## Organisation Development

The systematic application of behavioural science knowledge at various levels (group, inter-group and total organisation) to bring about planned change. A planned approach to interpersonal, group, inter-group, and organisation-wide change that is comprehensive, long-term and under the guidance of a change agent. Change-oriented activities.

- **Planned Organisational Change:** Any alteration in the environment, technology, structure, management process or decision process designed to help achieve organisational goals.
- **Grid OD**: A six-phase programme of organisation development based on Blake and Mouton's managerial grid.
- **Managerial Grid**: A system developed by Robert Blake and Jane Mouton for measuring management style based on both concern for people and concern for task accomplishment. A framework for simultaneously examining the concern

for production and people dimensions of leadership. Also an Organisation Development programme for teaching leaders team management—getting work accomplished through committed people. A nine-by-nine matrix outlining eighty-one different leadership styles. Framework of management styles based on the dimensions of concern for people and concern for production.

- *MAPS*: Multivariate analysis, participation and structure. A structural Organisation Development technique.
- *Intervention*: A particular organisation development technique, such as counselling or team building that is used to stimulate change in organisations.

# Performance Appraisal

Process of evaluating the performance of employees.

- *Performance Evaluation*: The assessment of a person's performance in achieving job objectives. The process by which an organisation obtains data about an employee's effectiveness.
- *Performance Feedback*: Providing performance evaluation both formal and informal. Timely provision of data or judgement regarding task-related results.
- *Performance Monitoring*: Observing behaviour, inspecting output, or studying documents of performance indicators.
- *Halo Effect*: Drawing a general impression about an individual based on a single characteristic. The process in which the perceiver evaluates all dimensions of another person solely according to one impression, either favourable or unfavourable.
- *Management by Objectives (MBO)*: A goal-setting process that involves managers and their subordinates jointly setting goals for work performance and personal development, evaluating progress towards these goals; and integrating individual, departmental and organisational goals. A management system based on achievement of well-defined, attainable, time-limited, quantitative goals and objectives at every level and by every person in an organisation. Process by which a superior and subordinate jointly determine the subordinate's performance goals, followed by an evaluation of the subordinate's performance based on these performance goals.
- *Objectives*: Those goals an individual or group decides must be accomplished. Good objectives are specific, measurable, assigned to individuals or groups and are time-limited (scheduled). The specific goals against which actual performance is compared. An integral part of MBO.
- *Objectivity*: In science, the degree to which a set of scientific findings is independent of any one person's opinion about them.

- *Productivity*: A performance measure including effectiveness and efficiency. Ratio that compares units of output with units of input.
- *Recency Effect*: Influence on the decision-maker through information discovered near the end of the search process.
- *Self-appraisal*: The process of asking individuals to identify and compare their strengths and weaknesses.
- *Stated Goals*: Goal statements that appear in formal documents made available to the public.
- *Evaluation*: Measuring the effectiveness of planned actions to determine whether additional action is required.

## Personality and Behavioural Traits

Tendencies or predisposition to respond to a stimulus (situation) in a particular way.

- *Traits and Abilities*: Early studies of leadership attempted to identify specific characteristics (traits) and skills (abilities) common to all leaders. Such studies have yielded very little useful results.
- *Type A Behaviour*: Aggressive involvement in a chronic, incessant struggle to achieve more and more in less and less time, and, if necessary, against the opposing efforts of other things or other persons.
- *Type A People*: Individuals who are aggressive and competitive, set high standards and put themselves under constant time pressures.
- *Type A Personality*: Characteristics of this personality type include: a chronic sense of time urgency; an extremely competitive, almost hostile orientation; an aversion to idleness; an impatience with barriers to task accomplishment.
- *Type B Behaviour*: Rarely harried by the desire to obtain a wildly increasing number of things or to participate in an endlessly growing series of events in an ever-decreasing amount of time. A behaviour patterns the opposite of Type A. A relaxed, patient, relatively contented approach to life.
- *Type B People*: Individuals who are relaxed and easygoing and accept situations readily.
- *Type B Personality*: Characteristics of this personality type include: unlikeliness to overreact to situations or to behave competitively or aggressively in situations where competitive behaviour is inappropriate. Lack of status and consciousness. Minimal need for recognition for achievement; and a contemplative orientation towards setting goals and examining alternatives.
- *Type Z Organisation*: A new approach to management in which an organisation would draw characteristics from both successful Japanese and US firms and blend them to fit the economic climate and culture of the United States.

- *Traits:* Tendencies or predisposition to respond to a stimulus (situation) in a particular way.
- *Traits and Abilities:* Early studies of leadership attempted to identify specific characteristics (traits) and skills (abilities) common to all leaders. Such studies have yielded very little useful results.
- *Transactional Analysis (TA):* Study of social transactions between people so as to develop improved communication and human relationships. Defines and analyses communication interactions between people. A theory of personality. A technique for improving interpersonal relationships that looks upon every human relationship as a transaction between the ego states (parent, adult, child) of people.

## Quality

Is a perceived criterion for a product or services one sets for oneself or standards that are universally set and accepted. It may be for an individual a state of mind, while for others a value for money.

- *Total Quality Management:* The process of getting every employee involved in the task of searching for continuous improvements in their operations.
- *Quality Circles:* A technique for encouraging genuine participation through worker–manager problem-solving groups that meets on a regular basis. A voluntary work group of employees, who meet regularly to discuss their quality problems, investigate causes, recommend solutions and take corrective actions. Voluntary groups that receives training in statistical techniques and problem-solving skills and then meet to produce ideas for improving productivity and working conditions. Small groups of employees who meet on company time to identify and resolve job-related problems.
- *Quality of Work Life (QWL):* An organisational philosophy that concentrates on development of a work climate that views both managers and employees as responsible for success or failure of the enterprise. Favourableness or unfavourableness of a job environment for people.
- *Quality of Work Life Movement:* Attempts to alter organisational structure and process to improve both the well-being of workers and the productivity of the organisation.
- *Quality Perspective:* An approach to job design in which elements of the efficiency and satisfaction perspectives are combined to improve the quality of goods or services produced.
- *Kaizen:* The widespread belief in Japan that everyone should constantly drive themselves to be seeking ways to improve the quality of everything around them.

## Research and Theory

The process of gathering and interpreting relevant evidence that will either support a behavioural theory or help change it. A systematic explanation of some phenomenon or phenomena based upon research or empirical knowledge. The popular meaning of the term 'theory' refers to speculative explanations for phenomena, or impractical ideas. A set of interrelated constructs, definitions, and propositions that present a systematic view of phenomena by specifying relations among variables.

- *Hypothesis:* A statement about the relationship between two or more variables. Statement or proposition usually based on observation or past information that is tested in an experiment or research study. It may be denied or supported but never proved conclusively. A specific, testable prediction derived typically from a theory, about the relationship between two variables.
- *Data:* Facts, statistics, or bits of knowledge from which conclusions can be drawn, thus converting them into information. Data is the plural of datum.
- *Theories:* Explanations of how and why people think, feel and act as they do.
- *Theory X:* The traditional management assumptions are that people do not like work, shun responsibility, are not normally creative, and must be controlled. The assumption about the employee is that he/she dislikes work and responsibility, is lazy, and must be coerced to perform. These are a set of autocratic and traditional assumptions about people. From the managerial point of view, it assumes that non-managerial employees have little interest in attaining organisational goals and must therefore be motivated to satisfy the needs of the organisation.
- *Theory Y:* According to Theory Y, the assumption is that work is as natural to people as play, and that under the right conditions, people enjoy work, seek responsibility, are normally creative, and are self-controlled. The assumption is that employees like work and can exercise self-direction. It is a human and supportive set of assumptions about people. The managerial point of view assumes that non-managerial employees readily direct their behaviour toward organisational goals if they are given the opportunity to do so.
- *Theory Z:* Model that adapts the elements of Japanese management systems to the US culture and emphasises both cooperation and consensus decision processes. Under this theory, the management and employee assumptions are that organisational success is dependent on managers and employees working in partnership, each sharing responsibility for the organisation's achievements or failures.
- *Close-Ended Questions:* Those questions presented in an interview or survey format, which direct the respondent to simply select and mark the answers, that best represent their own feelings.
- *Open-Ended Questions:* Interview or survey formats in which employees respond in their own words to express their feelings, thoughts and intentions.

- *Diagnosis*: Gathering information about a troublesome situation and analysing it to develop a problem statement.
- *Inference*: 'Jumping to conclusions'. Development of a belief about an event, person, or circumstance without full knowledge of factual data. Interpretation of symbols that is based on assumptions, not facts.

## Reward

It is recognition of a person's achievement of a task/target and its acknowledgement in a monetory or non-monetory form.

- *Reward Power*: The capacities to control and administer items that are valued by other people so as to influence them. The ability to distribute anything of value. Interpersonal power based on the ability to control how desirable outcomes is distributed.
- *Reward System*: A set of inducements allocated to attract, encourage, and retain valued organisational members.
- **Competitive Group Rewards:** Group rewards distributed in such a way that members receive equitable rewards in exchange for successful performance as individuals in a group.
- *Normative Reward/Punishment systems*: Systems of inducements that emphasise the opportunity to experience intrinsic reward satisfaction.
- *Cafeteria-Style Fringe Benefit Programme*: Reward scheme that allows individual employees to select the combination of benefits most suited to their needs within some stated limits.
- *Cost-Reward Comparison*: Process in which employees identify and compare personal costs and rewards to determine the point at which they are approximately equal.
- *Extrinsic Rewards*: Rewards that do not come from the work itself.
- *Gain Sharing*: Policy of giving employees a substantial portion of the cost savings produced when their jobs are improved. Gain sharing plan is a programme that established a historical base period of organisational performance, measures improvements and shares the gains with employees on some formula basis.
- *Intrinsic Rewards*: Rewards that come from the work itself. A reward that is inherent in a task rather than one that is externally imposed. For some people, problem solving is intrinsically rewarding.
- *Incentives*: Environmental factors that are established for the purpose of motivating a person.
- *Normative Reward/Punishment Systems*: Systems of inducements that emphasise the opportunity to experience intrinsic reward satisfaction.

- *Profit Sharing*: System that distributes to employees some portion of the profits of business.
- *Skill-Based Pay*: A system that rewards individual employees for what they know how to do. Also known as knowledge-based pay or multi-skill pay.
- *Flexible Benefits*: Systems that allow employees to select an individualised combination of benefits.
- *Wage Incentive*: Reward system that provides more pay for more production.

## Role

Behaviour that is shaped by the situation, expectations of others, learned experiences and observations of others. A set of expected behaviour patterns attributed to someone occupying a given position in a social unit. Pattern of actions expected of a person in activities involving others. The typical and expected behaviours that characterise an individual's position in some social context.

- *Role Ambiguity*: Feeling that arises when roles are inadequately defined or are substantially unknown. Uncertainty of appropriate behaviour in a situation or psychological-social setting. Lack of clarity about the expectations of a person's role in an organisation.
- *Role Conflict*: Feeling that arises when others have different perceptions or expectations of a person's role. When requirements are added to a role that were not anticipated or desired. A work group leader may understand both employee and management points of view and why they differ. Conflict occurs when the leader must take either management's view or that of the employee's. A situation in which an individual is confronted by divergent role expectations. Anxiety generated in a person when people have incompatible expectations of him or her or when two or more roles conflict with each other. Disagreements over behavioural expectations. Conflict or incompatibility between the demands facing a person who occupies a particular role.
- *Role Custodianship*: A product of socialisation in which a new group member adopts the means and ends associated with the role unquestioningly.
- *Role Expectation*: The expectation of behaviour of others or self in a particular psychological-social setting. How others believe a person should act in a given situation.
- *Role Identity*: Certain attitudes and behaviour consistent with a role.
- *Role Innovation*: A product of socialisation in which a new group member is expected to improve on both the goals for his or her job and the means of achieving them.

- *Role Models*: Leaders who serve as examples for their followers.
- *Role Negotiation Technique*: An interpersonal organisation development intervention of moderate depth intended to help people form and maintain effective working relationships by clarifying role expectations.
- *Role Occupant*: The current incumbent of an existing role.
- *Role Perception*: An individual's view of how he or she is supposed to act in a given situation. How people think that they are supposed to act in their own roles and others should act in their roles.
- *Role Playing*: Spontaneous acting of a realistic situation involving two or more people under classroom conditions.
- *Role Scope*: The total number of expectations that exist for the person occupying a particular role.
- *Role Set*: The entire group of individuals who have an interest in and expectations about the way that a role occupant performs his or her job.
- *Role under Load*: Situation in which a person has insufficient responsibilities and duties to perform. As a consequence, the person feels underutilised and therefore experiences stress.
- *Interpersonal Role*: A type of role arising directly from a manager's formal authority. Interpersonal roles include figurehead role, leadership role and liaison role.

## Staff

That part of an organisation whose members are engaged in support, advisory, planning, legal or other functions not directly associated with the end product or service of the organisation. In some cases, the word 'staff' is used to denote employees of the organisation or a special group of employees.

- *Staff Function or Responsibility*: The activities of departments or other subunits that contribute indirectly to an organisation's production of goods and services. Staff personnel generally supervise line personnel.
- *Staffing*: The selection, placement, training and development of appropriately qualified employees.

## Stress

A tension reaction to threat, fear of failure, attainment of goals, compressed schedules, poor interpersonal relations, or any of a variety of other anxiety or emotion-inducing job factors. A dynamic condition in which an individual is confronted with an opportunity, constraint or demand related to what he or she desires and for which the outcome is perceived to be both uncertain and important. A consequence of or a response to an action, situation, or force that places special physical demands, psychological demands, or both on a person. The general term applied to the pressure people feel in life. An unpleasant emotional state resulting from the perception that a situational demand exceeds one's capacity and that it is very important to meet the demand.

- **Stress Management:** The act of controlling and directing stress as an energising rather than a destructive force. Also, the act of creating working environments without undue or destructive stress.
- **Bottom-up View of Authority:** View that authority begins with the consent of subordinates and then flows upward in the organisation through acceptance of orders, commands and requests.
- **Burnout:** Conditions where employees are emotionally exhausted, become detached from their work, and feel helpless in accomplishing their goals. A condition of emotional, physical and mental exhaustion resulting from prolonged exposure to intense job-related stress.
- **Anxiety:** Tension. Generalised feelings of fear and apprehension usually resulting from a perceived threat and accompanied by feelings of uneasiness.

## Structure and Organisation Structure

The degree of complexity, formalisation, and centralisation in the organisation. The prescribed patterns of work-related behaviour that are deliberately established for the accomplishment of organisational goals. The formal arrangement of processes and functions within the organisation. Leader's task orientation.

- **Organisation Structure:** Division of work as well as levels of responsibility and authority in work organisations. The relatively stable network of interconnections or interdependencies among the people and tasks that make up an organisation.
- **Structure Variable:** The system of formal communication, authority and responsibility in the organisation.
- **Centralisation:** The degree to which decision-making is concentrated at a single point in the organisation. A concept that prevails when all major, and possibly many minor, decisions are made only at the top levels of the organisation. The concentration of authority and decision making at the top of an organisation. The opposite of decentralisation.
- **Adhocracy:** An organisation in which the dominant form or structure is made up of small, special-purpose (ad hoc) groups such as task forces or project teams.

Adhocratic structure is flexible, adaptive and responsive, organised around unique problems to be solved by groups of relative strangers with diverse professional skills.

- **Functional Structure**: A structure characterised by grouping similar and related occupational specialties together. The type of bureaucratic structure characterised by standardisation, functional departmentation, and centralisation.
- **Functionalisation**:: Division of work into different kinds of duties.
- **Geocentric Organisations**: Those, which largely ignore nationality while accenting ability in their work-related decisions.
- **Hierarchy**: A mechanism for obtaining integration between two groups through the use of a common superior. The pyramidal differentiation of rank that occurs as authority is assigned to individual organisation members according to their organisational status and responsibilities.
- **Line Organisation**: Organisational components and its members directly involved in producing the end product or service of the organisation.
- **Matrix**: A structure that creates dual lines of authority; combines the functional and product structures.
- **Matrix Structure**: A combination of functional Departmentation with another form superimposed at the same organisational level. The type of bureaucratic organisation structure that incorporates both functional and divisional departmentation, along with significant mutual adjustment at the top of the organisation.
- **Mechanistic Structure**: A structure characterised by high complexity, high formalisation and centralisation. Machine-like organisation structures designed to enhance efficiency; characterised by large amounts of formalisation, standardisation, specialisation and centralisation.
- **Modular Structure**: The type of post-bureaucratic structure consisting of autonomous teams of employees joined together by an intra-firm computer network (Intranet).
- **Organic Structure**: A structure characterised by low complexity, low formalisation and decentralisation. Organism-like organisation structures designed to enhance flexibility and innovation; characterised by large amounts of mutual adjustment and decentralisation.
- **Organic Organisation**: An organisation generally accepting of change and characterised by low amounts of job specialisation, high degrees of superior–subordinate interaction, autonomy for employees and a climate of participative decision making. Organisations characterised by flexible tasks and roles, open communications and decentralised decision making.
- **Bureaucracy**: A system or organisation with highly structured divisions of labour, specialisation of work, rules, regulations, reporting systems and controls. Large, complex administrative system operating with impersonal detachment from people.

- **Bureaucratic Form:** Refers to a system of management characterised by rules and regulations, and a clearly outlined hierarchy, division of labour, impersonal relationships among members and a rigid criteria of promotion and selection.
- **Bureaucratic Structure:** A structure characterised by high complexity, high formalisation, impersonality, career tracks, employment decisions based on merit, and separation of members, organisational and personal lives. A structure used in a large, complex organisation that involves significant standardisation.
- **Post-Bureaucratic Structure:** An extremely flexible structure that substitutes various information-processing mechanisms for hierarchy and incorporates significant mutual adjustment, decentralisation, and either functional or divisional departmentalisation among different autonomous units or allied organisations.
- **Pre-Bureaucratic Structure:** A structure used in a small, simple organisation, which lacks standardisation.
- **Pyramidal organisation structure:** Hierarchically shaped organisation in which the highest level of management has the greatest amount of formal authority. Each successive lower layer has much less formal authority.
- **Simple Structure:** A structure characterised by low complexity, low formalisation and authority centralised in a single person.
- **Span of Control:** The number of subordinates who report directly to a manager.
- **Multi-Unit Structure:** The type of bureaucratic organisation structure that is composed of autonomous, self-managed business units and is characterised by divisional departmentalisation and extreme decentralisation.
- **Virtual Structure:** The type of post-bureaucratic structure consisting of multiple companies specialising in different functional tasks and joined together by an intra-firm computer network (Internet).

## Task

Is a set of activities to perform.

- **Task Forces:** Special groups that consist of one or more representatives from each of the interdependent groups and have the responsibility for working on specific problems that is of mutual concern.
- **Task Group:** Those working together to complete a job task. A group that serves the primary purpose of accomplishing organisationally defined goals.
- **Task Identity:** The degree to which the job requires completion of a whole and identifiable piece of work.
- **Task Significance:** The degree to which the job has a substantial impact on the lives or work of other people.

- **Task Structure:** Activities directed toward accomplishing a task, set of tasks, or series of objectives. It is a necessary component of effective managerial leadership. A component of Fiedler's contingency theory that describes the clarity of goals and of means–end relationships in a group's task.
- **Task Team:** Cooperative small group in regular contact that is engaged in coordinated action and whose members contribute responsibly and enthusiastically to the task.
- **Task-Oriented Role:** Group members' roles that facilitate and coordinate problem-solving activities.

# Team

A type of group characterised by tight interdependence, cross-functional expertise and differential information among members.

- **Team Building (or Team Development):** High interaction among group members to increase trust and openness. An organisational change process by which members of an organisational group diagnose how they work together and plan changes that will improve their effectiveness. Organisation Development process of developing integrated, cooperative groups. An Organisation Development technique emphasising small discussion groups that attempts to bring about improved communication and cooperation in work groups. A deep, group-level extension of interpersonal sensitivity training in which a group of people who work together on a daily basis meet over an extended period to assess and modify group processes.
- **Team-Oriented MBO:** A Management by Objectives (MBO) process that contains the same basic elements of individual-oriented MBO but, in addition, includes entire work groups or teams jointly setting some objectives.
- **Teamwork:** The state that occurs when members know their objectives, contributes responsibly and enthusiastically to the task and supports one another.
- **Informal Group:** A group that is neither structured nor organisationally determined; appears in response to the need for social contact. Groups formed on basis of common interests, proximity and friendships.
- **Self-Managing Teams:** Groups that are given a large degree of decision-making autonomy and expected to control their own behaviour and results. Also known as self-directing or self-reliant teams. Teams of employees empowered with the authority to determine job procedures, work assignments, membership, and so on.
- **Stages of Team Development:** Movement of a group through the evolutionary phases of forming, storming, norming and performing.

## Training and Learning

Any relatively permanent change in behaviour that occurs as a result of experience. A relatively permanent change in behaviour that results from reinforced practice or experience.

- *In-Basket Exercises*: Training technique in which subject plays the role of a manager who must respond to a large number of memos, phone messages and other communiqués in a short period of time.
- *Retraining*: Providing opportunities to learn new skills to those employees whose jobs are replaced by technological change.
- *Sensitivity/T-Group Training*: Training groups that seek to change behaviour through unstructured group interaction. An intensive approach to Organisation Development in which participants share their feelings and attitudes about each other with the group. Designed to foster self-understanding and personal growth. The T-group is the core of sensitivity training. Training technically used to improve interpersonal skills through closure of peer's feelings about behaviour in a setting. A deep, interpersonal organisation development intervention that focuses on developing greater sensitivity to oneself, to others, and to one's relations with others through an intense, leaderless group experience.
- *Development*: Efforts aimed at increasing the breadth and scope of knowledge and skills.
- *Ability*: The skills and knowledge, which allow an individual to bridge the gap between motivation and performance.
- *Attitude*: Evaluative statements or judgements concerning objects, people or events. Feelings and beliefs that largely determine how employees will perceive their environment.
- *Experiential Learning*: Process in which participants learn by experiencing in the training environment the kinds of human problems they face on the job.
- *Training Multiplier Effect*: The process by which skilled people develop others, and these become the nucleus for developing still others.
- *Transfer of Training*: The use on the job of knowledge and skills gained through training.
- *Vicarious Learning*: A relatively permanent change in behaviour that results from a person's observing others performing the behaviour and/or experiencing the consequences of the behaviour.
- *Case*: An involved description usually based on fact that is useful in illustrating or studying a phenomenon. This book uses a number of case histories to illustrate the concepts discussed.

- *Case Study*: A written description of an organisation used as an educational tool. The examination of numerous characteristics of a person, group or organisation over an extended period of time.

# Value

Anything that has personal worth or meaning. Values are based largely on religious, moral and societal percepts learned at an early age and modified throughout a person's life. Basic convictions that a specific mode of conduct or end-state of existence is personally or socially preferable to an opposite or converse mode of conduct or end-state of existence.

- *Value Premises*: Personal views of the desirability of certain goals and activities.
- *Value Systems*: A prioritising of individual values according to their relative importance.
- *Humanistic Values*: Positive beliefs about the potential and desire for growth among employees.
- *Morals*: Basic values of right and wrong; good and bad. Usually cultural or religious in origin, as opposed to ethics, this is societal in origin.
- *Ethics*: Personal values of correct and incorrect behaviour. Societal values of honesty, truthfulness, fairness and equity.

# Work

Is an occupation or profession for a given set of activities.

- *Work Design*: The process of deciding what specific tasks each jobholder should perform in the context of the overall work that an organisation must accomplish.
- *Work Ethic*: Employee attitude of viewing work as a central life interest and desirable goal in life.
- *Work Measurement*: An area of industrial engineering concerned with measuring the amount of work accomplished and developing standards for performing work of an acceptable quantity and quality.
- *Work Modules*: The creation of two-hour time task units, four of which equal an eight-hour day; can be allocated in ways to give workers diverse tasks.
- *Work Motivation*: In general, physical and mental efforts expended toward meeting organisational objectives.

- *Work Redesign*: A technique of rearranging, changing, adding to, or deleting specific tasks to make a job more challenging, more interesting and affected employees more productive.
- *Workaholic (Work Addict)*: A person addicted to work to the extent that it has adverse consequences for family and personal life. The condition may also interfere with job effectiveness as the person often loses perspective and objectivity.
- *Work Flow Grouping*: Grouping people into units based on similarities in the products they make or markets they serve.
- *Workplace Trauma*: The disintegration of employee self-concepts and benefits in their capabilities arising from factors or experiences at work.
- *Works Council*: A committee of worker representatives who are elected by their peers and management representatives who are appointed by top management; it oversees policy formulation in industrial democracies.

## Commonly Used Terms in HRM

- *Competition*: A situation where one party seeks to achieve his goals or further his interests, regardless of the impact of this behaviour on others. Actions taken by one person to attain his or her preferred goal while simultaneously blocking attainment of a counterpart's goal.
- *Consultant*: A person who, on a fee or volunteer basis, provides advice and/or technical help or aid to an organisation in solving its own problem. In some circumstances, consultants provide services to individuals as well as organisations. Consultation is a level of participation in which supervisors make decisions jointly with their subordinates.
- *Creativity*: Generation of new ways of acting, new explanations, unique methods of solving problems, or any activity that utilises a previously unknown or unused approach to a human activity. The ability to process information in such a way that the result is new, original and meaningful.
- *Devil's Advocate*: A decision-making method involving a proposed course of action and a critique of the proposal. Intended to cause cognitive conflict for the decision-maker. Persons, who challenge the ideas of others, probe for supporting facts, provide constructive criticism and challenge logic so as to improve the quality of a group decision.
- *Divergent Thinking*: Thinking and learning that is more dependent on feelings, intuition and creativity than that of convergent thinking. Less dependent on rules, precision, detail; comfortable with ambiguity.
- *Electronic Brainstorming*: The use of personal computers to facilitate idea generation and recording during brainstorming sessions.

- *Electronic Grapevine*: The transmission of informal messages by the use of computers.
- *Electronic Mail*: A computer-based communication system that allows messages to be sent to multiple parties simultaneously.
- *Ergonomics*: Another name for human factors engineering; a type of methods engineering that focuses on designing machines to match human capacities and limitations.
- *Facilitation*: Supervisory behaviours characterised by (a) providing clear and salient goals, (b) guiding and coordinating employee efforts, (c) providing technical resources, and (d) making subordinate performance satisfying.
- *Flextime*: A form of work scheduling that allows the employee, within certain limits, to vary arrival and departure times to suit individual needs and desires. Employees work during a common core time period each day but have discretion in forming their total workday from flexible set of hours outside the core. Allowing workers flexibility as to when they begin and end their workday.
- *Frame of Reference*: Personal perception or viewpoint based on one's experience, cultural values, attitudes, beliefs and values. The assumptions a person makes; perspectives a person uses to form a 'cognitive map' for interpreting and coping with his or her world.
- *Goodwill*: In accounting terms, this is the difference between the fair value of a business as a whole and the aggregate fair value of its net separable assets. Historically, goodwill has been conceptualised as the positive disposition of a customer towards a particular business enterprise that causes the customer to continue patronising the business. The components of goodwill, however, are broader than just customer capital; they are all the intangible assets that are not valued separately on a firm's financial statements. Practically, then, goodwill comprises intellectual capital—human capital, structural capital and customer capital.
- *Innovation*: Utilisation of existing resources in new and different ways. Developing unique solutions or approaches to problems.
- *Intuition*: A feeling not necessarily supported by research. Direct perception of truth or fact that seems to be independent of any reasoning process. A keen and quick insight that can be very helpful to a knowledge worker.
- *Jargon*: Language associated with a particular job or type of work that has little or no meaning to those not associated with the work. The word 'scupper', for example, has little meaning to people outside the building trades. (Specialised vocabulary. Idiosyncratic use of language that is often useful among specialists but that inhibits their ability to communicate with non-specialists).
- *Law of Diminishing Returns*: Principle that a declining amount of extra outputs are received when more of a desirable input is added to an operation system.
- *Open System*: A system that engages in exchanges with its environment through its boundaries, receiving inputs and providing outputs.

- **Open-Door Policy:** Statement encouraging employees to come to their supervisor or higher managers with any matter that concerns them.
- **Professional:** Member of an occupational group characterised by (a) the presence of a systematic theory, (b) a high level of authroity, (c) standards of training prescribed by colleagues, (d) a code of ethics, and (e) a culture unique to the profession.
- **Quid pro quo:** Something for something. You scratch my back, I'll scratch yours. Do me a favour; I'll do one for you.
- **Red tape:** Procedure that appears to be unnecessary to those who are following it.
- **Reliability:** The degree to which a measure of an individual, group, organisational, or environmental attribute is free from random error and is thus replicable. Capacity of a survey instrument to produce consistent results.
- **Sexual harassment:** Any act, proposal, or suggestion of compliance in sexual conduct as a condition of work or promotion. Any sexual proposal or suggestion that interferes with the performance of work. The process of making employment or promotion decisions contingent on sexual favours. Also, exhibiting any verbal or physical conduct that creates an offensive working environment.
- **Simulations:** Comprehensive experiential approaches that create many dimensions of work life in organisations to help participants experience and understand behaviour within them. Training technique of exposing subject to an artificial environment that has the same essential characteristics and demands as the actual job.
- **Standardisation:** A basic coordination mechanism in which work is coordinated by providing employees with carefully planned standards and procedures that guide the performance of their tasks. In the context of scientific measurement, standardisation is the practice of ensuring that all people measure the same variables by applying the same instruments in the same manner. Procedures designed to regularise organisational activities.
- **State-of-the-Art:** Common consensus about the amount of knowledge currently available for problem solving in a particular area.
- **Strategy/Strategic Planning:** Integrative plan for the organisation to accomplish its goals in the context of environmental forces beyond the control of the organisation (time span of more than two years).
- **Survey Feedback:** An organisational development technique that utilises survey data that is summarised and given to the survey respondents who in turn interpret the data and suggest actions. The use of questionnaires to identify discrepancies among member perceptions; discussion follows and remedies are suggested. An organisational change approach that consists of collecting information from members of an organisation or work group, organising the data into an understandable and useful form, and feeding it back to the employees who generated the data. Organisation Development process of surveying members of an organisation and

reporting the results directly to the persons involved for their interpretation and action. A shallow, organisation-level organisation development intervention intended to stimulate information sharing throughout the entire organisation.

● *Technology*: How an organisation transfers its inputs to outputs. The knowledge, procedures and equipment used in an organisation to transform unprocessed resources into finished goods or services.

● *Whistle-Blower*: Employee who discloses alleged misconduct to an internal or external source.

● *Withdrawal*: A psychological retreat from conflicting, boring or threatening situations. Fantasy (day dreaming), falling asleep, physically leaving and suicide are all withdrawal behaviours.

## Reference and Further Reading

Blake, R. and J. Mouton. 1964. *The Managerial Grid: The Key to Leadership Excellence*. Houston: Gulf Publishing Co.

# Index

# About the Authors

**Ashok Chanda** is doctoral fellow at the School of Management, University of South Australia. He has nearly two decades of corporate experience as an HR professional. His last position was Vice President—HR with Reliance Energy, Mumbai. Earlier, he has worked with Gati Ltd., and Gujarat Gas Ltd., a subsidiary of British Gas. He is also a member of the Australian Human Resource Institute. His publications include articles published in various journals and a co-authored volume, *Human Resource Strategy: Architecture for Change* (2000).

**B. Sivarama Krishna** is General Manager, Human Resources with Frontline Corporation, Ahmedabad. In his 12 years' experience in the field of HR, he has worked with various large and reputed organisations dealing with HRM, corporate administration, industrial relations, etc. He is currently associated with various professional bodies.

**Jie Shen** is senior lecturer in Human Resource Management at the School of Management, University of South Australia. His research interests include international human resource management, industrial relations and HR practices in China and organisational behaviour. He has co-authored *International Human Resource Management in Chinese MNEs* (2006) and published numerous articles in various international journals. He is a member of the editorial board of *The International Journal of Organisational Transformation and Social Change* (OTSC) and also a member of several professional associations.

# About the Authors

**Ashok Chanda** is doctoral fellow at the School of Management, University of South Australia. He has nearly two decades of corporate experience as an HR professional. His last position was Vice President—HR with Reliance Energy, Mumbai. Earlier, he has worked with Gati Ltd., and Gujarat Gas Ltd., a subsidiary of British Gas. He is also a member of the Australian Human Resource Institute. His publications include articles published in various journals and a co-authored volume, *Human Resource Strategy: Architecture for Change* (2000).

**B. Sivarama Krishna** is General Manager, Human Resources with Frontline Corporation, Ahmedabad. In his 12 years' experience in the field of HR, he has worked with various large and reputed organisations dealing with HRM, corporate administration, industrial relations, etc. He is currently associated with various professional bodies.

**Jie Shen** is senior lecturer in Human Resource Management at the School of Management, University of South Australia. His research interests include international human resource management, industrial relations and HR practices in China and organisational behaviour. He has co-authored *International Human Resource Management in Chinese MNEs* (2006) and published numerous articles in various international journals. He is a member of the editorial board of *The International Journal of Organisational Transformation and Social Change* (OTSC) and also a member of several professional associations.